THE SCHOOL IN THE SERVICE
OF
EVANGELIZATION

STUDIES ON RELIGION IN AFRICA

SUPPLEMENTS TO THE JOURNAL OF RELIGION IN AFRICA

VI

THE SCHOOL IN THE SERVICE
OF
EVANGELIZATION

THE CATHOLIC EDUCATIONAL IMPACT
IN EASTERN NIGERIA
1886-1950

BY

NICHOLAS IBEAWUCHI OMENKA

E.J. BRILL
LEIDEN · NEW YORK · KØBENHAVN · KÖLN
1989

Library of Congress Cataloging-in-Publication Data

Omenka, Nicholas Ibeawuchi.
   The school in the service of evangelization : the Catholic
educational impact in eastern Nigeria. 1886-1950 / by Nicholas
Ibeawuchi Omenka.
      p.   cm. — (Studies on religion in Africa. ISSN 0169-9814 ; 6)
   Bibliography: p.
   Includes index.
   ISBN 9004086323
      1. Catholic schools—Nigeria, Eastern—History.   2. Catholic
Church—Missions—Nigeria, Eastern—History   I. Title.
   II. Series
   LC508.N542E186   1989
   377'.82'669—dc19   88-37555
                                                                              CIP

ISSN 0169-9814
ISBN 90 04 08632 3

PRINTED IN THE NETHERLANDS BY E. J. BRILL

To my Family
in Loving Gratitude

TABLE OF CONTENTS

CHAPTER FOUR

THE PROBLEM OF TEACHERS

CHAPTER FIVE

MISSION AND EDUCATIONAL ACTION

CHAPTER SIX

CATHOLIC SCHOOLS IN THE STRUGGLE BETWEEN
MISSION AND COLONIAL POLITICS, 1920-1950

CHAPTER SEVEN

SECONDARY EDUCATION AND NATIONAL CONSCIOUSNESS

APPENDIX A.

Copy of a Contract Made by Father E. Kuntzmann with a Catechist of the Mission, Onitsha, 18 May, 1896................................... 296

APPENDIX B

1. Temporary Scheme of Religious Moral Instruction in the Roman Catholic Mission Schools by Father J. Shanahan, Apostolic Prefect, Onitsha, 1915... 297
2. Approved Scheme of Religious Instruction for the Onitsha-Owerri Vicariate, 1944.. 299

APPENDIX C

1. Regulations on the Running of School Farms in Senior Primary Schools.. 300
2. Rural Science in Primary Schools: Circular by the Director of Education, Eastern Region, Enugu, 26 June, 1953........................ 301

APPENDIX D

Outline of Evidence Given Before the Eliot Commission on Higher Education by the Catholic Missions of Nigeria, 1944.............. 302

APPENDIX E

1. Press Release on a Proposed Catholic University by Father J. Jordan, Education Adviser to the Catholic Missions of Nigeria, 1955..... 306
2. Note on Financing the Catholic University by J. Jordan....... 308

LIST OF TABLES

LIST OF ILLUSTRATIONS

ABBREVIATIONS

AAS	Acta Apostolicae Sedis
AFER	African Ecclesiastical Review
AP	Archivio di Propaganda Fide, Rome.
Cf.	confer
C.K.C.	Christ the King College, Onitsha.
CMS	Church Missionary Society (Anglican).
C.O.	Colonial Office, London.
CSE	Archives, Congrégation du Saint-Esprit, Paris.
fol.	folio
F.C.O.L.	Foreign and Colonial Office Library, London.
F.O.	Foreign Office, London.
IRM	International Review of Missions
KM	Die katholische Missionen
Ms	Manuscript
n.d.	no date
N.S.	Nuova Serie (Propaganda Archives).
ODA	Onitsha Diocesan Archives
PRO	Public Record Office, London.
R.	Rubriche (Propaganda Archives).
r	recto (righthand page).
R.C.M.	Roman Catholic Mission
rpt.	reprinted
SC	Scritture riferite nei Congressi
SMA	Archives, Société des Missions Africaines, Rome.
Std.	Standard
TS	Typescript
v	verso (left-hand page).
ZM	Zeitschrift für Missionswissenschaft

PREFACE

The missionary factor, which reached its highwater mark in Nigeria in the first half of this century, is one of the greatest epoch-making events in the history of this important West African nation. Many Nigerians who were privileged to be witnesses to that great event still have some vivid memories of its course: they still remember the days when the missionaries lived and worked among them. However, as recent studies and enquiries have revealed, the degree of the authenticity to be accorded to the historical facts that are derived from oral communications of the natives often does not exceed that of a guess work. With the older generations slowly passing away, the need to see a detailed documentary exposition of the Nigerian history in its missionary setting is urgently voiced.

Several Nigerian historians have addressed themselves positively to this popular demand in recent times. However, in almost all the works on the general history of the Christian Missions in Nigeria, emphasis has been placed only on the Protestant endeavours. The profound impact which Catholicism has had on the Nigerian Society and culture has generally not received the attention it deserves. This became particularly obvious to me in the course of my work on a Licentiate thesis entitled, "Catholicism in Southern Nigeria, 1862 - 1914," which I presented in 1979 to the University of Innsbruck, Austria. Also transparent during my research in various mission and government archives was the central position which the school occupied in the evangelical activities of the Catholic Missions in Nigeria. These vital findings were instrumental in my decision to write a doctoral dissertation on the Catholic educational endeavours in Eastern Nigeria which I presented to the University of Regensburg, West Germany, in 1986. The present work is an improved version of that study.

The choice of 1950 as a limiting date for this study was influenced by two primary factors. Firstly, apart from the Onitsha diocesan archives, none of the archives from which the materials for this work were drawn allows researchers to examine mission records that date later than 1950. For any source work, this is a serious inhibition. Secondly, Nigeria attained the status of a Church hierarchy in 1950. With that the missionary era theoretically came to an end. Although Catholic education faced renewed challenges in the 1950s following the regional control of education by the Nigerian nationalists, its success in the intricate evangelization process was, by that time, already an accomplished task.

In the pages that lie ahead, we shall be looking at the different stages of this special achievement.

I wish to thank all those who in any way contributed to the success of this work. My special thanks and gratitude go to Professor Dr. K. J. Benz of the University of Regensburg, whose scholarly discussions, advice, and, above all, friendly dispositions were a source of great inspiration for my doctoral thesis. My gratitude also goes to Professor G. Winkler, now of the University of Salzburg, Austria, for giving this project definite perspectives at the initial stage. I am very much indebted to Professor Dr. B. Willeke of the Mission Institute of the University of Würzburg for his useful suggestions and help during the early stages of my investigations. It was he who, among other things, called my attention to what I did not particularly take notice of before our first meeting and what many Nigerians do not know today, namely, the decisive impact which Fr. Léon Lejeune had on the Catholic Mission in Eastern Nigeria. A word of gratitude and appreciation is very much due to Professor Dr. K. H. Göller of the Department of English, University of Regensburg, for reading through the manuscript. My friend and spiritual adviser, Professor Dr. M. Schmaus provided moral and material assistance at a time when this work was only an idea. For this I am particularly grateful.

I wish to thank the various archives and their staff for the immense assistance they rendered me during my quest for source materials. It is almost impossible to mention all the names here. However, I must not fail to thank in a special way the Very Rev. Dr. J. Metzler, Director of the Propaganda Archives, Rome. But for his guidelines, getting what I wanted from the huge record office would have been like searching for needles in a haystack. A word of thanks goes to the following archivists: Fr. Bernard Noël of the Holy Ghost Congregation, Paris, who kindly allowed me to consult the records even after the office hours, Fr. Douau Noël of the Society of African Missions, Rome, Fr. Rath of the German Province of the Holy Ghost Congregation in Knechtsteden, Dormagen, the archivists of the Public Record Office, Kew, London, and Dr. H. Adigwe, Archdiocesan Secretariat, Onitsha.

My gratitude also goes to the various libraries: Library of the Foreign and Colonial Office, London, the London University and Institute of Education Library, the Overseas Development Administration Library, London, Library of the International African Institute, Paris, Library of the Pontifical Urban University, Rome, the University of Regensburg Library, which was of immense help to my work through its most efficient inter-university exchange programme, and the Library of the Jesuit College, Innsbruck.

I am greatly indebted to Missio Aachen and the Bishop of Regensburg for financing my studies in Regensburg.

Last but by no means least, I express my sincere gratitude to Mr. W. Schönfeld of the Computer Centre of the University of Regensburg for the immense help he rendered me in the processing of the manuscript of this work. The amount of sacrifice and patience he put into this often frustrating undertaking is really praiseworthy.

Enugu, 29 April, 1988   Nicholas Omenka

CHAPTER ONE

INTRODUCTION:
HISTORICAL PERSPECTIVES

I. *The School In The Nineteenth Century Missionary Movement*

1. *The Re-Thinking of Missionary Motives*

A burning issue in the nineteenth century missionary movement was the necessity of re-defining the motives of the missionary enterprise with a view to re-establishing the Mission on a permanent basis. By the beginning of the century, the French Revolution had finally administered a *coup de grace* to the missionary edifice which had long been shaken by such factors as the extraordinary high mortality rate among the white missionaries, the *padroado* or "patronage" controversies,[1] and the suppression of the Jesuit Order. What was left after these scourges were mere ruins, and according to estimates, there were only about 300 Catholic missionaries in the whole world at the beginning of the nineteenth century. In the African continent, the number of Catholics—including the Coptic and Abyssinian Christians—amounted to only 47,000 souls.[2] The function to be assigned to the school in the impending restoration of the Missions depended, to a large extent, on a re-evaluation of the hitherto

---

[1] Eager to extend the Christian message to the lands opened to European trade in the fifteenth century, Pope Martin V (1417-1431) and his successors granted the monarchs of the Iberian Peninsular the right to appoint bishops and missionaries for the Missions. By virtue of these *padroado* or "patronage" accords, the most famous being the 1493 Bull of Demarcation by Pope Alexander VI, Africa and the East Indies fell under the Portuguese sphere of influence. For political and economic reasons, the Portuguese turned the control of their Missions into "a jealously guarded royal prerogative." See A.F.C. Ryder, "Portuguese Missions in Western Africa," *Tahrik*, 3, No.1 (1969), 1. This presented enormous difficulties in later centuries when the Portuguese, unable or unwilling to send missionaries to their mission lands, doggedly resisted the attempts of the Congregation for the Propagation of the Faith, founded in 1622, to send missionaries to these territories. The endless quarrels between Rome and Portugal led to the division of mission lands into two categories, the Padroada and the Propaganda.

[2] For a detailed account of the decay and revival of Catholic Missions, see M. Spitz, "The Growth of Roman Catholic Missions in Africa," *IRM*, 12 (1923), 360-372; R. Gray, "The Origins and Organization of the Nineteenth-Century Missionary Movement," *Tahrik*, 3, No.1 (1969), 14-22; W. Henkel, "Gestaltnahme von Bekehrungsvorstellungen bei Ordensgründungen im 19. Jahrhundert," *Mission: Präsenz, Verkündigung, Bekehrung?* Studia Instituti Missiologici Societatis Verbi Divini, No, 13 (St. Augustin: Styler Verlag, 1974), pp.102-114; A. Mulders, *Missionsgeschichte: Die Ausbreitung des katholischen Glaubens* (Regensburg, 1960).

accepted interpretations of the biblical command: *Docete omnes gentes* (Mt.28, 20; Mk.16,15).

In the past, opinions had varied among the Christian Missions about where to lay emphasis in the execution of that divine order to teach all nations. Some favoured the "conversion" or "evangelization" principle, which laid stress on the salvation of souls. Accordingly, the catechumenate was in this case the most logical missionary objective, which involved the admittance and instruction of the neophyte till he received baptism. If the neophyte died after baptism, the missionary would have accomplished his task all the same. By contrast, the advocates of the "plantatio" principle called for a systematic spreading of the visible Church through deep-rooted measures which would lead to the emergence of local clergies and hierarchies in the Missions.

The theological and intellectual impulses which ultimately led to the solution of this problem made their first appearances in Protestant pietism and evangelicalism, movements which had demanded personal religious independence and collaboration as a reaction against orthodox formalism. Apart from the influence which these movements had on the formation of Protestant missionary societies in England in the eighteenth century, they also provided the framework for the formulation of missionary theories in the nineteenth century. The Protestant scholar who most successfully sculptured missionary motives into acceptable theoretical structures was Gustav Warneck.[3] He understood "Christian Mission" to mean "the totality of an action which is aimed at planting and organizing the Christian Church among non-Christians."[4] For him, and indeed for most of the Anglo-American and German Protestant mission theoreticians of the nineteenth and early twentieth centuries, the goal of the Mission was the establishment of independent local Churches.[5] Seen against this background, the primary concern of the Missionary would be not so much the catechumenate, but rather activities which would lead to the organization of an indigenous clergy, a task which would not be thought of without education and the school.

Spurred on by the Protestant initiative in the re-definition of missionary motives, some Catholic theologians and scholars developed missionary theories and principles of their own. Prominent among these was

[3] Warneck's book, *Evangelische Missionslehre*, 5 vols. (Göttingen, 1892-1903), was a milestone in missionary history.
[4] Quoted in H. Berger, *Mission und Kolonialpolitik: Die katholische Mission in Kamerun während der deutschen Kolonialzeit* (Immensee, 1978), p. 109.
[5] Warneck conceded that the idea of independent local Churches first emanated from England and America. See P. Beyerhaus, *Die Selbständigkeit der jungen Kirchen als missionarisches Problem* (Wuppertal-Barmen, 1967), p.329, n.8.

Joseph Schmidlin, whose book on Catholic missiology—*Die katholische Missionslehre im Grundriss* (Münster, 1919)—had a popularity which reached beyond the frontiers of Germany. Although he relied on a number of Catholic authors who had lived before him, the greatest influence on his thoughts came from Warneck.[6] Like Warneck, he saw the object of the Mission in activities among pagans,[7] and made a distinction between individual and personal conversion of a pagan on the one hand, and the organization of independent local churches on the other.[8] But unlike Warneck, Schmidlin leaned rather too heavily on the evangelization principle, which highlighted the salvation of the individual soul. Accordingly, the Church and the doctrine of a universal concept of salvation received little attention in his teachings.[9] However, Schmidlin's merit lay chiefly in his establishment, for the first time in the history of the Catholic Church, of a department of Missiology at the University of Münster in 1911.[10]

Contrary to the teachings of the Münster school, as the followers of Schmidlin were called, another school of thought, the Louvain school, emphasized the organization of indigenous clergy and hierarchy as the primary purpose of all missionary endeavour. The founder and most articulate defender of this school, Pièrre Charles, a Belgian Jesuit, called on missionaries to "planter l'Eglise visible."[11] A major feature of his

---

[6] Cf. H. Berger, *Mission und Kolonialpolitik*, p. 83f. For details on the Catholic missionary theoreticians prior to the nineteenth century, see J. Schmidlin, "Katholische Missionstheoretiker des 16.und 17. Jahrhunderts," *ZM*, 1 (1911), 213-227; R. Streit, "Die Missionsliteratur des 19. Jahrhunderts," *ZM*, 7 (1917), 108-115.

[7] This position was however challenged by other Catholic thinkers. T. Grentrup, for instance, took the object of the Mission to be conversion to Catholicism of all non-Catholics. See "Die Definition des Missionsbegriffes," *ZM*, 3 (1913), 265-274. Grentrup's position was very much in line with the official teaching of the Church. In his Bull, "Inscrutabili," with which the Propaganda Congregation was established in 1622, Pope Gregory XV spoke expressly of "non-Catholics" as being the object of the missionary enterprise. See J. Glazik, "Die neuzeitliche Mission unter Leitung der Propagandakongregation," *Warum Mission: Theologische Motive in der Missionsgeschichte der Neuzeit.* Kirche und Religion (St. Ottilien: EOS Verlag, 1984), Vol. III, pp. 28-30. Torn asunder by the Reformation, the Church understandably focused the efforts of the Counter-Reformation primarily on the apostatized faithful of Europe. It was not until the 1830s—during the Pontificate of Gregory XVI, the great missionary Pope—that Propaganda began to devote its attention chiefly to the pagans of the Third World.

[8] See J. Schmidlin, *Die katholische Missionslehre*, p. 241.

[9] Cf. J. Glazik, *Mission—Der stets größere Auftrag: Gesammelte Vorträge und Aufsätze* (Aachen, 1979), p. 105.

[10] Following his example, other centres made Missiology a university disciple: Munich (1919), Rome, at the Propaganda College (1919), Nimwegen (1930), Ottawa (1932), Vienna (1933), and Freiburg in Switzerland (1940). Cf. A. Mulders, *Missionsgeschichte*, p. 430.

[11] P. Charles, *Les Dossiers de l'action Missionaire* (Louvain, 1932), quoted in H. Berger, *Mission und Kolonialpolitik*, p. 120. See also J. Glazik, *Mission*, p. 105.

"plantatio" doctrine was a rather excessive ecclesio-centric emphasis which placed an overriding priority on the socio-cultural values of missionary enterprise. Accordingly, the school acquired a more than evangelical character in his teachings. In one of his many works on this subject, he wrote:

> How would one meet the objection which considers as a kind of pious dissipation of energy, or as a spurious manoeuver, the use which the mission makes of its resources and activities in the field of education...? One may reply that because the goal of the mission is to convert pagans, we establish schools in order to bring about conversion and to entice to our missionary enterprise those who would otherwise not come to us and listen to us in our churches. But this answer would rather be grotesque. The goal of the mission is not only to convert the unbelievers; it is also to sustain and ameliorate the converts.... If you teach arithmetic, it is your duty to make sure that your pupils also comprehend [and utilize] it; otherwise do not teach it.... The religious objective simply disappears and is superseded by a humanitarian goal. You may entertain the secret hope that your educational effort may produce religious results, but you should not make that hope the primary motive of your enterprise....[12]

The findings of the theoreticians found a belated acceptance outside the academic world of the universities. Nevertheless, there emerged among the leaders of the Church an awareness of the necessity of a revision of missionary motives. The call for local Churches demanded, above all, that systematic measures be taken to create social and cultural backgrounds from which indigenous leadership—native clergy, catechists and teachers, and social workers—would be drawn. Such an objective would be totally illusive without a formal education of the masses. Consequently, the papal encyclicals of the first half of this century devoted much attention to the importance of the school for the Missions.

A milestone in this changed missionary attitude was Benedict XV's encyclical, "Maximum Illud," (1919). Here the Pontiff underlined the central position of the native clergy in the establishment of independent local Churches, and urged the missionaries to make the education of the indigenes the primary purpose of their missionary enterprise.[13] Speaking in a similar vein, his successor, Pope Pius XI, wrote in "Rerum Ecclesiae" (1922) that the clergy of the Apostolic era were chosen not from people of alien cultures, but from the inhabitants of the local communities.[14] In a revolutionary departure from the practice of the

---

[12] P. Charles, "Le problème de l'enseignement aux missions," *Katholiches Missionsjahrbuch der Schweiz*, 4 (1937), 5.
[13] Cf. "Maximum Illud," *Acta Apostolicae Sedis* (AAS), 11 (1919), 444f.
[14] "Rerum Ecclesiae," AAS, 18 (1926), p. 74.

medieval church, he urged the missionaries to build hospitals and schools instead of magnificent churches and palaces. These latter establishments, he reasoned, would be taken care of in their appointed time.[15] To substantiate his commitments to the promotion of local Churches, he consecrated six Chinese bishops to take charge of the Apostolic Vicariates of their homeland.

It was under Pope Pius XII that the enthusiastic approbation of the school was carried out with the greatest élan. In the encyclical, "Evangelii Praecones" (1951), the Pontiff gave expression to his commendation of the school apostolate with an unprecedented lucidity:

> The youth, especially those of them who have gone through high schools, will control the destiny of their countries in the future. The importance of education at the elementary, secondary, and university levels is generally recognized as deserving of the greatest care. For this reason, therefore, we exhort mission leaders with fatherly endearment to spare no effort or expense in the development of these institutions.
>
> The elementary and secondary schools have, in addition, the advantage of creating valuable relationships between the missionaries and the natives. The youth in particular, who are as flexible as wax, can easily be educated to understand, value, and accept Catholic doctrines. The well-educated among them shall one day have leading positions in Government, and the masses shall have them as their leaders and teachers.[16]

Worthy of note in this admonition is the emphasis placed on the importance of the school for the social and political aspirations of native societies. Whereas former papal instructions to missionaries accentuated the exigencies of local Churches, "Evangelii Praecones," without losing sight of these objectives, directed attention on the totality of society. This was hardly surprising: by 1951, it was not so much the determination of missionary goals as the creation of cordial relationships between the Missions and the rising nationalist movements that needed official guidelines in the formulation of mission policy. With the leaders of the European

---

[15] Ibid., p.80f. The reports from the West African Missions between the fifteenth and eighteenth centuries reveal a close adherence to the medieval missionary strategy of building monasteries and churches in important centres. In 1688, for instance, Father Francesco da Monteleone, the Apostolic Prefect of Sao Thomé, highlighted his establishment of monasteries and churches in Angola and Sao Thomé. See "F. Monteleone to Propaganda," Sao Thomé, 8 July, 1688, quoted in R. Streit, J. Dindinger, *Bibliotheca Missionum*, XVI (Freiburg: Herder, 1952), 723. In 1692 he reported that Father Guiseppe da Venasca, his co-worker in the Mission of Sao Thomé, had also built a monastery and a church on the Island of Principe. See "F. Monteleone to Propaganda," Sao Thomé, 28 August, 1692, quoted in ibid., p. 724. But his reports and those of other missionaries before and after him are conspicuously silent about the establishment of schools for the masses. By contrast, the foundation of schools is a regular feature in the missionary reports of the nineteenth and twentieth centuries.

[16] "Evangelii Praecones," AAS, 43 (1951), 514-515.

Governments, Pius XII shared the conviction that the success of future relations with the rising states depended solely on cooperation with the nationalists. That conviction had in fact already found expression in the granting of partial self-government to the natives in a number of African colonies. On the ecclesiastical level, "Evangelii Praecones" was a sequel to the Apostolic Constitution, "Laeto Accepimus," of 18 April, 1950, with which the Pontiff created church hierarchies in the British West African dependencies.[17] By emphasizing the place of the younger generation in the political future of their countries, Pope Pius XII therefore brought his ardent commitments to the furtherance of independent local Churches in line with political developments in the mission lands.

By bringing the school to the centre stage of the missionary enterprise, the Church revealed a determination to avoid the grave mistakes of the past centuries. That the Missions failed to take firm roots in Africa after three hundred years of tireless efforts was a clear indication that there were serious flaws in missionary motives and methods. These defects were often products of some ill-conceived assumptions, such as the theological error which saw no salvation outside the Church. The missionaries, who, to a large extent, had received that theological background, went to the Missions (often on short-time basis) to save as many souls as possible. In the Congo, for instance, 2,700 baptisms in 25 days were reported as being a moderate number.[18] By contrast, of the 47,000 catechumens who were registered at Emekukwu in 1929, many were said to have waited for their baptism for as many as seven years.[19] Although this was by no means an ideal norm, its lack of urgency was indicative of a permanent character which was lacking in former missionary attempts. Since the greater majority of the catechumens at Emekukwu, as in all parts of the Lower Niger Mission, were school children, the missionaries had the opportunity of adding thoroughness and lasting features to the work of evangelization.

Furthermore, the apostolate of the school, so characteristic a feature in the missionary movements of the nineteenth and twentieth centuries, grew out of the conviction that the success of missionary labours depended not so much on the pious enthusiasm of the missionary as on

---

[17] See AAS, 42 (1950), 615-619.

[18] See A.F.C. Ryder, "Portuguese Missions," p. 8. This is hardly surprising in view of the often sporadic nature of the missionary contacts. According to a report reaching the Propaganda Congregation in 1646, the missionaries in Sao Thomé came to Benin every six years to stay for about fourteen days. Cf. L. Kilger, "Die Missionsversuche in Benin," ZM, 22 (1932), 310. Given such circumstances, the missionaries generally carried out mass baptism wherever they got the opportunity and permission to do so.

[19] See CSE:554/V, J. Soul, "General Report to the Superior General on the Visit to the District of Southern Nigeria," Onitsha, 12 November, 1929, p. 18.

his sincere commitment to the work of civilization. This trend of thought accordingly found expression in the constitutions of the new religious congregations.

2. *The Educational Character of the New Congregations*

Of all the missionary societies that worked in Africa in recent times, Cardinal Lavigerie's White Fathers, Libermann's Holy Ghost Fathers and Brésillac's Society of African Missions were undoubtedly the most successful. Like the majority of their kind, these congregations were founded in the nineteenth century, when there was yet no definite missionary theory and strategy to go by. Nevertheless, the apostolate of the school was more or less a common characteristic of their missionary "plans." This was no accident: it was, to a large extent, a reflection of the general pedagogical trend of the nineteenth century, which advocated the education of the masses. Two Enlightenment thinkers who greatly influenced that zeitgeist were Jean-Jacques Rousseau and Johann Heinrich Pestalozzi. Both experimented with innovatory teaching methods which were later widely adopted in the development of elementary education in the nineteenth century, especially in Prussia, France, Holland, and England.[20] In all these countries, as in all Europe, the slogan: "whoever has the youth has the future" was passionately acclaimed.

This popular spirit of enlightenment exerted no small influence on the Church. The old religious orders which had survived the Secularization owed their continued existence chiefly to their educational and social activities. Was it any wonder then that the new congregations had such a general recourse to the school? Since the majority of them had their origin in France, the country in which anti-clericalism was at its strongest, the school became for them an existential factor. Consequently, their constitutions generally followed two models which had placed emphasis on the involvement of religious houses in social activities: the scheme drawn up by St. Jean-Baptiste de la Salle for School Brothers, and the seventeenth century model which had stipulated a plurality of apostolic activities for French religious priests.[21]

---

[20] The introduction in 1870 of an Education Act in England made elementary education compulsory for the masses, and inspired the first moves of the British Government towards the education of the natives in the colonies.

[21] For more details on the special features of the new congregations, see R. Aubert, "Die Wiedergeburt der alten Orden und das Aufblühen neuer Kongregationen," *Handbuch der Kirchengeschichte*, ed. H. Jedin (Freiburg: Herder, 1971), VI/1, pp. 247-259.

The missionary society which was to extend the educational ideal to Eastern Nigeria was the Holy Ghost Congregation. It came into existence in 1848 after the amalgamation of the Holy Ghost Society, founded in 1703 by Claude François Poullat des Places, with the Society of the Immaculate Heart of Mary, founded in 1841 by Francis Maria Paul Libermann. A major factor in Libermann's missionary conception was the idea of organizing local clergies and hierarchies, a viewpoint which was strengthened by the precarious experiences of his society in the West African Coast in the 1840s.[22] Convinced that the localization of the Church was a task which could not be achieved without a certain measure of civilization, he accordingly gave the education of the natives a central position in his missionary programme which he sent to Propaganda in 1846.[23] Among other things, the plan envisaged the establishment of elementary schools in every mission centre for the education of the general public. To enable the missionaries to come into more intimate contact with their pupils, it also recommended the establishment of boarding schools for younger children. In both categories of schools only the first basics of education were to be given. However, children who showed some exceptional aptitudes were to be sent to central schools for a more elevated primary education suitable for priest candidates, catechists, and artisans.[24]

The "Libermann plan" brought order and uniformity into the various pioneer missionary quests along the West African Coast. Hitherto the absence of a functioning formula, which was caused sometimes by inexperience and bizarre experiments, had greatly hampered the progress of the Missions.[25] After some initial scathing attitudes towards Libermann's missionary programme, the leaders of the Missions finally arrived at the consensus that the school was the most suitable method of evangelization among native societies. This judgment was given expression in a letter to Propaganda in 1853 by Mgr. Aloyse Kobès, the Pro-vicar of Senegambia:

---

[22] See P. F. Moody, "The Growth of Catholic Missions in Western, Central and Eastern Africa," *Sacrae Congregationis de Propaganda Fide Memoria Rerum, 1622-1972*, ed. J. Metzler (Freiburg: Herder, 1975), III/1, pp. 204-208.

[23] See L. Dohmen, "Missionsstrategische Gedanken des ehrwürdigen P. Libermann," ZM, 36 (1952), 153-155.

[24] See F.M.P. Libermann, "Mémoire à la Propagande," quoted in A. Engel, *Die Missionsmethode der Missionare vom Heiligen Geist auf den Afrikanischen Festland* (Neuß, 1932), p. 82.

[25] In Dakar, for instance, Mgr. Truffet had made abortive attempts to realize his dreams of an Afro-Roman Church that was free from all foreign influences. To achieve that goal, he had insisted that classes be taught only in Latin and the native languages, and that no books be used other than the Holy Bible. See A. Engel, *Die Missionsmethode*, p. 89.

We are in complete agreement with Mgr. Barron on following the mission formula proposed by M. Libermann, that schools and a central establishment must be started to ensure the formation of a native clergy. The reason is that the unhealthy climate does not allow missionaries to stay long enough to learn the native languages, and so these missions will never be sufficiently cared for by European workers.[26]

Nevertheless, it took the school method of evangelization some time to emerge as the missionary strategy par excellence. Among the early missionaries in Africa, there were some who wanted to be known only as missionaries and not as schoolmasters, and some who argued that much of Western education was in fact detrimental to the Africans. The views of Father Carlo Zappa of the Society of African Missions—the French congregation which evangelized the greater part of Nigeria—come to mind here. In a letter that has now become famous, he outlined the reasons for his misgivings about the apostolate of the school as follows:

It is well known amongst all my brethren of the Mission at least until recently, that I have not favoured or much encouraged the work of schools, I believe, as I still do, that in encouraging them to be instructed we are pushing our young people towards the European business house and towards Government employment, and I don't think we ought to be the first to push them in this direction. In such work they are far from the guardianship of their families and the missionaries, and are naturally led into places of corruption where their morals and their faith are practically certain to be lost... For this reason I have always thought the school method involves a misunderstanding of our mission which is simply an apostolic affair; we would virtually be committing a crime against the souls of these children, if we were to be the first means of leading them into this dangerous situation, without being actually forced to do so.[27]

Such views as expressed in this passage seem to reinforce the popular belief that the French missionaries in Nigeria were less enthusiastic about the school than their Irish counterparts.[28] Father J. Jordan, an Irish missionary, has tried to explain this alleged strand in French missionary enterprise with a reference to the bitter memories which the French Fathers had of the *école laique* in France.[29] Highlighting the preeminence of Irish educational endeavours, he pointed out that the school was for the French merely "'ancillary to the main work of evangelization through

---

[26] Quoted in F. Moody, "The Growth of the Catholic Missions," p. 208.

[27] "C. Zappa to Mgr. Pellet," 12 February, 1911, quoted in J. U. Todd, *African Mission* (London, 1962), p. 121f.

[28] Father Carlo Zappa was Italian and his views about the school were undoubtedly personal. However, our discussion here is on the French missionary society which he represented.

[29] Cf. J. P. Jordan, *Bishop Shanahan of Southern Nigeria* (Dublin: Clonmore & Reynolds, 1949), p. 30.

the Christian village and the community of redeemed slaves.''[30] This
attempt to exclude the French from basking in the glow of the educational
triumphs of the new congregations of which they were founders and
innovators was received with great indignation by the Society of African
Missions, a fact which becomes most apparent from the reaction of an
archivist of the Society in 1949. When Father M. J. Walsh, an Irish
member of the Society, was about to write a thesis that year on the contribution of the Catholics to education in Western Nigeria, the archivist
requested him to devote special attention to Father Jordan's utterances
which, he said, were ''absolutely untrue'' as far as his congregation was
concerned. In what may well be a representative opinion of all French
missionaries, he went on to emphasize that ''all the missions, without
exception, began with a school.''[31] That Father Walsh made the refuta-
tion of Jordan's views the subject of the very first chapter of his work
shows how seriously he took the task that was put before him.[32]

Although the secularization in France had adverse effects on French
missionary movement, it would indeed be unrealistic to suggest that the
French missionaries failed, as a result, to avail themselves of the advantages of the school in the Missions. The mission records are full of proofs
that long before the Irish missionaries were, for political reasons, called
to Nigeria, the French pioneers had adopted the school apostolate as their
primary missionary strategy. In 1885, for instance, Bishop Planque, the
Superior General of the Society of African Missions, asked Propaganda
Fide to take disciplinary measures against a rebellious young missionary,
James Hennebery, who ironically must be Irish or English, for his anti-
school sentiments and propaganda in the Gold Coast Mission. The
observations of the Mission leader prove beyond doubt that for the
Society of African Missions, as indeed for all the new missionary congregations, which were either French or had French beginnings, the
school had an overriding priority in the work of evangelization. He
wrote:

> James Hennebery knows very well that our Mission prospers primarily
> through the education of children. Yet, on arriving at Elmina [Gold Coast]
> he intends, in his youthful pride, to change everything in the Mission; it
> would be more appropriate to say that he wants to suppress a Mission
> which finds it impossible to progress without the youth. It was through the
> schools that Elmina had more than 300 baptisms in 1884.[33]

----

[30] Ibid., p. 35.
[31] SMA:4/955, 14/2W/1949, "The Archivist to M. J. Walsh," 30 August, 1949.
[32] See M. J. Walsh, "The Catholic Contribution to Education in Western Nigeria,
1861-1926," (unpubl. M. A. Thesis, Univ. of London 1951), pp. 115.
[33] AP: SC. Angola, vol.8, "Planque to Prefect of Propaganda," Lyon, 10 May, 1885.
Recounting the great difficulties which the Society of African Missions experienced in

A point which emerges from our discussion so far is that the use of the school as a medium for proselytization was not a prerogative of the Irish. As a matter of fact, it was a Frenchman, Father Léon Lejeune, who initiated the revolutionary process which ultimately placed the school at the centre stage of Catholic missionary enterprise in Eastern Nigeria. Nevertheless, Father Jordan's observations concerning the attitude of the French towards the school were not totally unfounded. As we shall see in later chapters, the French missionaries did receive the extraordinary drive towards education in Nigeria with dampened enthusiasm. But that was an attitude whose cause lay more in their educational and missionary backgrounds than in any political imperatives. If the Irish were more willing than the French to follow an accelerated pace in the educational race, it was chiefly because they were a new generation of missionaries prepared specially for that task.

The success of the school as a means of evangelization was by no means instantaneous. In Eastern Nigeria, as indeed in all Africa, it came after many trials and failures. Not until after the acquisition of some vital field experiences and better knowledge of the social and political realities in the mission lands did the missionary congregations begin to translate their educational theories into meaningful results.

II. *Political and Missionary Struggles on the Niger*

1. *French and British Pretensions on the Niger*

For several centuries, the European nations maintained a steady contact with the West African coast without however venturing into its hinterland. They depended exclusively on native middlemen for the smooth running of the infamous slave trade. Nor did sporadic foreign incursions into the "darkest" continent via the Saharan caravan routes go beyond the northern frontiers of the inland kingdoms of West Africa. This long isolation of the mysterious West African hinterland was ended in the nineteenth century following the discovery of the true course of the Niger by adventurous British explorers. Thereafter, the Niger and Benue territories became a scene of the greatest political upheavals in nineteenth century Africa.

Almost simultaneously with the European penetration of the West African hinterland, the Christian Missions were endeavouring to make

Lagos in the 1860s and 1970s, Sir James Marshall, a very keen observer and long-time friend of the Catholic Missions in West Africa, confirmed that the French Fathers saw in the school "their best hopes of success." J. Marshall, *Reminiscences of West Africa and its Missions* (London: St. Anselm's Society, 1885), p. 29.

good their long neglect of the Africans in their missionary enterprise.[34] Soon the Niger was to become, in the words of Bishop Taylor of the Vicariate of Western Nigeria, "God's liquid road between sea and desert."[35] By 1901 Nigeria alone possessed three of the nineteen Apostolic Vicariates and Prefectures that had been established along West Africa from Senegambia to Angola.[36]

Much of the political wrangle that took place on the Niger in the nineteenth century between the European Powers was centred on the quest for raw materials which the opening of the Niger waterway promised in abundance. At first, the struggle was carried out by private factories which had established themselves along the Niger and Benue river banks. However, to the chagrin of the French, the National African Company, a private British enterprise, endeavoured from the onset to secure the Niger territory for the Crown. The British Government, for its part, apparently showed no territorial ambitions in Africa during the first half of the nineteenth century. Her primary interest in the West African coast was the extermination of the slave trade. It was largely the expansionist colonial policy of the French that eventually forced the British to reconsider their own policy. By 1852 they had placed Lagos under their "protection." Continued mistrust of the French led to the occupation of the town in 1861. In the following year, Lagos and its environs were made a British colony with a Governor and a Legislative Council.

An event which precipitated a definitive partition of Africa was the Berlin Conference held in 1885. Article 26 of its general Act granted freedom of navigation on the Niger and the Congo, and assigned the responsibility of protecting the subjects and establishment of the European nations on the Niger to Britain. Through a royal charter, the Niger Company was in turn authorized by Britain to exercise imperial authority and administration in the Niger territory, a mandate which allowed this private enterprise to assume the name: Royal Niger Company. Its most celebrated head, George Taubman Goldie, was accredited

---

[34] As a matter of fact, a missionary group of the Anglican Church Missionary Society accompanied the ill-fated Niger Expedition of 1841. On the Catholic side, the Congregation of the Immaculate Heart of Mary, founded in 1841 by Father Libermann, was one of the first missionary societies to make the conversion of Africans their raison d'être. The venerable founder wrote: "For many centuries legions of apostles have been rushing...to the farthest ends of the Earth...while millions of souls are languishing in uncertainty and misfortune at the very door of Europe." Quoted in L. Dohmen, "Missionsstrategische Gedanken des ehrw. P. Libermann," p. 153.
[35] Quoted in *Bulletin de la Congregation des Pères du Saint-Esprit* (cited hereafter as CSE:*Bulletin*), 37 (1935-1936), 541.
[36] For a list of the mission territories, see AP: N.S. R.141/1901, Vol. 214, p. 232.

with being more of a statesman than a businessman.[37] Under his leadership, the Company took measures to prevent the other European nations
from securing a foothold on the Niger. When a French explorer named
Mizon ascended the Niger in 1890, for instance, he was allegedly
attacked by the natives at the instigation of the Royal Niger Company.
The answer of the Company to the charges made afterwards against it
was that what was legal in the Niger territory was the use of the waterway
but not the acquisition of land without authorization—the Company's
authorization. The French regarded this bold usurpation of authority as
an undisguised infidelity to the stipulations of the Berlin Conference and
threatened to close the Congo if the Company went on to "confiscate"
the Niger.[38] The monopoly of the Royal Niger Company also constituted
a subject for debate in the German Parliament in 1889, with Bismark
promising to intervene in person.[39] However, probably with the support
of the British Government, the Royal Niger Company remained
undaunted during the course of the popular agitations against it in
Europe. Outmanoeuvred and frustrated, the French companies sold off
their possessions and withdrew from the Niger.[40] The era of British
hegemony in Nigeria had begun.

A boundary dispute over the British possessions in the Benue region
and the German possessions in Northern Cameroons was settled in
1893.[41] Through a diplomatic convention signed in Paris on June 14,
1898, the delimitation of French and British West Africa was achieved,
making Britain the sole master of the Niger Countries.[42] The following
year, the British Government withdrew the charter of the Royal Niger
Company, and in 1900 the southern part of the territory administered by
the Company was merged with the Oil River Protectorate to form the
Protectorate of Southern Nigeria under a High Commissioner. This was
the first time the name "Nigeria" was used officially.[43]

---

[37] For more details on the impact of Goldie on the Nigerian colony, see J. E. Flint,
Sir George Goldie and the Making of Nigeria (London: Oxford Univ. Press, 1960).

[38] Cf. *Le Soleil*, 24 June, 1891.

[39] Cf. CSE:191/A/IV, "La Question Coloniale au Parlement Allemand," Berlin, 26
November, 1889.

[40] See AP:SC Angola, Vol.9, "Planque to Prefect of Propaganda," Lyon, 27 June,
1889, p. 187ᵛ. See also CSE:191/B/XI, "Father Lutz to Superior General," Akassa, 18
December, 1885; Bishop A. LeRoy, "Les missions françaises de la Nigeria," *Echo de
Paris*, 3 April, 1904.

[41] See KM, 33 (1904), 202.

[42] Cf. Ministère des Affaires E'trangères, *Documents Diplomatiques, Afrique: Convention
entre la France et la Grande Bretagne* (Paris: Imprimerie Nationale, 1898).

[43] Cf. M. J. Bane, *Catholic Pioneers in West Africa* (Dublin: Conmore & Reynolds, 1956),
p. 171.

The political feud that existed throughout the nineteenth century between the French and the British in West Africa was not without consequences for Catholic missionary enterprise. If complications arose here, it was chiefly because of flawed approaches to the all-important question of the relationship between Mission and colonial politics. Some official guidelines on this issue were contained in Instructions of the Propaganda Fide and in papal Encyclicals. In these the missionaries were enjoined to avoid involvement in politics.[44] However, the question of national propaganda in the Missions was a pit into which almost every missionary fell, and by all account, the French fall was the heaviest of all.[45] It was not unusual, especially in the nineteenth century, for French missionaries to make overt their political predilections.[46] No less a personality than Bishop Alexander LeRoy, the Superior General of the Holy Ghost Fathers, publicly criticized the French Government for ''abandoning'' the French Niger Company by whose courtesy the French missionaries came to the Niger. Had the company been given official backing, he argued, the Niger and Benue countries would have been secured for France in such a way that would have made it possible to travel from the Atlantic to Lake Chad without leaving French territory.[47] It was such expressions of territorial ambition by French missionaries that brought them into conflict with the British colonial authorities.

---

[44] For the Instructions of Propaganda to the first Apostolic Vicars in 1659, see *Collectanea Sacrae Congregationis de Propaganda Fide* (Rome, 1893), No. 300; for the Instructions to the Apostolic Vicars of China in 1883, see also ibid., No. 328. The catastrophe of World War One gave Pope Benedict XV the occasion to warn missionaries against excessive nationalism in the Missions. Cf. ''Maximun Illud,'' AAS, 11 (1919), 446f.

[45] For more details on the political and nationalistic inclinations of the missionaries, see F. Schwager, ''Missionstätigkeit und nationale Propaganda,'' ZM, 6 (1916), 109-134.

[46] Bishop Angouard, a French missionary who worked in the Congo, took it to be a great compliment when people said he was more of a French politician than a Catholic missionary. F. Brunnetières conceded in his book: *Les Missions Catholique Française au XIXᵉ Siècle* that the spreading of the Christian faith also advanced the cause and civilization of his fatherland. Perfectly in agreement with him, his publishers easily decorated his mission history book with a more patriotic sub-title: *La France au dehors*. Cf. F. Schwager, ''Missionstätigkeit...,'' p. 109f.

[47] A. LeRoy, ''Les Missions Françaises de la Nigeria,'' *Echo de Paris*, 3 April, 1904. The Superior did not say precisely which of the French missionary societies was invited to the Niger by a French Niger Company. However, since there were no more French factories at Onitsha or Lokoja by 1885, when the Holy Ghost Fathers first came to the Niger, we may presume he spoke of the Society of African Missions which made an extensive tour of the Niger territory in 1883. However, if he referred to his own congregation, the Holy Ghost Fathers, then these must have accepted the invitation of the French Company rather too late, for by 1885, the French Niger Companies had, as has been seen, sold off their businesses to the English, a thing which ought to have been common knowledge both in Gabon and in Paris.

In Western Nigeria, the Lagos colonial Government was at odds with the French Society of African Missions in 1888 for the latter's knowledge and active support of a treaty which a French explorer named Viard signed that year at Abeokuta. In that agreement the Egba chiefs placed their country under French protection. Thereafter, a serious campaign was carried out to introduce English missionaries into British West Africa.[48] In the Niger country, a strained relationship existed between the Royal Niger Company and the French Holy Ghost Fathers largely because of the political leanings of the latter. However, it must be conceded that the British did not make the replacement of French missionaries with English missionaries an issue in official government policy. As the Propaganda Congregation rightly judged, the campaign pursued in 1889 to give the Niger Catholic Missions an English character was the personal undertaking of Sir James Marshall alone with the support of Cardinal Manning.[49] Goldie's position was that the Royal Niger Company was prepared to accept missionaries of all nationalities and denominations.[50] It was the necessity of having English-speaking missionaries to run the mission schools that eventually led to the replacement of the French missionaries by the Irish.

2. The Catholic Missions in Southern Nigeria before 1885

The African continent was sealed off from the Christian religion by the conquests of the Moslems in the seventh and eighth centuries. It was not until the fifteenth century that efforts were made, in the wake of the geographical discoveries in that century, to re-introduce Christianity in Africa. Supported by their political leaders, Portuguese priests undertook missionary activities on the western coast. According to Joâo de Barros,

[48] For details on the Viard case and the efforts made to give Catholic Missions in Western Africa an English character, see AP:SC Angola, Vol. 9. "J. Marshall to Mgr. Stonor," Rochampton Park, 9 February, 1889, pp. 144r-147v. He calls the involvement of the SMA in the Viard case "a mischievous interference in political matters." See also ibid., "Planque to Prefect of Propaganda," Lyon, 27 June, 1889, pp. 185r-190r; ibid., "Planque to Prefect of Propaganda," Lyon, 4 October, 1889. p. 237rv; CSE:191/B/I, "Planque to Superior General of the Holy Ghost Fathers," Lyon, 14 June, 1889; The African Times (London), February, 1889.
[49] Cf. CSE:191/B/I, "Propaganda to Father Eschbach," 5 July, 1889. Among the many letters of Sir James Marshall on this issue to Church dignitaries, see AP:SC Angola, Vol. 9. "J. Marshall to Propaganda," London, 12 March, 1889, pp. 153-154; ibid., "J. Marshall to Mgr. Stonor," Rochampton, 27 March, 1889, pp. 158r-165r (in this letter he doubts whether Father Chause, if made a bishop, would "be at all anxious to lessen the French character of the Missions," p.159); ibid., "J. Marshall to Propaganda," London, 17 April, 1889, pp. 179-171; CSE:191/B/XI, "J. Marshall to Father Lutz," Rochampton Park, 28 May, 1989; "Cardinal Newman and West Africa," Illustrated Catholic Missions (April, 1891), p. 193.
[50] Cf. CSE:191/B/I, "Propaganda to Father Eschbach," 5 July, 1889.

a Portuguese royal chronicler, the first Portuguese to reach the Benin coast in 1485 was Fenao de Po.[51] Thereafter, a number of abortive efforts were made to establish the Christian religion at the Oba's court.[52]

In spite of the repeated presence of white missionaries in Benin, Christianity failed to take firm roots there.[53] Nor did the missionary undertakings in Warri in the seventeenth century, when Italian Capuchins, operating from Sao Thomé, succeeded in establishing Christianity at the Olu's court, produce the desired results.[54] In 1733, a report reaching Propaganda said that the Missions of Benin and Warri, like the other Missions in the West African coast, had to be abandoned for lack of missionaries.[55] By the close of the eighteenth century, all that remained of the Catholic missionary endeavours in Southern Nigeria were "a few names and the addition of crucifixion to native punishment of criminals."[56]

It is now generally believed that the motives of the kings of Benin for demanding missionaries must have been anything but religious. Accordingly, the failure of the Missions among the inhabitants is often attributed to lack of cooperation from their rulers.[57] However, given the

---

[51] Cf. L. Kilger, "Die Missionsversuche in Benin," ZM, 22 (1932), 305.

[52] For more information on the Missions of Benin and Warri, see ibid., pp. 305-319; A.F.C. Ryder, "The Benin Missions," *Journal of the Historical Society of Nigeria*, 2 (1961), 231-259; A.F.C. Ryder, "Portuguese Missions in Western Africa," *Tahrik*, 3, No.1 (1969), 113; J. A. Cavazzi, *Relation Historique de l'Ethiopie Occidentale*, Vol. III (Paris, 1732), pp. 432-462; J.F. Ajayi, *Christian Missions in Nigeria* (London: Longman, 1956), pp. 14.

[53] For three hundred years Catholic missionaries made sporadic contacts with Benin mainly from the Portuguese settlements in the islands of Sao Thomé and Principe. However, the only years when it can, with certitude, be said that they settled down in Benin were: 1515-1516, 1651-1653, 1664-1674, 1695 (the year Father Francesco da Monteleone went personally to Benin only to die at Qwato in November of the same year), and 1713-1714. See L. Kilger, "Die Missionsversuche in Benin," p. 319.

[54] For more details on the work of the Capuchins at Warri and Benin in the seventeenth century, see R. Streit, J. Dindinger, *Bibliotheca Missionum*, XVI, pp.685-686; 723-725.

[55] Cf. AP:Acta 1733, fol. 579, quoted in L. Kilger, "Die Missionsversuche in Benin," p. 319.

[56] E. D. Morel, *Nigeria: Its Peoples and Its Problems* (London: Frank Case, 1968), p. 214. In 1921 an old mission chapel was reported to be still standing in Warri, a discovery which showed that Christianity attained a more permanent character at Warri than in Benin.

[57] Somehow the missionaries failed to comprehend the complexities of the African society and the depth of its allegiance to its traditional ties. Accordingly, they easily overestimated the powers of the chiefs and kings, and doggedly held to the misguided notion that once a native ruler was won over to Christianity, the victory over his subjects would be piecemeal. Father Monteleone's evaluation of missionary success in Benin was that "It only needs the king to give the word that they should become Christians and all...will embrace the Faith." Quoted in A.F.C. Ryder, "The Benin Missions," p. 250. See also ibid., p. 255.

political intrigues that existed among the European Nations, and the strategy and scope of the Missions themselves, it is very much open to question whether Christianity would have taken a different course in Benin, as indeed in all West Africa, had the native rulers shown a more enthusiastic attitude.

Because of the lucrative trade in human beings, the English, the Dutch and the Danes did not hold the evangelization of the slave coast in great esteem. Is it any wonder, therefore, that Father Francesco da Monteleone, the Apostolic Vicar of Sao Thomé from 1684 to 1695, regarded them as the most dangerous enemies of the Missions on the West African coast?[58] Similarly, the restrictive policy with which the Portuguese endeavoured to safeguard their waning authority along the West African coast exerted a heavy toll on the progress of the Missions. In fact, the last mission station in Benin in the eighteenth century was said to have been "confiscated" by a Portuguese official.[59]

Furthermore, the scarcity of missionaries and their fleeting contacts with the natives could not have made lasting impacts on the African society. The records of the efforts of the Italian Capuchins to revive Christianity in Southern Nigeria between 1684 and 1714 reveal several sporadic and short-lived endeavours that did not go beyond mere flirtations with the royal courts at Benin and Warri. At the root of these superficial encounters lay always the lack of missionary personnel. In his letter of May 24, 1692, Father Francesco da Monteleone said that the chiefs of Calabar, Futu, Popu, and Accra, had expressed the wish to have missionaries among them. In December of the same year, he wrote that he could not start Missions at Calabar and Benin for lack of missionaries.[60] When two of the three Fathers who had settled at Warri died in 1692, the sole survivor, Father Protasio da Brescia, abandoned the Mission despite the pleas of the king of Warri.[61]

The only places where the Missions attained some measure of permanence were in the territories where there were European settlements, especially in Angola and Congo. To the chagrin of Father Monteleone, the preference of the majority of the Fathers who came to the African Missions was always with the areas where the Europeans exercised administrative powers. In November, 1693, for instance, he complained

    [58] ''F. Monteleone to Propaganda,'' Sao Thomé, 25 April, 1691, quoted in *Bibliotheca Missionum*, XVI, p. 724.
    [59] Cf. AP:Acta 1714, fol. 657, quoted in L. Kilger, "Die Missionsversuche in Benin," p. 319.
    [60] ''F. Monteleone to Propaganda,'' Sao Thomé, 29 December, 1692, quoted in *Bibliotheca Missionum*, XVI, p. 724.
    [61] Ibid.

that although there were 25 missionaries in Angola, none wanted to come over to Sao Thomé from where they would be sent to places without European settlements.[62] This state of affairs lends credence to Ryder's contention that the priesthood of Loanda and its environs was in fact not a missionary force, but rather "a parochial clergy serving the needs of a Europeanized community and a native population subject to it."[63] This may explain why there were in the missionary enterprise of the fifteenth to eighteenth centuries along the West African coast no recognizable attempts to educate the natives in order to relieve the white missionaries of their often precarious tasks. This lack of an extensive educational programme is the greatest single factor which distinguishes the missionary endeavours of these centuries from the labours of the nineteenth and twentieth centuries.

The pioneer of Catholic evangelism in colonial Nigeria was the Society of African Missions. Founded in Lyon in 1856 by Mgr. de Marion Brésillac, the Society embarked upon the evangelization of Dahomey in 1861.[64] From Whydah, Father Borghero, the leader of the Dahomey Mission, visited Lagos in March, 1862, the year the British annexed Lagos after having occupied it in 1861. He was warmly received at Lagos by a group of about 200 Catholics who were mainly ex-slaves from Brazil. The existence of so many Catholics at Lagos was particularly encouraging. Among the positive results of this first visit was also the generosity with which the British received the prospects of a future Catholic Mission in Lagos, a favour which the French missionaries did not easily get in the French-dominated Porto Novo.[65] From the Governor of Lagos a piece of land was acquired for a church and a school, but it was not until 1868 that a Mission was finally established at Lagos. By 1872 the existence there of an active Catholic community, which conducted its religious services in the Portuguese language, and which had a strong devotion to the Blessed Virgin, had become "a source of consolation and a cause of optimism," for the missionaries.[66]

By all account, the establishment of a Mission at Lagos was a landmark in the history of the Society of African Missions in West Africa. The first person to address himself to this reality was Father Borghero. The impression he received during his first visits to Lagos between 1862

---

[62] "F. Monteleone to Propaganda," Sao Thomé, 18 November, 1683, quoted in ibid., p. 725.

[63] A. F. C. Ryder, "Portuguese Missions in Western Nigeria," p. 5.

[64] See AP:SC Angola, Vol. 8, 1861-1868; P.F. Moody, "The Growth of Catholic Missions," p. 211f.

[65] Cf. M. J. Walsh, "The Catholic Contribution to Education," p. 4.

[66] "Father Deniard to Superior General," 4 April, 1872, quoted in Les Missions Catholiques (July, 1872), p. 407.

and 1864 was that because of its growing fame as a trading seaport, and in view of the emerging British influence along the West African coast, Lagos offered the greatest prospects for a succesful Mission among the Africans.[67] He was not mistaken: the success of the Society of African Missions in Lagos was a source of great inspiration for future missionary endeavours in the whole of Nigeria.[68]

A factor of major significance in the first Catholic missionary enterprise in Nigeria during the nineteenth century was the unique language situation which came about as a result of the political and social structures of the Lagos colony. By the close of the eighteenth century, Portuguese influence in West Africa was already on the wane. Nevertheless, the Portuguese language continued to be the lingua franca, as it had been since the fifteenth century. It is no wonder, therefore, that the first Catholic community in Lagos conducted its religious services in that language. What may cause eyebrows to be raised is the fact that under the guidance of French missionaries, Brazilian Catholics were conducting services in the Portuguese language in an English colony where Yoruba was spoken. This perfect confusion was to be assuaged in later years following the triumph of English as the language of commerce, but throughout the 1870s, the language problem was as acute as it was frustrating, especially with regard to the establishment of Catholic schools in Lagos.

The first Catholic school in Lagos was established on February 15, 1869, with 30 pupils, 16 boys and 14 girls.[69] Although it was not specifically stated, we may presume that since the majority of the Catholics were Portuguese-speaking, the school was also Portuguese. It is also possible that there was a mixture of Portuguese and English in the school, a likelihood which is strengthened by Father Bouche's remark that the school was not well organized. However, by 1872, there were two distinct Catholic schools in Lagos, one English and the other Portuguese, with the latter having more pupils than the former.[70]

Since the French Fathers were not conversant with English, they relied

---

[67] For Father Borghero's numerous reports and letters to Propaganda and to his Superior General, see AP:SC Angola, Vol. 8 (1861-1866).

[68] By 1883 the Lagos Mission had become so important as to be separated from Dahomey and raised to a metropolitan See with Father John Baptist Chause as Pro-vicar. It retained the name: Apostolic Vicariate of the Bight of Benin. The following year, the Apostolic Prefecture of the Upper Niger was created and was also assigned to the care of the Society of African Missions. It included most part of Northern Nigeria and the territories west of the Niger. Asaba later became the headquarter of the Mission. See KM, 13 (1885), 7; Annales de la Propagation de la foi, (1894), p. 2.

[69] SMA:17059, 14/80 200, "Father Bouche to Planque," Lagos, 25 February, 1869.

[70] See Les Missions Catholiques, (July, 1872), p. 467.

on Protestant teachers to keep their English school running.[71] However, recognizing the great importance of the school for the success of their enterprise, and given the fact that the colonial Administration in Lagos had made its grants to mission schools dependent on English being taught in them, the Society of African Missions began in 1876 to think seriously about giving their personnel some English character. A recommendation to this effect had been made by Father Borghero in 1862.[72] Following the appeal of the Superior General, Mgr. Planque, to the Irish to aid the French in the evangelization of Africa, an Apostolic College for African Missions was established in 1878 at Cork, Ireland.[73] In the same year, an Irishman, Brother Timothy Doyle, arrived in Lagos to take charge of the Catholic English school. He thus became the first Irish male missionary to reach Nigeria. By bringing in English-speaking missionaries to direct its educational activities, the Society of African Missions set a precedent which was later adopted by the Holy Ghost Congregation in Eastern Nigeria.

3. The Foundation of the Lower Niger Mission

It was not until 1885 that a Catholic Mission was finally established in the eastern part of the Niger. Behind this belated execution of a long-standing missionary project lay two main factors—the struggle between the French and the English over West African territories, and a protracted disagreement between the Society of African Missions and the Holy Ghost Congregation.

As long as the African continent was not yet clearly partitioned, Rome tended not to be in a hurry about creating new mission provinces, especially in territories where rivalry and conflict prevailed between the colonial powers. However, the inhibition caused by the political contentions on the Niger was a mere trifle in comparison with the effects of the dispute which existed between the two French missionary societies over the boundaries of their mission territories. In fact, Mgr. Schwindenhammer, the Superior General of the Holy Ghost Fathers, conceded in 1867 that the French Government had given up hope of establishing a Protectorate in Nigeria. He blamed the failure of his congregation to found a Mission there on misunderstandings with the Society of African Missions.[74]

---

[71] Cf. M. J. Walsh, "The Catholic Contribution to Education," p. 9.
[72] See AP:SC Angola, Vol. 8, pp. 230-235.
[73] See ibid., p. 10; J. Marshall, *Reminiscences*, p. 51.
[74] Cf. P. F. Moody, "The Growth of Catholic Missions...," p. 212.

If boundary disputes arose between the missionary societies operating on the West African coast, it was chiefly because the northern limits of their Missions remained largely undefined in the years when the African continent was still unexplored. Even the boundaries between the Vicariate of Benin and the Prefecture of the Upper Niger, two Missions belonging to the same congregation—the Society of African Missions—were not definitively fixed until 1894.[75] The Holy Ghost Congregation, whose Vicariate of the Two Guineas included a vast area of Western and Central Africa, had felt its jurisdiction encroached upon in 1861, when Father Borghero made his first visit to Lagos. It was probably against this background that Schwindenhammer wrote in 1867. However, Propaganda must have felt that it was better to cede territories to the society which was best disposed to carry out missionary expansion, namely, the Society of African Missions. In 1883, Fathers Holley and Chause made an extensive missionary exploration of the Yoruba country, going as far as to Bida in Northern Nigeria.[76] When the Prefecture of the Upper Niger was created in 1884, much of its southern boarder extended into territories originally assigned to the Vicariate of the Two Guineas.[77] In 1885, Mgr. Planque, the Superior General of the Society of African Missions, expressed his willingness to allow the Holy Ghost Fathers a free hand in the territories east of the Niger on the condition that they sent missionaries there without delay.[78]

It can be said, therefore, that the evangelization of Eastern Nigeria was expedited by pressure from the Society of African Missions. Bishop Le Berre, the Apostolic Vicar of the Two Guineas, was apparently not in a hurry to extend missionary activities in the Niger and Benue territories. By contrast, both the Society of African Missions and Propaganda were most anxious to establish Catholic presence in these territories which many reports had often recommended as a virgin land for effective Christian evangelism. The speed with which the Prefecture of the Upper Niger was created in 1884 underscored the urgency with which Rome received these recommendations. There was no doubt that Propaganda would have allowed the Society of African Missions to extend the southern boundary of its new Mission further into the mission

---

[75] See AP:N.S. R.141/1894, Vol. 49, "C. Zappa to Prefect of Propaganda," 20 September, 1894, p. 665f; see also ibid., "Planque to Prefect of Propaganda," Lyon, 18 January, 1889, p. 651; ibid., "Planque to Prefect of Propaganda," Rome, 24 December, 1892, p. 653rv.

[76] See KM, 13 (1885), 7-10, 30-33, 78-80, 101-104.

[77] See AP:N.S. R.141/1902, Vol. 237, p. 319.

[78] Cf. AP:SC Angola, Vol. 8, "Planque to Prefect of Propaganda," Lyon, 29 June, 1885.

territory of the Holy Ghost Fathers. To salvage their threatened jurisdiction, therefore, Paris and Gabon decided to found a Mission on the Niger in 1885.[79]

The man chosen to lead the new Mission was Father Joseph Lutz, a native of Dauendorf in the diocese of Strassburg. Hitherto, he had been Superior of the Mission of Boffa in the Rio Pongo district of French Guinea. The other members of his team included: Father Johann Horne, and Brothers Hermas and Jean-Gotto. Departing from Liverpool on October 8, 1885, they arrived at Akassa on November 20.[80] Their request at Akassa to be taken up the Niger in a vessel belonging to the Royal Niger Company was unfortunately refused, and they had to go to Brass for a passage inland.

The Akassa incident has become a topic for debate among historians in recent times. The controversy concerns a statement by Father Lejeune, the Prefect of the Lower Niger Mission from 1900 to 1905, that Father Lutz and his men were told that no missionaries other than the Protestants were needed in the Niger country.[81] Why did Father Lutz fail to mention such a serious matter in his rather detailed report to the Superior General on their journey to the Niger?

There is compelling evidence in Lutz's report that the *refusal* was political rather than religious. The Royal Niger Company had received information in advance from its leaders in London that some French missionaries were heading for the Niger. When these arrived at Akassa, they were, in the words of Father Lutz, ''denounced as agents of a new company.''[82] This fits well into the picture of the political situation on the Niger which we have so far been following in this chapter. Aware of the political bent of the French missionaries, the chief agent of the Royal Niger Company, a man named Serjant, had given orders that no unidentified travellers be allowed passage up the Niger in his absence. He no doubt knew that the French missionaries were not in possession of a letter of recommendation from London. His instruction was designed to prevent them from signing treaties with the native chiefs or carrying out

[79] See CSE:191/B/I, R. Daly, ''Reverend Father Lutz of Onitsha,'' undated notes _d on the diaries of the Prefect; CSE: *Bulletin*, 13 (1883-1886), 877 & 1054.

[80] See CSE:191/B/XI, ''Lutz to Superior General,'' Akassa, 18 December, 1885; CSE:*Bulletin*, 14 (1887-1888), 459-460.

[81] CSE:191/B/II, L. Lejeune, ''Report for *Les Missions Catholiques*,'' Onitsha, 1902. The controversial passage reads as follows: ''Le 20 Novembre [1885]... ils étaient à Akassa et sollicitaient un passage à bord d'un de bateaux de la Royal Niger Company pour remonter le fleure, passage qui leur fut refusé sous pretexte qu'on ne les connaisait pas et qu'il n'était nul besoin d'avoir dans ce pay des missionnaires autre que les protestants.''

[82] CSE:191/B/XI, ''Lutz to Superior General,'' Akassa, 18 December, 1885.

political activities in his absence, and was not aimed at excluding
Catholic missionaries from the Niger country. When Father Lutz eventually met Mr. Serjant at Onitsha, the latter in fact apologized for the
action of his representative at Akassa. His hospitality and friendliness
towards the Catholic missionaries, as reported by Father Lutz, now
appear very much at variance with Lejeune's version of the story.[83]

Yet, it would be wrong to suggest that the Prefect deliberately distorted
the facts. Writing seven years after the Akassa incident, he told the story
from the perspective of the prevailing relationship between the Catholics
and the Anglicans, which was one of bitter rivalry and open hostility. By
the 1890s, the Protestants had begun to regard the Catholics as introducing unfair competition in their sphere of influence, especially with regard
to what they saw as an aggressive Catholic educational policy. The active
support which the Anglicans received from the Royal Niger Company,
and the Company's discriminating attitude towards the Catholics were
factors which vindicated Lejeune's interpretation of the Akassa incident
as a rejection on denominational grounds.

Departing finally from Brass on November 26 with the help of an
English seaman named Townsend, Father Lutz and his men arrived at
Onitsha on December 6, 1885. They were welcomed with open arms by
the king and people of Onitsha, and promised any piece of land of their
choice.

For the pioneer missionaries, it was nearness to the Niger—the only
means of communication in the area—and a source of palatable water
that were decisive in the choice of a site for the future Mission. These
conditions were found fulfilled at a place called *Nkissi* near the wharf, and
it was here that the Catholic missionaries secured a site for the Mission.
For a while, Father Lutz and his men stayed in a house put at their
disposal by agents of the Royal Niger Company. But on April 8, 1886,
they were able to take permanent quarters in their own simple house built
on the mission grounds with the help of the natives.[84] On Easter Sunday,
April 25, 1886, the first Catholic Mission in Eastern Nigeria was blessed
and dedicated to the Holy Trinity.[85].

Among the many problems that faced the new Mission in its first years
at Onitsha was that of communication with the Vicariate of the Two
Guineas to which it was attached. It was not only the long distance that

[83] Ibid. : Il avait appris qu'on nous avait refusé le passage à Akassa.... Il nous reçut
très bien, s'exusa d'abord de la conduite qu'on avait tenue à notre égard à Akassa, disant
que son agent été obligé de se conformer aux ordres qu'il avait reçu.... Il s'offrit en même
temps de nous rendre tous les services possibles dans notre entreprise.''
[84] See CSE:191/B/XI, ''Lutz to Emonet,'' Onitsha, 14 May, 1886.
[85] See CSE:191/B/I, R. Daly. ''Reverend Father Lutz of Onitsha,'' p. 4.

separated the small team of missionaries from their headquarters in Gabon that mitigated against the smooth running of the new station, but also the political barriers that lay between Gabon—which was French— and the Niger country—which was English. Given its large pagan population and its freedom from Moslem domination, Onitsha was seen as holding ideal prospects for a successful Mission. Although the Protestants had been there since 1857, they had not yet made lasting impacts on the society. It was argued that a Catholic Mission would provide a necessary counter to their influence. These were the factors which had induced Father Lutz to choose Onitsha as a starting-point for a Mission in Eastern Nigeria, and not Igbebe as was originally envisaged.[86] They were also to be instrumental in the decision to separate Onitsha from Gabon. Furthermore, it was realized that raising the Onitsha Mission to the status of a Prefecture would not only solve its administrative problems, but also enable it to get financial aid from charitable organizations in Europe.[87]

A proposal to that effect was made to Rome in February, 1889, by Mgr. Emonet, the Superior General of the Holy Ghost Congregation.[88] However, his request coincided with Sir James Marshall's campaign for an English mission province in West Africa, a call which received sustained impetus from the intervening support of the English episcopacy. Had there been enough English missionaries at the time, Propaganda would have ceded the Niger countries to their charge.[89] But the Society for Foreign Missions at Mill Hill, whose members were in fact largely people from Belgium, Germany, Holland, and France, was in no position to undertake a Mission in the Niger territories.[90] This knowledge, and the assurance from the Royal Niger Company that non-British missionaries would not be discriminated against, disposed Rome to announce the creation of the Prefecture of the Lower Niger in May, 1889.[91]

The new Prefecture was limited in the East by the German possessions in the Cameroons, in the South by the Atlantic Ocean, in the West by

---

[86] See CSE:191/B/XI, "Lutz to Superior General," Onitsha, 20 January, 1886.

[87] Cf. CSE:191/B/XI, "Lutz to Superior General," Onitsha, 28 January, 1888.

[88] CSE:191/B/I, "Emonet to Prefect of Propaganda," Paris, 4 February, 1889; see also CSE:*Bulletin*, 15 (1889-1891), 357-360.

[89] See CSE:191/B/I, "Propaganda to Father Eschbach," 5 July, 1889. By June 1889, the Superior General of the Society of African Missions was ready to confide the Prefecture of the Upper Niger to the charge of English missionaries if that would "satisfy Mr. Marshall" (AP:SC Angola, Vol.9, "Planque to Prefect of Propaganda," Lyon, 27 June, 1889, p. 190).

[90] Cf. CSE:191/B/I, "Propaganda to Father Eschbach," 5 July, 1889.

[91] See CSE:191/B/I, "Propaganda to Emonet," 10 May, 1889; CSE:191/B/XI, "J. Marshall to Father Lutz," 28 May, 1889; CSE: *Bulletin*, 15 (1889-1891), 360.

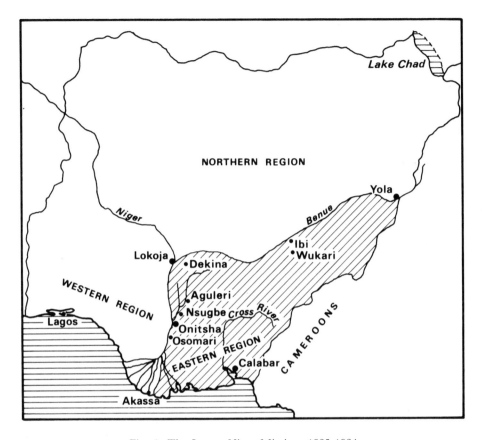

Fig. 1: The Lower Niger Mission, 1885-1934.

the Niger, and in the North by the Benue, from Lokoja to Yola.[92] It retained these boundaries till 1934, when the Mission was split into three—the Onitsha-Owerri Vicariate, and the Calabar and Benue Prefectures.[93] In 1919, the name "Prefecture of the Lower Niger" was changed to "Prefecture of Southern Nigeria," a name whose raison d'étre was alone the need to conform to the government styling of the colony.[94] Otherwise, it took little notice of the fact that there were other Missions in Southern Nigeria, namely, those of the Society of African Missions in Western Nigeria.

---

[92] See CSE:*Bulletin*, 15 (1889-1891), 360.
[93] Cf. AAS, 27 (1935), 323-325.
[94] Cf. CSE:191/B/III, "LeRoy to Prefect of Propaganda," Paris, 29 September, 1919.

III. *The Land and Peoples of Eastern Nigeria*

The political boundaries of Nigeria in the period covered in this study—
1885 to 1950—were not usually coterminous with the ecclesiastical divisions. The Igala and Munshi countries, for instance, which were
included in the vast Prefecture of the Lower Niger until 1934, were
politically never a part of Eastern Nigeria. However, except for brief missionary endeavours at Dekina, Ibi, and Wukari during the prefectship of
Father Lejeune, these regions were not effectively evangelized until 1934.
The missionary and educational activities of the Lower Niger Mission
(later Vicariate of Southern Nigeria) were carried out almost exclusively
in that part of Southern Nigeria which, until the Nigerian civil war in
1967, was known as Eastern Nigeria. The greater part of this region lies
within the rain forest zone of West Africa.

The chief ethnic groups of the Eastern Region are the Igbo,[95] the Ijaw,
the Ibibio, and the Efik. Their profound linguistic differences are at the
same time the most prominent cultural features that distinguish one
group from the other. Although English has remained the official
language of the academic and business worlds of these peoples, the prominence of their various native vernaculars as the chief means of communication in their social and family lives has never been broken.

The Ijaw are the inhabitants of the great Niger delta. Of all the peoples
of South-Eastern Nigeria, they were the first to have contacts with the
Europeans, when in the fifteenth century the Portuguese began to pay
visits to their coastal towns. Some of their chief ports like Bonny,
Okirika, Buguma, Abonnema, Degema, Brass, Nembe and Akassa
became famous (or infamous) as a result of the slave trade. In the nineteenth century, they served not only as outlets for industrial raw-
materials, but also as landing grounds for Christian missionaries. The
chief occupation of the Ijaw is fishing and trade along the delta
waterways.

The Ibibio and the Efik, two ethnic groups with close linguistic
affinity, are the second largest group of peoples in Eastern Nigeria. Two
of their towns, Anua and Calabar, became very important Catholic
strong-holds. Like the Ijaw, the Efik had early contacts with the Europeans in connection with the slave trade. The Presbyterian Church of
Scotland Mission established a Mission among them as early as 1846.

A distinct group from the Ibibio and the Efik are the peoples of the

---

[95] As a result of the phonetic problems which the Europeans generally had with
African digraphs, the word *Ibo* was widely employed by them instead of the locally used
form, *Igbo*. This latter form shall be used throughout this work, with the former appearing only in quotations from other sources.

north-eastern region. They live chiefly in and around Ogoja, Abakiliki and in the district north of Calabar. Their chief occupation is farming.

The most numerous and influential ethnic group in Eastern Nigeria are the Igbo. They are at the same time the second largest national unit in the whole of Nigeria and are found on both sides of the Niger. The Igbo had no kingdoms or powerful city states like the other major tribes of Nigeria. Until the nineteenth century, they lived in self-governing and democratic villages. Much of their early history is shrouded in mystery and legend. However, some concrete information about Igbo history and culture in the ninth century A.D. have been acquired from archaeological findings in 1936 at Igbo-Ukwu, a small village near Onitsha. The bronze figures discovered there are a testimony to a highly developed culture in ancient Igbo country.[96] The main centres of Igbo population east of the Niger are Owerri, Orlu, Umuahia, Onitsha, Enugu, and parts of Abakiliki and Port Harcourt provinces. These regions are among the most densely populated in all tropical Africa. The Igbo are primarily farmers and enterprising businessmen.

Igboland was the centre of Catholic missionary and educational endeavours in Nigeria in the nineteenth and twentieth centuries. A popular saying in the missionary era was: "The Igbos make good Catholics," a maxim whose promise the Fathers endeavoured to exploit to the fullest. "We like them," said one, "because they are so ready to be converted."[97] To a large extent, Igbo susceptibility to change in general, and to education in particular, had an important bearing on their readiness to accept Christianity. If they exhibited a natural tendency towards Catholicism, it was perhaps because, of all the Christian denominations, the Catholics best satisfied their propensity to seek external influences—better education, more profound liturgy, ample opportunity for contact with the white man. Even where the degree of real conversion in the Igbo became difficult to estimate, most Fathers believed "the Church could wait with patience for the spiritual to oust the material."[98] One cannot say for sure how long the Church's patience sustained this kind of exercise, but the fact remains that by the early 1950s, Igboland had become the most important stronghold of Catholicism in Nigeria, if not in all Africa.

From the onset, the Catholic Church in Nigeria also profited from another peculiar feature of the Igbo—their predilection for emigration.

---

[96] See E. Isichei, *A History of the Igbo People* (London: Macmillan, 1976), pp. 10-16.
[97] Quoted in S. Leith-Ross, *African Women: A Study of the Ibo of Nigeria* (1939; rpt. London: Routledge Kegan Paul, 1978), p. 356.
[98] Ibid., p. 170.

Unable to sustain a large population on a very poor and overwhelmed soil, the Igbo were forced to seek their livelihood "abroad" in other Nigerian towns and villages.[99] They brought their religion along with them wherever they went. By 1955 as many as 70 per cent of the Catholics in Northern Nigeria, and 30 per cent in Western Nigeria, were Igbo, a development which prompted some observers to style the Igbo tribe as "The Irish of West Africa."[100] It was among them that the French began a successful missionary work which was completed by the Irish.

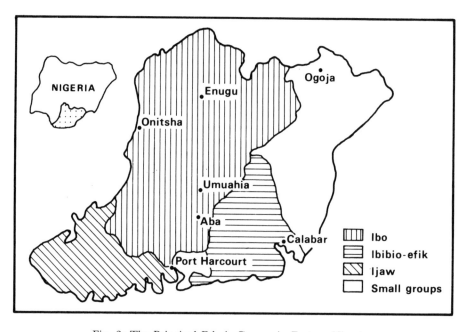

Fig. 2: The Principal Ethnic Groups in Eastern Nigeria.

---

[99] See G. Cockin, "The Land and Education in the Ibo Country of South East Nigeria," IRM, 33 (1944), 274-279; B. Floyd, *Eastern Nigeria: A Geographical Review* (London: Macmillan, 1969), pp. 28-31.

[100] ODA: J. Jordan, "Background Note to Nigeria, With Special Reference to Catholic Education," 31 May, 1955.

CHAPTER TWO

THE DEVELOPMENT OF CATHOLIC EDUCATION IN EASTERN NIGERIA, 1886-1905

I. *The Years of Experiments, 1886-1899*

According to a report on the Lower Niger Mission in the period from November 1885 to January 1888, the pioneer Catholic missionaries started a school at Onitsha "shortly after [their] arrival."[1] This vague statement is certainly of little help in determining the actual date of the beginning of Catholic educational efforts in Eastern Nigeria. However, since Father Lutz and his confrères lived temporarily from December 6, 1885, to April 7, 1886, in a house belonging to the Royal Niger Company,"shortly" must be sometime after they had occupied their new mission house in April 1886.[2] According to the report mentioned above, 20 of the 40 pupils of the school in question were said to be living in the Mission with the missionaries, a clear indication that the school must have taken off after the Mission had been blessed and opened to the general public, an event which took place on April 25, 1886. Father Richard Daly confirmed, in a study based closely on the personal diary of Father Lutz, that children were taken into the Mission "a few days" after this blessing ceremony.[3] One can therefore say with certitude that the inception of Catholic educational programme in Eastern Nigeria took place in April 1886, and not 1893, as has been suggested by Dr. Peter Clarke.[4]

It is true that the school was of a very rudimentary character, being largely a quasi catechism class in which one Father or Brother did his utmost best to communicate strange ideas to excited children in a language the latter could hardly understand. Nevertheless, the basic instructions that are given to infants in any normal school—reading, writing, and arithmetic—were offered in 1886 in the Onitsha-Wharf school from the onset. Father Lutz taught the children English, while

---

[1] CSE: *Bulletin*, 14 (1887-1888), 462.

[2] As has been seen, Father Lutz arrived at Onitsha on December 5, 1885, with Father Horne. But he went back to Brass shortly afterwards to collect their luggage and the two Brothers left behind there. It was not until December 29, 1885, that the team finally came back to Onitsha. It would be hard, therefore, to imagine that they undertook any missionary activities at Onitsha in 1885, let alone running a school.

[3] Cf. CSE:191/B/I, R. Daly, "Reverend Father Lutz of Onitsha," n.d., p. 4.

[4] See P. B. Clarke, "The Methods and Ideology of the Holy Ghost Fathers in Eastern Nigeria, 1885-1906," *Journal of Religion in Africa*, 6 (1974), 85.

Father Horne taught them arithmetic and writing. When the latter was forced to take a sick leave in 1887, his educational responsibilities were taken care of by Father Lecuyer and Brother Astier. In 1889, these two missionaries returned to France on health grounds, and Brother Hermas had to add teaching work to his many duties.[5]

The educational experiments of the first years of the Catholic Mission in Onitsha were remarkable from the point of view of the importance attached to them by both the Catholic missionaries and the leaders of Onitsha. To Fathers Lutz and Horne, the special function of the school as an effective means of propaganda became apparent during their first meeting with the Obi of Onitsha and his ministers on December 6, 1885. The aim of that eventful encounter with the native rulers of Onitsha was "to obtain permission to establish a Mission."[6] Although the speech made by Father Lutz to the assembly on the purpose of such a Mission was not recorded, some clues to its content are to be found in the following report by one of the Fathers on the reactions of the people:

> With regard to those present [at the meeting], they could not contain their astonishment and admiration for the fact that we have come from a distant country of the whites, not to engage in trade and money-making like the other Europeans, but to render them services and to educate their children.[7]

Although the proposal "to render them services" (*pour leur faire du bien*) may have included soul-saving activities, it certainly was made and understood in a humanitarian context. Especially the offer to make better persons out of the children through education was clearly designed to make good impression on the people.[8] This strategy was productive of good and instant results: the Obi of Onitsha promised to hand over two of his sons to the Fathers and to cede to them any piece of land they would chose.

Having demanded and obtained 20 hectares of land, Father Lutz and his team signed a land contract with the leaders of Onitsha on January 6, 1886.[9] The terms of the agreement underscored the great importance

---

[5] Cf. CSE:191/B/I, R. Daly, "Reverend Father Lutz," p. 5f.

[6] CSE.*Bulletin*, 14 (1887-1888), 460.

[7] Ibid.

[8] The civilizing mission of the Catholic missionaries was understood and greatly coveted beyond the frontiers of Onitsha at a very early stage. When the chief of Abutshi brought his one-year-old baby to the orphanage at Onitsha, his lengthy laudatio to Father Lutz contained, among other things, the following words: "White man, I salute you. God is with you, man from the country of the *Oyibos*. It is the gods who have sent you to this country to do us good: you teach the children to read books and to speak like one speaks there across the great sea." Quoted in CSE:*Bulletin*, 15 (1889-1891), 541.

[9] The Waterside, where the Catholics chose a site for the Mission in 1885, was largely uninhabited by 1860. But its population quickly experienced a phenomenal increase,

which the rulers of Onitsha attached to the civilizing mission of the Catholic missionaries. The Obi and his chiefs granted land to the Catholic Mission "in perpetuity," and declared it free from "all tributes and dues." However, in return for this favour, they got the missionaries to make a written pledge "to undertake the fostering care of children, their tuition in religion and secular teaching with the consent of their parents or guardians."[10]

That the leaders of Onitsha chose to seal their deeds with the foreign missionaries with written contracts showed the influence on native society by its contact not only with European commercial enterprise, but also with the Protestant Missions. Onitsha witnessed a tremendous transition in the nineteenth century. By 1856, Macgregor Laird and other trading companies had established commercial firms there. But it was in the 1880s, when the Royal Niger Company intensified its activities in the Niger territory, that Onitsha attained its popularity as a commercial centre. Treaty making between its leaders and the trading companies was a regular feature in its political and economic life. By the time the Catholics arrived at Onitsha in 1885, the Obi and his chiefs still retained sovereignty over their lands and the freedom to make non-political alliances. However, as soon as the Royal Niger Company began to exercise imperial authority on the Niger, the native rulers gradually lost their administrative powers.[11]

The Catholic pioneers benefited in many ways from the fact that the Protestant Missions were in the Niger territory before them. On arriving at Onitsha for the first time, Father Lutz and his companions did not find themselves in a savage land where no European language was spoken. On the contrary, they witnessed a civilized social routine at the Obi's court.[12] They must have spoken to the Obi directly or with the help of a native interpreter. To show them around the town was one of the Obi's men who spoke "a little English."[13] The terms of the land contract between the leaders of Onitsha and the Catholic missionaries, which was written in an unblemished legal English, was most probably formulated to a large extent by native agents of the Obi's court. These and other

following the activities of the European trading companies and of the Christian Missions there. By 1902, the population of Onitsha-wharf, as the Waterside was popularly known, was estimated at 6000 (see CSE:*Bulletin*, 21, 1901-1902, p. 519). But by 1937 it had risen to about 14,000. By contrast, the population of the Onitsha Township decreased from 17,969 in 1931 to 1,300 in 1937. Cf. C. K. Meek, *Law and Authority in a Nigerian Tribe: A Study in Indirect Rule* (Oxford, 1937; rpt. New York: Barnes & Noble, 1970), p. 14.

[10] CSE:192/A/VIII, *Journal of Southern Nigeria* (January, 1886).

[11] For more details on the history of Onitsha and the influence which contact with the Europeans had on its society, see C.K. Meek, *Law and Authority*, pp. 11-15.

[12] See CSE:*Bulletin*, 14 (1887-1888), 460.

[13] Ibid.

facts show the effect of Protestant educational enterprise on the Eastern Nigerian society prior to the coming of the Catholics. Most of the pioneer Catholic catechists and interpreters were men who had been educated in Protestant schools at Onitsha.

The success of Protestant educational labours in West Africa in the nineteenth century was an extraordinary by-product of the slave trade. As one of its programmes to rehabilitate freed slaves, the Anglican Church Missionary Society founded the Fourah Bay College in Freetown, Sierra Leone, in 1827. Many of the ransomed slaves who attended this first post-primary institution in West Africa were originally from Nigeria. They later emigrated to their motherland where they enthusiastically strove to put their learning at the disposal of their townsmen. It was with the help of these "Sierra Leonians," as the ex-students of Fourah Bay were popularly styled, that Bishop Samuel Ajayi Crowther of the Church Missionary Society founded a Mission at Onitsha in 1857.

To all appearances, the people of Onitsha were not as enthusiastic as their Obi to avail themselves of the educational services of the Catholics. The first signal to this attitude was given in that curious clause of the land contract which made the religious and secular education of the children dependent on the consent of their parents and guardians. As Father Lutz and his co-workers were to discover afterwards, this consent was not always easy to obtain. This experience had been made before them by the Anglicans, who most probably must have endeavoured to bring children to their schools through means that were displeasing to their parents. The Obi and his chiefs apparently tried, in their contract with the Catholics, to guide against this "malpractice" by emphasizing the rights of parents over the education of their children.

Two main factors seem to have been responsible for the people's reluctance to send their children to school. Firstly, the Onitsha district, as indeed the whole of the Anambra valley, was an agricultural country where children were traditionally expected to help their parents in the farms. When the boys were not engaged in this activity, they usually whiled away their time either by hunting or by making various handicrafts. Is it any wonder that the first Anglican school at Onitsha was opened for girls and not for boys? The latter felt themselves not drawn to the funny and effeminate class-room drillings.[14] Secondly, the parents and guardians must have sensed that the missionaries, by insisting that pupils should renounce their traditional religion and be baptized as

[14] Cf. A. B. Fafunwa, *History of Education in Nigeria* (London: George Allen & Unwin, 1974), p. 82f.

Christians, were indulging in an untoward angling for adherents. Since they held the beliefs of their ancestors in very high esteem, they consequently received the efforts of the missionaries to indoctrinate their children with other views with indignation.

In view of their strategy of using the school as a means of evangelization, the Catholic missionaries, for their part, saw this hitch in the acquisition of school children as a serious hindrance to their enterprise. By opting for a charity-orientated evangelism in which the school occupied a place of prominence, the Catholics hoped to secure a foothold on the otherwise impregnable pagan fortress. They understandably felt disappointment and frustration in the face of a trend in which parents showed a liking for mission social establishments—the schools, the orphanages, the refugee homes, the dispensaries, and hospitals—and resentment for the larger aim of these institutions—conversion. Sister Marie Claver of the Onitsha Convent expressed the feelings and views of the Catholic pioneer missionaries in the following passage:

> One thing...which causes us much pain is ingratitude. Parents in extreme anguish bring their children... [with the promise to leave them] with us once they regained their health. But was such a promise kept? ... We now make them sign an agreement to leave the children with us till they reach the age of marriage, in the hope of making them good Christians, who will in turn raise Christian families....[15]

A consensus in the opinions of the Catholic missionaries was that a total separation of the neophytes from their pagan families and friends was necessary in order to safeguard their Christian faith and way of life. This explains the special care and devotion shown to school children who were boarders. The desire to keep this category of pupils in the Mission until they got married and established Christian households made the natural urge of the parents to see their sons and daughters reunited with them look like ingratitude.

This brings us to the constitution of the Catholic schools. As a general rule, they were open to children of all social standings—freeborn and slaves, sons of chiefs and sons of the poor. However, the preference of the Fathers was largely with the boarders and not the externes who attended the Catholic schools from their homes. In 1886, there were 20 of the former and 20 of the latter in the Onitsha wharf school.[16] But by

---

[15] "M. Claver to Director of Sainte-Enfance," 1891, quoted in *A Hundred Years of the Catholic Church in Eastern Nigeria, 1885-1985*, ed. C. A. Obi (Onitsha: Africana-Fep, 1985), p. 40.

[16] Cf. CSE:*Bulletin*, 14 (1887-1888), 462.

1891, the number of boarders had risen to about 47, and that of the externes had decreased to about 10.[17]

In the main, there were three groups of boarders in the care of the Fathers and Sisters: 1) children ransomed from slavery, 2) children entrusted to the care of the Mission by their parents and guardians, 3) abandoned children, orphans, and refugees. Since each of these groups was of vital importance to the inception of Catholicism in Eastern Nigeria, it would be appropriate to discuss them in some detail.

1. *Children Ransomed from slavery*

As has been seen, there were 20 boarders in the Onitsha school in 1886. According to the Fathers, all of them were children who had been ransomed from slavery. Unlike in Lagos where Father Borghero started a Mission with a fairly large number of former slaves who had already regained their freedom, Father Lutz had to buy, house and feed his first Catholic adherents in Onitsha. The "slave method" was a celebrated missionary strategy in the nineteenth and early twentieth centuries. It involved the practice of freeing slaves by purchase and confining them in quasi Christian ghettos, where they were systematically instructed in the truths of the Christian faith. It was first practiced in Africa by Cardinal Lavigerie, the founder of the Congregation of the White Fathers. Following an outbreak of famine in Algiers, Lavigerie had taken care of about 1,800 orphans who otherwise would have perished in the catastrophe. He later got permission from the French colonial Government to bring up the children as Christians. As it were, he was forced by circumstances to settle the orphans in what were to become "Christian villages." Having made this experiment with the orphans, he tried it on redeemed slaves and encouraged other missionary societies to do the same. "Slaves, especially children," he wrote, "could be bought and gathered in Christian settlements; these would form the nucleus of a growing Christian Church."[18]

The Cardinal had drawn his inspiration largely from the controversial Christian state organized and governed by the Jesuits in Paraguay from 1608 to 1767. To facilitate the conversion and education of the Indianers of Paraguay, the Jesuits freed them from the oppressive rule of the Spanish conquerors and settled them in small independent Christian towns known as *Reductions*. Greatly disliked by the Spanish authorities for

---

[17] Cf. CSE:*Bulletin*, 16 (18911893), 335.
[18] Quoted in S. Neill, *A History of Christian Missions* (Middlesex: Penguin, 1964), p. 428.

being a state in a state, the *Reductions* were finally dismantled in 1767 following the expulsion of the Jesuits from Paraguay in that year. The extinction of the *Reductions* is considered by many today to be a major gap in mission history. Nevertheless, the experiment by the Jesuits had a lasting impact on foreign Missions.

For a long time, the "slave method," which was usually employed in connection with the "Christian village" method, was considered to be the right missionary strategy for Africa, where slavery had made deep inroads in the social lives of the natives. Although international slavery had been abolished by the second half of the nineteenth century, domestic slavery was carried out with unbroken regularity, especially in West Africa—the great slave coast. It was customary for a rich West African man to measure his wealth in terms of the number of wives, children, and slaves in his possession. At Onitsha, where the Catholic Mission in Eastern Nigeria was started, slaves were publicly exhibited for sale in both regular and makeshift markets. Writing to Propaganda in 1912, Father Shanahan recalled the experiences of the pioneer missionaries with the infamous trade in human beings:

> On the sandbank before our eyes, in Onitsha, slaves were once publicly marketed, and our Fathers redeemed them daily to the extent their meagre resources permitted. Soon hundreds of these unfortunates were living in the Mission, and it was no small task to feed, clothe and house them; no easy task to dress their hideous wounds and gradually to instruct them and change them to a Christian way of life.[19]

The ransoming of slaves was a major objective in the activities of the charitable organizations of the nineteenth and early twentieth centuries. Propaganda Fide, for its part, was sending over 20,000 Francs annually to each of the Catholic Missions on both sides of the Niger for anti-slave activities.[20] Though relatively insufficient, this money was of immense help to Catholic missionary enterprise in Eastern Nigeria in the early years when the redeemed slaves were about the only adherents to the Catholic faith. As has been seen, the Fathers went to the "slave bank" at Onitsha and bought their future neophytes in a measure that was commensurate with the meagre funds at their disposal. By 1888, the price of a slave varied from 25 to 250 Francs, depending on his age, health, and physical features. The Catholic pioneers preferred little children, the sick and the aged because, as they said, this group of persons most attracted the sympathy of the missionaries and cost less money.[21]

---

[19] "Shanahan to Cardinal Gotti," 1 September, 1912, quoted in J. Jordan, *Bishop Shanahan of Southern Nigeria*, p. 89.

[20] See CSE:192/B/III, "Lejeune to Superior General," Onitsha, 20 October, 1903.

[21] Cf. CSE:*Bulletin*, 14 (1887-1888), 464.

The redeeming of sick and aged slaves was a proof that the anti-slavery activities of the Catholics had genuine humanitarian motives—to alleviate the plights of the unfortunate victims of the heinous trade. However, an overriding priority was always given to the redeeming of children, who formed the pupils of the first Catholic schools at Onitsha. Their availability had become for the Catholic missionaries an indispensable factor in the work of evangelization. In 1899, Father Pawlas supported his plans to found a Mission at Brass with the argument that a large number of slaves would be readily available there.[22] In fact the dependence of the Fathers on the slaves had become so absolute that they expressed deep concern in 1888 when Major MacDonald, an official of the British Government, forbade the sale of slaves at Onitsha.[23]

However, there is compelling evidence that the slave method of evangelization had begun to wane during the last decade of the nineteenth century. The records of the Mission show that fewer slaves were bought in the 1890s than in former days. The mission accounts for 1892, for instance, reveal that no slaves were bought that year, even though a total of 50,000 francs had been received from the Sainte-Enfance and Propaganda Fide expressly for "le rachat et l'entretien des esclaves."[24] The slave method of evangelization lost its importance as soon as the people began to soften their prejudice over the school and the Christian religion. Thereafter, the number of children of free-born citizens began to preponderate in the boarding schools in a measure that made the purchase of slaves superfluous and, to a large extent, inexpedient. Of the estimated 95 boarders of the Onitsha Catholic schools in 1899, only 15 were redeemed slaves.[25] The rest were pupils who had come to the Mission by virtue of the wish and free choice of their parents. This was a sign that by the close of the century, the slave method of evangelization was already on the road to extinction. Seen against this background, Father Lejeune's dogged opposition to its use in the early 1900s was merely a *coup de grace* to a practice which many church leaders had come to regard as an aberration in the evangelical methods.

---

[22] Cf. AP:N.S. R.141/1899, Vol.168, "R. Pawlas to Prefect of Propaganda Fide," Onitsha, 8 August, 1899.

[23] CSE:*Bulletin*, 15 (1889-1891), 540: "Cette décision nous empêchera désormais de racheter des esclaves, comme nous l'avons fait jusquà présent. Mais le bon Dieu nous envoie de temps à autre de petits enfants soit orphelins, soit voués à la mort...."

[24] Quoted in P. B. Clarke, "The Methods and Ideology of the Holy Ghost Fathers," p. 85.

[25] See AP:N.S. R.141/1899, Vol.168, "R. Pawlas to Prefect of Propaganda Fide," Onitsha, 8 August, 1899.

2. Children Entrusted to the Care of the Mission by their Parents and Guardians

There were 85 of these in 1899 in the two schools run by the Fathers and Sisters at Onitsha—52 boys and 33 girls.[26] The majority of these children came from towns and villages around Onitsha which the Fathers had visited but where they were not yet in the position to establish a Mission or a school. School children from Onitsha usually accompanied the Fathers during such inland visits, and the "knowledge" and good looks of these privileged mission "boys" often influenced the decision of parents to send their own sons to Onitsha to be educated. In this way children from Adekwe and Atani were brought to Onitsha in November 1887.[27] When Father Bubendorf went to Aguleri for the first time in February, 1890, chief Idigo handed over one of his sons to be educated at Onitsha.[28] Similarly, ambitious parents and guardians in distant towns like Brass and Oguta also sent their sons or "boys" to Onitsha to have them trained by the Catholic missionaries.

The Fathers accepted these children with open arms and probably without placing any financial obligations on their parents. The reason for this benevolent programme was two-fold. In the first place, the Catholic missionaries hoped that the children trained at Onitsha would, in their turn, form the nucleus of the Christian communities that were envisaged in their respective villages. Accordingly, many of these children were trained as catechists and pupil-teachers, and it was they who laid the foundation of the Christian faith in many parts of Eastern Nigeria. This was by far the greatest fruit of Catholic educational programme in the early years. Secondly, the benevolence of the Catholic missionaries towards children entrusted to them had also a social implication. The idea of having to build the Catholic Church exclusively on the dregs of society—redeemed slaves and outcasts—was loathsome to many mission leaders. Their wish was always to have the free-born citizens also in their following. They were only too glad, therefore, to see children of the middle and upper classes entrusted to their care.

3. Abandoned Children, Orphans, and Refugees

The third group of boarders in Catholic schools consisted of orphans and those who, as babies, had been rejected by their parents for being twins, or for having one bodily defect or another. According to Father Pawlas, between 15 and 20 of such babies were adopted each year by the Fathers

---

[26] Ibid.
[27] Cf. CSE:191/B/I, R. Daly, "Reverend Father Lutz," p. 5.
[28] Cf. CSE:*Bulletin*, 16 (1891-1893), 355.

and Sisters. Only a very small number actually survived their precarious infancy to become pupils in the schools. The refugees were usually old women who had been condemned to death on charges of witch-craft. About 12 of these and nine sick adults were taking refuge in the mission house at Onitsha in 1899.[29] As would be expected, these old people were not fit for the school, but they took active part in the catechism classes.

A day in the life of a boarder was a bundle of activities, comprising, more or less, five hours of classes, five hours of manual labour, five hours of recreation and prayer, and nine hours of sleep.[30] Catechism classes and school work were usually done in the afternoons, when the weather was too hot for work in the fields. The morning and evening hours were devoted to industrial activities in the workshops, the cultivation of the land, and work in the fruit and vegetable gardens. During the prefectship of Father Lejeune, the boarders were made to work for the Mission to compensate for the expenses incurred in educating, housing, feeding and clothing them.[31]

In distributing labour and responsibility to the boarders, the Fathers must have taken the social backgrounds of these children into consideration. According to Father Pawlas, the pupils who were taught various trades, such as tailoring, carpentry, and shoe-making, were usually the boys who had been entrusted to the care of the Mission by their parents and guardians. The freed slaves and orphans were employed in the farms and gardens.[32] This latter group of pupils must have been emotionally and intellectually inferior to the former. However, there is a strong possibility that the Fathers must have felt themselves under compulsion to give their best to the free-born boarders on whom they had placed much hope for a growing Christian Church. Furthermore, the ambitious parents and guardians of these children had sent them to Onitsha precisely for the trades they would learn there, a thing which the Fathers knew rather too well.

An event which had important consequences for Catholic educational efforts at Onitsha was the arrival in 1893 of Brother David Doran. His impact on Catholic education may have induced Dr. P. B. Clarke to regard 1893 as the actual beginning of Catholic educational endeavours in Eastern Nigeria. Of course the educational labours of the Catholics did not begin with Brother David. As has been seen, many capable Fathers, Brothers, Sisters, and experienced native catechists had, before him,

[29] Cf. AP:N.S R.141/1899, Vol.168, "R. Pawlas to Prefect of Propaganda Fide," Onitsha, 8 August, 1899.
[30] Cf. CSE:*Bulletin*, 22 (1903-1904), 786.
[31] See CSE:*Bulletin*, 21 (1901-1902), 516f; ibid., 22 (1903-1904), 786.
[32] See AP:N.S. R.141/1899, Vol.168, p. 160.

taken turns at teaching both religious and secular subjects in the schools at Onitsha and Aguleri. However, of all the teachers seen by the Mission so far, Brother David was about the only one who had received formal training as a school master. His arrival on the educational scene was therefore a major step forwards in the Catholic educational race. For more than fifteen years, he was to play a central role in the development and direction of Catholic education at Onitsha.[33]

Catholic educational activities continued to be centred in Onitsha throughout the 1880s. Although pastoral ministries were carried out in the immediate neighbourhoods of the town—Adekwe, Atani, Obosi, Nkwelle and Ogidi—no schools could yet be run in these centres. By 1890, there were still only two schools at Onitsha, one for boys and one for girls. The number of pupils in both schools was about 65, of which 30 boys and 25 girls were boarders.[34] Given the enormous size of the Prefecture, these figures would certainly appear ridiculous. Yet, the achievement they represented was the best that could be expected from a few missionaries whose morale was permanently put at a low ebb by constant deaths and ruined health. With the arrival of more hands in the early 1890s, arrangements were made to expand the missionary and educational activities of the Mission.

An event which precipitated that long overdue crusade was the conversion of chief Idigo of Aguleri. He had expressed the desire to have the Catholic faith brought to his village as early as 1887. But it was not until February 1890 that Father Bubendorf was able to visit Aguleri and its saintly chief. In December 1891, the chief was baptized together with seven of his children.[35] As would be expected in a society where religion and politics had an inseparable co-existence, the acceptance of Christianity by a native ruler was received with consternation and indignation in his village. Doggedly eager to follow his religious persuasion, chief Idigo forfeited his chieftaincy, and all his rights and privileges as a native doctor. With his family and a handful of followers, he left his home and settled in the outskirts of the village. There he hoped to pursue his new vocation without molestations from the pagan community. Thus was called into existence the first and only real Christian village in Eastern Nigeria. Unlike the Christian enclave at Onitsha which in reality was the

[33] See CSE:*Bulletin*, 17 (1893-1896), 418.

[34] Cf. CSE:*Bulletin*, 16 ((1891-1893), 335.

[35] For more details on the conversion of chief Idigo, see CSE:*Bulletin*, 16 (1891-1893), 354-364; CSE:191/B/I, R. Daly, "Reverend Father Lutz," p. 8; AP:N.S. R.141/1897, Vol.118, "J. Reling to Prefect of Propaganda Fide," Rome, 23 December, 1896; *Les Missions Catholiques*, 27 (1895), 433-437.

mission compound with its schools and humanitarian establishments for the redeemed slaves, the orphans, the poor and the sick, the Christian village at Aguleri was a dwelling site for Christian families which, from the onset and to a large extent, included free-born citizens. It was organized and governed along the lines of a free state. Its population grew from year to year with the arrival of new converts and their families. By 1899, there were about 270 Christians living there in total isolation from the pagan community of Aguleri.[36] No other place in the then Eastern Nigeria would have been more adequate for a Father's residence. Accordingly, Father Pawlas moved permanently to Aguleri in May 1892, five months after chief Idigo's baptism. With that Aguleri became the first Father's residence to be established outside Onitsha since the foundation of the Prefecture. As was the practice wherever a Father or a catechist resided, a school was quickly established there.

The education of children acquired new features in Aguleri following the establishment of a Christian village there in 1891. Hitherto, the small number of pupils under instruction at Onitsha were kept as boarders in the Mission. Most of these children were, as has been seen, not allowed to come in contact with their pagan families and relatives. Since all the families of the Christian village at Aguleri were, by contrast, adherents to the Catholic faith, the Fathers felt free to leave the pupils with their parents. In 1897, there were 90 school children in the village—20 boarders and 70 externes.[37] But by 1899 all the pupils of the school, except four who were at the service of the Fathers, were attending classes from their homes.[38] This certainly marked a definite departure from the policy which had hitherto made the boarders the focus of Catholic educational endeavour. But, as the Fathers were soon to discover, the abandonment of the boarding system was counter-productive, at least for the school. This becomes evident in the following report from Aguleri in 1902:

> The school is giving us less consolation. Among the 40 to 50 children who attended classes regularly two years ago, only a very small number has continued to answer the call of the bell. However, the fact is that the parents put three-quarters of the year into farm work, and the children are obliged to spend much time with them using the hoe. Besides, the latter prefer the free life of the bush to going to school. Nevertheless, there has not been any loss in the religious sector: the young people who are engaged in agriculture

---

[36] Cf. AP:N.S. R.141/1899, Vol. 168, "R. Pawlas to Prefect of Propaganda Fide," Onitsha, 8 August, 1899, p. 159.

[37] Cf. CSE:*Bulletin*, 19 (1898-1899), 340.

[38] Cf. CSE:*Bulletin*, 20 (1899-1900), 318.

are usually better Christians. Those of them who acquire some education seek employment in the factories, where they are very much exposed to perdition.[39]

The rationale of this negative verdict on the school by those who, at Onitsha, had insisted on educating the children, sometimes against the will of their parents, can only be sought in the function which the school was expected to fulfil for the Mission. It was not so much the desire to improve the material well-being of the natives as the need to lure them to the Catholic faith that inspired the educational endeavours of the early missionaries. Accordingly, emphasis on the school tended to wane wherever the pursuit of this major objective was not of immediate concern. This was the case in the Christian village at Aguleri. In 1902, when the above report was made, there were about 300 souls living in the village—240 baptized Christians and 60 catechumens. Catechism classes were held every morning for children and every evening for adults. As many as 50 of the former were said to have attended these classes regularly. There were a total of 56 baptisms between September 1900 and March 1902, a record which was comparatively higher than that of Onitsha.[40] Seen against the background of the guaranteed missionary success at Aguleri, therefore, the momentary depreciation of the value of the school by the Fathers would appear less paradoxical. Furthermore, the religious security that was felt in the Christian village would also make the unusual separation of the school from the catechism classes less surprising.

The missionary and educational experiments carried out at Aguleri acted as a spur for further expansion in the interior. Covetous of the civilization of the mission house, other chiefs in the neighbourhood of Aguleri tried to emulate chief Idigo; they began to express the wish to have Catholic missionaries among them. The Fathers welcomed this popular longing for missionaries in spite of their awareness that much of it was inspired by hopes of economic gains. "For some year," they said, "material interest shall not be alien to [the people's desire for missionaries]: the presence of the whites would give them influence, and open avenues for commerce, etc."[41]

The first major village after Aguleri to receive special attention was Nsugbe. A station catechist was installed there in March 1892, and his duty consisted mainly in running catechism classes for the catechumens.

---

[39] CSE:*Bulletin*, 21 (1901-1902), 523. In July 1899, Father Pawlas, Prefect from 1898 to 1900, expressed the same views about educational activities at Osomari. See CSE:*Bulletin*, 20 (1899-1900), 314.

[40] See CSE:*Bulletin*, 21 (1901-1902), 522-523.

[41] Ibid., p. 524.

Fathers Cadio and Xavier Lichtenberger took permanent residence at Nsugbe in April, 1894. However, the Mission was to enter into a chequered existence soon afterwards. Frequent deaths and sick leave of the European missionaries took their toll on the progress of the Mission, and in April, 1897, the lone priest there, Father A. Ganot, returned to Aguleri. The residence was temporarily closed, but monthly visitations continued to be made to Nsugbe by the Fathers of Onitsha.

Further expansions were made to Igbariam and Ossomari. These centres had got station catechists by the end of 1898, and in 1899 schools were established in both outstations.

By August, 1899, fourteen years after the foundation of the Lower Niger Mission, there were about 350 school children in all the Catholic schools.[42] Quantitatively, this achievement would certainly be no cause for jubilation. Yet, it was a great source of encouragement for the pioneer missionaries. Their encounter with a society that doggedly held on to its pagan beliefs and practices had caused them excruciating mental and physical pains. The criticism was made during Father Lejeune's prefectship (1900-1905) that Father Lutz and his immediate successors dissipated their energy on charitable services to redeemed slaves, orphans, and the rejects of society. In fairness to the pioneer Fathers, however, it must be conceded that they had little room for manoevres. Their humanitarian activities were, as has been seen, their only doorway to the nineteenth-century Nigerian society. Furthermore, although the school was a part of their missionary programme from the onset, they could not develop it to any meaningful level because of serious financial handicaps. Compelled by a strong moral obligation to honour the will and intentions of the donors and benefactors (such as *L'Oeuvre Anti-esclavagiste and the Sainte-Enfance*), Rome insisted that the money sent to the Mission be used exclusively for the ransoming of slaves and the running of orphanages and charity homes. If the pioneer Fathers failed to make the mass education of the villagers the focus of their missionary enterprise, it was largely because of this financial inhibition. Yet, they did not lose sight of the utility of the school in the work of evangelization. After many trials and disappointed hopes, a functioning system at last emerged from their preoccupation with the younger generation. As has been seen, the school played a major role in the expansion of the Mission in the 1890s, when boys trained "abroad" at Onitsha were actively involved in the evangelization of their townsmen.[43] This success was a major incen-

---

[42] Cf. AP:N.S. R.141/1899, Vol. 168, "R. Pawlas to Prefect of Propaganda Fide," Onitsha, 8 August, 1899.
[43] See CSE:*Bulletin*, 20 (1899-1900), 314.

tive in the determination of the pioneer missionaries to carry on the struggle.[44]

However, the willingness to follow up this break-through with some advantage was greatly undermined by another trial of a different sort. Father Lutz, the founder and first Apostolic Prefect of the Lower Niger Mission, fell mortally sick and returned to France in August, 1894. He died there in December, 1895. Father Joseph Reling was chosen as his successor in October, 1896, while he was on sick leave in France. Being unable to return to the Niger, the new leader tried to govern his Prefecture from Senegal. But his health obliged him to resign his post in June 1898. He was succeeded by Father René Pawlas, who returned to Onitsha in December, 1898, only to die there in March 1900. Meanwhile other Fathers too had fallen sick and left the Mission. Under these circumstances, no new residences could be established, and consequently no new schools could be opened, especially at some strategic points like Onitsha Town, Brass and Oguta, where there were long-standing projects to found new Missions. Even a promising Mission like Nsugbe had to be abandoned in 1897 for lack of personnel. These searching trials made the last decade of the nineteenth century the darkest period, perhaps, in the history of the Lower Niger Mission. What was mostly needed to illuminate its bleak future was a stable leadership and a new beginning.

II. *New Orientations in Catholic Education Policy, 1900-1905*

1. *The Lejeunean Revolution*

Father Léon Alexander Lejeune was appointed Apostolic Prefect of the Lower Niger Mission on 23 May, 1900. As has been seen, the years between 1895 and 1900 were a period of constant changes in the leadership of the Mission. This was, to a large extent, responsible for the stalemate that was discernible in its progress. Father Lejeune brought not only a period of relative stability, but also a number of imaginative innovations. Since much of what follows in this chapter will concern him and his revolutionary administration, it will be appropriate at this point to expatiate on his life-history.

He was born on March 24, 1860, in Tournai-sur-Dives, in the diocese of Séer, France. He did his priestly studies in the major seminary at Séer. After his profession in 1885, he was sent to the Vicariate of the Two

---

[44] Among the many reports of the Fathers on the importance of school children for the success of the Mission, see CSE:*Bulletin*, 17 (1893-1896), 418; ibid., 19 (1898-1899), 336.

Guineas in Gabon. It must be recalled that the Onitsha Mission was from 1885 to 1889 a part of the Vicariate of the Two Guineas. Incidentally, it was Father Lejeune who furnished his Mother House and the Propaganda Congregation with the reports which expedited the foundation of the Lower Niger Mission in December, 1885. On his way to Gabon early 1885, he had made a stop at the Niger Delta and obtained reliable information on the land and peoples of the Niger country from a native chief.[45] Arriving at Gabon, he quickly distinguished himself as a great missionary, especially in the Mission of Lambarene, where he was the superior for 15 years. His greatest achievements were made in the field of catechetics.[46] Apart from his numerous erudite reports and articles, he also published a number of important works in the vernacular, including a catechism and a dictionary in the Fang language.[47] Father Lejeune's abilities as a leader did not escape the notice of his superiors in Gabon— Bishop Le Berre and Bishop Alexander LeRoy. The latter became the Superior General of the Holy Ghost Congregation in 1896, and when the question of a new Prefect for the Lower Niger Mission came up in 1900, he did not hesitate to recommend him for the office.[48] Father Lejeune successfully directed the Prefecture from September 1900 till April 1905. Returning to France on account of an illness, he died at Chevilly on September 6, 1905.

In the words of Father Shanahan, Lejeune was the only missionary in Africa "who was capable of achieving the impossible."[49] This was a reference to Father Lejeune's approach to the intractable problems of the Lower Niger Mission. Very few Missions in Africa had had a more frustrating and pestiferous beginning. The principal cause of this misfortune was, besides the political intrigues and extortions of the Royal Niger Company, the debilitating climate. The average stay of a missionary there was only two years, after which he either died or returned invalidated to Europe. Is it any wonder that by the late 1890s the Lower Niger Mission had attained the unenviable reputation of being the most dreaded in the whole world?[50] However, because of its dense population,

[45] Cf. J. Jordan, *Bishop Shanahan of Southern Nigeria*, p. 8.

[46] His expertise and originality in this field are evident in the pages of his long article, "Les Catéchistes de l'Ogowé," *Les Missions Catholiques*, 28 (1896), 556-557; 570-574; 584-587; 597-599; 603-606; 619-621.

[47] See R. Streit, J. Dindinger, *Bibliotheca Missionum*, XVIII, p. 293.

[48] See AP:N.S. R.141/1900, Vol. 193, Bishop A. LeRoy, "Notes au sujet des Pères proposé pour la charge de Préfet apostolique du Bas-Niger," Paris, 15 May, 1900, p. 593rv.

[49] Quoted in J. Jordan, *Bishop Shanahan*, p. 20.

[50] See J. Gosson, "The Apostolate of the School in Southern Nigeria," *Pagan Mission*, 13 (1940), 45.

and the relatively good disposition of the natives towards Catholicism, the Mission was generally regarded as the most important in Africa. A Mission with such good prospects for the future should not, in Father Lejeune's opinion, be allowed to die off. He declared that the misfortunes of the Mission, more than anything else, induced him to accept the office of Apostolic Prefect.[51] This was in keeping with his usual reaction in the face of difficulties, an attitude he gave expression with his characteristic utterance: *laissez-moi faire*!

His appointment as Prefect of the Lower Niger Mission came to him while he was on sick leave in France. In his letter of intent to the Prefect of the Propaganda Congregation, he blamed the misery of the Mission solely on the high mortality rate of its missionaries. He must have got reliable information from former Niger veterans about the shabby and unhealthy huts which served the Catholic missionaries as dwelling places.[52] In a rather satirical reckoning, he pointed out that it cost the Holy Ghost Congregation and the various charitable organizations about 5000 francs to train one missionary.[53] To let him perish soon afterwards, he argued, was bad economy. Father Lejeune was led to this view-point by his experiences in Gabon. As superior of the Lambarene Mission, he had constructed brick houses for his missionaries with 10,000 francs, and after 15 years, he had lost none of them. With the same amount of money he hoped to save the Lower Niger Mission from its impending breakdown.

Accordingly, the revolutionary innovations which he tackled *par la base*, as he put it,[54] included, first and foremost, the provision of solid buildings at Onitsha and Aguleri. A considerable improvement of the health of the missionaries was the result, and this in turn enhanced the material and spiritual growth of the Mission.

The greatest aspect of Father Lejeune's revolutionary administration, however, was his radical departure from the charity-orientated evangelism of his predecessors. He became, for his part, an articulate defender of the school apostolate. Some critics like Andrew Porter have spoken of this change in Catholic missionary strategy as having the

---

[51] Cf. AP:N.S. R.141/1900, Vol. 193, "Lejeune to Prefect of Propaganda Fide," Beauvais, 6 June, 1900, p. 596ᵛ.

[52] See ibid., p. 596ᵛ-597ʳ; see also CSE:*Bulletin*, 21 (1901-1902), 511.

[53] AP:N.S. R.141/1900, Vol. 193, p.597ʳ. Father Lejeune must have meant 50,000 francs because the training he was referring to included: "études littéraires et théologiques, noviciate, trousseau et voyage, tout compris." It would be impossible, even in his day, to pay for all these with only 5000 francs.

[54] CSE:192/B/III, "Lejeune to Superior General," Onitsha, 28 September, 1903.

"appearance of intensified aggression aimed at its rivals."[55] This view rests on a most superficial understanding of Catholic motives and aspirations. In his realistic way of looking at things, Lejeune believed that the exclusive choice of outcasts and slaves as adherents to Catholicism was fraught with very unsavoury consequences for the developing Church in Eastern Nigeria. Father Lutz, he argued, had laid much emphasis on a method of evangelization which directed attention not to the entire population, but only to a particular group of persons—redeemed slaves, orphans, outcasts, and condemned criminals. Going through the list of candidates for baptism in 1902, he discovered that there were 500 of these rejects of society in Onitsha alone. "Good harvest," he said, "but the free-born, the chiefs, the ruling class if you will, where are they?"[56] In his opinion, the free-born and the upper class of society were made to look with spite on an institution which gave refuge to "their outcasts, their criminals, and the accursed of their gods," namely, the Catholic Mission.[57]

To a large extent, therefore, the school-orientated evangelism which Father Lejeune advocated was an attempt to make Catholicism appeal to the Nigerian society in its entirety. It was not, as Andrew Porter unfairly termed it, a move "to exacerbate division within Christendom."[58] In having recourse to education, the Catholics did no more than imitate the method, inspiration and motives of their Protestant counterparts. As Father Lejeune noted in 1902, the ruling class at Onitsha was "entirely Protestant."[59] He castigated his predecessors for missing the opportunity of breaking this monopoly in the 1890s, when the Church Missionary Society suffered a stinging set-back following a crisis over its leadership in Nigeria.[60]

---

[55] A. Porter, "Late Nineteenth-Century Anglican Missionary Expansion: A Consideration of Some Non-Anglican Sources of Inspiration," *Religious Motivation: Biographical and Sociological Problems for the Church Historian*. Studies in Church History. Vol. 15, ed. D. Baker, (Oxford: Blackwell, 1978), p. 354.

[56] CSE:191/B/II, "A Report by Lejeune," Onitsha, 1902.

[57] Ibid.

[58] A. Porter, "Late Nineteenth-Century Missionary Expansion," p. 354.

[59] CSE:191/B/II, "A Report by Lejeune," Onitsha, 1902.

[60] Led by Rev. Henry Townsend, some European members of the CMS began in the 1880s to advance theories which strongly opposed the promotion of a native clergy in Africa. The bellicose schemes of the Townsend faction were shelved for a time, thanks to the pro-African bent of Rev. Henry Venn, the honorary Secretary of the Society. But when Venn died, his successors felt free to assert the superiority of the whites over the blacks in their policies over the leadership of the Mission. This culminated in the humiliation and tactful displacement of Bishop Ajayi Crowther in 1891. Thereafter the CMS experienced mass desertions and apostasy of its black adherents, who felt that the unscrupulous policy of their white leaders was incompatible with the teachings of Christianity. Cf. J. F. A. Ajayi, *Christian Missions in Nigeria, 1841-1891* (London: Longman, 1965), pp. 180-204.

At first Father Lejeune's educational policy did not receive the sympathy of Propaganda Fide. The authorities in Rome must have believed that the practice of ransoming slaves would ultimately eradicate the heinous slave trade. Lejeune, for his part, was not convinced that one could possibly put an end to the slave trade simply by buying off the slaves. The readiness to buy slaves, he argued, encouraged the dealers to ensure a regular flow of their *goods.* "My opinion," he wrote, "and the opinion of our Superior General and of many African bishops is that slavery shall never be abolished by buying slaves, but by evangelization properly so-called."[61] It was during his intensive but short-lived campaign to win support for his conception of "evangelization properly so called" that he developed and employed the educational principles which Father J. Jordan has unfairly attributed to Bishop Shanahan.[62] It was Father Léon Lejeune, and not Shanahan, who gave definite direction to the practice of preaching Christianity to the village people by way of the school. As has been seen, the maxim: "whoever has the youth has the future" was a popular pedagogical principle in the nineteenth and early twentieth centuries. It was not Lejeune's invention. But it was he, and not Shanahan, who first discovered its relevance and great importance for success in Eastern Nigeria. "The schools," he wrote in 1903, "are for us an excellent means of propaganda. It is the youth that we educate, and the youth are the future."[63]

Similar utterances on the importance of the school for the work of evangelization in Nigeria are found in numerous letters and reports sent to Paris and Rome by Father Lejeune between 1900 and 1905. On May 28, 1901, for instance, He wrote to his Superior General saying: "Les école, celles des garçons surtour, sont un de nos moyens d'évangélisation."[64] Later in the year he wrote: "Il faut des écoles, c'est le plus sur moyens d'évangélisation."[65] Then in 1902 he wrote: "Une méthod d'évangélisation, employée ici, et qui fait merveille, échouerait entièrement ailleurs. Ici, ce sont les école qui fournissent tous les succès."[66] In spite of his awareness of Rome's uncompromising support for the slave method of evangelization, he courageously told the directors of Prop-

---

[61] CSE:191/B/III, "Lejeune to Cardinal Ledochowski."

[62] Father Jordan propagated the popular but erroneous view that it was Shanahan who launched the Catholic educational policy in Eastern Nigeria. See J. Jordan, *Bishop Shanahan*, pp. 26-46.

[63] CSE:192/B/III, "Lejeune to Superior General," Onitsha, 25 February, 1903.

[64] Quoted in CSE:*Bulletin*, 21 (1901-1902), 516.

[65] CSE:191/B/II, "A Report by Father Lejeune," Onitsha, 24 October, 1901.

[66] CSE:191/B/II, "A Report by Father Lejeune," Onitsha, 1902.

aganda Fide in 1904 that "education in Africa is the surest means of converting the races. It has, in fact, become the only means."[67]

Worthy of special note are the progressive changes in the stress which Lejeune placed in these passages on the importance of the school. In May 1901, the school was just one among other means of evangelization. But by October of the same year, it had become "the surest means." By 1902 there was not the slightest doubt about the utility of the school: it was responsible for all the success hitherto. With this conviction, he urged Catholic leaders to give a more sustained impetus to the only method of evangelization that was capable of placing Christianity on firm grounds in Africa. Through education, the natives would be gradually persuaded to distance themselves from the unworthy aspects of their pagan heritage. Through education he hoped to bring Catholicism out of the confines of the Mission houses and spread it to the village people.

Furthermore, Father Lejeune regarded the school as an absolute necessity for the Catholics in their struggle for survival in an English colony, where the Protestants had a place of influence. This point was stressed in his letter to the directors of Propaganda Fide, part of which reads as follows:

> The 1,200 pupils in our schools are, in fact, our only hope, but what a disaster and what a pity if it became impossible for us to continue [the work of education]. Without schools we shall be nothing, just as the Catholics are nothing in English territories where Protestant establishments have the advantage.[68]

Meanwhile, however, Father Lejeune found himself confronted with a vast array of opposition not only from his confrères, but also from the natives. His radical educational ambitions, his uncompromising disregard of the hitherto accepted missionary methods, and his high-handedness in putting through his revolutionary ideas had touched off fears in many circles. With regard to his confrères, there were some specific and, in part, genuine reasons for their trepidation over his educational policy. As has been seen, both the Society of African Missions in Western Nigeria and the Holy Ghost Fathers in Eastern Nigeria were French missionary societies. The majority of the members of these two societies were French and Alsatians of German origin. These had come to West Africa when the territorial struggle between France and Britain was still largely unresolved. But as soon as the Niger country came under the tutelage of Britain, a search for English-speaking missionaries

---

[67] CSE:192/A/IV, "Lejeune to the Directors of Propaganda Fide," Calabar, 20 October, 1904.
[68] Ibid.

became inevitable. Although he was a Frenchman, Father Lejeune made no bones of his preference for Irish missionaries with good academic qualifications. His main contention was that the education which the other Fathers had received in France and Germany, and the language handicap which they brought along with them to an English colony were factors which were not conducive to the educational contest going on there.[69] This policy soon irritated the sensitive patriotism of the French and German missionaries, who had come to the Mission immediately after their ordinations and had had no formal training as school masters. They understandably saw in Lejeune's educational policy a threat to their missionary careers, for the consequences of the radical move towards education would be their being either superseded by the Irish or reduced to second-class missionaries in a Mission they had built up with so much suffering and sacrifice.[70]

It is not surprising, therefore, that a group of Fathers in the Mission, mostly the Alsatians, resolved to get rid of Father Lejeune by all means. For this purpose they received active support from some members of the Prefecture of the Upper Niger in Asaba who shared their sentiments. Two priests from this Mission were particularly mentioned by Father Lejeune as being the ring-leaders of the *complot* formed against him. "I took the liberty," he wrote to his superior in 1903, "to rebuke Fathers Hummel and Scherrer very vehemently for criticizing my administration in my presence."[71]

The seriousness of the opposition formed against Father Lejeune can best be assessed from a letter of Bishop Gorman of Sierra Leone to the

---

[69] When Shanahan succeeded Lejeune, he echoed this view of his master in more concrete terms: "What we need here most are confrères who know English. If one arrives here without being able to say *yes*, then it is a great damage to the Mission...Usually the young priests do not have the slightest idea of the basic requirements of a primary school. They would teach rhetoric and philosophy very well, but it becomes a different story when it comes to teaching A. B. C. or *Our Father*. But the fact is that the school is the most important thing out here." CSE:192/B/IV, "Shanahan to Superior General," 14 April, 1907.

[70] The fears of the French and German missionaries were in fact not unfounded. For in 1939, the Ordinaries of Nigeria actually adopted a resolution which, among other things, urged Propaganda Fide to direct the religious orders and congregations with Missions in British Africa to train their missionaries in the best modern methods necessary for a University degree and Teacher's diploma. Cf. CSE:554/I, "Conference of the Ordinaries of Nigeria and the British Cameroons held at Lagos, August 31 September 3, 1929," (Lagos, 1929), Resolution xiv, p. 15f. Commenting on this decision, Father Joseph Soul, a Visitor of the Holy Ghost Congregation, emphasized that their Society in Nigeria was resolutely of the opinion that missionaries sent to Nigeria without the said academic qualifications should be regarded as second-class missionaries, good only for the ministry. Cf. CSE:554/V, J. Soul, "General Report to the Superior General on the Visit to the District of Southern Nigeria," Onitsha, 12 November, 1929, p. 20.

[71] Cf. CSE:192/B/III, "Lejeune to LeRoy," Calabar, 20 June, 1903.

Superior General. Responding to the Superior's demand for information on Nigeria, Gorman expressed the view that Lejeune was in a situation which would jeopardize his authority as a bishop of the Lower Niger Mission. He went on to say:

> This Mission has well the same rights as Sierra Leone to be raised to the status of a Vicariate. However, I shall pity the new Apostolic Vicar if the old *clique* which organized an opposition against Father Lejeune has not disbanded.[72]

The records of the Holy Ghost Congregation show that Rome and Paris were seriously contemplating making Lejeune a bishop. But his sudden death in 1905 set the idea to rest. The fact that no bishop was appointed after his death until 1920, when Shanahan, an Irishman, was made bishop, shows that Rome and Paris were not unmindful of the national intrigues which went on in the Mission.

A more serious opposition to Father Lejeune's revolutionary policies came from the natives of Onitsha. The shift from a charity-orientated evangelism to a new missionary policy which emphasized labour and self-help had alienated many Catholic adherents who had been used to the pampering they got from Lejeune's predecessors. When the Prefect arrived in the Mission in September, 1900, he saw a very large number of persons who were completely dependent on the Mission for their upkeep. These included, first and foremost, the redeemed slaves, the orphans, refugees, the sick and the old; then there were the school boarders, the catechists, interpreters and other helpers in the Mission. As has been seen, he questioned the propriety of founding the Church exclusively on the first group. However, if his criticism of his predecessors for their dependence on these persons was ideological, his determination to change the relationship of the Mission to all its dependents was practical. As soon as he arrived in the Mission, he embarked upon many construction works at Onitsha and Aguleri. He needed money and, above all, manpower.

The best way to get the former was to reduce the expenses of the Mission. Accordingly, his first deed as Prefect was the order not to buy any more slaves and not to accept, even in his absence, refugees and babies deprived of their mothers. To get the much needed labour, he got both the school boarders and all the inmates of the refugee homes to work at the construction sites. Even the externes (about 110 boys and girls in January 1901), who had hitherto attended the Catholic schools

[72] CSE:200/A/II, "Gorman to LeRoy," Sierra Leone, 16 June, 1905.

gratuitously, were made to work one hour each day for the Mission.[73]

The unfortunate state of the Mission and the priority and urgency which its resuscitation demanded had seemingly pushed the Prefect to extremes. Yet, it must be conceded that he was not unmindful of the plights of the poor, as is evident in his commentary on the new measures:

> It is a pity, a great pity; it hurts me to see the lepers, the crippled, these human debris, bending over the axe in the heat of the sun...But what else can one do?... It was necessary to come to [these severe measures] in order to be able to meet all our expenses. Besides, one may add that nothing is more important than to inculcate in the young Africans a sense of labour.[74]

The propriety of Lejeune's policy can hardly be doubted. Yet, whatever merits it gained from its good intentions were lost in the abruptness and firmness with which it was executed. For many, the humanitarian activities of the Mission had become the hallmark of Catholicism, and Lejeune passed for a great enemy of the Church for going against them.

The leaders of the people's opposition to Father Lejeune's rule were the catechists. There were about 12 of these at Onitsha when the Prefect came to the Mission in 1900. Since the majority of them were converts from Protestantism, Lejeune developed an obsessive dislike for them. Some of the catechists added salt to injury by attaching pre-conditions to their conversion. Appendix "A" shows that Ephrem, the most famous and perhaps the most highly paid Catholic catechist, was actually given a written assurance that he would never be transferred to any station outside Onitsha. Employment at Onitsha seemed to have been the focus of the aspirations of many of the pioneer catechists. Father Lejeune destroyed that dream in 1900. As soon as he took office, he began to post the catechists to the outstations. He was to regret in 1902 that he did not dismiss all of them instead. But as he wisely judged, sending away the catechists would have caused out-right revolt.[75] The only course of action open to him was to keep their number down as long as this did not affect the progress of the Mission. In 1902 he dismissed four catechists, a measure he described as being "to the discontentment of certain Fathers and to the detriment of my popularity."[76]

Economic considerations had an important bearing on Lejeune's quarrel with the lay helpers in the Mission. A catechist was paid between £2

---

[73] Cf. CSE:*Bulletin*, 21 (1901-1902), 511-512; see also CSE:192/B/II, "Lejeune to LeRoy," Onitsha, 23 January, 1901.
[74] Ibid.
[75] See CSE:192/B/II, "Lejeune to Superior General," Onitsha, 19 February, 1902.
[76] Ibid.

and £5 a month. This, in his opinion, was out of character with the practice in other African Missions. He claimed, for instance, that he would
have maintained 50 catechists at Lambarene with the 4,600 francs which
Father Pawlas spent on 5 catechists in 1899.[77] However, this estimate did
not take into account the economic disparity which existed between
Nigeria and Gabon. According to Lejeune's own estimate, the economic
growth of Nigeria by 1904 was higher than those of Senegal, Gabon,
Congo, and Guinea put together.[78] As would be expected, the cost of living was correspondingly higher in Nigeria than in Gabon.

The best opportunity for the disgruntled catechists to give vent to their
rage offered itself on Saturday, April 25, 1903. On that day the inmates
of the Onitsha wharf school went on a strike which lasted until Monday,
April 27, 1903. The incident, which started as a protest against poor
feeding conditions in the school, took new dimensions when Father
Lejeune revealed his intention to transfer Brother David Doran to
Calabar. As has been seen, Brother David was for the people of Onitsha
the most beloved of all the European teachers. Much of the popularity
of the Wharf School was hinged on his person. When he was transferred
to Onitsha Town in 1906, for instance, as many as 50 pupils changed
camp and followed him to his new station. As a result, the grants-in-aid
which the Wharf School received that year from the Colonial
Administration fell short of expectation.[79] Is it any wonder that the
outrage of the Onitsha people knew no bounds at the thought of Brother
David being removed from their midst?. Led by the teachers and
catechists, the Catholic population of Onitsha rose up in revolt, the first,
and perhaps the last, of its kind in the history of the Catholic Mission in
Eastern Nigeria. In protest letters sent to Bishop LeRoy, the Superior
General of the Holy Ghost Congregation in Paris, the Catholics of Onitsha demanded the immediate removal of Father Lejeune from the
Mission.[80]

The boldness of this demand and the fact that the petition was sent
directly to the Superior General in Paris are indications that the natives
must have received active support from very high quarters in the Mission. Lejeune's account of the incident confirms this and brings out the
intricate nature of the whole sad affair:

---

[77] CSE:192/B/II, "Lejeune to LeRoy," Onitsha, 13 September, 1900.
[78] CSE:192/A/IV, "Lejeune to Directors of Propaganda Fide," Calabar, 20 October,
1904.
[79] See CSE:*Bulletin*, 24 (1907-1908), 146.
[80] Cf. CSE:192/B/III, "The Christians of Onitsha to Bishop LeRoy," Onitsha, 26
April, 1903. This letter was signed by 23 men and 17 women. However, the majority
of the names were written by the same hand. See also ibid., "B. Ejo to Bishop LeRoy,"
Onitsha, 16 April, 1903.

The brains behind the war which our Onitsha Christians waged against me are Fathers Joseph and Vogler. Each time Father Joseph shows up there something always goes wrong. Father Vogler has said at Old Calabar that I would no longer be on the Niger within six months. I shall not be here anymore only when I am dead. But as long as I am alive I shall continue to be here, even if those apostates of Onitsha were to accuse me before the Pope. They reprobate me for being: 1) a hypocrite, 2) a pharisee, 3) a Pharaoh who delights in making bricks, 4) for not distributing clothings like my predecessors, 5), for not ransoming slaves, 6) for not knowing how to differentiate good Christians from bad ones, 7) for baptizing people who do not merit baptism (the townspeople), 8) for calling them monkeys sometimes and for having told them that it is their fault if they are poor. I am very glad that they have nothing other than these to reproach me with.[81]

To go through these charges is to discover the depth of the structural changes which had taken place in the Mission in less than three years of Lejeune's leadership, changes which have all the symbolic character of a great revolution—the *Lejeunean Revolution*. Of great significance are charges 4) and 5). Father Lejeune regarded the distribution of clothings and the ransoming of slaves as not belonging to evangelization "properly so-called." His radical break with the charity-orientated apostolate of former days produced ineluctable reactions from those who were directly affected. From charges 6) and 7) one sees that for the hitherto pampered Christians the assurance of staying in the special favour of the Mission had blurred into a notion of personal righteousness. The extension of the Christian message outside the privileged confines of the Mission house had become for them a movement in the wrong direction.

Lejeune's contention in charge 8) would be that it is through hard work that people are led to a state of honour and dignity. In his letter of intent to Propaganda Fide before he came to Nigeria, he had strongly argued for the provision of solid buildings in the Niger Mission in order to reduce the high mortality rate among the European missionaries. When he came to the Mission in September 1900, he embarked on a brick making project that was unprecedented in Nigeria. It is no wonder therefore that the people called him a Pharaoh in charge 3).

Father Lejeune had a resolute character and was easily moved to anger. He revealed this side of himself in that story of his encounter with Fathers Hummel and Scherrer of the Prefecture of the Upper Niger. As can be seen in charges 1) and 2), the people mistook this human weakness for badwill and were led to call him names. They failed to reconcile his inflexible will with his priestly status. In the opinion of Bernard Ejo, one

---

[81] CSE:192/B/III, "Lejeune to Superior General," Old Calabar, 20 June, 1903.

of the protesters at Onitsha, Lejeune was "not a Father but a man, and severe monster, who never pity unto [sic] his dog.[82]

Lejeune's extremely bad temper accounted very much for the fact that he failed where Shanahan succeeded, namely, the ability to elicit local support and admiration. When Shanahan assumed the leadership of the Mission in 1905, he carried out Lejeune's schemes and policies to the very letter without at the same time alienating himself from the people. With an incomparable adroitness, he managed to fill the cleft left over by the break with the old order. However, credit must be given to Lejeune for his originality, his sincerity, and, above all, his selfless commitments to the good of the people. C. S. Lewis has written that "all discoveries are made and all errors corrected by those who ignore the climate of opinion."[83] Lejeune was such a man. He did not allow public hostility to deter him from his purpose. The Onitsha revolt of 1903, in particular, caused him a moment of despair. "I passed a most terrible week," he wrote afterwards "and feared an apostasy of about 40 to 50 members of our Wharf Church."[84] But being conscious of working for a very high ideal, and being doggedly enthusiastic about a success, he readily sacrificed his popularity and his health in its pursuit. The success of his educational policy and, in consequence, the resuscitation of the Lower Niger Mission were the rewards of that unparalleled steadfastness.

2. The Triumph of the School Apostolate

The era of Father Lutz and his successors, which was superceded in 1900 by the Prefectship of Father Lejeune, was largely a period of missionary experiments in which the slave method, the Christian village and the apostolate of the school were collectively employed with varying degrees of emphasis. As has been seen, Lejeune rejected the first two methods of evangelization on economic and ideological grounds. This perforce led to a concentration of attention on the school method of evangelization.

During the first meeting of his Mission Council in September 1900, Father Lejeune left no doubts to the fact that he was going to shift the school to the centre stage of missionary enterprise. Among other things, he proposed the establishment of an outstation at Onitsha Town to be run by a catechist whose duty would include school activities. Hitherto, the combination "catechist-teacher" had been employed with success only at Onitsha Wharf and Aguleri, where there were Fathers'

---

[82] CSE:192/B/III, "B. Ejo to Bishop LeRoy," Onitsha, 16 April, 1903.
[83] C. S. Lewis, *The Problem of Pain* (London, 1940; rpt. Glasgow: Collins, 1977), p. 122.
[84] CSE:192/B/III, "Lejeune to Superior General," Onitsha, 1 May, 1903.

residences. Under Lejeune, it became a major devise in the evangelization of the outstations. Of special importance was his proposal at the Mission Council meeting to found an *école supérieure* at Onitsha in the
immediate near future. It was to have about 20 pupils from whom candidates to the priesthood were to be drawn. Worthy of special note is also
the order given by the Prefect to his confrères and lay helpers in the Mission to promote the production of Christian literature in the vernacular.[85]

The success of Father Lejeune's educational policy can be measured
in practical terms. As a result of the elaborate construction works which
were undertaken in the Mission in 1900, the execution of most of the
decisions of the council meeting was deferred to 1901. In this year, the
Fathers' residence at Nsugbe, which had been closed down in 1897, was
re-opened by Father Ganot. Thereafter, about 60 children made daily
attendance to the mission school and catechism classes. Catholic education in this centre took a wider dimension after the baptism of chief Obi
Fatu of Nsugbe, an event which took place on the feast of Assumption
in 1901. Together with eight other chiefs of the village, he promulgated
a law which enjoined all parents and guardians to send their children to
school. Heavy fines were to be imposed on anybody who did not comply
with the ruling.[86] This concerted action in favour of education was the
first of its kind in Eastern Nigeria by native rulers, the majority of whom
were pagans. It elicited in the Fathers such a strong expectation of a pros-
perous Mission at Nsugbe that they envisaged the establishment there of
a Catholic post-primary institution.

From a missionary point of view, the educational developments at
Nsugbe were a great victory for Father Lejeune. For the first time, his
theory that the hitherto impregnable pagan fortress could be penetrated
received credence and support from the conversion of chief Obi Fatu and
the promise of school children by a popular decision. His dream of
preaching the gospel to the ruling class and to the townspeople was
already becoming a reality. In fact some journals reported that the entire
village of Nsugbe accepted baptism with chief Obi Fatu. However,
Father Ganot's response to that benign rumour was: "Would that it were
so!"[87] This underscored the transient nature of the sensational success at
Nsugbe. In keeping with Lejeune's strong disapproval of the methods of
his predecessors which had confined missionary and educational
activities to the Christian enclaves, only a perfunctory attention was paid
to the boarding system at Nsugbe. The result was a drastic fall in the

[85] For more details on the decisions of this Mission Council meeting, see
CSE:192/B/II, "Lejeune to Superior General," Onitsha, 14 September, 1900.
[86] See ibid., p. 522; see also *Les Missions Catholiques* (December, 1901).
[87] Quoted in CSE:*Bulletin*, 21 (1901-1902), 521, n. 1.

number of pupils who attended the schools. The educational law of their chiefs notwithstanding, the parents and guardians sent their children to the farms and not to the schools. As has been seen, this experience was also reported in Aguleri in 1902. But unlike in the Christian village, where the Mission had nothing to lose without schools, the effect of the set-back in the schools of Nsugbe had disastrous consequences. After many years of failures there, the Fathers' residence was finally transferred to Ntedje in 1908, and Nsugbe once more became an outstation.[88]

This turn of events shows how justified Father Lutz and his immediate successors were in attaching great importance on the use of boarders in their schools. Of the 65 pupils in the two Catholic schools at Onitsha in 1890, for instance, only 10 were externes. The rest were boarders and were the only ones who attended classes regularly.[89] Given the socio-economic imperatives in native society which gave the use of children in the farms an overriding priority, it was certain that no educational programme would have succeeded in the early years without the boarding system.

Meanwhile, progress was being made at Onitsha. By the beginning of 1901, the number of school children at the wharf school had risen to more than 100. The time was ripe for Lejeune to implement his designs on an école superieure. Accordingly, the wharf school was split into two classes. One class comprising 100 pupils was looked after by Brother David and was located in the old site at Onitsha Wharf. The other class comprising 20 "most advanced pupils" was given the name High School and moved to Onitsha mainland. It was directed by Father Cronenberger and Ephrem, the native catechist who had been closely associated with the wharf school since the days of Father Lutz.[90] Writing to the Superior General in 1902, Father Lejeune said that the foundation of the High School was "absolutely necessary" in order to prevent Catholic pupils from going to Protestant schools.[91]

As shall be seen later, the High School founded by Father Lejeune in Onitsha Town was not a secondary school. Nor had it the standard of an intermediate school in 1901. Rather it was a more advanced kind of primary school than the simple elementary schools run at the Wharf for boys and girls. There brilliant boys in the upper primary classes were given special instructions as pupil-teachers. That the school was called a High School is an indication of the educational influence which came from the Lagos colony, where both the Catholic and Protestant Missions were

---

[88] Cf. CSE:*Bulletin*, 24 (1907-1908), 523.
[89] See CSE:*Bulletin*, 16 (1891-1893), 335.
[90] Cf. CSE:*Bulletin*, 21 (1901-1902), 516.
[91] CSE:192/B/II, "Lejeune to LeRoy," 19 February, 1902.

running such schools, and where there was government regulation and control of education. Father Lejeune adopted the name because it suited his educational ambition. However, since there was yet no recognized system of education, and no government control of schools in the Protectorate of Southern Nigeria in 1901, it is difficult to assess the scope of studies offered in the Onitsha *High School*. All we know with certitude is that catechism and religion were given priority in the school.[92]

The decision of the colonial administration at the beginning of 1900 to carry out military expeditions into the hinterland of Eastern Nigeria offered Lejeune a welcome opportunity to intensify Catholic educational activities among the village people of the interior. Prior to 1900, government control of Southern Nigeria was limited to an insignificant area along the coast. Given the unsettled nature of the interior, it was realized that the establishment of British rule there depended largely on the extension of the *pax Britannica* behind the coastal regions. This often meant subjugation by force of arms, followed by a formal education of the people. For the latter, the Government needed the help and co-operation of the only agents involved with education at the time—the Christian Missions. With a prophetic insight, Father Lejeune reckoned that it was only through education and concerted effort with the Government that the Catholic Mission would take a place of influence in the territories to be opened.[93] It was against this background that the Catholics began at this period to follow government educational programmes with unquestioning resolve. Such subjects as English, Mathematics, and various other industrial subjects, which the Anglicans regarded as too "secular" and "ambitious",[94] were passionately taught in Catholic schools. This willingness to follow the official scheme of education accounted much for the success of Lejeune's educational policy. Among other things, it won him the personal friendship and co-operation of the High Commissioner, Sir Ralph Moor, who happened to be a professing Catholic.

During his visit to Onitsha in 1901, the High Commissioner invited the Catholic school to take part in a general competition for the schools of the Protectorate, a practice which was designed to spur the individual schools towards better results. The Onitsha Mission also got encouraging compliments for its marvellous achievements in brick-making, carpentry

---

[92] Ibid.

[93] Cf. CSE:192/A/IV, "Lejeune to Directors of Propaganda Fide," Calabar, 20 October, 1904: "Le gouvernement de la Nigéria, southern et northern, a maintenant pénétré toutes les provinces.... Si nous pouvions répondre favorablement à toutes ses demandes, toute l'influence dans l'intérieur serait à nous."

[94] Quoted in P. B. Clarke, "The Methods and Ideology of the Holy Ghost Fathers," p. 100.

and masonry. The High Commissioner was so impressed that he decided to recommend these industrial undertakings to the colonies of Sierra Leone and Gold Coast.[95] In June 1901, Moor informed Lejeune that "an Inspector of schools would...be shortly appointed and that examination would be held and grants made to various missions in accordance with results."[96] By 1902 the Protectorate of Southern Nigeria had got its Inspector of Schools, and in December of the same year the Catholic schools at Onitsha, Aguleri, and Ossomari were officially inspected. This first official inspection of schools in Eastern Nigeria revealed that by 1902 the Catholics had begun to take an edge over the Protestants in primary and industrial education, in spite of the fact that the latter had a lead of over 25 years. According to Lejeune's account, the Protestant schools in and around Onitsha were inspected in one single day, whereas it took three full days to go through the Catholic schools.[97] A grant-in-aid of about 5000 francs was received from the Government for the three Catholic schools, and a special grant was promised for a future Catholic industrial school.[98] This financial assistance strengthened the Prefect's decision at the beginning of his office to make the school his primary means of evangelization. "Since a part of the expenses incurred in these schools shall, in reality, be defrayed by the colonial Government," he wrote to his Superior General, "we are directing our efforts towards the schools."[99]

The results of this fervent commitment to education were not long in coming. By virtue of the expansive educational programmes that were carried out in Onitsha, the authorities were able to meet the urgent demands for schools which came from the towns and villages around Onitsha. Boys who had completed their training at Onitsha as teachers were sent to these centres to run the schools founded there.[100] A new era of Catholic evangelism in Eastern Nigeria had set in: the apostolate of the school was carried out by pupils who had been trained by the Catholic missionaries themselves or under their supervision.

Our survey so far has been concerned with the expansion of schools in the Onitsha district. Father Lejeune was the first Prefect to embark upon a constructive missionary programme designed to embrace the whole of the large Prefecture. This included missionary and educational activities

---

[95] See CSE:*Bulletin*, 21 (1901-1902), 518.

[96] PRO:C.O. 520/8, No. 157, "Moor to Colonial Office," 12 June, 1901.

[97] Cf. CSE:192/B/II, "Lejeune to Superior General," Onitsha, 25 December, 1902.

[98] Ibid.; see also CSE:*Bulletin*, 22 (1903-1904), 39.

[99] CSE:192/B/III, "Lejeune to LeRoy," Onitsha, 25 February, 1903.

[100] See CSE:181/B/I, R. Daly, "Reverend Father Lutz," p. 11.

in the Niger delta area, in the Calabar and Cross River districts, and in the Benue region.

He visited Oguta after only two weeks of his arrival in September 1900, and a month later a school was established there by Father Xavier. In October of the same year he undertook a missionary journey to Brass with Father Bubendorf.[101] His greatest achievement outside Onitsha, however, was at Old Calabar. By 1900 the town had an estimated population of about 30,000. It became famous as a commercial centre towards the close of the nineteenth century, when exports in palm oil, rubber, ivory and timber were replacing the slave trade. It was the head-quarters of the Protectorate of Southern Nigeria, and by 1903 its population included immigrants from other British colonies, and about 300 Europeans.[102] By all account, Calabar possessed good prospects for a successful Mission. Having been impressed by the educational efforts of the Catholics at Onitsha, Sir Ralph Moor, the High Commissioner, was very eager to see their influence spread in the capital of his Protectorate.

The first instance of the presence at Calabar of Catholic missionaries was in October 1900, when Father Lejeune visited the town with Father Bubendorf. In January 1903, Moor was again at Onitsha and during this visit conclusive arrangements were made for a Catholic Mission at Calabar. In February the Calabar Mission was finally founded by Lejeune and Father Patrick MacDermott.[103] Here, as in all new stations, schools were made the focus of missionary activities. A convent was also built for the Sisters of St. Joseph of Cluny, who were to work in a hospital for the natives, and to run a school for girls. The Government and the people showed their appreciation by donating 2,500 and 4,000 francs respectively.[104]

Writing shortly after the foundation of the Calabar Mission, Father Patrick MacDermott, the first superior of the Mission, spoke of the great success achieved in the school. He said that about 140 pupils were attending classes daily, and that a second school sponsored by a native chief named Essieni was under construction. This latter school was officially inaugurated on July 3, 1903 with a colourful town festival.[105] In a letter

---

[101] Ibid.

[102] See CSE:192/B/III, "Lejeune to Superior General," 19 July, 1903.

[103] See CSE:*Bulletin*, 22 (1903-1904), 131.

[104] Ibid., p. 798. It is hardly surprising that the natives of Calabar were capable of donating generously to the Catholic cause. The numerous Efik and Ibibio chiefs had amassed great wealth in the past through the slave trade. Their villas were usually storey buildings which were furnished like most aristocratic homes in Europe (see ibid., p. 800). It was these "gentlemen," as they were popularly called, who were behind the promotion of education at Calabar and the Niger-Delta city-states.

[105] Cf. CSE:*Bulletin*, 22 (1903-1904), 342f.

to the Mother House in September, 1903, Father Lejeune revealed that there were a total of 360 registered pupils in the two Catholic schools established so far at Calabar, with 250 attending regularly.[106] This was the result of only seven months of educational efforts in the town. Its magnitude becomes apparent in comparison with the results of 1899, when there were about 335 attendances in all the schools of the Prefecture. In the opinion of Father Lejeune, this "extraordinary success" at Calabar was possible only because of the exclusive preoccupation of the Catholic missionaries with the school.[107]

Perhaps the greatest expression of official recognition of Father Lejeune's educational labours in Eastern Nigeria was a proposal made to him in 1903 by the High Commissioner to found a special "Institute" for the education of about 150 sons of the chiefs of Calabar. The school was to run a four-year-course for pupils intending to enter the Government High School, where students were prepared for the Cambridge Certificate.[108] Nothing could have conformed better with the Prefect's missionary aspirations than the invitation to take the education of the ruling class in his own hands.

Although Father Lejeune preferred to call the proposed Catholic school an "Institute," it is to his French designation of it that we should turn in order to determine the standard of education to be offered in it. In a more detailed report to Propaganda Fide, he called the proposed school both a "Training Institute" and *une école intermédiaire*.[109] As shall be seen in the next chapter, there was no definite system of education in the Protectorate of Southern Nigeria as late as May 1902.[110] By October 1902, Moor had finally worked out a scheme of education which distinguished between four types of schools, namely, Primary school, Intermediate school, High school, and Technical school.[111] There was only one Training Institute in Eastern Nigeria by the time Lejeune wrote his report in October 1903, namely, the Presbyterian Hope Waddell Institute. According to Moor, the scheme for the High School (also called Government College) was the same as that of Hope Waddell. Since the proposed Catholic *Institute* was to prepare pupils for the Government

[106] Cf. CSE:192/B/III, "Lejeune to Superior General," Old Calabar, 13 September, 1903; see also CSE:*Bulletin*, 22 (1903-1904), 343 & 799.

[107] Ibid.: "Jusqu'ici, on ne s'est guère occupé que des écoles; mais on l'a fait avec un suceès extraordinaire."

[108] See CSE:192/B/III, "Lejeune to Superior General," Old Calabar, 13 September, 1903; see also 192/B/III, "Lejeune to Superior General," 20 October, 1903.

[109] Cf. CSE:192/A/IV, L. Lejeune, "Compt-rendu pour la Propagande," Lokoja, 20 October, 1903.

[110] See PRO:C.O. 520/14, "Moor to Colonial Office," 27 May, 1902.

[111] PRO:C.O. 520/15, No. 483, "Moor to Colonial Office," 29 October, 1902.

High School, there is no doubt, therefore, that it falls under the category of Intermediate school, a more advanced primary school. It was to have the same character as the *High School* which Lejeune founded at Onitsha Town in 1901. The fact that the Prefect chose to call it an "Institute" shows that he was aiming at something much higher than just an intermediate school.

However, the opportunity of establishing a Catholic institution of higher learning was missed during Father Lejeune's prefectship. In fact there is no indication that a special Catholic school was ever established at Calabar for the privileged sons of the aristocracy. There is no doubt, however, that the education of this group of persons was carried out in the existing Catholic school at Calabar. As shall be seen later, the Catholic authorities in Paris were yet not as enthusiastic as Father Lejeune to get deeply involved with secular education in the Mission. Furthermore, whatever chances there were for Lejeune to put up a fight for his designs on a Catholic training institute was greatly undermined by the Prefect's renewed missionary quests in the Benue region between 1903 and 1905. Realising "the most excellent work" done by the Catholics in Southern Nigeria, Lord F. D. Lugard, the High Commissioner of Northern Nigeria, had invited Lejeune to open a freed-slave home at Dekina.[112] The proposal to establish a special school at Calabar would have given Lejeune an edge over his Protestant rivals. But he failed to parley this advantage into something substantial by directing all his attention forthwith on the project at Dekina.

A remarkable thing about the project at Dekina was that both leaders, Lugard and Lejeune, were forced to modify their policies in order to bring it about. Anxious to secure the assistance of the Christian Missions in his Government's efforts to settle the slaves freed under the Slavery Proclamation of 1900, Lugard was forced for the first time to moderate his Government's policy of non-interference with Islam.[113] This change of mind surprised even Lejeune himself. The Prefect seemed not to have forgotten Lugard's persecution of the Catholics in Uganda. "How is it possible," he wondered, "that he, the arch-enemy of the Catholics in the past, is now procuring for us every possible facility for the foundation of Missions on the Niger and the Benue? This is certainly a divine mystery.[114] There is no doubt, however, that Lugard's urgent need of

---

[112] See CSE:192/B/IV, F. D. Lugard, "Report to Colonial Office," 1903.

[113] See P. B. Clarke, "The Methods and Ideology of the Holy Ghost Fathers," pp. 88-93. As many as 500 slaves were liberated early 1902 from the captivity of the soldiers of the Sultan of Kano. Cf. AP:N.S. R.141/1902, Vol. 237, "Lejeune to Cardinal Gotti," Onitsha, 1 October, 1902.

[114] AP:N.S. R.141/1902, Vol. 237. "Lejeune to Cardinal Gotti," Onitsha, 19 August, 1902.

missionaries to aid his Government in its fight against Hausa slave raiders in the North had a very important bearing on this mystery. Following a series of military actions against the Igala tribes of Bassa and Okpoto in 1903, he called upon the Catholics to resume their abortive missionary ventures on the Benue in 1902.[115]

Lejeune's willingness to found freed slaves homes in the North, a method of evangelization he had despised and fought against in the South, may smack of contradiction. Yet, there were some cogent reasons which vindicated it. A guiding force in the Prefect's change of policy was what he saw as a rare opportunity for a concerted action by Church and State against Mohammedanism, one of the three most dangerous threats to Catholicism in Africa, the other two being Protestantism and Fetishism.[116] By joining the government campaign against the slave raiders, Lejeune hoped to contribute to the destruction of the economy of the Moslems. Furthermore, he argued that the foundation of Christian enclaves along the Benue would prevent them from spreading southwards.[117]

The Catholic missionary venture in Northern Nigeria had a most precarious existence. Shortly after its foundation on October 14, 1903, the Mission of Dekina was completely destroyed by fire. The greatest foil to its existence, however, came from the bitter strife between the Moslems and their pagan neighbours. Lejeune dwelt on this stingy problem in a letter to Lord Lugard:

> The unsettled state of the country has not permitted us to get into contact
> with the natives. No workmen to be had, no children for our schools. Con-

---

[115] See CSE:*Bulletin*, 22 (1903-1904), 438. In response to a special appeal in 1902 by Cardinal Ledochowski, Prefect of Propaganda Fide, Lugard granted Lejeune his Government's protection and assistance, which enabled Lejeune to undertake his first exploration tour of the Benue region of his Prefecture. He went as far as Ibi and Wukari, and by the end of 1902, two Missions had been founded in these centres, Holy Cross at Ibi and St. Peter Claver at Wukari. See AP:N.S. R.141/1902, Vol. 237, "Lejeune to Cardinal Gotti," Onitsha 1 October, 1902, p. 812ᵛ. Lejeune proposed the foundation of schools in these stations and reckoned with a successful ministry among the pagan population. But this hope was stifled by the deep-seated Moslem-pagan hostilities in the area. Work was defered at Ibi and Wukari and was never resumed in Lejeune's life-time.

[116] In the words of Father Pied of the SMA in Lagos, "the most formidable adversary of Christianity in Africa is by no means fetishism, but rather Mohammedanism [especially when it is] supported by the representatives of the European Governments." AP:N.S. R.141/1894, Vol. 49, "Pied to Ledochowski," Lagos, 10 July, 1894, p.560ᵛ. In the main, the Catholics in Eastern Nigeria were spared the ordeal of direct dealings with the Moslems. However, they lived in constant fear of Mohammedan infiltration in the East. Father Lejeune wrote in 1901, for instance, that the Moslems had come as near as Asaba, and he expressed the fear that Onitsha and its neighbours might be infected. See CSE:191/A/II, "Report by Lejeune," Onitsha, 1901.

[117] Cf. AP:N.S. R.141/1902, Vol. 237, "Lejeune to Cardinal Gotti," Onitsha, 1 October, 1902, p. 812ʳ.

sequently nothing to be done.... As the Okpoto tribe seems to be composed of intelligent and hardworking people, we tried to get their children to frequent our schools, unfortunately such is the racial enmity between Pagans and Hausas in this country that it looks an impossible task, for the present, to have them together in the same school or workshop. The Hausas refuse to come to our school, nor, if the report be true, will they allow the pagans to attend.[118]

The inestimable value of the school in the work of evangelization becomes very apparent in this letter. Called to Dekina to found a Christian village for liberated slaves, the Catholic Fathers nevertheless aimed at spreading beyond the frontiers of the slave home and evangelizing the neighbouring tribes. Accordingly, they tried to lure the people to their schools, a strategy which failed only because of the strangulating effect which the local feuds had on these schools.

The educational schemes carried out in the slave home were designed to provide useful trades for the liberated slaves. Besides lessons on writing and English, the boys were taught gardening, methods of agriculture, cooking, carpentry and various other trades. A workshop with a good supply of European tools was built for the industrial subjects. The aim of these educational projects was to make the freed slaves self-supporting citizens and useful assets to the Protectorate.[119]

The education of women in the Dekina slave home presented some special problems. There were no European Sisters there to take charge of them, and since the Fathers considered it necessary to form the girls on the same principles as those devised for the boys, they proposed that from 10 to 15 slave girls be sent annually to Onitsha, where they would be taught domestic science by the Sisters of Cluny. After a few years at Onitsha, the girls were to be sent back to Dekina and married to the boys of the slave home.[120] Lugard expressed no objections to this plan on the condition, however, that a special application was made in accordance with government "Standing Order 150," which prohibited the sending of freed slaves from the North to the South.[121]

However, there is no indication that the government Standing Order 150 was ever relaxed in order to enable freed slave girls to be sent to Onitsha for training. It was for another purpose that the order was relaxed in August 1905. Having failed to produce results in a measure that was commensurate with the difficulties and expenses that were incured in

---

[118] CSE:192/B/IV, "Lejeune to Lugard," Bassa, 15 January, 1905. This letter was written by Father Shanahan on behalf of the Prefect.
[119] Cf. Ibid.
[120] Ibid.
[121] CSE:192/B/IV, Lugard to Lejeune," 2 February, 1905.

running it, the Dekina Mission was abandoned in August 1905 with the sanction of the Mother House of the Holy Ghost Fathers.[122] This happened the same year that the proposal was made to send some girls to Onitsha for training. In accordance with the terms of the Standing Order 150, the Lugard Government ordered Shanahan to hand over the children of the slave home to government officials at Lokoja.[123] However, after some negotiations, he was allowed to take the children to the South. A team of 2 Fathers, 1 Brother, and 15 children returned to Onitsha on August 26, 1905.[124] Given the fact that 15 out of the 16 children, and the entire staff, of the Dekina slave home were involved in this exodus, the claim by G. O. Olusanya that the settlement did not fold up at their departure must be open to question.[125]

Two factors were chiefly responsible for the failure of the Dekina project, namely, Muslim hostility and the pro-Islam politics of the Northern Nigerian Government. As has been seen above, all efforts to get children of pagan parents to attend the Catholic schools were frustrated by the Muslim Hausas, who, for their part, would not send their own children to the schools. This baneful attitude towards the school—the principal medium of evangelization—had disastrous consequences on the Dekina Mission. However, despite this case of Muslim hostility, it still would have been possible to establish a flourishing Christian village at Dekina if the Government had kept its promise to send about 100 liberated slaves annually to the Mission. This promise was made prior to actual armed expeditions into Northern Nigeria,[126] but soon afterwards Lugard realized the grave danger inherent in alienating his Government with the powerful Sultans and Emirs. Consequently, he slowly and tactfully returned to the "non-interference" policy, a move which inhibited government action against the slave raiders.[127] Lejeune complained bitterly in January 1905 that the pro-Islam politics of the Government jeopardized the success of the Mission at Dekina.[128] His fears were not unfounded, for as early as January 1905, there were only 8 freed slaves at the Dekina settlement, which had accommodation and facilities for 60

[122] See CSE:*Bulletin*, 23 (1905-1906), 354.

[123] See CSE:192/B/IV, "Shanahan to Superior General," 23 August, 1905.

[124] Cf. CSE:192/B/IV, "Vogler to Superior General," Onitsha, 27 August, 1905; see also CSE:*Bulletin*, 23 (1905-1906), 354.

[125] See G. O. Olusanya, "The Freed Slave Homes: An Unknown Aspect of Northern Nigerian History," *Journal of the Historical Society of Nigeria*, 3 (1966), cited in P. B. Clarke, "The Methods and Ideology of the Holy Ghost Fathers," p. 93.

[126] See AP:N.S. R.141/1902, Vol. 237, "Lejeune to Cardinal Gotti," Onitsha, 10 October, 1902, p. 812v.

[127] See ibid., pp. 812v-813r: "Les officiers ont l'ordre de ne pas s'opposer encore à la traites."

[128] Cf. CSE:192/B/IV, "Lejeune to Superior General," 6 January, 1905.

children. He promised to send a carpenter from Onitsha to the slave home "should the Government supply us with a sufficient number of slaves—say from 50 to 60 to give occupation to the men in charge."[129] The slave home was abandoned only after the Northern Nigerian Government under Lugard had broken its pledge.

Generally speaking, the missionary fiasco at Dekina was not unpredictable: it was just one among a series of failures experienced by the Christian Missions in Muslim Northern Nigeria. The Protestant and Catholic missionaries of the nineteenth century were often tempted to look upon Northern Nigeria as possessing better prospects for the work of evangelization than the South. Accordingly, at the beginning of their enterprise in Nigeria, they all headed northwards, especially to Lokoja, a commercial town with a predominantly Muslim influence. From this strategic position they hoped for a piecemeal victory of the Cross over the Crescent. But they invariably missed the mark with a very wide margin. The Society of African Missions, which had established a Mission at Lokoja in 1884, was forced to retreat to Asaba in 1888 after all its efforts to win the sympathy of the Muslim population had failed. By 1900, the Anglican Church Missionary Society had also come to a full awareness of the futility of preaching the gospel in Islamic Northern Nigeria.[130] Seen against this background, the withdrawal of the Holy Ghost Fathers from Dekina in 1905 was an unfortunate repetition of a gross miscalculation in missionary strategy.

It is not certain who took the final decision to abandon the slave home, but since Lejeune was already in France by August 1905, when the establishment folded up, it must be presumed that Shanahan took the decision. He was the superior of the Dekina Mission from 1903 to 1905 and his personal experiences with Muslim hostilities must have had a significant bearing on the fact that he did not resume missionary quests in the Benue region during his long term of office as head of the Prefecture.

Although Father Lejeune did not live to see most of the fruits of his labours, the success of his educational policy was already an accomplished task even in his last days in the Mission. In its Annual Report on the Education Department for the year 1906, the Southern Nigerian Government gave special credit to the Onitsha Roman Catholic Mission for "the excellent educational work of the past three years."[131] This cor-

---

[129] CSE:192/B/IV, "Lejeune to Lugard," Bassa, 15 January, 1905.
[130] Cf. E. A. Ayandele, *The Missionary Impact on Modern Nigeria, 1842-1914* (London: Longman, 1966), pp. 133-137.
[131] PRO:C.O. 592/3, *Annual Report on the Education Department for the Year 1906*.

responds, to a large extent, with the time when Lejeune began, in spite of fierce opposition, to shift the school forcibly to the centre stage of missionary enterprise not only in the Onitsha district, but also in the Calabar and Benue regions. A look at the statistics in Table 1 shows that between the end of 1899 and 1904 the number of schools in the Prefecture had more than doubled and that the number of pupils had tripled. A comparison of the figures of 1904 with those of 1906 shows a more interesting growth. With less European missionaries, the number of schools had risen from 16 in 1904 to 24 in 1906, and the number of pupils from 1200 to 3000. There is only one explanation to this: the availability of more African catechist-teachers, thanks to the schools established at Onitsha and Calabar. Lejeune's school children had become teachers in the schools.

The success of Lejeune's educational policy was aided by a number of factors. Firstly, unlike Father Lutz, Lejeune had the advantage of starting his ministry in Eastern Nigeria at a time when there was already a considerable Catholic influence on the society. The choice of Samuel Okosi Okolo, a Catholic catechist, as the Obi of Onitsha may serve here as an illustration. This event took place at the beginning of November 1900, barely a month after Lejeune's arrival in the Mission. Samuel was a former Protestant who was converted to Catholicism in 1893. He served as a catechist at Nsugbe and Aguleri. According to Father Lejeune, his *concitoyens* (fellow-townsmen or compatriots) presented him as their candidate for the office of the Obi of Onitsha. Vying for the kingship were also the son of the deceased pagan Obi and another unidentified Protestant candidate.[132] The question that must be asked here is: who were Samuel Okolo's *concitoyens*? Given the strained relations between the Catholics and the Protestants in Eastern Nigeria, there is little likelihood that there were Protestants among them. Since the Catholic population at Onitsha in 1900 was very insignificant, we must presume therefore that the overwhelming majority of the votes which made Samuel Okolo the Obi of Onitsha came from the pagans.

The choice of an educated Christian, instead of an illiterate pagan, to be the leader of the people shows the direction which the social wind was blowing at the beginning of this century: it highlights the importance which the natives attached to education and Western civilization. One of the first deeds of the new "enlightened" leader was to turn his royal palace into a provisional school so that the children of the town could receive instructions—given personally by himself—while a proper school

---

[132] "Lejeune to Cardinal Ledochowski," 15 November, 1900, quoted in CSE:*Bulletin*, 21 (1901-1902), 77-79.

Table 1

The Lower Niger Mission: Its Growth and its Schools, 1899-1917.

	1889	1901	1904	1906	1909	1912	1917
Fathers	8	9	13	10	15	17	17
Brothers	3	7	8	7	12	10	6
Catechist-Teachers	12	14	19	33	42	124	506
Principal Stations	3	3	5	5	7	8	9
Outstations	a	a	a	a	16	38	280
Schools	7	11	16	24	24	46	287
School Children	334	828	1,200	3,000	2,591	6,578	20,000
Catholics	a	2,000	3,000	a	2,894	5,563	10,289
Catechumens	a	a	a	a	1,671	5,368	32,449
Baptisms	133	323	a	569	670	1,199	2,326

Source: Sacred Returns as given in CSE: *Bulletin*, 21 (1901) to ibid., 29 (1918-1920).
a = Figures not given.

was being built for them.[133] The elevation of a Catholic catechist to the highest office in the Onitsha society underlines the degree of Catholic influence in the town at the beginning of Father Lejeune's ministry. The decision of the Prefect to launch an educational programme which had the totality of society, rather than just the Christian villages, as its orbit, must have rested, to a large extent, on his awareness of the sympathy which the Catholic cause had among the people.

Secondly, the good relationship which existed between Lejeune and the colonial Government had profound implications for his educational policy. The beginning of his office corresponded with a change in the administration of the Protectorate of Southern Nigeria. The Royal Niger Company—the biased imperial law enforcement agent—was replaced by a co-operative colonial Government under Sir Ralph Moor. The missionary gains in the interior which resulted from intensified government activities in the hinterland, and the government grants in aid of education were some of the favours which eluded Lejeune's predecessors. His appraisal of the disposition of the colonial government towards the Catholic Mission was accordingly at variance with the experiences of those he succeeded. Speaking of the assistance he got from Moor's Administration at Calabar, he said:

> Whereas the religious are being expelled everywhere in France, the English Government here in Nigeria... [gives] aid to the work of construction. So far it is very true to say that the Holy Church gains from one side what it loses on the other.[134]

Finally, the existence of a government controlled system of education during Lejeune's prefectship played an important role in the success of his educational policy. Prior to 1902 the choice of subjects for the mission schools was completely at the discretion of the Fathers and Brothers in charge of them. The education offered in these rudimentary schools was generally of a very elementary character. With the introduction of official regulations and control, new élan and purpose were added to the work of education. This was of immense help for the teacher and the taught.

It must be emphasized, however, that all these advantages would have come to nothing if Father Lejeune had not been a man of originality and extraordinary foresight. In less than five years, he succeeded in saving a dying Mission by courageously bringing its methods and ideals in line with contemporary changes. To direct the Prefecture after his death in September 1905 was Father Joseph Shanahan, his right-hand man in the

---

[133] Ibid., p. 78.
[134] L. Lejeune, "Report to Propaganda Fide," 20 October, 1904, quoted in CSE:*Bulletin*, 22 (1903-1904), 798.

Mission and personal choice as successor. Shanahan had closely followed and imbibed the ideas and plans of his great master. It was under him that the triumph of the school apostolate attained its plenitude. But he never failed to give credit to Lejeune, who master-minded, directly or indirectly, most of the epoch-making decisions in the Lower Niger Mission.[135]

---

[135] After five years of serious efforts to establish a Catholic Training Institute, Shanahan made a tentative start in 1910. In a report to the Mother House, he tried to calm the rage of his displeased Superior General by saying: "The question of a High School dates from the time of Rev. Father Lejeune; I have done no more than executing the plan very well conceived and commenced by him." CSE:191/B/VI, J. Shanahan, "Training School for Southern Nigeria," Onitsha, 6 May, 1910.

CHAPTER THREE

COLONIAL AND MISSION INTERESTS IN EDUCATION

I. *Government Intervention in Education, 1887-1919*

Before the colonial administrators decided at the beginning of this century to exercise some measure of control over education, the Christian
Missions had the choice and direction of education firmly in their hands.
It has become customary to deplore the Mission schools of these years of
unchallenged monopoly for the low-grade education they actually
offered. The most famous critic of Mission education in the early years
was, perhaps, Mr. Henry Carr, the Inspector of Schools for the Lagos
Colony. After his inspection of the Mission schools in Calabar and
Bonny between 1899 and 1900, he endeavoured to pin-point the cause
of the inferiority of "school-learning" in the Mission schools. In his
opinion, "the Missionaries look upon schools as instruments for making
converts, other men view them as instruments for making good and
useful citizens."[1] Professor A. Afigbo has written in a similar vein when
he suggested that the missionaries "would have pursued instead a policy
of concentrating on a few well-equipped and properly-staffed schools
which would turn out tolerably well-educated men."[2]

These views had grown out of considerations of the place of education
in the art of nation-building, and if the task of inserting education into
the national plan belonged as much to the Missions as to the Government, then credit ought in fact to be given to the party that took the
initiative, however ineffectively, to provide some education for the
people. Given the meagre resources at their disposal, the Missionaries
could not but provide the simplest form of education. With government
assistance and control, they were able to demonstrate in a more definite
manner that national considerations in education were not alien to their
purpose. But that aid was unduly long in coming their way.

It took the British Government quite a long time to come to terms with
the complexities of the educational issue not only in her colonies, but also
in England itself. As late as the second half of the nineteenth century,
there was no effectively planned educational system in England. For

---

[1] PRO:C.O.520/3, No. 35281, *Annual Report on Southern Nigeria, 1899-1900.*
[2] "The Background to the Southern Nigerian Education Code of 1903," *Journal of the
Historical Society of Nigeria*, 4 (June, 1968), 209.

many centuries, educational policies were firmly in the hands of private education bodies and voluntary agencies—usually the Christian Churches. A significant departure from this norm occurred in 1870 with the passage of an Education Act introducing a compulsory primary education for all. The impulse had come from France, where the French Revolution had inspired a number of measures aimed at building up a central administrative framework to take charge of the education of the common man. The discussions that followed in England over the relationship between elementary education and industrial prosperity corresponded with, and greatly influenced, the very first steps taken in the colonies towards education.

1. The Educational Influence From Lagos

In 1864, the Imperial Government in London sent Commissioner Ord to the British possessions in West Africa to study the state of education there. Motivated by this visit, the Colonial Administration in Lagos began in 1877 to make annual grants of £200 to each of the three missionary bodies engaged with educational work in Lagos—the Wesleyan Methodist Mission, the Church Missionary Society, and the Roman Catholic Mission.[3] In the same year, the first official statement on colonial educational policy was made, suggesting, among other things, that education be left completely in the hands of the missionaries.[4] Accordingly, the grants to the Mission schools were made without government control of any kind.

A persistent government dissatisfaction with the quality of Mission education led in 1882 to a modification of that policy of non-interference. In that year, a West African Education Ordinance was promulgated and was applied to the Lagos colony. The Ordinance made grants-in-aid to Mission schools dependent upon discipline and good organization, the number of attendance, and the result of examinations. An Inspector of Schools was appointed to ensure that these conditions were met.

Although the education Ordinance of 1882 marked a turning-point in the history of education in West Africa, the scope it gave to government involvement in education nevertheless remained basically insignificant. It did not, for instance, set up an independent department to take charge of education. Rather it merely provided for a general Board of Education consisting of the Governor, the members of the Executive Council, and four other nominated members, who were usually representatives of the

[3] See S. Phillipson, *Grants in Aid of Education in Nigeria* (Lagos, 1948), p. 11.
[4] See M. J. Walsh, "The Catholic Contribution to Education in Western Nigeria, 1861-1926" (unpub. M. A. Thesis, University of London, 1951), p. 164.

local Christian Churches.[5] Even the provision of an inspectorate was not a thing to be taken seriously in view of the fact that only one Inspector of Schools was saddled with the task of inspecting the whole of the then British West Africa, which included the settlements in Gambia, Sierra Leone, the Gold Coast, and Lagos. The inspection of the schools in these territories were, to a great extent, dependent upon "the wanderings or leave of the Inspector."[6]

A purely Nigerian Education Ordinance was enacted in 1887, a year after Lagos was detached from the Gold Coast and once more made a separate Crown Colony. Under this Ordinance, the Legislative Council was constituted the Board of Education. To render grants-in- aid strictly dependent upon merit, emphasis was laid on a more effective control of the schools.[7]

The Lagos Education Ordinance of 1887 was in many respects a high-water mark of the West African educational movement. It greatly influenced the educational decisions of other British West African administrators in subsequent years. Among these was Sir Ralph Moor, one of the most notable political figures of colonial Southern Nigeria. As has been seen, Southern Nigeria was by 1887 not a political entity. Only Lagos was a Crown colony and the rest of Southern Nigeria was regarded as a Protectorate. Sir Ralph Moor was Commissioner and Consul-General of the Niger Coast Protectorate from 1896 to 1899. In dealing with the natives, he lacked the tact and patience of his predecessor, Sir Claude Macdonald, preferring the "shelling and burning" of towns and villages to peaceful persuasion.[8] Nevertheless, in spite of his bad temper, Moor was the first administrator in the Protectorate to show great interest in the education of the masses. As acting Commissioner and Consul-General in the Niger Coast Protectorate, he began in 1894 to give financial assistance to the Protestant Missions in the Niger Delta city-states.[9] He saw in such aids the only means of determining what should be done in the Mission schools, over which he had no control whatever. However, the deplorable nature of most of the mission schools

[5] See PRO:C. O.147/61, "Governor A. Moloney to Sir H. Hollang, Secretary of State for the Colonies," 18 November, 1887. The inclusion of Mission representatives in the Board of Education underscored the dependence of the Colonial Governments on the Voluntary Agencies in educational matters.

[6] PRO:C. O.147/61, "Minutes to a Meeting of the Legislative Council of the Colony of Lagos," 3 November, 1887.

[7] See PRO:C. O.147/60, "Education Ordinance, 1887," Notice by E. G. Woolhouse, Acting Colonial Secretary.

[8] See PRO:F. O.2/84, "Moor to Foreign Office," 26 October, 1895.

[9] See A. Afigbo, "The Background to the Southern Nigerian Education Code of 1903," pp. 210-211.

mitigated against Moor's educational endeavours, and by 1899 there were only three schools in the Protectorate receiving grants- in-aid from the Government—the Hope Waddell Training Institute belonging to the United Presbyterian Mission at Calabar, the school of the Pastorate Mission at Bonny, and the school of the Church Missionary Society at Brass.[10]

Moor's contention was that government control of schools was the only sound system under which educational policy could be satisfactorily implemented. Since there were yet no education ordinances in existence in his Protectorate, he naturally grasped at the preconditions for grants-in-aid which were demanded in other British West African colonies, especially in lagos. "It will...be advisable in future years," he wrote in 1897, "that the educational grants shall be dependent on results and that the schools shall be subject to the inspection of a school inspector in the same manner as in the colonies."[11]

Encouraged by the efforts of Moor's Government to give financial assistance to mission schools, and given the fact that the Niger Coast Protectorate was part of the Prefecture of the Lower Niger, Catholic authorities at Onitsha endeavoured to extend their missionary and educational activities to the coastal regions. In 1898 Father Bubendorf contemplated installing "a good Catechist" at Brass, meaning one who would be capable of running a school, in order to have rights over the grant of 5000 francs promised by the Government.[12] This was a clear indication that Moor and his Government were implementing the Lagos Education Ordinance of 1887, and its general rules of 1891 and 1896 which stipulated the qualifications a teacher must have in order to be allowed to teach in a school.[13]

---

[10] See PRO:C.O.444/1, "Moor to Colonial Office," 10 May, 1899.

[11] Quoted in A. Afigbo, "The Background to the...Code of 1903," p. 211.

[12] See CSE: 191/B/XII, "Bubendorf to superior General," Onitsha, 10 January, 1898. Father Bubendorf made frequent contacts with the Niger Coast Protectorate, especially during his caretaker years between 1895 and 1898. He revisited Brass in 1895 accompanied by King Koko's son, who was being educated at that time at the Onitsha Wharf school. The King's son was one of the four boys that Father Lutz took with him to Onitsha during his visit to Brass in January 1891 (see CSE: *Bulletin*, 16, 1891-1893, pp. 338-339). Father Bubendorf's plans to found a school at Brass came at a time when the Lower Niger Mission was going through the grimmest trials of its history. The absence of a resident Prefect from 1894 to 1898 inhibited efforts to expand the Mission beyond the Onitsha district.

[13] See F.C.O.L./10940, "Report by the Committee of the Education Board," Lagos, 1903. During its meeting on 19 February, 1903, this committee revised the General Education Rules of 1896 and agreed that Head teachers should have at least a second-class certificate, and every other teacher a third-class certificate.

To lend more substance to his doctrine of government intervention in education, Moor invited Henry Carr, the Inspector of Schools for the Lagos Colony, to make an inspection of the schools at Old Calabar and Bonny and to enquire into the condition of education in the Protectorate. The inspection which was carried out between 1899 and 1900 resulted in a comprehensive report on education in Southern Nigeria in which Mr. Carr stressed, like Moor, the necessity of government control of schools. "Bright as the prospects for education in Nigeria may appear to be," he said, "I am persuaded that that prospect will not be realised until the Government takes an active part in organizing and promoting public institutions."[14] By means of Government inspection, Carr hoped that such anomalies as insufficiency of qualified teachers, and what he described as "the multiplicity of subjects without thorough grounding in the elementary matters of instruction," would be eliminated.[15]

This official out-cry for Government control of education was a reflection of a controversy which dominated educational debate in England in the nineteenth century. Matthew Arnold argued, for instance, that an effective system of public education could only be thought of in terms of a municipal organization.[16] He noted that other countries, especially France and Germany, had taken the lead by replacing "the defective public establishment made by the middle ages for their education with a new one, which provides for the actual condition of things."[17]

The urge to provide for the actual condition of things was also felt in the colonies by the administrators. And such evidence as history affords shows that economic considerations accounted for much of the new order of things in the colonies. The Colonial Government in Nigeria felt that Mission education was not making adequate contribution towards economic growth in the colony. In the words of Governor H. MacCallum of Lagos, Mission interest in the upper standards was "not for the advancement of general progress in the colony...but only because they must rely on those scholars as the recruiting ground for helpers in the Mission field."[18] The wish to couple education with the fulfilment of an economic need inspired the first moves of the colonial administrators towards education.

---

[14] PRO:C.O.520/3, No. 35281, *Annual Report on Southern Nigeria, 1899-1900.*
[15] Ibid.
[16] See "A French Eton or Middle-Class Education and the State," in *Matthew Arnold and the Education of the New Order: A Selection of Arnold's Writings on Education,* ed. P. Smith and G. Summerfield (Cambridge: The Univ. Press. 1969), pp. 76-156.
[17] Ibid.
[18] PRO:C.O.147/132, No. 122, Governor MacCallum, "Memorandum on Secondary Education in the Lagos Colony," 1 May, 1898.

2. Sir Ralph Moor's Scheme of Education

Active government collaboration in education in Eastern Nigeria was preceded by a historic event at the turn of the century, namely, the creation of the Protectorate of Southern Nigeria in 1900. The Royal Niger Company lost its charter in 1899, and the southern portion of the territories administered by it was united with the Niger Coast Protectorate in 1900 to form the Protectorate of Southern Nigeria under a High Commissioner.[19] The educational interest shown by the Administration thereafter can be seen as the result of an enthusiastic response to the need of providing an effective British control over the new political creation. The High Commissioner of the Protectorate, Sir Ralph Moor, responded to this educational need more positively than any other administrator in Nigeria at that time. In a memorandum sent to the Secretary of State in 1901, he highlighted the importance of education in the administration of the territories:

> I would submit that the provision of adequate educational opportunities for the Natives is one of the primary duties devolving on local administrations consequent on the powers assumed by Her Majesty's Government in Nigeria and one that required and is deserving of immediate attention. As a matter of policy it is a duty that should be at once coped with for permanent peace cannot be established in the territories until enlightenment and education are introduced....[20]

In 1899, Moor proposed an amalgamated education department for Lagos, the Niger Coast and Northern Nigeria.[21] In the following year, he got Sir William MacGregor, the new Governor of Lagos, to agree to a joint scheme of education for the whole of Nigeria. The scheme envisaged the formation of one Education Board for the three provinces with Lagos as headquarter. A competent Inspecting staff would ensure that control was effective. In or near Lagos, an educational establishment was to be started for secondary and higher education under the direct control of the Education Board. A High School for the training of teachers was envisaged as a supplement to secondary education. Furthermore, it was anticipated that the Mission schools throughout the territories would undertake all primary education and that the Government would establish primary schools in suitable centers only when the Missions had failed.[22]

---

[19] For more details on the decline and fall of the Niger Company, see J. E. Flint, *Sir George Goldie and the Making of Nigeria* (London: Oxford Univ. Press, 1960), pp. 295-312.

[20] Quoted in A. E. Afigbo, "The Background to the Southern Nigerian Education Code of 1903," p. 200.

[21] See PRO:C.O.444/1, "Moor to Colonial Office," 10 May, 1899.

[22] See PRO:C.O.520/1, No. 59, "Moor to Colonial Office," 28 February, 1900.

This scheme of education resembled Governor MacCallum's 1898 memorandum on education in two respects, namely, the call on the Government to take charge of secondary education, and the implicit recognition of missionary excellence in primary education. However, the first joint scheme of education for the whole of Nigeria turned out to be nothing other than a short lived triumph of Moor's political dreams. By 1901, Moor had failed not only to elicit Lugard's support, but also to uphold the concerted effort with MacGregor, as can be seen from the following report:

> [The] question of education was discussed in April last [1901] at Lagos by Sir William MacGregor, Sir Frederick Lugard, and myself with the result that the cooperation of Lagos in the establishment of the Joint High School cannot at present be obtained; and Sir Frederick Lugard is not at present prepared to deal practically with the question of education though most anxious to obtain and give employment to the natives of Nigeria in the Government service of Northern Nigeria.[23]

Three factors were chiefly responsible for the failure of the colonial administrators to work in concert. Firstly, there was the question of rivalry and struggle for power between the leaders of the various political entities - the Royal Niger Company, the Niger Coast Protectorate, and the colony of Lagos. With the elimination of the Royal Niger Company in 1900, Sir Ralph Moor became doggedly enthusiastic about his being made the Governor General of an amalgamated Southern Nigeria. In 1901, he drew up an administrative scheme on a proposed 'Maritime' province without seeking the opinion of Sir MacGregor, the new Governor of Lagos. MacGregor reacted by proposing an impossible union between Lagos and Northern Nigeria,[24] and by withdrawing his former support for a joint scheme of education for the whole of Nigeria.

Secondly, there was a problem arising from the economic disparity between Northern Nigeria and the Southern territories. Since the move towards education was closely allied with economic development, it was not surprising that Northern Nigeria, economically less viable than the

---

[23] PRO:C.O.520/8, No. 157, "Moor to Colonial Office," 12 June, 1901; see also PRO:C.O.520/14, No. 145. Although Sir Lugard was anxious to have educated natives in the service of his Government, that need was never as acute in the North as it was in the South. Given the well organized administrative structures of the Moslem North, his Administration found it more convenient to exercise British control through existing native administrative institutions. In the Pagan South, where traditional authority was more or less decentralized, British control became effective only by direct control, and that meant in practical terms, control by the help of new-breed Africans who had contact with the British through education. See D. B. Abernethy, *The Political Dilemma*, pp. 76-78.

[24] See J. C. Anene, *Southern Nigeria*, p. 278.

South, did not respond effectively to an overall policy of commercial exploitation. Furthermore, the *pax Britannica* was easily achieved in the South, the Aro Chukwu expedition of 1901-1902 being the last major move against resistance to British rule.[25] By contrast, resistance in the North was more formidable and more protracted, growing in intensity between 1903 and 1906. Whereas early attention was paid on economic development in the South, it was considered inexpedient to do the same in the North as long as the territories remained unsettled. It was against this background that the Imperial Government in London described as "premature" Moor's move to include Northern Nigeria in a joint education scheme.[26]

Finally, the idea of Government control of education in a concerted effort failed because of the hesitation of the Imperial government to make rules and laws that were binding on all the Crown possessions in Nigeria. Prior to 1900, the administration of these territories was shared between three more or less independent organs—the Colonial Office, the Foreign Office and the Royal Niger Company. Until absolute command was conferred on the Colonial Office in April 1899, no serious decision could be taken on education, especially in the Protectorate.[27] Thereafter, the Colonial Office still preferred not to be firm on policy in Nigeria. In the words of Miss Margery Perham, "The Colonial Office does not impose or even guide policy," and "decisions upon questions of native administration are left largely to successive Governors."[28] In defence of this strand in British colonial policy, Lord Lugard noted that the emphasis on decentralization was a logical corollary to the effective administration of London's diversified possessions.[29]

Meanwhile, Moor was encouraged to go after his educational designs without Lagos and Northern Nigeria. He saw the prerogative of his Government in the establishment of Government schools. In 1899 he had argued that

> a system of Government schools properly conducted and supervised would be more economical and give better results from a purely educational point of view than the present system of grants to the various missions where the

---

[25] See D. B. Abernethy, *The Political Dilemma*, p. 75f; see also A. E. Afigbo, "The Calabar Mission and The Aro Expedition of 1901-1902," *Journal of Religion in Africa*, 5 (Leiden, 1973), 94-106; A. E. Afigbo, "Patterns of Igbo Resistance to British Conquest," *Tahrik*, 4, No. 3 (1973), 14-23.

[26] PRO:C.O.444/1, Colonial Office Commentary to Moor's Despatch of 10 May, 1899.

[27] See PRO:C.O.520/3, No. 35281, *Annual Report on Southern Nigeria, 1899-1900.*

[28] Quoted in F. D. Lugard, "British Policy in Nigeria," *Africa*, 10 (1937), 398.

[29] See ibid.

methods and systems vary according to the ideas of the various denominations.[30]

The first government school in the Protectorate of Southern Nigeria was founded at Bonny in April 1900 and was called the "Ogugumanga Government School."[31] Another government school was founded at Benin in 1901, and like the Ogugumanga school, it was supported by contributions from the local chiefs and by fees collected from the pupils.[32]

Since there were no mission schools in the Benin City territories, the establishment of a government school there represented the administration's determination to provide elementary education in areas where mission education was lacking. It also represented a tactical procedure chosen by the Government to implement its policy without getting into undue confrontations with the Missions. The Commissioner's intention was also to establish government schools in or around Onitsha, a stronghold of the Missions. But he was careful not to enter into conflict with the Catholics and wise not to duplicate schools unnecessarily:

> I was...influenced in delaying the start of the school in this locality by the representatives of the Roman Catholic Fathers. The Father Superior, Father Lejeune, who had only lately been transferred there, appeared to be an able and energetic manager, and he informed me that his intention was to improve the system of general and industrial education which was being carried on and he hoped that the Government would assist him in carrying this out. I informed him that an Inspector of schools would, I hope, be shortly appointed and that examinations would be held and grants made to various missions in accordance with results.... I am consequently of opinion that there is fair chance of the Roman Catholic Mission schools at all events being rendered effective with some little government assistance and it is therefore wise to postpone the establishment of new schools until there has been a fair trial given to the Missions.[33]

This was the first time attempts were made by the Government to control education in territories outside the coastal city states. To ensure that this control was effectively carried out, an Inspector of schools was appointed in 1901. Meanwhile, the Imperial Board of Education in London demonstrated an awakening interest in education in the colonies by despatching circulars to different colonial administrators, asking them to produce an account of the educational systems in their territories. Moor was not yet in the position to produce one for the Protectorate of

[30] Quoted in A. E. Afigbo, "The Background to the Southern Nigerian Education Code of 1903," p. 213.

[31] See PRO:C.O.521/15, No. 485, "Moor to Colonial Office," 29 November, 1902.

[32] See PRO:C.O.520/7, "Moor to Secretary of State for the Colonies," 6 February, 1901.

[33] PRO:C.O.520/8, "Moor to Colonial Office," 12 June 1901.

Southern Nigeria, because, as he said, his newly appointed Inspector of schools, Mr. Gordon, had not yet visited the schools on the Niger. He went on to say that "any report without particulars of the Church Missionary Society schools and the schools of the Roman Catholic Missions there would be practically valueless."[34]

By October 1902 a scheme of education for Southern Nigeria had been worked out proposing four kinds of schools—Primary school, Intermediate school, Normal or High school, and Technical school.[35] The scheme for primary school took to the already existing mission schools at Asaba and Onitsha. Although Moor rated the Intermediate school next in importance to the High school, yet it was in the former that he clearly depicted his ideas of a secular education firmly in the hands of the Government. Like the Ogugumanga government school at Bonny, all Intermediate schools were, according to his plan, to have some scope for industrial education:

> In conjunction with these Intermediate schools there will be a system of apprenticeship in all the government workshops under the Public Works at Old Calabar and on the Niger, and the Marine Department Engineering branch at Old Calabar and Akassa, and the pupils more fitted for industrial training will be sorted out by the Principals.[36]

The provision in a school for general education of such a wide scope for industrial training made the establishment of separate Technical schools superfluous. Moor realised this in 1902, and although he included Technical school in his scheme of education, he remarked that such a school was not "immediately required but will be necessary in the near future."[37] Had his educational plans come to fruition, Nigeria would have had a most useful system of education. But, unfortunately, Moor left the Niger for good in 1903 before any of his dreams could come true. His successors insisted on a complete separation of industrial education from general education, thus laying the foundation of a serious flaw in Nigerian education, namely, the eagerness to place a premium on book-learning rather than on practical skills.

The scheme for the Normal or High school was the same as the one already operating in the Hope Waddell Training Institute. Apart from being a comprehensive school, the Institute was the only post- primary school in the Protectorate. However, the High Commissioner was dissatisfied with the work it had been able to do so far and saw in the

---

[34] PRO:C.O.520/4, No. 232, "Moor to Colonial Office," 27 May, 1902.
[35] See PRO:C.O.520/15, No. 485, "Moor to Colonial Office," 29 October, 1902.
[36] PRO:C.O.520/15, No. 485, "Moor to Colonial Office," 29 October, 1902.
[37] Ibid.

establishment of a separate government model school as his best choice. In this question of providing a High school for the Protectorate, Moor was not as ready to avoid confrontation with the Missions as he was with regard to primary schools. "If the missions are not prepared to fall in with the views of the Government in establishing efficient schools for higher education," he wrote to the Secretary of State, "there would appear to be no course open but the organization of government schools."[38] His determination to go against the Missions was strengthened by pressure from the natives of Calabar, who were also displeased with the educational results produced hitherto by the Presbyterian Hope Waddell Institute. In a letter dated 18 April, 1902, the Efik National Committee expressed the wish that "there should be founded in this place [Calabar] a government Model school on the principles of, and on the same lines as, those of other Colonies."[39]

However, the only real course open to Moor's Government was the ruling by London that it should rely "on the Hope Waddell Institute for the purpose of continuation education."[40] The Imperial Board of Education laid emphasis on the importance of a training school for teachers, and since Hope Waddell was fulfilling this function, Moor was strongly advised to improve and expand it to the level of his envisaged High school.

The work of expansion began at the Institute in 1902 and Father Lejeune put the figure of government expenditure on the project at 125,000 francs.[41] Although the Government was careful to emphasize the non-denominational character of the newly reconstructed High School, the School Board of Education included only members of Government and officials of the Presbyterian Church, who owned the Hope Waddell Institute. Besides, the entire teaching staff remained the monopoly of the Presbyterians. This and similar arrangements inhibited the progress of cooperation between the Catholics and the government schools. Early in

---

[38] PRO:C.O.520/14, No. 195, "Moor to Colonial Office," 28 April, 1902.

[39] See PRO:C.0.520/14, Petition by the Efik National Committee, attached to No. 195, "Moor to Colonial Office," 28 April, 1902; see also A. E. Afigbo, "The Background to the Southern Nigerian Education Code of 1903," pp. 206-207. As Afigbo rightly pointed out, the chaotic grammar of this petition is a sure evidence of the nature of the education the people had got from the Presbyterians at Calabar. A part of the petition reads as follows: "It is now fifty-six years since the Missionaries established at Calabar and there is no competence proof show by their education. For it is disgraceful to us to see the foreigners coming in and occupied offices and the benefits of our country which should be our positions had we better education from the Missionaries since April 10th 1846 up to even date."

[40] PRO:C.O.520/8, No. 160, "Moor to Rev. J. Buchanan, Secretary to the United Free Church of Scotland," 15 June, 1901.

[41] See CSE:192/B/II, "Lejeune to Superior General," 25 December, 1902.

this century, there were no clear-cut distinctions between government schools and Protestant schools. As C. G. Wise rightly pointed out, the government schools were usually under the direction of Protestant Ministers who were often part of the civil administration.[42] Given the fierce nature of denominational rivalry in the Protectorate, it was no wonder that the Catholics were reluctant to send their pupils to government schools run by Protestants.

Father Lejeune seemed to have been strengthened in his willingness to support government plans with regard to the Hope Waddell Institute by the fact that Sir Ralph Moor, the Chairman of the Institute's Board of Education, was himself a Catholic. But as soon as Moor left the scene in 1903, denominational squabbles were allowed to make non-sense of the neutrality of the government High school. When the overwhelming educational victory of the Catholics in Calabar threatened the very existence of the Presbyterian Mission in that region, the Hope Waddell Institute became a centre from which devastating attacks on Catholic missionary methods and religious tenets originated.[43]

3. The 1903 Education Code and Its Effect On Catholic Schools.

In June 1903, the first education code for the Protectorate of Southern Nigeria was issued by the Acting High Commissioner, Sir Leslie Probyn. The code contained all the features of the education scheme already worked out by Sir Ralph Moor—the grading of schools into Primary, Intermediary, High and· Technical Schools, the creation of a central Board of Education to exert some measure of control over all schools in the Protectorate, and the provision of Rules and Regulations relative to grants-in-aid to schools. A distinction was made between government schools and assisted schools or schools belonging to the Voluntary Agencies, which, by 1903, were made up exclusively of the Christian Missions. The few government schools were placed under the management of local authorities, and the Voluntary Agencies were required to comply with the stipulations of the code in order to have their schools taken into the list of assisted schools.

The policy of making grants-in-aid dependent on the fulfilment of the conditions of education rules and regulations was the only course open to the Government to achieve some measure of central control over

---

[42] See C. G. Wise, *A History of Education in British West Africa* (London: Longman, 1956), p. 31.

[43] See PRO:C.O.520/21, No. 599, "W. Forsbery, Acting High Commissioner, to Colonial Office," 29 December, 1903. More details on the conflict between the Presbyterians and the Catholics in Calabar shall be given later in this chapter.

education. It was a method applied in England and in most of her colonies. More often than not, however, the aids offered by the Government were surrounded with coercive measures designed to induce the Voluntary Agencies to make educational changes. Desirous of financial assistance, the Missions were often willing to comply, however painfully, with official regulations. In the Lagos Colony, for instance, the three most influential missionary bodies engaged in educational work there— the Church Missionary Society, the Wesleyan Methodist Church, and the Roman Catholic Mission—pursued some specific subjects, such as Latin and Greek, at the expense of Geography and History. To demonstrate its disapproval, the Lagos Board of Education passed a resolution in 1905 whereby no grants were to be accorded for passes in Latin and Greek. By contrast, huge rewards were promised for proficiency in practical English.[44] In a similar measure, the Education Code of 1903, which applied to the Protectorate of Southern Nigeria, made ''Plant Life'' and ''Law of Health'' compulsory in all standards in spite of a general awareness that there were no teachers capable of handling these subjects.[45]

In choosing subjects for their schools, the missionaries took the training of their future ministers into consideration. The Government, for its part, was guided by considerations of what would be of immediate practical use to the colony. Indeed, the measures against Latin and Greek cannot be taken as intrinsic apathy of the Lagos Board of Education towards these subjects. In fact, the Education Code of 1908, the first of its kind to apply to the whole of Southern Nigeria, included Latin on the list of compulsory subjects for secondary schools.[46] But this was a luxury which the Lagos Board of Education could ill-afford in 1905. Accordingly, it felt that other matters of public interest should be given priority in the distribution of public funds to private institutions.

However, in spite of the bullying threads in the grants, it was hard not to recognize the utility of government intervention in education. At the expense of considerable sums of public funds, the Government endeavoured to bring into existence a well ordered system of education

---

[44] See PRO:C. O.520/58, No. 105, H. Carr, Inspector of Schools for Lagos Colony, ''Memorandum on Education,'' 29 January, 1908.

[45] See PRO:C. O.520/19, No. 278, ''Probyn, Acting High Commissioner, to Colonial Office,'' 13 June, 1903.

[46] When the Code Finally became law in 1911, Latin and French were introduced in some Catholic primary schools in the East, and according to Father Shanahan, that measure was taken not only to bring Catholic schools in line with other schools, but also with the hope that the new subjects would eventually give birth to a minor Seminary. See CSE: *Bulletin*, 26 (1911-1912), 877; see also CSE: 192/B/VI, ''Shanahan to Superior General,'' Calabar, 18 January, 1910.

in the Protectorate. Mr. C. J. Gordon, the first Inspector of schools in the Protectorate of Southern Nigeria, noted in 1902 that the mission schools lacked uniformity and central control. "Until quite recently," he said, "there was little organization even among the schools maintained by one Mission. In most cases the management of each appears to have been left entirely in the hands of the local representative."[47] The objectivity of this observation can hardly be doubted. In spite of their educational victories since 1900, the Catholics, for instance, did not think of ensuring uniformity in their schools until 1905. In that year, Father MacDermott was appointed Inspector General of all Catholic schools in the Prefecture and on him fell the task of drafting regulations for the various classes and their teachers.[48] As Father Shanahan revealed, the guiding force behind this measure was the eagerness to meet the conditions of the Code for government grants.[49]

Government grants-in-aid of education were therefore fulfilling a dual function. In the first place, they provided the Voluntary Agencies with much needed fund for educational and missionary expansions. Secondly, they induced the Missions to improve the quality of education offered in their schools. The inspection of Catholic schools in Onitsha Town, Aguleri, and Osamari in 1902 brought 5000 francs into the mission coffer, and this aid played a decisive role in Father Lejeune's determination to plunge into the complexities of the educational issue.[50] However, when in 1905 the Catholic schools were examined for the first time according to the stipulations of the 1903 Code, the grant they got amounted to only 1000 francs.[51] Some schools like Aguleri and Onitsha Town which had qualified for aid in 1902, namely, before the code came into existence, were no longer on the assisted list in 1905. This touched off fears in Father Shanahan, the new proprietor of Catholic schools. "All our prestige in this country," he said, "lies in the fact that we are looked upon as great educators. If this prestige is lost, then all is lost."[52]

The Catholic authorities also knew rather too well that greater efforts were needed in order to salvage their threatened educational image and no time was lost in bringing this about. Since the stinging set-back of 1905 was caused primarily by the unsatisfactory nature of the qualifications of teachers, measures were taken to supply the schools at Onitsha

[47] PRO:C.O.520/14, No. 86, "Report on Education," 7 February 1903.

[48] See CSE: 192/B/IV, "Rapport pour la Sainte Enfance," Onitsha, 4 December, 1905.

[49] Ibid.: "Le travail, la discipline, la bonne tenue de nos enfants y gagnéront beaucoup; puis surtout nous espérons avoir une meilleure allocation du Gouvernement."

[50] See CSE: 192/B/II, "Lejeune to Superior General," Onitsha, 25 December, 1902.

[51] See CSE: 191/B/IV, "Shanahan to Superior General," 13 November, 1905.

[52] CSE: 191/B/IV, "Shanahan to Superior General," 13 November, 1905.

Town and Aguleri with capable Irish Fathers in order to bring them back
to the assisted list in 1906.[53] Similar measures were carried out in other
schools of the Prefecture with remarkable results.   In its Annual Report
for the year 1906, the Education Department regarded the progress made
by the mission schools as "the most satisfactory feature of the year's
work."[54] The Onitsha Catholic Mission was given special credit for its
excellence in educational work. The Catholic schools in Onitsha alone
were able to present 630 school children for public examinations, as
opposed to only 200 in 1903. Eleven new schools in the surroundings of
Onitsha were taken into the assisted list. The number of assisted schools
in the Central Province at the beginning of 1906 was eight, comprising
schools in the Asaba and Onitsha districts.[55] With the exception of the
Industrial Mission school belonging to the Church Missionary Society,
all these schools were managed by the two Roman Catholic Missionary
Societies in the Niger district—the Society of African Missions in Asaba,
and the Holy Ghost Congregation at Onitsha.

Mission success in education was generously rewarded by the Government. According to Catholic sources, the amount received in 1906 in
grants-in-aid was £500 or 12,000 francs.[56] The grants for the years 1907
to 1909 were described as "appreciable."[57] These scores were usually
made with considerable pains as a result of the searching and strict rules
of the codes. Initially, the grants were based merely on the number of
attendance in the schools. But Moor's successors considered this measure
as being too lenient, and in addition to official annual examinations, the
practice of surprise inspection was gradually introduced to ensure greater
efficiency in government control of the schools.

---

[53] See CSE: 192/B/IV, "Vogler to Superior General," Onitsha, 3 October, 1905.

[54] PRO:C.O.592/3, Annual Report on the Education Department for the Year 1906.

[55] PRO:C.O.592/3, "Report on the Inspection of Schools in the Central Province,"
1906. It is important to bear in mind that the Missions ran numerous other schools which
did not appear on official government lists, namely, the so-called 'unassisted' schools.
The great majority of these were schools which did not measure up with the standard set
up by the grant codes and which were therefore considered unworthy of government
assistance. A small number of the unassisted schools included schools whose managers
did not apply for admission into the Assisted List for fear of government meddling with
religious matters. There is no telling for sure how many unassisted schools existed in
Southern Nigeria, especially before 1916. Lord Lugard estimated that as many as six-
tenths of the total number of pupils attending schools were in unassisted schools, compared with one-tenth in government schools, three-tenths in mission-assisted schools. Cf.
F. D. Lugard, *Report on the Amalgamation of Northern and Southern Nigeria, and Administration,
1912-1919*, (London: His Majesty's Stationary Office, 1920), p. 59.

[56] Cf. CSE: 192/B/IV, "Shanahan to Superior General," Calabar, 26 November,
1906; see also CSE: *Bulletin*, 24 (1907-1908), 144.

[57] CSE: *Bulletin*, 25 (1909-1910), 368.

Table 2

Grants in Aid in Schools in Southern Nigeria, 1900-1908

Year	Proprietors of Schools	Number of Schools	Average Attendance	Grants to Schools
1900	Catholic	7	445	5,000 fr.
	Protestant	20	615	50,000 fr.
	Government	—	—	— fr.
1907	Catholic	22	1940	8,000 fr.
	Protestant	43	1720	200,000 fr.
	Government	34	2166	190,000 fr.
1908	Catholic	24	2793	9,000 fr.
	Protestant	53	2120	200,000 fr.
	Government	42	3138	231,000 fr.

Source: CSE: 192/B/IV, "Shanahan to Propaganda," Onitsha, 10 October, 1909.

There are indications that some discrimination existed in government grants to mission schools. A look at the figures in Table 2, which were taken from an official government gazette and sent to Propaganda Fide in 1909 by Father Shanahan, shows that some other criterion must have been at play in the distribution of public funds to the mission schools. The figures for 1908 show that the pupils in Catholic schools were more than half of those in all the Protestant and Government schools put together. Yet the Catholic schools received grants in a measure that was not commensurate with this reality. A possible explanation for this discrepancy could be that the Government tended to favour Protestant schools in its distribution of grants. In 1906, for instance, seven Catholic schools in the Central Province received only £ 315.18.0., whereas one Protestant school alone, the Onitsha Industrial Mission School, received £200.0.0.[58] One would be tempted to think that the Government distributed grants to the various missionary bodies on a quota basis, irrespective of the number and quality of their schools. But that would lessen the credibility of government policy of making grants dependent on merit. Furthermore, the very fact that the payment of grants was usually made to the educational agencies rather than to the individual schools did not make for efficiency in the supervision of, and creativity in, the individual schools.[59]

[58] See PRO:C.O.592/3, "Report on the Inspection of Schools in the Central Province," 1906.
[59] Cf. F.C.O.L./LA 1611, "A Study of Education Policy and Practice in British West Africa," A Report to the Secretary of State for the Colonies (TS. 1951), p. 89.

4. The Political And Educational Changes of 1906

In 1906, the Protectorate of Southern Nigeria was absorbed into the Lagos Colony to form one political entity known as the Colony and Protectorate of Southern Nigeria under a Governor, an Executive Council and a nominated Legislative Council. This amalgamated "Colony" of Southern Nigeria was divided into three provinces: a) The Western Province, which included Lagos and its Protectorate. b) The Central Province with headquarters at Warri. c) The Eastern Province with headquarters at Calabar. With this political change, the Lower Niger Mission found itself lying within two administrative units, the Central and the Eastern Provinces.

The creation of an amalgamated Colony of Southern Nigeria in 1906 necessitated a major educational change in the same year. In June, the Education Departments of the Protectorate of Southern Nigeria and Lagos Colony, which had hitherto been carried on separately, were united and Mr. J. A. Douglas, who had been the Director of Education in the Protectorate of Southern Nigeria, was appointed the Director of Education in the amalgamated colony of Southern Nigeria.[60] In spite of this unification, however, two distinct Codes of Education continued to be in operation, the 1887 Education Ordinance in the Western Province, and the 1903 Code in the Central and Eastern Provinces.

The division of the Protectorate of Southern Nigeria into two provincial administrations had far-reaching consequences on Catholic education on Eastern Nigeria. Among other things, it led to a gradual loss of emphasis in Catholic educational efforts in Calabar and to a growing concentration of attention on Onitsha. For some time, the consensus among the leadership of the Holy Ghost Congregation was that Calabar would become the principal center of religious and educational activities in Nigeria.[61] Father Léna had in fact suggested to the Mother House that Calabar be made the Headquarters of the Prefecture, arguing that Onitsha was no longer the suitable centre to contend with the rapid growth of the Mission.[62] As the capital of the Protectorate of Southern Nigeria and the seat of the High Commissioner, Calabar played host to many important meetings on education. It was at Calabar that Father Lejeune took most of his educational decisions, and his quarrel with the Onitsha people intensified his attention on, and presence at, Calabar between 1903 and 1905. On succeeding Lejeune in 1905 as Apostolic Prefect, Shanahan continued this move towards Calabar. His good disposition

---

[60] See PRO:C.O.592/38, *Annual Report on the Education Department for the Year 1906.*
[61] See CSE: *Bulletin*, 24 (1907-1908), 591.
[62] See CSE: 192/B/IV, "Léna to Superior General," 23 August, 1907.

towards Calabar had some bearing on his decision in 1908 to close the Convent at Onitsha in order to reinforce the educational work of the Sisters at Calabar.[63] But, the political changes of 1906 led to serious speculations about the future of Catholic educational influence in Calabar, as can be seen from the following report:

> The colony of Lagos has been united with Southern Nigeria; the center of politics has been transferred from Calabar to the Town of Lagos, which has become the capital. Here, as in Europe, the capital attracts people, and when Lagos gets a government college, many of the sons of chiefs shall elude our influence in order to come under those of teachers who, though capable, are under obligation not to teach religion.[64]

After 1910, the scale of Catholic education tilted permanently to the direction of Onitsha, a development which was aided by the discovery of coal at Enugu and the concentration of government establishments in that region.[65]

5. The Education Code of 1908

Speculations about the effect of the concentration of educational policy-making in Lagos began to take on some real substance in 1908. An Education Ordinance for the whole of the Colony of Southern Nigeria was issued at the beginning of the year and came into operation in April. A code was drawn up but did not become law yet.[66] According to Father Shanahan, these changes were made in Lagos without the consultation of the former Protectorate of Southern Nigeria. "Since the amalgamation with Lagos," he said, "Southern Nigeria has, as it were, disappeared."[67]

Shanahan's indignation over this changed relationship was understandable. In 1906, he was appointed a member of an Education Advisory Council, which was commissioned shortly before the amalgamation with the task of drafting a new code for the Protectorate.[68] For the first time, the proprietor of Catholic schools got the best opportunity of exercising a decisive influence on education in the colony. But this rare opportunity quickly vanished with the creation of a new Board of Education in Lagos after the amalgamation in 1906. Shanahan's

---

[63] Cf. CSE: 192/B/IV, "Shanahan to Superior General," Onitsha, 22 May, 1908; see also CSE: Bulletin, 24 (1907-1908), 591.

[64] CSE: Bulletin, 24 (1907-1908), 159.

[65] See CSE: Bulletin, 26 (1911-1912), 863.

[66] See PRO:C.O.592/5, Annual Report for the Year 1908.

[67] CSE:192/B/V, "Shanahan to Superior General," Calabar, 21 January, 1908.

[68] See CSE: 192/B/IV, "Shanahan to Superior General," Calabar, 21 March, 1906.

demand in 1908 that the former Protectorate be restored to its place of influence was coupled, in the main, with his intention to salvage Catholic interests from the clutches of an Education Board in Lagos which was predominantly Protestant in its constitution.[69]

While conceding that the Code of 1908 contained some "excellent points", Father Shanahan strongly objected to some other points which, according to him, were "carefully concealed" with a view to "killing" Catholic schools.[70] He enumerated these alleged adverse points as follows:

> 1. That all teachers should have teaching certificates.
> 2. That the vernacular should be obligatory in all schools.
> 3. That there should be only one Board of Education for Lagos and Southern Nigeria, that is to say, our Mission in its entirety shall have only one representative for each province (there are only two provinces). This representative may happen to be a Protestant, a member of the C.M.S. 4. That all teachers should go through a Teaching College (all belong to the Protestants at the moment) in order to qualify for a teaching certificate. 5. That all teachers could become Inspectors of Schools if they passed an examination in an institute set apart for this purpose (this institute exists in Lagos and in Sierra Leone). 6. That grants-in-aid should be 9 shillings for each unit of average attendance in Primary schools, 25 for each unit of average attendance in Training Institutes. 7. That the Legislative Council (three-quarters of which are Blacks) should elect the Board of Education, which Board shall judge over everything, leaving no room for appeals.[71]

The points enumerated above were contained in the first draft of the code, the contents of which were most probably generally known by the end of 1907. Writing to the Superior General in May 1907, Father Shanahan said that a code was "being prepared for the Niger (this code has already become law in the Gold Coast), which shall prohibit all men and women from teaching without the possession of teaching certificates."[72] Given the havoc which the suppression of teachers without certificates was doing on Catholic schools in the Gold Coast, it was no surprise that Shanahan spoke of the 1908 Education Code in terms of a concealed plan to "kill" Catholic schools.

The points which arguably had *killing* effects on Catholic schools were those concerning teachers. An implementation of government ruling on teachers would have meant either to close down most of the Catholic

---

[69] See CSE: 192/B/V, "Shanahan to Superior General," Calabar, 21 January, 1908: "Ce code a été fabriqué à Lagos par un petit comité composé en majeure partie des représentant du C.M.S."

[70] Ibid.

[71] CSE: 192/B/V, "Shanahan to Superior General," Calabar, 21 January 1908.

[72] CSE: 192/B/V, "Shanahan to Superior General," Onitsha, 28 May, 1907.

schools, or to go on running them without government grants, a measure which would have led, sooner or later, to a total collapse of the Catholic educational set-up. The question of teachers was, therefore, an existential problem for Catholic schools. It had important bearings on almost all of Shanahan's objections to the first draft of the 1908 Code, including the unfortunate campaign against the vernacular.[73] The only teachers who were qualified to teach were the Fathers and Brothers of the Mission and their number was not enough to meet the challenge posed by the rapid growth of schools. The Catholics had therefore to depend on Africans trained hastily in the elementary schools and who had no officially recognized teacher certificates. Since all the Teacher Training Institutes in the then Nigeria belonged to the Protestants, Father Shanahan determined to oppose the exclusive use of certificated teachers in schools until the Catholics were ready to meet that demand by establishing their own training institutes.

A welcome chance to redress some of the adverse clauses of the code offered itself in the existence of hostility between Southern Nigeria and Lagos. For the first time, the rival factions in the former Protectorate were induced to form a common front in their fight against Lagos. Accordingly, a meeting of the old Board of Education for Southern Nigeria was held in January 1908 at Calabar, and according to Shanahan, the primary aim of the meeting was "to thwart the disastrous effects of the Code."[74] The proprietor of Catholic schools was determined to use his influence in the Board to secure the best possible changes in the code that would favour Catholic schools. "I took it upon myself right from the beginning of the meeting," he said, "to defend vigorously our schools in Southern Nigeria."[75] In a carefully documented speech, Shanahan got all the members of the Board, including the chief representative of the Presbyterian Church, to endorse five of his proposals, which he enumerated as follows:

> 1. There should be one independent Board of Education in each of the three colonial provinces (this is to counterpoise Lagos and the Central Board). 2. Certificated Teachers shall not be required in the schools of Southern Nigeria. Teachers shall be elected by the Provincial Commissioner on the recommendation of school Managers and Provincial Inspectors of schools. 3. The Vernacular shall not be obligatory in schools (this is to counterpoise Black Inspectors of schools and also to put a check on Protestant publications in the native language with which the whole country is swarming). 4.

---

[73] The Catholic approach to the vernacular problem shall be discussed in a later chapter.

[74] CSE: 192/B/V, "Shanahan to Superior General," Calabar, 21 January, 1908.

[75] Ibid.

> The Governor of the Colony and Protectorate of Southern Nigeria shall be
> free to dispense with each of the clauses of the code in favour of certain
> schools (this is to ensure that one could appeal directly to the Governor
> above the heads of all the employees of the Colony). 5. Technical schools
> in Southern Nigeria shall be recognized with a grant of £10 per annum for
> each pupil. Training Institutes... should also be recognized in each pro-
> vince and should enjoy the same financial privileges and assistance as those
> in Lagos, namely, £25 per annum for every student.[76]

A sub-committee was appointed to study the code itself, and after five
days of hard work, its proposals were sent to Lagos for consideration.
Writing to the Superior General in September 1908, Father Shanahan
said that the new code had not yet been published, and added that he was
confident that most of the articles would be in Catholic favour.[77] An
amended code was finally published in August 1909, but it was not introduced until 1911.[78]

To a great extent, the amendment of the 1908 Education Code was a
triumph for Father Shanahan. Three Provincial Boards of Education
were created in 1908 and they approved the new code in 1909.[79]
Shanahan himself and Father Léna, the superior of the Catholic Mission
at Calabar, were appointed members of the Provincial Board of
Education.[80]

With regard to the sensitive question of certificated teachers, several
stings were taken out of the former proposal. The amended code recognized three types of teachers—Pupil Teachers, Assistant Teachers, and
Schoolmasters or Principal Teachers.[81] Of these, only the Schoolmasters
or Principal Teachers were obliged to possess certificates, and even here,
the Director of Education reserved to himself the right to make excep-
tions "in special cases."[82]

Although the code insisted on making the vernacular obligatory in

---

[76] Ibid.

[77] Cf. CSE: 192/B/V, "Shanahan to Superior General," Onitsha, 9 September, 1908.

[78] See PRO:C.O.592/13, *Annual Report on the Education Department of the Colony and Protectorate of Southern Nigeria for 1911.*

[79] See PRO:C.O.592/7, *Annual Report for 1909.* The fact that the new code needed the
approval of the Provincial Boards of Education indicated that absolute authority was no
longer concentrated in Lagos as was initially envisaged. However, by the time an Annual
Report for 1926 was made, the three Provincial Boards of Education had long "ceased
to take any active part in the general development of educational policy" (quoted in S.
Phillipson, *Grants in Aid of Education*, p.15).

[80] See CSE: 192/B/IV, "Shanahan to Propaganda Fide," Onitsha, 26 September,
1908.

[81] See Colony of Southern Nigeria, Education Department, *Code of Regulations for
Primary and Secondary Schools, Government and Assisted* (Lagos: Government Printer, 1909),
pp. 7-9.

[82] Ibid., p. 8.

primary schools, its final ruling on the issue was too loose to be binding. To test the ability of the pupils to read English passages "with intelligence", the code required them to make translations of what they read into the Vernacular.[83] Consequently, the Vernacular in Primary schools, as well as in Infant and Trade Schools, was made a part of Reading. The only place it was offered as an independent subject was in Training Institutions for teachers, schools which absorbed only an insignificant fraction of the school children in the Colony and Protectorate of Southern Nigeria.

In the main, the 1908 Code of Education embodied a firm basis for co-operation between the Government and the Missions. Of remarkable significance was the detailed scheme of government financial help to assisted schools, which included grants to schools, grants to teachers, and maintenance and building grants. In shaping educational policy in the colony, Mr. E. G. Rowden, the Director of Education, showed a readiness to be influenced and guided by the counsels of the Missions. In his Annual Report on the Education Department for the year 1910, he explained the changes in the new code as follows:

> The most important changes introduced under the new code are designed to realize the modern conception of education by enlarging and enriching the ordinary school curriculum of reading, writing, and arithmetic. Provision is accordingly made for colloquial English, drawing, kindergarten, object lessons, nature study, and physical exercises and musical drill. It is also required that some definite form of moral instructions shall be given in every school.[84]

The new code was introduced in 1911 and remained in force in Southern Nigeria until it was superseded in 1916 by Lugard's Education Ordinance.

6. Lugard And The Direction of Educational Policy, 1914-1919

Following the amalgamation of the Southern and Northern Provinces in 1914 to form what is now known as Nigeria, Lugard "sought to lay down principles, alike for Government and for assisted schools, which it was hoped would in course of time produce better results."[85] He accordingly drafted a new code early in 1914, which became law in December 1916. The Lugard Education Ordinance and Regulations laid emphasis on "the function of a school in forming character, in inculcating habits of

---

[83] Ibid., pp. 4 & 18.
[84] PRO:C.O.592/9, *Annual Report for the Year 1910.*
[85] F. D. Lugard, *The Amalgamation of Northern and Southern Nigeria*, p. 62.

discipline, self-control, and good manners.''[86] To facilitate the realization of these objectives, Moral education was recognized in mission schools as a regular course of instruction.

Like his predecessors, Lugard eagerly sought co-operation between Government and Mission in matters educational. By including selected representatives of the missions in the Boards of Education, he hoped, as he said, to solve the problem of education in Africa ''with the good will and assistance of those who have daily experience of the practical work of education.''[87]

As is evident in this chapter, the Catholic Mission in Eastern Nigeria played a major role in this hearty co-operation between the Government and the Voluntary Agencies. A Catholic chronicler rightly attributed the good standing of the Catholic educators in the eyes of the Government exclusively to merit rather than to a special favour.[88] The Catholic schools in Eastern Nigeria excelled in various educational performances which could not escape the notice of the Government.

In the main, co-operation between the Government and the Missions was, to a large extent, a marriage of convenience. Desirous of a healthy economy in the colony, the Government endeavoured to ensure the existence of good and efficient schools. The Missions, for their part, needed the schools in the fulfilment of their evangelical ideals.[89] This community of interest remained the most important factor in deciding the scope of co-operation the parties were prepared to offer each other. Friction almost always resulted whenever a party felt that its interests were at stake, and this happened particularly in the case of educational rivalry not only between the Missions and the Government, but also between the various Christian denominations.

II. *Conflict and Rivalry Between the Educating Bodies*

1. *Catholic Objections to Government Schools*

Many years after he had left the political scene in Nigeria, Lord Lugard spoke of Mission education as having done nothing ''to inculcate civic

---

[86] PRO:C.O.657/5, Sessional Papers, No. 8 of 1916, Annual Report on the Education Department, 1916.

[87] F. D. Lugard, *The Amalgamation of Northern and Southern Nigeria*, p. 62.

[88] See CSE: *Bulletin*, 25 (1909–1910), 368 : ''Auprés des Anglais les missionnaires Catholiques jouissent d'une réputation de travailleurs acharnés et d'hommes pratiques.''

[89] See CSE: 192/B/V, ''Shanahan to Superior General,'' Onitsha, 28 May, 1907: ''L'école c'est la base de tout... et sans les écoles je ne sais où la Mission serait aujourd'hui. Je me suis permis de parler peut-être trop longuement sur cette question. Mais l'avenir de la Mission dépend de la solution qu'on lui donnera.''

duties, or to develop native societies into units of local government."[90]
He felt, like most Colonial Administrators, that the best way to achieve
these objectives was by establishing government non-denominational
schools—schools that were managed by District Officers in collaboration
with Native Authorities.[91]

The Catholic Mission in Eastern Nigeria did not receive such designs
without misgivings. When the Administration announced its intention to
open a school at Onitsha in January 1906, Father Vogler spoke of an
unfortunate introduction of competition into the educational field.[92]

If the Government had hitherto avoided establishing its schools in mission strongholds, it demonstrated a shift in its policy after 1905.
Thereafter, it was no longer unusual to see government model schools in
mission-dominated centres. According to Catholic sources, there were as
many as twenty-five government schools in Southern Nigeria in 1906.[93]
By 1919, the number of government schools in the South had risen to
forty-three.[94] Though modest by modern standard, this school offensive
by a hitherto inactive Administration gave rise to some serious speculations. Was this merely local competition or the result of an external influence from the British Government?

The Catholic authorities tended to see the new development in the
light of the second option. They suspected that there could be behind this
measure an imperial move to secularize education in the British colonies.
This lurking suspicion grew in intensity between 1907 and 1910 in connection with the controversy over the establishment of Catholic Training
Institutes for teachers.[95] In this period Catholic authorities spoke
repeatedly of "neutral" or "godless" government training schools. In
1907, for instance, Father Shanahan said that the establishment of
government "High Schools" was a development which would force
Catholic primary school leavers into "the godless schools of the Government."[96] Father Lichtenberger wrote in a similar vein in 1910 when he
warned that sending Catholic boys to the "atheistic school of Bonny"
would lead to the loss of their faith.[97]

---

[90] "British Policy in Nigeria," in *Africa*, 10 (1937), 389f.
[91] Ibid., p. 389f
[92] See CSE: 192/B/IV. "Vogler to LeRoy," Onitsha, 3 October, 1905.
[93] CSE: 192/B/IV. "Shanahan to LeRoy," Calabar, 26 November, 1906; also CSE: *Bulletin*, 24 (1907-1908), 144.
[94] See T. J. Jones, *Education in Africa: A Study of West, South, and Equatorial Africa by the African Education Commission* (New York: Phelps-stokes fund, 1924), p. 156.
[95] This shall be treated in the next chapter.
[96] CSE: 192/B/V, "Shanahan to LeRoy," Onitsha, 28 May, 1907.
[97] CSE: 191/B/V, "Report by X. Lichtenberger," 1 April, 1910.

The language employed in speaking of government schools clearly showed that the Catholics linked the school issue in Nigeria with political controversy in England over education. Eager to fulfil its electoral pledge, the new Liberal Government in Britain attempted, between 1906 and 1908, to pass a number of education Bills which sought to establish a uniform system of education under popular control, and to confine religious education outside the school.[98] Although the measures were intended to break the monopoly of denominational control of education by the Anglican Church, Shanahan and his confrères feared the repercussions such Bills would have had on all Mission schools—Catholic and Protestant—in the colonies, where the Imperial Government would not have hesitated to extend them. In a letter to the Superior General, the Prefect in fact suggested that the Administration, by introducing a secular education in Nigeria, was merely acting on orders from London:

> The Government has made itself the apostle of godless schools. It wants, just itself alone, to have absolute control over the body and the soul of both the old and the young. The officials here are very kind to us; they do not oppose us in anything..., they are merely executing the orders which emanate from above, the very orders which dictate the current politics of the Government on education in England.[99]

The Prefect of the Lower Niger Mission wrote in these early years with the consciousness of a leader of a French congregation in an English colony. The French—the innovators of the missionary movement in recent times—came to Africa in the eighteenth and nineteenth centuries with sad memories of the secularization in their home country, especially with regard to the *école laique*, or what the Church in France regarded as "godless schools." Given this painful stigma on their national history, it was not surprising that the French congregations became nervous at the thought of grappling with the French experience also in English colonies. Hitherto, they had admired and praised the Liberality of the British in matters of religion, a fact which becomes evident in an article written by Father Lejeune in 1902:

> In some Missions, you find a government that would frustrate you by controlling your activities and almost every step that you take. By contrast, the Government on the Niger leaves you undisturbed and free, except for the customs, which are becoming heavier each day. [Here] you can baptize, preach, and join people in marriage; the Government follows everything with keen interest, knowing that you are rendering it assistance through

---

[98] See M. Cruickshank, *Church and State in English Education: 1870 to the Present Day* (London: Macmillan, 1963), pp. 90-112.

[99] CSE: 192/B/V, "Shanahan to LeRoy," Onitsha, 28 May, 1907; see also CSE: 192/B/IV, "Shanahan to President of Propaganda Society in Paris," 11 July, 1907.

these great acts of civilization, which minimize its own spending. It gives you encouragements... verbally at least: "Very well," "very glad", "all right."[100]

A shadow of doubt was cast on this liberality of the British when the anti-religious politics of the Liberals corresponded with the establishment of government "neutral" schools in Southern Nigeria. In relating this doubt to their superiors, the Fathers did not hesitate to use terms and expressions that were familiar in France in connection with the *école laique*.

But one cannot, in fairness to the Administration, take the state model schools to be "godless." If the Government established neutral or non-denominational schools, then it was, in part, an attempt to circumvent the often-acrimonious divisions between the various Christian Missions in Nigeria. To a large extent, in fact, Catholic opposition to the government model schools was as a result of Protestant influence in them. As has been seen earlier, the government schools were closely associated with the Church Missionary Society and its ministers, and more often than not, the Catholic Fathers mixed their description of these schools as "godless" with charges of a strong Protestant bias in them. In fact, Shanahan's real quarrel with the government school at Bonny was not its godlessness, but its strong Protestant ethos:

> Bonny has a government school where all the teachers are Protestants and where the Principal is a Protestant Minister, the Reverend MaCauley! Never have we sent a child there; never shall we send any of our children there![101]

However, since the school was for the Protestants also a medium for proselytization, Catholic objections to government schools—which were to a large extent Protestant—received ample justification, no matter how strange this attitude may appear today.

Nevertheless, some other reasons behind Catholic disapproval of state schools were, though understandable, pragmatic. The most notable of these was the fear that the Government, by establishing numerous schools, would escalate the grim struggle over education in such a way that Catholic educators would not be able to remain in contention. Between 1906 and 1910, they repeatedly spoke of a "gloomy point" in

---

[100] CSE: 191/B/II, Lejeune, "Rapport pour *Les Missions Catholiques*," Onitsha, 1902.

[101] CSE: 191/B/VI, J. Shanahan, "Training School for Southern Nigeria," Onitsha, 6 May, 1910. Father Vogler spoke in a similar vein concerning the Bonny school: "Bonny is a place where there is no Catholic Mission. To send our young fellows to a school where everything is Protestant, even though it is supposed to be neutral, would certainly mean exposing [them] to the danger of losing their faith" (CSE:191/B/V, Vogler, "Question des Frères et des Ecoles").

the future of the Mission. The demand made on the tiny teaching staff
was so great that in spite of their educational success so far, the Fathers
often wondered if they would ever be a match to this new genre of
evangelization.[102] For the Prefect in particular, the escalation of the
educational struggle was not an infinite blessing. "The Government has
already established twenty-five schools...," he wrote in 1906. "This is
real madness. From every corner, one hears nothing more other than
talks of schools, schools!"[103]

Unfortunately for the Fathers, this unprecedented quest for education
in Nigeria was going on at a time when Paris was taking measures to
guard against what it considered to be an untoward involvement in
education by its Congregation in Southern Nigeria. In separate
enquiries, the Mother House demanded in 1910 that the Fathers give a
detailed and honest justification of the school as an indispensable factor
in the missionary work of Southern Nigeria. The Catholic Missionaries
had therefore not only to cope with the extraordinary challenge posed by
the Government and the Protestants, but also to labour very hard to
obtain the approval of their superiors in Europe in order to remain in the
struggle. At one point in his detailed review of the prominent place the
school had assumed in Nigeria, the Prefect made no attempt to hide his
annoyance over the misgivings of his Superior General:

> I do not understand what is meant by 'evangelization in its real sense.'
> Would one say that we are not evangelizing the country in which we find
> ourselves when we have all its children in our hands? The discipline in the
> school, the missionary, who is in steady contact with the pupils, the facility
> that one has to bring them to the sacraments, the Masses that are being said
> all these years, are all these not true evangelization?.... Let me say it once
> again that the school does not preclude any other system of evangeliza-
> tion.... Moral instruction shall go hand in hand with intellectual instruc-
> tion; so it was [in past ages]...and shall not be different with regard to the
> moral and intellectual education of the immense population of Southern
> Nigeria.[104]

Whereas Shanahan endeavoured to link the school apostolate with his
superior's conceptions of a true and healthy Christian evangelism,
Fathers Vogler and Léna emphasized the fact that the political and social
realities in Nigeria did not admit of other alternatives. The former noted
that the Government and the Protestants were opening schools every-

---

[102] See CSE: *Bulletin*, 24 (1907-1908), 159.
[103] CSE: 192/B/IV, "Shanahan to LeRoy," Calabar, 26 November 1906; also
CSE:*Bulletin*, 24 (1907-1908), 10f.
[104] CSE: 191/B/VI, J. Shanahan, "Training School for Southern Nigeria," Onitsha,
6 May, 1910.

where and warned that "if we lag behind, then we shall lose control over the youth and, eventually, the future [of the Mission]."[105] In his own report, Father Léna regarded the campaign against the school as a flawed measure. "Our schools have not been a failure," he said, "why to go [sic] against it?"[106] To be more precise, he enumerated three factors which made it imperative for the Catholics to run schools, namely, government "godless" schools, Protestant challenge, and the eagerness of the natives to have schools. Certainly, these and similar danger signals did not go unheeded in Paris.

The difference between government and missionary objectives in education had an important bearing on Catholic opposition to government schools. From the start, it was clear to everybody that the Administration, by establishing its own schools, was out to demonstrate what it had long been preaching, namely, the use of the school in the provision of the right kind of civil servants. For their part, the Catholic Fathers thought that the school should serve the primary interests of the Mission. A report from Onitsha-Town in 1906 threw some light on this contrariety in missionary and governmental educational designs:

> Our objective would not be to train clerks or employees for commerce or for the Government. Our aim, especially in this big town [Onitsha], which is like a gate to the interior, is to form future catechists and future school masters for the Igbo country…. In accordance with the strict demands of the government education regulations, the pupils are scrupulously drilled in reading, writing, arithmetic, geography, English composition, and some elements of science. However, the emphasis is on religious instructions, catechism, church songs, and the Scriptures.[107]

The chronicler of this humble letter of intent was motivated by a need to assure his superiors that the excellent performances of the Catholic school at Onitsha-Ogboli in 1906 and the attractive reward of £ 97 were not going to bind the Mission to the wishes of the Government. But reading between the lines, one discovers that he had also realised that with state intervention in education, the days of the simple catechism school were numbered.

If the Catholics failed in the early years to be doggedly committed to their declared educational objectives, then it was because of the need to respond to the exigencies of the time. Three main factors were instrumental in coercing them into modifications, namely, pressure from

---

[105] CSE: 191/B/V, Vogler, "Question des Frères et des Ecoles." See also CSE: 191/B/IV, X. Lichtenberger, "A Report," 1 April, 1910. p. 6.

[106] CSE: 191/B/VI, L. Léna, "Report on Schools," Onitsha, 6 May, 1910.

[107] CSE: *Bulletin*, 24 (1907 -1908), 151.

the Government, pressure from the natives, and the struggle for
supremacy between the Christian denominations.

The stipulations of the education regulations made it increasingly
impossible for the Catholics to limit instructions in their schools to the
explicit needs of the Mission. As the above passage reveals, the *modus
agendi* in the Onitsha school was no longer exclusively dictated by
intimate mission designs on religious instructions, but also by the "strict
demands" of the education codes. These searching regulations had in
fact pushed the secular subjects to the centre stage. Anxious to obtain
grants-in-aid from the Government, Missions inevitably sought intense
preoccupation with subjects which had grown out of economic
imperatives. "The Government is generously remunerating all trade
schools," Shanahan wrote in 1907. "We shall require carpenters and
bricklayers here at all costs."[108] Since only the schools which met government requirements were taken into the assisted list, the Voluntary Agencies were therefore forced to improve the quality of education offered in
their schools. In 1914, Father Shanahan lamented bitterly that out of the
102 Catholic schools in Eastern Nigeria, only 17 were actually following
the programme of education set down by the Government. In what was
undoubtedly a conspicuous departure from Catholic educational policy
in 1906, the Prefect regretted that only a few Catholic schools were training their pupils to be employees of the Government "either as school
teachers or as clerks in the commercial firms."[109]

Another factor that led to the "secularization" of Catholic schools was
the pressure from the natives. In Eastern Nigeria, more than in any other
part of West Africa, this pressure accounted for much of the extraordinary involvement of the Missions, and indeed of the Government,
in education. At the beginning of this century, the people of Eastern
Nigeria, especially at Calabar and Onitsha, became increasingly indig-
nant over the practice of using educated African "gentlemen" from
Lagos and Sierra Leone as civil servants in their regions. In protest letters and petitions, they urged the Government to create educational
opportunities which would lead to a just participation of their children in
the economic growth of their country.[110]

Knowing the educational ambitions of the parents and guardians,
therefore, Shanahan was convinced that the pupils would be drawn to
any school which offered the best instructions. When in 1906 he des-

---

[108] CSE: 192/B/IV, "Shanahan to LeRoy," 14 October, 1907.
[109] CSE: 192/B/VII, "Shanahan to LeRoy," Onitsha, 5 June 1914.
[110] See PRO:C.0.520/14, Petition by the Efik National Committee, attached to
No.195, "Moor to Colonial Office," 28 April, 1902.

cribed the foundation of a government "neutral" school at Onitsha as "a real madness," he also clearly emphasized the fact that the black "gentlemen" who directed the new school had come "too close" to his children. His fears were not unfounded: in the same year, some progress-seeking parents and guardians forced their boys to change to the government school.[111]

To forestall this danger from escalating, desperate efforts were made to make Catholic schools more attractive for the natives. The most notable of the steps taken in this regard was, besides the introduction of industrial subjects, the prominence given to the English language in Catholic schools. Throughout the colonial era, English was considered as a symbol of progress—the surest guarantee for all job opportunities in the colony. Since the Protestants gave special attention to the vernacular rather than to English, the Catholics were, as a result of the premium they placed on English, able to attract more children to their schools than their rivals in Eastern Nigeria.[112]

Finally, a change in Catholic education policy was considered inevitable in the face of the often-bitter struggle for supremacy between the Christian Missions. With the establishment of a lawful Government in Southern Nigeria, and the opening of the interior to economic exploitation, the need to secure the best possible positions for their adherents became a common obsession for the various denominations. In 1904, for instance, Father Lejeune called the attention of the Directors of Propaganda Society in Paris to the fact that a position of influence would belong to any Mission which furnished the Government with "political agents, indigenous judges, secretaries to the native councils, medical doctors and so on."[113] This observation was again made in 1910 with greater emphasis by Father Lichtenberger:

> The one thing that is now absolutely important is to get our Christians a place in the Colony, otherwise all the positions shall be taken by the Protestants. One may confidently say that each employee, each clerk in an English territory, where every thing is done by Blacks, has great influence on the future of the country or the locality where he works. If we take our place in this new Colony, we shall be able to carry on the struggle with advantage; if not, the Catholic cause shall lag way behind.[114]

---

[111] See CSE: *Bulletin*, 24 (1907-1908), 146.

[112] Cf. F. K. Ekechi, *Missionary Enterprise in Igboland, 1857-1914* (London: Frank Cass, 1972), pp. 102-104.

[113] CSE: 192/A/IV, "Lejeune to the Directors of Propaganda Fide," Calabar, 20 October,1904. In 1914 Father Shanahan expressed the same views when he wrote that the Catholics "do not want to leave these good positions to the Protestants." CSE: 192/B/VII, "Shanahan to LeRoy," Onitsha, 5 June, 1914.

[114] CSE: 191/B/V, "Report by F. X. Lichtenberger," 1 April, 1910.

This desire to get right in the foreground had serious repercussions for the new Colony. Before too long, the denominational rivalry that ensued acquired almost all the hallmarks of the religious controversy that is going on in present Northern Ireland. In their struggle for religious, economic and political influence, Catholics and Protestants raised propaganda to the level of permanent attacks on almost everything in the opposite camp, and, as a result, the school and the people became segregated along strict religious lines, a divisive mold which nothing has succeeded in breaking, from its inception to the present day.

2. *Denominational Divisions and the Growth of Schools*

A decisive factor in the rapid growth of schools in Eastern Nigeria was the existence of rivalry between the Christian Missions. Since the denominations used the school as a medium for winning adherents, they endeavoured to establish as many of them as possible. As one Catholic chronicler would have it, the conquest of the hearts of the children would be ensured by "the entrance into the care of the Catholic Church of the greatest number of them."[115] The result was the proliferation of schools by both the Catholics and the Protestants to the advantage, no doubt, of the people.

But, the multiplication of schools was done without much value being placed on standard or quality. There were, for instance, 167 Assisted Schools—Catholic and Protestant—in 1917, compared with 1,142 Unassisted Schools in the same year.[116] The stringent education rules were geared to the reduction of the number of the inferior Mission schools. As Father Biéchy observed, the government measures hurt the Catholics as equally as it hurt the Protestants:

> The Protestants launched into schools right from the start. They established them everywhere and organized them according as it pleased them. In the past, it was relatively easy to do so, the Government having only a small control over the country. It is all different now that the Government has claimed absolute control over all the schools in the country. The Protestants, and we ourselves, have been surprised and, in some ways, inhibited by these new regulations.[117]

Government regulations on education began to have greater effects on Voluntary Agency schools in later years. In the 1950s, for instance, the

---

[115] CSE: *Bulletin*, 24 (1907-1908), 151.

[116] See S. Phillipson, *Grants in Aid of Education*, p. 16. The numerical strength of the Unassisted Schools is clearly evident in Table 3.

[117] CSE: 191/B/IX, Biéchy, "Protestantisme, obstacle à l'expansion du Catholicisme au Niger," Anua, 1930.

number of schools failed to grow in a measure that was commensurate with the increase in the number of pupils. In Calabar, the number of school children increased from 44,028 in 1957 to 87,345 in 1959. In the same years, the number of schools decreased from 470 to 293.[118]

Beyond their immediate aim of using the school as a means of evangelization, the Catholic missionaries, who had been formed under the influence of anti-modernism, had a larger purpose of preserving the young mission lands from doctrinal and intellectual errors. Basing their teaching mission on the tradition of the Church, they often did not hold the concept of the equality of religions in any great esteem. It was in this regard that Father J. Jordan, the long-time Education Adviser to the Catholic Missions, wrote in 1947 that "the Catholic tradition is the only full Christian educational tradition."[119] The occasion was a controversy within the Catholic School Board of Governors over the use of the word 'Christian' in paragraph 2 of its constitution. Mindful of the possibility of a misinterpretation, some members of the Board had demanded that the word *Christian* be substituted with *Catholic*. Father Jordan, the President of the Board, did not see a need for such a terminological precision because of his conviction that the Catholics were the only religious group that had a valid claim to the Christian tradition. Father Flanagan, the chief contender for a substitution, had a more cautious approach to the problem. Without firmly disagreeing with the views of the Education Adviser, he nevertheless had some misgivings about the universal acceptance of the Catholic position. "Few Protestants (if any)," he argued, "would admit that the 'Catholic Tradition' is the only 'full Christian Education Tradition.'"[120]

However, the consensus in the opinions of most of the Fathers was that the salvation of the people was best guaranteed only in Catholic schools. Accordingly, they looked on the multiplication of Protestant and government schools with genuine trepidation:

> The administration, for its part, is establishing government neutral or godless schools.... For their part, the Presbyterians, the Church Missionary Society, the Methodists, the Wesleyans, the Native Pastorate, the Anabaptists, etc. have resolutely rushed to the establishment of numerous schools. Everybody knows that once the childhood is won, then all is won. It is in the school that the mind and the spirit of the child are formed; it is there that he acquires the habits that will guide him all his life. We want to save

[118] See C. M. Cooke, "Church, State and Education: The Eastern Nigeria Experience, 1950-1967," *Christianity in Independent Africa*, ed. E. Fasholé-Luke, et al. (London: Rex Collins, 1978), p. 194.

[119] Onitsha Diocesan Archives (ODA), "J. Jordan to M. Flanagan, Principal of Christ the King College (C. K. C.)," Onitsha, 20 June, 1947.

[120] ODA: "Flanagan to Jordan," Onitsha, 26 June, 1947.

the souls of our thousands of children; behold the reason why we, more than all our rivals, ought to direct all our efforts towards the school, and we are doing just that.[121]

Given the existence of similar view-points and aspirations in the Protestant camp,[122] it was no wonder that the battle over education on the Niger was particulary fierce, and that an unwritten law—never leave the opponent alone in any locality—was meticulously kept.

By 1899, the Protestants had three schools in Onitsha town, and the Catholics, who had settled in the outskirts of the town, proposed in the same year to found a Catholic school on the mainland. As has been seen, that plan was executed in 1901 by Father Lejeune, who became Prefect of the Mission in 1900. According to him, the new school was necessary not as a means of evangelization, but as a check on Protestant influence in Onitsha main township.[123] Given the relatively small number of Christians at Onitsha in 1899, the Catholics would certainly not have bothered about having a second school at Onitsha had the Protestants not been there.

However, the venture was a great success. Before 1904, Ogboli, as this part of Onitsha was called, was run practically as an outstation. In 1904, Father Patrick MacDermott took permanent residence there, and the coming in 1906 of Brother David, the veteran school-master of the Onitsha people, placed Onitsha-Obgoli on the way to being the most famous centre of Catholic education in Eastern Nigeria.[124]

As one would expect, the stepping up of educational efforts in Onitsha by the Catholics was received with indignation by the Anglicans, the pioneer missionary workers in the town. In retaliation, they deliberately located one of their schools on the Wharf, the Catholic stronghold at Onitsha, thanks to the help of the Royal Niger Company:

[Archdeacon] Denis...requested for a piece of land at Onitsha-Wharf for the purpose of establishing a Protestant school. The Company granted his request, and today an Anglican school is attracting all the children around

---

[121] CSE: *Bulletin*, 24 (1907-1908), 144.

[122] In 1930, Father Biéchy quoted the Protestants as saying: "We have the alternative of either following the programme and proposition of the Government, or leaving our entire system of education to break down, thereby losing contact with the youth of the country" CSE: 191/B/IX, P. Biéchy, "Protestantisme, obstacle à l'expansion du Catholicisme au Niger," Anua, 1930.

[123] See CSE: *Bulletin*, 21 (1901-1902), 518; also CSE: 192/B/II, "Lejeune to LeRoy," Onitsha, 19 February,1902.

[124] By 1910, there were 1,200 school children at Ogboli and its dependent outstations, compared with only 573 at the Wharf, and 1,200 in the whole of the Calabar district. See CSE:192/B/VI, "Shanahan to LeRoy," Onitsha, 16 June, 1910.

us. But we are not scared at all; we are only waiting for a fresh reinforcement of Brothers to redouble our efforts.[125]

The active support given to the C.M.S. by the Royal Niger Company
proved counter-productive on the long run. Because of its harsh extortions and punitive reprisals in the territory under its control, the Company was loathed everywhere by the natives. Though the Africans were
able to differentiate between White missionaries and White Company
officials, they were prone to extend their anger to all Whites who allied
themselves with the Company. The Anglicans, for their part, were
prepared to risk hostility with the people rather than lose the good relationship they had with a constituted authority.[126]

As a result of an internal crisis, caused chiefly by a scathing attitude
of the Europeans towards the African leadership of the Mission, the
Church Missionary Society in Nigeria was plagued in the 1890s with
apostasy. Although this did not necessarily lead to mass conversions to
Catholicism, it did lead at Onitsha to a considerable desertion of school
children from Protestant schools. So bleak was the future of the CMS in
1903 that the Anglicans temporarily withdrew from Onitsha, after
having demolished one of their schools for girls.[127] For some time, they
confined their educational efforts to the famous Onitsha Industrial Mission School.

Denominational rivalry and divisions took a radical turn for the worse
at Calabar, the stronghold of the Presbyterian Church of Scotland since
1846. The physical presence there of the Catholics in 1903 and their
ambitious educational programmes were for the Presbyterians extremely
unacceptable developments. Having failed to secure a legal ejection of
the "intruders",[128] the Church of Scotland missionaries gave vent to
their anger in fierce attacks on the Catholics in the media, especially in
the *Calabar Observer*, the Mission's chief propaganda organ. If one of such

[125] CSE: *Bulletin*, 18 (1896-1897), 415f.

[126] According to A. Porter, the Anglican Church was, as an arm of State, compelled
to support government imperialistic policies. He described its conformity to the secular
ideology of expansion as "a congruence arising from its lack of any real source of
authority, from the facts of establishment, and an education common to lay and
ecclesiastical leaders alike." A. Porter, "Late Nineteenth-Century Anglican Missionary
Expansion," *Religious Motivation: Biographical and Sociological Problems for the Church
Historian*. Studies in Church History, vol. 15, ed. D. Baker (Oxford: Blackwell, 1978),
p. 350.

[127] See CSE: *Bulletin*, 22 (1903-1904), 790.

[128] See CSE: 192/B/IV, "Father Vogler to Superior General," Onitsha, 3 October,
1905: "On veut nous enlever l'école d'Old Town et P. Léna ne veut absolument pas
céder. Il a écrit au chef de la mission Presbytérienne qu'il continuera à faire l'école "till
legally ejected.""

press attacks is dwelt upon here, it is to demonstrate how far denominational squabbles were allowed to go in the African missions during the first half of this century.

A *reflection* on the Catholic Mission was published in the *Efik* supplement of the *Calabar Observer* on March 2, 1903. The article was so embarrassing that the Colonial Secretary, Mr. Chamberlain, felt a compulsion to intervene in person. He demanded, through the Secretary to the United Free Church of Scotland Mission, that Mr. Luke, the Acting Superintendent of the Hope Waddell Institute and editor of the *Calabar Observer*, express a public apology for his defamatory article.[129] Following this demand, an "explanation" was published in the April issue of the *Calabar Observer* under the title *"Nte Me Roman Katholic Esu Nsu?"* (Do the Roman Catholics Not Tell Lies?) which was in fact more outrageous than what it was supposed to explain. The content of the *explanation* ranged from stereotypes of religious controversies to political conflicts among the nations of Europe. Our interest shall be focused only on the part which is relevant to our subject:

> We have been censored by some for the statement published in the *Observer* that the Roman Catholics tell exceeding lies. All those who have read the history of Germany, Switzerland, Scotland, and England, at the time when the eyes of thousands of people in the fifteenth century were opened by the Spirit of God will be convinced that the Roman Catholics tell exceeding lies....
>
> I wish to ask: why are all the nations which are Roman Catholics humiliated? They fall back [sic]. France fought war with Germany, and the latter which is not a Roman Catholic conquered. Spain too fought with America, and the latter which is not a Roman Catholic conquered. The Spaniards having been aware that the Priests have ruined their country, picked up stones and pelted them with it in the streets at day-time. France also does not wish the Priests to educate its children at school. Why? Because the French Government has found that the Priests tell lies, and also deprave the minds of the children. This statement is true, let anyone who doubts it read newspapers. It will be exceedingly worse with the Efik people when their children enter schools in which Priests teach.[130]

As would be expected, this mixture of denigration and historical fallacy did not impress anybody. On the contrary, it was counter-productive. For in the wake of this controversy, several papers, most of them Protes-

---

[129] See PRO:C.O.520/21, Document attached to No.599, "Fosbery, Acting High Commissioner, to Colonial Office," 29 December, 1903.

[130] PRO:C.O.520/21, Document attached to No.599, "Fosbery, Acting High Commissioner, to Colonial Office," 29 December,1903. The grammatical errors in this passage are not necessarily those of the author, since what is here cited is a translation of the original Efik "procured" by the Commissioner.

tant, came out boldly in defence of the Catholics.[131] Since these papers enjoyed wide publicity in Africa and Europe, the Presbyterians merely succeeded, to their chagrin, in directing the attention of the whole world on Catholic endeavours in Eastern Nigeria. For the Catholics, the outcome was most encouraging. In defiance to the appeals of the United Free Church, many chiefs and well-to-do of Calabar withdrew their children from Presbyterian schools and placed them under the care of priests. However, as Father Lejeune rightly observed, the pupils and their parents were motivated not by any religious conviction, but by a quest for better education.[132]

The nature of traditional government in Eastern Nigeria provided a fertile ground for denominational divisions in the region. Instead of being governed by a single symbol of authority, Igboland, for instance, was filled with a conglomeration of independent chiefs whose spheres of influence hardly extended beyond their respective clans and villages.[133] This unusual phenomenon was a thorn in the flesh of the Administration and a welcome tool in the hands of the Missions in their struggle for influence in the hinterland. Accordingly, being in alliance with a local chief was an important consideration in any decision to found a catechist post—usually a bush school—in any given locality. When Father Bubendorf installed one Mr. James as catechist-teacher at Igbariam in August 1904, the chiefs of the vicinity gathered at Igbariam to deliberate upon the best means of procuring pupils for the school. The success of the educational venture and the desired influence of the Catholics in the village thus rested on the. cooperation of the local chiefs, a fact which becomes more evident in Bubendorf's report:

> [The chiefs] told me that I have only to give the orders and the town would belong to me, that they would do anything which I would demand; but...I preferred that they decide themselves what measures are to be taken.[134]

More often than not, local chiefs resorted to coercive measures in their efforts to obtain school children for the Mission schools. A much publicized instance was a resolution passed at Nsugbe in 1901 by nine

---

[131] Some of these papers included: *The West African Mail*, *The Lagos Standard*, *The Sierra Leone Weekly News*, and *The Month*.

[132] See CSE: *Bulletin*, 22 (1903–1904), 783-785; 797-799. The struggle discussed here was made over primary education. For some time, the Presbyterians maintained an unchallenged superiority in post-primary education.

[133] For more details on the political and administrative machinery in Igboland, see S. N. Nwabara, *Iboland: A Century of Contact with Britain, 1869-1960* (London: Hodder & Stoughton, 1977).

[134] "Bubendorf to Father Lejeune," 5 August 1904, quoted in CSE: *Bulletin*, 22 (1903-1904), 793.

chiefs of the village requiring parents to choose between sending their children to school or paying heavy fines.[135] The optimism instilled into the missionaries by such facile measures rested on a misconception of the true scope of the authority of the chiefs of Eastern Nigeria. As A. F. Ryder rightly pointed out, the pioneer missionaries started their work in Africa with the belief that the conversion of a ruler would lead to a piecemeal victory over the souls of his subjects. They generally overlooked the "variations in the nature of African 'kingship' and the numerous checks and balances to which it was subjected."[136]

Although the patronage of the chiefs played an indispensable role in the work of evangelization, the Fathers in Eastern Nigeria learnt, after many cases of disappointed hopes, to accept the conceited, and often pretentious, claims and promises of some of the local chiefs with caution. Having promised the Fathers some 120 children in 1907, the chiefs of Ozubulu were able to procure only 60, a matter that the disappointed missionaries quickly described as a "deception."[137] Hard though it was, this judgment nevertheless contained some elements of truth. Eager to have the Catholics establish a school in their area, some chiefs often deliberately attempted impracticable measures, such as the resolution at Nsugbe in 1901. They readily made ostensible promises that were not within the bounds of their authority. For their part, the missionaries failed to see the chiefs as representatives or speakers of a highly democratic society that had not, in the first decade of this century, been fully convinced of the utility of educating its children outside the home or the farm. Here was no culpable indulgence in a known error; it was a mistake whose correction was only possible through experience. When in 1906 the Fathers at Onitsha began to grasp the complexity of traditional government in the Eastern Nigerian society, they spoke of chief Samuel Okosi, the Obi of Onitsha, in a correspondingly new out-look. They appreciated his services to the Mission by emphasizing the fact that he was aiding the Mission "as much as his very limited authority allowed."[138]

Given the squabbles that often existed between the many chiefs of one town or village, it was no wonder that their patronage of schools also helped to exacerbate denominational divisions. Warring factions usually preferred different denominations in the same village to having just one. Sometimes it was inter-village jealousy that stimulated interest in several

---

[135] See CSE: *Bulletin*, 21 (1901-1902), 522.
[136] A. F. C. Ryder, "Portuguese Missions in Western Africa," in *Tahrik*, 3, No. 1 (1969), 2.
[137] CSE: *Bulletin*, 25 (1909-1910), 371.
[138] CSE: *Bulletin*, 24 (1907-1908), 153.

denominational schools—the highest symbol of progress—in a locality where one school would have been sufficient.

Both Protestant and Catholic records show that the hostilities that inevitably resulted from such physical contacts were either encouraged or resolved by the local chiefs. According to Protestant sources, local chiefs in Owerri district used personal violence to force Roman Catholic teachers out of their midst.[139] Similar cases were reported in the Onitsha district by the Catholics:

> The Protestant chiefs have placed all sorts of obstacles on our way, intimidating by threat those who invited us, and having the audacity to come as far as our grounds and removing the demarcations of the new grants of land made to us. However, the Government has condemned the most powerful of them all, the king of Oguidi [Ogidi], in the [legal] action he brought against our chief of Oumwodji [Umuodji]. This judgment has already borne its fruits: by a curious sudden change of mind, the king of Oguidi no longer wants the agents of the Church Missionary Society who are with him; rather he is building a school for us.[140]

Such incidents as these were rampant in the years of missionary expansion, and they should serve here as an illustration of the dividing effect which denominational rivalry had on local communities.[141] The structure of village life in Eastern Nigeria was based chiefly on the principle of communal effort, and this system of rural government tended to collapse as soon as different Missions established their schools in one village or town. For the colonial administration, this was a source of great concern. Requiring functioning units of local Governments for the execution of his policy of indirect rule, Lord Lugard was made to regard mission education as having a disintegrating influence. It was against this background that his Education Ordinance of 1916 endeavoured to control the course of missionary expansion. Accordingly, the Missions were required to obtain government permission before establishing new stations and new schools in any locality. To guard against squabbles, different denomina-

---

[139] See F. K. Ekechi, *Missionary Enterprise*, p. 224.

[140] CSE: *Bulletin*, 24 (1907-1908), 149. The word "king", as used in this report, should not be understood in an European context. Igboland, as has been said, was governed by numerous chiefs and elders whose authority varied from place to place. The clear distinction made in the report between "chief" and "king" simply means that the chief of Ogidi had more power and influence than the chief of Umuodji.

[141] When the question of the state take-over of schools came up in Eastern Nigeria in the 1950s, the divisions in towns and villages caused by sectarian differences became one of the strongest arguments of the nationalists who opted for a complete exclusion of the Missions from educational activities in the region. See A. E. Afigbo, "The Missions, the State and Education in South-Eastern Nigeria, 1956-71," *Christianity in Independent Africa*, ed. E. Fasholé-Luke, et al. (London: Rex Collins, 1978), p. 185.

tions were discouraged from establishing themselves in the same village.[142]

The good intentions of the Government notwithstanding, the effort to confine the various missionary bodies in definite localities destroyed more things than it solved. Among other things, it encouraged permanent divisions where experiments in peaceful co-existence should have been given a chance. Since the Missions insisted on having their members educated in accordance with their ethos, it meant unnecessary hardships for school children in areas where such education was not available. It was usual for school children to walk long distances to their mission schools rather than go to 'alien' ones next door. Sometimes whole families had to leave their homes for good in order to settle near their mission schools.[143] The flight to denominational schools thus became a religious pledge which was broken in later years only on very stringent conditions, as can be seen from a promulgation in 1924 by Shanahan concerning Catholic pupils attending Protestant schools:

> 1) In places where there are Catholic schools no Catholic is allowed to attend a Protestant school.
> 2) Where there are no Catholic schools a Catholic may attend a secular instruction in a Protestant school, but on no account is he to attend religious instruction or Divine Service at any time. When a Catholic school is set up in the place this privilege ceases.
> 3) A Catholic must not enter on any account a Protestant institution as boarder. To do so would mean excommunication for him on account of the proximate occasion of the danger of perversion, heresy, apostasy etc.[144]

This official regulation reveals not only the degree of inter-denominational hostility, but also the plight of the natives who became victims in such religious controversies and machinations. However, the people were not deterred in their quest for knowledge and religious experience.

From the foregoing, it becomes evident that proselytization was the decisive factor in the proliferation of schools by the Christian Missions. So intense and extensive was the indulgence in the school apostolate that some critics were inclined to rate lowly the degree of true conversion obtainable in such a method of evangelization.[145] However, using as

---

[142] See CSE: 192/B/VIII, "Shanahan to LeRoy," 26 January 1917.

[143] See CSE: *Bulletin*, 26 (1911-1912), 873-874.

[144] CSE: 191/B/III, J. Shanahan, "Promulgation of Directions Relative to the Administration of the Sacraments in the Vicariate of Southern Nigeria and Some Other Matters of General Importance," Circular No. 10, August, 1924.

[145] Some Protestants tended to regard the Roman Catholics, in view of their extraordinary success in Africa, as having "insufficient conditions for Church membership." A. Porter, "Late Nineteenth-Century...," p. 354.

illustrations the sacred returns for 1912 and 1917, which have been reproduced in Table 1 of this work, father Shanahan endeavoured to convince the adversaries of Catholicism and the opponents of the school that the Catholics did not indulge in indiscriminate proselytization:

> The statistics [for 1917] show 21,000 pupils and only 10,829 Catholics; this is a useful verification for those who might suspect the existence of mass or rapid baptisms. We are prudent enough. Every school that is established is not, for that very fact, a new Christendom. Catechism class, which has been recognized by the Education Code [1916] as a principal part of the moral formation of the child, is taught one hour each day, and it is not until after three to four years that examinations are held for admission to the sacrament of baptism.[146]

In making this remark, the Prefect did not deny the indispensability of the school in the making of converts. In fact, he admitted in the same report that the growth of the number of Christians kept pace with the number of school children. For the Christian Missions in general, the school was, in the long term, a useful investment.

If denominational rivalry was more pronounced in the East than in the West, it was chiefly because of the susceptibility of the Easterners to change and new ideas.[147] Their eagerness to follow the appeals of education led to an escalation of the educational struggle between the Missions. As can be seen in Table 3, the Calabar and Owerri provinces had become, by 1928, the main centres of this struggle, with as many as eleven Christian denominations in Owerri alone. The consequences for the people were lasting changes on their socio-cultural structures.

III. *The Impact of Western Education on Native Society*

1. *The Imperatives of Law And Order*

The effects of Christianity and Western education on non-European cultures constitute an incessant theme in modern missionary history, and

---

[146] J. Shanahan, "Aperçu Général, 1912-1917," quoted in CSE: *Bulletin*, 29 (1918-20), 183. During his visit to Nigeria in 1929, Father Joseph Soul noticed that among the 47,000 catechumens of the Emekuku Mission, there were some who had been waiting for their baptism for as many as seven years. According to his report, the Fathers either had no time to conduct the obligatory catechism examinations, or they deliberately kept them waiting for fear of having to deal with a very large number of Christians, a situation he described as "deplorable" (CSE: 554/V, J. Soul, "General Report to the Superior General...," Onitsha, 12 November, 1929, p. 18).

[147] By 1911, the number of attendance in Catholic primary schools in the Western Provinces was far out-numbered by the figures in the Anglican schools. But in the Central and Eastern Provinces, the Catholics had achieved a lead over the Protestant Missions. See PRO:C.O.592/13, *Annual Report on the Education Department for 1911*.

Table 3

Mission Primary Schools in South-Eastern Nigeria, 1928

Province	Denomination	Number of Schools		Enrolment				Attendance			
				Assisted		Unassisted		Assisted		Unassisted	
		Asst.	Unas.	Boys	Girls	Boys	Girls	Boys	Girls	Boys	Girls
Calabar	United Free Church	22	34	4,069	1,656	1,325	412	3,414	1,403	965	251
	Roman Catholic	3	104	671	288	9,902	49	536	262	5,792	41
	Qua Ibo Mission	8	481	1,118	167	18,805	1,436	870	130	8,795	779
	Primitive Methodist	8	130	1,254	140	5,531	269	1,081	122	2,771	168
	Wesleyan Methodist	3	10	425	34	335	12	344	23	298	7
	Niger Delta Pastorate	2	—	246	52	—	—	180	42	—	—
	African Church	2	23	580	194	3,204	335	491	159	2,494	272
Cameroons	Roman Catholic	2	4	342	9	260	50	261	7	195	38
	Basel Mission	—	255	—	—	5,296	549	—	—	3,531	366
	American Baptist	—	18	—	—	240	54	—	—	160	40
Ogoja	United Free Church	2	13	204	16	504	10	157	15	380	7
	Roman Catholic	2	13	204	16	504	10	157	15	380	7
	Roman Catholic	1	22	51	2	729	13	47	3	530	6
	Primitive Methodist	—	1	—	—	14	—	—	—	8	—
	Anglican	—	1	—	—	16	10	—	—	8	8
Onitsha	Anglican	13	206	2,345	524	4,368	1,023	2,194	459	2,771	597
	Roman Catholic	14	136	3,477	325	50	—	—	—	32	—
	African Church	—	1	—	—	50	—	—	—	32	—
	Primitive Methodist	—	18	—	—	622	4	—	—	415	2
Owerri	Niger Delta Pastorate	9	—	1,660	354	—	—	1,508	279	—	—
	United Free Church	7	22	865	59	1,140	156	783	46	962	182
	Primitive Methodist	7	147	1,162	76	3,477	128	989	59	2,042	109
	Roman Catholic	5	145	1,190	5	11,449	49	847	3	6,782	42
	Anglican	4	136	780	184	9,346	1,593	682	140	6,587	1,006
	Seventh Day Adventist	1	—	129	12	—	—	102	7	—	—
	African Church	1	26	146	8	946	47	128	6	667	34
	Niger Delta Native Mission	1	—	125	6	—	—	95	4	—	—
	Niger Delta Baptist	1	—	98	4	—	—	89	3	—	—
	Christ Army Church	1	—	95	6	—	—	88	5	—	—
	Qua Ibo Mission	—	37	—	—	831	14	—	—	402	11

discussions on this have followed several lines. Over the decades, for instance, the idea that Christian missionaries were merely destroyers has been steadily gaining currency among nationalists in former mission lands. In most cases, reflections on the issue have stimulated bitter feelings which tend to depreciate the great merits of the Christian Missions in alien lands. While it would be totally wrong to suppress or ignore the harm done on traditional societies by Western education, it would serve a more useful purpose to judge the missionary in the light of his age, and the restrictive influences on his decisions.

The desire to create a peaceful atmosphere in which to carry out effective missionary work was one of the determining factors in the decision of Christian Missions to go against native customs and usages. In Africa, the existence of such heinous practices as cannibalism, the killing of twins, human sacrifice, and the willful destruction of war prisoners, persuaded the Europeans to regard the natives as dangerous savages, lacking intelligence, and devoid of culture. In order to inject the Christian message in a healthy body, therefore, it became imperative to carry out experiments in blood-letting and blood transfusion: local customs and habits were unsympathetically called out of existence. This practice was so firmly acclaimed that the discovery afterwards that the African did indeed possess a culture was not strong enough to temper the European cliché image of him. As Andrew Porter rightly pointed out, the Missionaries recognized the damage done on traditional society by Western culture, and yet they encouraged it "in order partly that new fields might be opened for effective missionary work, the only answer to the social and moral degradation with which they felt themselves confronted."[148]

This feeling of insecurity, and the need to maintain law and order for economic and administrative purposes, also ruled the actions of the colonial Governments in their dealings with the natives. A common interest of commerce and Christianity, therefore, was seen in the education of the people in the acquisition of higher ideals. Mr. E. J. Hussey, the Director of Education in Nigeria from 1929 to 1936, defined the features and aims of such an education as follows:

> In a country which is under the tutelage of a European Power, the term education can with propriety be applied to all the local activities of the 'tutoring' Power—the general administration and maintenance of law and order, the work of technical departments of government, the day-to-day undertakings of the European planters in countries where there is a European settlement, and last, but by no means least, the self-sacrificing labours of the missionaries, who, quite apart from the instruction provided in their

---

[148] A. Porter, "Late Nineteenth-Century Anglican Expansion," p. 352.

schools, do so much through the examples of their lives and through the force of the religion which they preach to educate the people up to nobler ideals and more civilized standards.[149]

This benign government recognition of the valuable contribution of the Christian Missions to the work of civilization had precedents in the history of education in Nigeria. Having come to the conclusion that Mission education had, by 1900, no economic value, Mr. Henry Carr, the then Inspector of Schools in the Lagos Colony, nevertheless extolled it on the grounds that it created new social conditions by battling with superstition and the old order of things.[150] Of all the Prefects of the Lower Niger Mission, none, perhaps, was so infinitely conscious of the inestimable value of the Missions for the work of civilization as Father Léon Lejeune, Prefect from 1900 to 1905. He went so far as to regard such religious activities as baptism, marriage, and sermons as deeds which minimized government spending on rural development, a service for which the Administration ought to be grateful.[151] When he was invited by Lugard to found a freed slave home in Dekina, he firmly asked the High Commissioner to give the Catholics the encouragement they needed "to devote all [their] energies in helping the Government promote its civilizing influence in Northern Nigeria."[152]

The concourse of Christianity and civilization brought enormous benefits for Catholic efforts in Eastern Nigeria. Given the uncharted nature of the country during the prefectship of Father Lejeune, the alliance between the Mission and the Government was a natural corollary to combating the common danger which faced every European venture into the mysterious and often perilous hinterland. Accordingly, the Prefect embraced the military expeditions of the Government with dogged enthusiasm. Writing to the Superior General about the British Arochukwu Expedition of 1901-1902, he said:

> We are at war, a war which is going to have great consequences. If the Niger Company, during the time it was master here, had been brave enough to undertake it, if it had not retreated from the Arochukwus as it did... things would have been different. This war is necessary ...to abolish slavery, human sacrifice, the killing of twins, the assassination of women

---

[149] E. R. J. Hussey, "Some Aspects of Education in Nigeria," *Some Aspects of Education in Tropical Africa: Three Joseph Payne Lectures for 1935* (London: Oxford Univ. Press, 1936), p. 7.

[150] PRO:C.O.520/3, No. 35281, *Annual Report on Southern Nigeria, 1899-1900.*

[151] CSE: 191/B/II, Lejeune,"Report Prepared for *Les Missions Catholiques*," Onitsha, 1902.

[152] CSE: 192/B/IV, "Lejeune to Lugard," Bassa, 15 January, 1905.

who have the bad luck of bringing into the world three girls in succession, and it is necessary to destroy the long juju of the Aros to which one hundred human victims are offered each day.[153]

Besides their consensus on the need to establish law and order in the hinterland, both the Mission and the Administration had clearly different and, by far, larger objectives in their decision to subdue the Aros in a concerted action. In Father Lejeune's judgment, the invitation to send a Catholic priest as chaplain to the Aro Field Force was a special honour for the Catholic Mission: to be the first to deal a deadly blow to the greatest symbol of paganism in Eastern Nigeria.[154] The need, therefore, to extend Catholicism in the pagan areas to be "opened" was the primary factor in the Prefect's willingness to ally with the Government. Consequently, he was able to forget for a while the fact that for several decades, the Catholic Mission had strongly condemned the military campaigns of the Royal Niger Company against the natives, a position which had earned it hatred and hostility from the Company. But the armed expedition of 1901-1902 against the Aros was something different: it was directed against a formidable obstacle to Christian evangelism in Eastern Nigeria. By actively supporting it, the Prefect hoped that the Catholic Mission would afterwards "assert itself once more on the immense interior."[155] This hope of immediate missionary gains was also expressed by Father Shanahan during subsequent military expeditions in the hinterland of Eastern Nigeria.[156]

For the Administration, it was neither the urge to suppress a pagan hegemony nor a desire to·establish Christianity firmly in Igboland that primarily induced it to carry arms against the Aros. Rather, it was some economic and administrative imperatives. These latter objectives were set down in a despatch to the Foreign and Colonial Offices by Sir Ralph Moor:

---

[153] CSE: 191/B/II, "Lejeune to LeRoy," Onitsha, 24 December 1901. That the "Long Juju" was a scene of abominable crimes, is today incontrovertible; but that as many as 100 human victims were slaughtered there each day is certainly an exaggeration.

[154] See CSE: 192/A/IV, Lejeune, "Comptes-rendus annuels à la Propagation de la Foi," Onitsha, 29 October, 1901. Since Presbyterian chaplains and medical personnels also accompanied the Field Force from Ikoroffiong in the Calabar region, the honour of championing a crusade against paganism in Arochukwu cannot be regarded as a Catholic prerogative. In fact, there are suggestions that the Presbyterian Mission master-minded the decision to subdue the Aros by force, a position which has though been refuted with striking clarity by Professor Afigbo. See A. E. Afigbo, "The Calabar Mission and the Aro Expedition of 1901-1902," *Journal of Religion in Africa*, 5 (Leiden, 1973), 94-106.

[155] CSE: 192/A/IV, Lejeune, "Comptes-rendus...," 1901.

[156] See CSE:192/B/V, "Shanahan to LeRoy," Calabar, 21 January, 1908: "A military expedition has just opened all the territories from Onitsha on the Niger to Afikpo on the Cross River. Afikpo is a big town on the same latitude as Onitsha. It shall be an ideal place for new series of stations which shall have Calabar as their base."

There are... grounds that render it advisable... that this work should be done as early as possible connected with the coming changes in the administration of the territories. The Headquarters of the proposed Colony of Southern Nigeria will undoubtedly require to be established at Onitsha or Asaba on the Niger and it is of utmost importance that telegraphic and road communications should be opened up thence to the Cross River and onto Old Calabar. This will be quite impossible to do until the Aros have been effectively dealt with, and any delay in the matter must be exceedingly dangerous to peace and general welfare of the territories and the revenue of the administration. Until the work is done, it will be impossible to rely on any stability in the trade or to establish accurately the revenue derivable from the territories of Southern Nigeria.[157]

It is noteworthy that these larger objectives of the Government not only served the interests of the Catholic Mission, but also affected the structure of its administration. To ensure a successful pacification of the hinterland and an effective harnessing of its resources, the Government built roads, railways, and nets of telecommunications. With the assurance of security and better means of communication, the Catholic Mission experienced its greatest era of expansion between 1906 and 1914.

Furthermore, the changes in the political administration of Southern Nigeria, which culminated in 1906 in the division of the colony into three provinces, were perforce a potent factor in the divisive mold which overshadowed the administration of the Lower Niger Mission. As has been seen, Onitsha and Calabar, the two main centres of the Catholic Mission by 1906, gradually drew apart as soon as the Prefecture found itself lying within two distinct political administrative units—the Central Province and the Eastern Province. Following the pacification of these territories, Father Shanahan expressed the wish to have the Prefecture divided into two. "The country of the Ibibios has just been opened," he wrote in 1910, "and I think it shall be an excellent thing if we divide the Prefecture, joining the Efiks, the Ibibios and the Okunis to the Calabar Mission."[158] Although this plan did not materialize until 1934, Calabar attained some measure of autonomy after 1910.[159]

The pacification of the hinterland also had an important bearing on the sudden movement of the people towards education after 1906. As the letters and reports of the missionaries between 1906 and 1914 bear witness, the demand for schools was made from "every corner" of Eastern

---

[157] Quoted in A. E. Afigbo," "The Calabar Mission...," p. 104.
[158] CSE: 192/B/VI, "Shanahan to LeRoy," Onitsha, 27 September 1910.
[159] See CSE: 192/B/VI, "Shanahan to LeRoy," Onitsha, 29 April, 1911.

Nigeria.[160] Realizing that education was the only key to progress, no village or town was prepared to lag behind in its pursuit. This trend was not without immense consequences for the work of evangelization, as can be seen from the following report from Onitsha:

> The work which has experienced a most welcome development recently is that of the catechists. We have more than 15 out-stations to visit, where the natives have built schools, chapels, and dwelling houses for the Fathers and catechists. When one recalls that a year ago all the territories of the hinterland, except around Nsube and Aguleri, were closed to us, one appreciates the grounds covered...for the Mission.[161]

In the main, the influence of the Christian Missions on government measures against crimes and social injustice was considerable. Since most of the social evils stood in the way of evangelization, mission leaders were often parties to official decisions to eliminate them. When Sir James Marshall, a Chief Judge of the Royal Niger Company, arrived at Asaba in 1888, he quickly summoned up about 300 chiefs and elders of the Asaba and Onitsha districts to a gathering where he promulgated a law which abolished human sacrifice. Father Lutz, the first Prefect of the Catholic Mission in Eastern Nigeria, was said to have been very instrumental in bringing about this government action.[162] On the thorny problem of polygamy and native marriage customs in particular, the Administration relied on mission leaders for acceptable solutions. Given the Christian uncompromising position on the issue of marriage, a consensus between Mission and State was looked upon as very essential. When, for instance, some District Agents demanded in 1902 that divorce be introduced in the Protectorate of Southern Nigeria, Sir Ralph Moor was wise to seek the opinion of Father Lejeune. The issue was shelved after the Prefect firmly objected to what he regarded as a measure that was ruinous to native marriages in general, and to Christian marriages in particular.[163] By contrast, he welcomed Moor's edict of 1901 which prohibited bigamy, the contracting of marriage with already married persons, and the possession of false marriage documents.[164] Similarly, he supported, and in part initiated, Moor's ten-point proclamation of 1901

---

[160] See for instance J. Krafft, "Aus der Mission von Calabar," in *Echo aus Afrika*, 19 (1907), 131f: "Since the high repute of our school became known in the whole country, the people are coming to us from every corner, requesting that we establish among them. There is hardly any locality that would not wish to have a school directed by us."

[161] CSE: *Bulletin*, 24 (1907-1908), 148.

[162] See CSE: *Bulletin*, 14 (1887-1888), 628.

[163] CSE: 192/B/II, "Lejeune to LeRoy," Onitsha, 21 March 1902.

[164] CSE: *Bulletin*, 22 (1902-1903), 513.

in which the use of poison as a means of prosecution, witch-craft, and the worship of idols were prohibited.[165]

The behavioural traits of traditional society got a transformation through another means that was different from the use of force, namely, peaceful persuasion on the part of the Missionaries. They did this through good examples, charitable works, and, above all, through formal education. The effect of the latter on the temper and mentality of the people can hardly be overemphasized. It was the school, more than any other thing, that led to the elimination of the social evils which had superstition and ignorance as their bases. In a gradual and systematic way, Christian education uncovered the absurdities of some ill-practices in traditional society.

The killing of twins, for instance, was a phenomenon which no amount of official compulsion would have succeeded in eradicating had such an action not been accompanied by a peaceful enlightenment of the people. Many African societies regarded the issue of twins as a disruption in the normal rhythm of nature. To kill the twins was to appease the gods, and, by so doing, to bring nature, in the interest of the whole community, back to harmony. Peaceful measures which sought to prove this strange conception wrong succeeded where the use of force had failed. This was Father Léna's experience at Calabar in 1912. Having picked up and nursed abandoned twins in that year, he noticed that the natives were stupefied when nothing like a general calamity descended on the town. According to his own report, this "extraordinary event" was worth more than a thousand sermons and a thousand Christian teachings.[166]

In general, Christianity and Western education brought peace and harmony to the otherwise turbulent Eastern Nigerian society. The people showed gratitude, and the Missionaries exhilaration, as is evident in the following report:

> [Our] ministry ranges from evangelization to formal education of the people... We are on friendly terms with all the natives; they love and respect us. If any serious dispute exists among them, it is to us that they come for a solution. Most of the barbarous customs have disappeared from the country, thanks to our admonitions, and thanks, occasionally, to our threats.[167]

---

[165] See KM, 31 (1903), 278; see also CSE: *Bulletin*, 22 (1903-1904), 202-203.

[166] L. Léna, "Aus Barbarei ins Gnadenlicht," in *Echo aus den Missionen der Väter vom heiligen Geist*, 14 (1913), 176.

[167] CSE: *Bulletin*, 18 (1896-1897), 420.

2. *The Mission as a Culture Bearer*

As an integral part of its existence in an alien land, a Mission develops a variety of cultural works. The milestones which the Christian Missions have set in Nigeria in such fields as industrial education and the development of the vernacular come to mind here. Even critics of the Mission emphasize this strand in its enterprise, namely, its obligation to promote and encourage studies of science, literature and Art. It is against this background that Martin Schlunk has written that "all educational work in a mission ought to be justified by the fact that it combines a definitely religious aim with a real cultural value."[168] By virtue of its structure and obligations, a Mission in a foreign land becomes a cultural centre where the natives eagerly seek new ideas. Through the Missions, they gain access to the new ways of life bursting upon them.

In Eastern Nigeria, the school served as the most direct link between the cultures. Besides being taught to read and write, the pupils were consciously and unconsciously introduced into the ideas of the Western world. Aware of the changing values in their society—new social order, and new elements in religious persuasion—the natives turned to the school in their quest for new status. An official report in 1912 from the Catholic Mission in Aguleri observed that

> ...the people are realizing that they are at the mercy of the greediness of the interpreters and other [government] employees, and would want to be liberated. They are demanding schools from us from every corner in order to learn the language of the White man and to be in direct contact with him.[169]

Only a small fraction of the population exploited the appeals of Western education from the time of its inception to the First World War. The educational sail received a favourable wind as soon as the merits of the school began to exert a considerable pressure on the socio-economic structures of traditional society. Noticing, for instance, that qualification for elevated social status no longer depended on traditional norms but on membership to the rising new educated class, the highly competitive Easterners quickly adjusted whatever prejudices they initially had towards education.

Meanwhile those who had had an early start had taken full advantage of job opportunities that came from the establishment in the hinterland of government offices, commercial centres, native courts, and Mission stations. If dissension arose between the educated and the uneducated,

---

[168] M. Schlunk, "Mission and Culture," IRM, 12 (1923), 543.
[169] CSE: *Bulletin*, 26 (1911-1912), 866.

it was not only because of the envious position of the former—better income, and a raised social standing—but also because of their discrimination and ill-treatment of the latter.[170] It was no wonder, therefore, that the people looked on the school as a panacea for all their troubles.

Since admission into a school was generally hinged on membership to a Christian Mission, the school consequently became a factor of determinate significance in the work of evangelization. With an eye on the school, most people willingly became Christians, and, as F. K. Ekechi put it, "it became fashionable to be called a Christian."[171] However, the hankering after Western education left some undesirable marks on the people and their society.

3. Catholic Attitudes Towards Native Customs

As would be expected, the physical contact with European culture was not without adverse effect on traditional society. Given the Igbo and Ibibio susceptibility to change and new ideas, the disintegration of the distinctive patterns of native society was particularly grave in Eastern Nigeria. The erosion of local usages and customs which inevitably resulted from a wholesale acceptance of a foreign culture was further expedited by unreflected actions and intolerance on the part of the Mission Fathers.

Urged by an unparalleled missionary zeal, the Catholics, as well as the Protestants, resolutely moved, *ad gloriam Dei*, against a variety of local customs in Eastern Nigeria. If Father Paul Biéchy, a man of deep religious conviction, whose administrative qualities made the Anua Mission a model for all the other Missions in the Prefecture of Southern Nigeria, was particularly uncompromising in his attitude towards traditional plays and usages, it was because of his firm belief that he acted in the interest of the Church. "From the very start," he wrote to Shanahan in 1929, "we had always to fight very hard against certain native plays and customs like *Ekpo*, and 'Fattening'. It is clear now that Christian [sic] cannot join, and generally they keep away from it."[172] The *Ekpo* or *Mmo*, it must be said, is a society of masquerades which appears seasonally or during important village feasts. It is found in varying forms and shades throughout West Africa. "Fattening" is an initiation rite for

---

[170] The exploits of the loathed court messengers, the shabby stooges of the native courts, have found popular expression in folk-tales in all parts of Nigeria.

[171] F. K. Ekechi, "Colonialism and Christianity in West Africa: The Igbo Case, 1900-1905," *Journal of African History*, 12 (1971), 103.

[172] CSE: 191/B/VIII, P. Biéchy to "Bishop Shanahan," Anua, 31 July 1929.

girls and young women. Practiced among the Igbos and Ibibios of
Eastern Nigeria, the educational value of the fattening- room in the
preparation of a young woman for a married life is so apparent that a
Catholic nun has successfully compared it to the institution of Novitiates
for religious women.[173]

Father Paul Biéchy has been mentioned above because of the
unprecedented wave of punitive measures he set in motion between 1926
and 1930—through decrees and regulations—to eradicate native customs
and recreational sports in the Uyo district. However, he should be looked
upon merely as a speaker of Catholic opinion, for his regulations were
officially approved by the Apostolic Vicar himself. In one such regulation, hunting was added to the list of things which the Christians were
not allowed to take part in.[174]

Precedents for such uncompromising attitudes towards native cultures
are not hard to find in the history of the Christian Missions. During the
era of geographical expansion of the Church in modern times, the special
merit of Christianity as a custodian of cultures was put to the test. After
a period of hesitation, a good start was finally made in Asia in the seventeenth century. In its Instruction of 1659 to the Apostolic vicars of China,
the Propaganda Congregation produced a famous guiding principle on
the relationship between Missions and native cultures. Among other
things, it firmly enjoined the missionaries to uphold and respect local
customs and habits which were not opposed to religion and
righteousness.[175]

To a large extent, this rare sanction from Rome was part of the
measures taken in the seventeenth century to give official support to the

---

[173] See J. Nwaokpoh, *Religious Novitiate, A Fattening Room: Some Insights into This Aspect
of the Nigerian Cultural Value in the Novitiate Formation of the African Sister* (Rome, 1979).

[174] CSE: 191/B/VIII, P. Biéchy, "Regulations Newly Approved by Bishop
Shanahan," n. d.

[175] See "Instructio Vicariorum Apostolicorum ad Regna Sinarum, Tonchini et Cocin-
cinae proficiscentium 1659," in *Sacrae Congregationis de Propaganda Fide Memoria Rerum
1622-1972*, Vol. III/2, ed. J. Metzler (Freiburg: Herder, 1976), pp. 702-703: "You
Should not attempt, by any means, to persuade these peoples to change their customs
and habits, provided that these are not clearly opposed to religion and righteousness. For
nothing would be more unreasonable than carrying France, Spain, Italy, or any other
European country to China. This is not your mission; what you should bring to them
is faith, a faith which does not despise or destroy the usages and customs of any land but
wishes to see them intact, provided that they are not bad. Since it belongs to the nature
of man to value and love national identity more than any thing else, nothing causes more
hate and alienation than the abrogation of local customs, especially when they have been
handed down by the ancestors from time immemorial; and worse still if one suppresses
them by substituting one's own habits in their place. Therefore, never compare the
usages of these peoples with European habits; rather you should endeavour diligently to
adapt yourselves to them. Admire and praise whatever merits praise...."

efforts of the Jesuits in China to adapt the Church to local traditions and
habits, efforts which had come under fierce attack from the Franciscans
and Dominicans. Made to believe that the Chinese Rites—local
ceremonies performed in honour of Confucius and the ancestors, and
other concessions made to Chinese Christians—were out of character
with the tradition of the Church, Pope Clement XI took restrictive
measures against them in 1704 and in 1715. Under pressure from conser-
vatives in Europe, Pope Benedict XIV finally put an end to the Chinese
Rites Controversy in 1742 with the Bull, *Ex quo singulari*.[176] Thereafter,
Catholic Missions all over the world were to have the same uniformity
in language, liturgy, and tradition as in Rome and the rest of Europe.[177]
Accordingly, for more than 200 years, the Church resolutely opposed the
very thing that had been the hallmark of Christianity in former days—
the interaction of cultures.

The belief that religion and culture were not necessarily identical had
enabled the first Christian community—a group that was culturally
inferior to the hellenistic and Roman worlds—to adapt itself to the more
advanced cultures around it. Thanks to the distinction made between
Christian faith on the one hand, and the projection of this faith on a
socio-cultural background on the other, it was possible, in the course of
the history of the Church, to give Christian interpretations to Greek philosophy, Roman organization, and pagan rites, symbols, and feasts. The
mediaeval Church continued and perfected this process of inculturation
to the extent that Christianity was brought to an intimate union with
Western civilization and culture. Seen against this background, *Ex quo
Singulari* was as unrealistic as it was destructive.[178]

Although Pope Pius XI saw, in 1926, a need for a second thought on
the Church's stand on alien cultures, it was not until 1951 that Pope Pius
XII, in his encyclical *Evangeli Praecones*, gave an official recognition to the
content and value of non- European cultures. Among other things, the
pontiff spoke of human nature as having something that is naturally

---

[176] For more details on the Chinese Rites Controversy, see G. H. Hunne, *Generation
of Giants: The Story of the Jesuits in China in the Last Decade of the Ming Dynasty* (Notre Dame,
1962), pp. 282-302; A. Huonder, "Die chinesische Ritenstreit," *KM*, 39 (1911), 112-
115, 167-169, 219-224, 268-274; J. Brucker, "Chinois (Rites)," *Dictionnaire de Théologie
Catholique*, II (1905), 2363-2391; B. Biermann, *Die Anfänge der neueren Dominikanermission
in China* (Münster, 1927); O. Maas, *Die Wiedereröffnung der Franziskanermission in China in
der Neuzeit* (Münster, 1926), pp. 81-134.

[177] F. Köster, "Ricci und Nobili: Der Ritenstreit," in *Warum Mission?: Theologische
Motive in der Missionsgeschichte der Neuzeit*. Kirche und Religionen, Vol. 3/1, ed. H. Fries,
F. Küster, F. Wolfinger (St. Ottilien: EOS Verlag, 1984) p. 56.

[178] Cf. F. Küster, Ricci und Nobili," p. 60; see also M. Schlunk, "Mission and
Cultures," pp. 532-544.

Christian (*naturaliter Christiana*),[179] a position held by Tertullian about the year 200.

Meanwhile, the conception of the superiority of European culture had been given full reign in the Mission lands. The reports and letters of the missionaries disclosed it in various forms. There were, for instance, descriptions of "primitive" peoples who lived in total ignorance.[180] There was need, therefore, to bring to them a culture that was worthy of Christianity. Joseph Schmidlin, a renowned Catholic missiologist, went as far as making this "culture mission" an integral part of colonization. Speaking on behalf of the European colonialists, he said:

> [We] shall be truly and inwardly justified to subjugate the native peoples under our dominion only when we bring them a higher ideal for the loss of their freedom, when we impart to them, as compensation, our higher civilization, our moral concepts and our better methods of work.[181]

However, several scholars did not share Schmidlin's view. Their awareness in the nineteenth and early twentieth centuries was strongly in favour of upholding native cultures and adapting them to Christianity. Gustav Warneck, for instance, was loud in his criticism of any distinction made between *Kulturvölkern* and *Naturvölkern*. No race, he said, can be judged to be absolutely devoid of culture. The differences in cultures come about as a result of differences in geographical locations, climatic conditions, and political and economic circumstances.[182] Herder was more precise when he said: "Where nature has divided the nations through language, habit, and disposition, let no one unite them through artefacta and chemical óperations."[183] P. Charles, the advocate of independent local Churches, called for an unconditional accommodation of the diversity of cultures which God himself has made manifest in the world.[184]

Whereas the liberal leanings of the Church in former days stopped at adaptation—a superficial accomodation of a few symbols and gestures— a consensus in the opinion of theologians today speaks of inculturation, or the incorporation of "the Christian faith into a particular culture in

---

[179] See AAS, 43 (1951), pp. 521-525.

[180] Pope Benedict XV spoke of people sitting "in tenebris et in umbra mortis." Cf. "Maximum Illud", AAS, 11 (1919), p. 442.

[181] J. Schmidlin, "Deutsche Kolonialpolitik und katholische Heidenmission," in KM, 2 (1912), 35. This argument also lay at the root not only of the Church's sanction of imperialism, but also of its propensity to Europeanism in the Missions.

[182] Quoted in J. Eggert, *Missionsschule und Sozialer Wandel in Ostafrika* (Bielefeld, 1972), p. 45.

[183] Quoted in ibid., p. 43.

[184] Quoted in H. Berger, *Mission and Kolonialpolitik: Die katholische Mission in Kamerun während der deutschen Kolonialzeit* (Immensee, 1978), p. 123.

such a way that the Christian experience is not only expressed in terms specific to the host culture, but also becomes a source of inspiration and action within that culture.''[185] This latter judgment is based on the fact that native peoples cannot truly open themselves to the Gospel if they are first uprooted from their coherent social backgrounds. Those Christians in Nigeria, for instance, who were called upon to disassociate themselves from the world of the *profanum vulgus* did so only because they feared apprehension. Christians who joined the Ekpo society in the Uyo district were submitted to public penance and made to pay double the fees demanded by the society. The fate of Christians who entered a fattening room was grimmer, as the following regulations show:

> Fattening of any kind — Pagan or the so called Christian — is strictly forbidden. Breaking this law: Husbands, fine £2. Wife ...£1. One pound is added if the husband is a Teacher:
> a) Head Teacher fattening his wife: fine as above, reduced to a substraction for at least a year; goes back to his rank when he marries.
> b) Teacher: fine as above, and dismissed as teacher.
> c) Christians: fine as above, and stopped from the sacraments till they marry.
> d) Catechumens: fine as above, baptism postponed for six months or till they marry.[186]

The urge to fill the vacuum created in those who, out of fear of these reprisals, disassociated themselves from their native customs and pastimes, was so strong that they ran back to their cherished habits at the slightest opportunity and through any back door. Here was no show of disrespect for the tenets of Christianity; nor was it a manifestation of a depraved nature. It was rather an evidence that a man cannot be complete who empties himself of his being—his joy, his senses and sensibilities.[187] It was a proof that Christianity, and indeed any religious experience, can only thrive on a complete and emotionally balanced personality.

Few missionaries took issue with this anthropological and psychological truth, even after some bitter experiences. Speaking of his dealings

---

[185] J. Scheuer, "Matteo Ricci and the Inculturation of Christianity, 1583-1983," in *Lumen Vitae*, English ed. XL/1 (1985), 7.

[186] CSE: 191/B/VIII, P. Biéchy, "Regulations newly Approved by Bishop Shanahan," n. d.

[187] A group of Nigerian nationalists made the following remark in 1962: "In the souls of most of us...there lurks an aching void for the games and pastimes of our childhood days, for the joy of the village green. Most of these have been ousted by imported games which are not bad because they are imported, but which should remain side by side with those of our own culture and mode of expression." Quoted in A. E. Afigbo, "The Missions, the State and Education in South-Eastern Nigeria, 1956-1971," *Christianity in Independent Africa*, ed. E. Fasholé-Luke, et al. (London: Rex Collins, 1978), p. 186.

with local rulers who became Christians, Bishop Crowther of the Church Missionary Society once said: "It is our experience in this field that influence is not worth having; for it parts like a rope of sand the moment a faithful attitude is resumed."[188]

This was also the experience of the Catholic authorities in 1913 when chief Sami, the Catholic Obi of Onitsha, turned apostate together with a good number of the Onitsha Catholic community. The measure which was taken to guard against this development failed to come to terms with its real cause. Although the main cause of the mass apostasy at Onitsha was given as the unpopularity of the First commandment among native Africans, the general meeting that was held in 1913 to rescue the Catholic faith discussed only one issue—marriage customs. As the report goes, the chief later re-joined the Church after having done a public penance.[189]

However, the seriousness of the matter called for further measures some two years later. Summoned by the Prefect, some 35 representatives of all the Missions of the Prefecture came together at Onitsha in 1915 for the first Catholic Congress ever held in Eastern Nigeria. The aim was to discuss the crisis which had beset the Prefecture since 1912. Three problems were chosen as subjects of discussion, namely, 1) pagan titles, 2) the masquerades and their public manifestations, 3) pagan customs on marriage.

1) The pagan title that was given exclusive treatment by the Congress was the *Ozo* title, whose holders can, with propriety, be compared with the feudal lords of Europe.[190] After some deliberations, the title was "unanimously condemned, in spite of the murmurs of the extreme right."[191] It is not specified in the report whether the "extreme right" were Whites or Blacks. Judging from the procedure of the Congress, however, one cannot truly speak of a "unanimous" decision. Since the Fathers considered Africans to be "indefatigable speakers," the number of the representatives at the Congress was "limited in advance," and

---

[188] Quoted in A. F. Walls, "Black Europeans, White Africans: Some Missionary Motives in West Africa," *Religious Motivation: Biographical and Sociological Problems for the Church Historian.* Studies in Church History, Vol. 15, p. 348.

[189] See CSE: *Bulletin,* 29 (1918-1920), 187-188.

[190] An Ozo man has a firm control over the economic, political, social, and religious development of his community, and this accounts for the popularity and attraction of the title among the natives. It is found mainly in the Onitsha and Nsukka districts, and the absence of the movement in other parts of Eastern Nigeria led Father Shanahan to the conclusion in 1912 that the Onitshas were originally not Igbos: "The Onitshas are not Igbos; they are former slaves who ran away from Benin City and established themselves at Onitsha about 200 years ago" (CSE: 192/B/VI, "Shanahan to LeRoy," Onitsha, 4 June 1912).

[191] CSE: *Bulletin,* 29 (1918-1920), 182.

their speeches "measured."[192] For the democratically minded Igbos and Ibibios, this handicap was particularly frustrating, and it is anyboby's guess where the murmur came from.

2) With regard to the second issue—the masquerades and their public manifestations—the Christians were strictly forbidden to belong to the *Ekpo* or *Mmo* societies, or to take part in their public processions.

3) Finally, pointing out the exploitations and enslavement of women by their husbands, the Congress resolved to inculcate in the youth—the future husbands—the awareness of Christian truths, the horror of vice, and the love of virtue. The importance of education in the achievement of these objectives was once more emphasized. "This latter conclusion of the Congress," it was stressed, "strengthens the path we have been following in Nigeria in order to have good Christians and, afterwards, good husbands: that is to say, through the school."[193]

The final resolutions of the Congress on the first two subjects—pagan titles, and masquerades—were, in many respects, unfortunate, short-sighted, and ill-advised. The first Catholic Congress in Eastern Nigeria missed a golden opportunity of allowing the natives to give expression to their Christian faith through their culture and prevailing social habits. In 1937, the Conference of Nigerian Ordinaries did make an attempt to revise the attitude of the Missions towards native titles. Its resolution contained, among other things, the following observation:

> In some areas what are known as native "titles" cause much trouble to the missionary.... The Conference considered that by reason of the influence these titled men have, and in virtue of the promise given [that Christians were to be exempt from making ritual sacrifices] it would be advisable to urge some faithful Christians who may be entrusted to withstand secret pressure to become "titled" men. In this way some control of the system may be acquired and the practice of sacrificing abolished.[194]

However, this concession did not temper the deep-seated prejudice which the individual Mission leaders had already had against pagan titles for so many decades. It is no wonder that even today Christians are very seldom allowed to decorate themselves with titles like the Ozo. One must concede that most of the local usages, like all primitive rites, were sur-rounded with myth, mystery and magic. But divorced of these elements, there was nothing in them that was opposed to religion and righteousness. Father Shanahan himself noted in clear terms that some of the Ekpos were harmless pastimes which called to mind "the carnivals

---

[192] Ibid., p. 181.

[193] Ibid., p. 182.

[194] CSE: 554/II, "Extracts from the Minutes of the Meeting of the Ordinaries of Nigeria, 1937," p. 23.

of Europe.''[195] Yet, he allowed no concessions that would have made it possible for Christians to participate in them. This was a good indication that the missionaries had restrictions on their decisions. Unlike the Ordinaries of normal dioceses, the Apostolic Prefects and Vicars, for instance, possessed only mandatory powers in the Missions they headed. As a result, they were extremely inhibited in their efforts to provide lasting solutions to actual problems on the spot. Since it was impossible to conform to the usages and customs of the natives without going contrary to the known wishes of their sovereigns in Rome, the mission leaders turned to paternism as the only way out of the impasse they often found themselves in. More often than not, decisions were made not *by* the people, but *for* the people, and very seldom *with* the people.[196]

The suppression of traditional habits and pastimes had adverse effects of another sort on native society: it inflicted irreparable damage on a number of rural economies and the traditional modes of education that they entailed. Behind the creation and realization of the masquerades and other native plays lay series of local industries and their craft gilds, such as the blacksmiths, weavers, and carvers, whose existence were terminated together with the disappearance in a locality of traditional entertainments. Since the ancestral mode of education in many African societies was based on association rather than formal instruction, many age-long experiences, art and knowledge, especially among the musicians, died out as soon as local plays and festivals fell into disuse.

The consequences for the craft gilds were bitter. When, for instance, leg rings, a set of graduated brass spirals worn by women as part of the out-fit for the fattening ceremony, were forbidden by Catholic authorities in the Onitsha district, the Awka people, the famous blacksmiths of the Igbo country, fought unsuccessfully to salvage their only source of sustenance. The Fathers themselves reported the incident as follows:

> Another progress [in the Mission] is the disappearance, not without troubles, of the enormous brass rings and ornaments which the women wear on their legs. Following a great meeting of all the chiefs of the region, we decided to suppress them, despite strong objections from the Okas, the blacksmiths of the country.[197]

This kind of ''progress''—the disappearance of traditional habits— was in fact counterproductive: what took the place of the native customs did not always produce the desired results. School children and students were required, for instance, to speak only English, to wear uniforms, and

---

[195] CSE: *Bulletin*, 29 (1918-1920), 182.
[196] J. Glazik, ''Die neuzeitliche Mission...,'' p. 36f.
[197] CSE: *Bulletin*, 26 (1911-1912), 866.

to assume a civilized physical appearance. The result was the production of a new breed of Africans who have been described severally by Europeans in such terms as "half Blacks, half Whites", or "black Europeans, white Africans". This cultural phenomenon was first observed by the Anglicans among the "Sierra Leonians", the pioneer Black evangelists in West Africa. Deprived of their African backgrounds as a result of slavery, the "gentlemen" readily adopted the European habits which Christianity offered them. This instilled a spirit of pride and, in part, arrogance in them. And as A. F. Walls rightly pointed out, "their European contemporaries assumed that the Sierra Leone reaction could and should be typical of African reaction to Christianity."[198] It is hardly surprising, therefore, that Catholic leaders in Onitsha were obsessed by the possibility of their adherents imitating the "disdainful" habits of the Black foreigners in the area:

> Whatever education they [the Black "gentlemen of the coast] have received has swollen their pride. You need to see them pass with their polished boots, their latest fashion in suit, and their insolent heads raised stiffly to the height of a large detachable collar. Although they are devotees of Protestantism, they typify the greatest scorn for everything that is connected with religion.
> To protect our Christians from this contagion, we are counterpoising it with the remedies of frequent sacraments, and the practice of charity.... Finally, going to communion every first Friday of the month ...is contributing forcefully to assure the perseverance of our faithful.[199]

The mission authorities were right, no doubt, in decisively taking measures to guard against the danger that threatened religion as a result of changes in society. But one issue was conspicuously over-looked, namely, the dilemma of the individuals involved in those changes. On the one hand, they were displaced from their coherent society, and on the other hand chastised for adopting the habits of another society. As Sir Ralph Moor himself conceded, the aping of European modes of life by educated Africans would have been superfluous had their education and spiritual formations taken adequate consideration of their distinctive native characteristics.[200]

4. The Break With The Old Order as a Generation Crisis

One other strand in Western education was the conflict it touched off between the generations. Since the success of the Christian Missions

---

[198] A. F. Walls, "Black Europeans, White Africans," p. 341.
[199] CSE: Bulletin, 24 (1907-1908), 147.
[200] Quoted in F. K. Ekechi, Missionary Enterprise and Rivalry in Igboland, 1857-1914 (London: Frank Cass, 1972), p. 180.

pivoted on the response of the youth, the missionaries concentrated their influence on school children. Little attention was, understandably, paid to the contemporary adult world. Doggedly attached to their native roots, the older people looked with awe on the new changes taking place in traditional society. If their attitude towards the new order of things was generally one of resignation, it was out of consideration for the new-found hopes and desires of their sons and daughters. But now and again, they gave some expression to their indignation over the exploits of their children and their new mentors.

The suppression of native customs, for instance, very much alienated the older generation and hardened them in their resolve to stand resolutely by their traditional way of life. As Father Lejeune learnt on the feast of Immaculate Heart, December 8, 1903, the older people did not run into the arms of the Church after the violation of their cherished pastimes. On that eventful day (the pagans themselves were also out feasting) the Prefect had interrupted a street dance and driven away the masquerades. To test the faith of the crowd, he said: "Those who wish to serve God and renounce the Devil should follow me!" He was followed by "70 children."[201] Although the Fathers rejoiced afterwards over their "victory over the Devil," they certainly were not unmindful of the defiance of their appeal by the older people.

The consequences of the break with the old order were also pronounced in the Owerri district. The bitter experiences of the Catholic authorities in this region affords a paradigm for the nature of the generation crisis in the early years of contact with Western civilization:

> The older people either do not want us or are indifferent. The younger ones on the contrary are most anxious. In many of our interviews with the chiefs we were badly treated. No sooner did we leave the compound than hundreds of young men and grown-up boys would come and beg us not to abandon them on account of the insolence of their chiefs.[202]

Like the chiefs in the Onitsha and Calabar regions, the chiefs and elders of Owerri were also enthusiastic about Christianity and Western education. It was for these objectives that they sent "deputation upon deputation" to the Calabar Mission between 1909 and 1911, inviting the

---

[201] CSE: 191/B/III, "Lejeune to LeRoy," Onitsha, 8 December 1903; also CSE: *Bulletin*, 22 (1903-1904), 790f. In 1895, the Catholics disapproved of a similar action by Archdeacon Denis of the Anglican Mission in Onitsha. However, the Archdeacon did not have the luck of the Prefect, for he was violently assaulted by the youth, who were, to a large extent, still one with their elders at that time. See CSE: *Bulletin*, 18 (1896-1897), 416.

[202] CSE: 192/B/VI, "Shanahan to Father Neville," Calabar, 20 September, 1912.

Catholics to their area.[203] If they were later hostile to the Fathers in spite
of their former dispositions, then it was probably because of the preconditions which the missionaries made known during their preliminary
meetings with the natives.[204] Three of such prerequisites are implicit in
Shanahan's letter to Father Neville, namely, the call on the chiefs to
renounce cannibalism, Mohammedanism, and slave trade.[205]

Another major cause of the conflict between the generations was the
encroachment of Western education upon the distribution of labour in
traditional society. The old order had definite functions for every
individual in the community, and it was the duty of children to aid their
parents in the home and in the farm. It was no wonder that the older
generation showed disapprobation in the face of a trend in which children
not only spent most of the working hours at school, but also stayed away
from home completely if they were boarders. This *zeitgeist* was particulary
loathed by parents at the early stages of Western education in Eastern
Nigeria. When, for instance, the Government opened a school at Bonny
in 1900, a curious problem threatened to cripple its existence—the lack
of school children. The parents, who did not want to take the risk of
educating "ungrateful" children, refused to send them to school. To
crack this hard nut, Sir Ralph Moor quickly introduced a Native Rule
which required the "Head of a house and the boy sent to school" to come
to an agreement, whereby the boy promised to refund the money spent
on him with an additional interest of 50 per cent.[206] The law worked and
the number of pupils in the government school rose from 28 in
November 1900 to 83 in June 1901.

At the very highest level of confrontation between the old and the
young was the contemptuous attitude of the youth towards local
authorities and institutions. More often than not, the younger generation
was led to civil disobedience by their mentors. Some government
officials, for instance, considered it expedient to give educated young
men a share in local administration on the grounds that they "no longer

---

[203] See CSE: *Bulletin*, 25 (1911-1912), 878; see also CSE: 192/B/VI, "Shanahan to
Superior General," Onitsha, 7 July 1911.

[204] Father Krafft of the Calabar Mission met with the chiefs of Owerri for the first time
in July 1911. Fathers Shanahan and A. Bindel joined him there later in the month. See
CSE: 192/V/VI, "Shanahan to LeRoy," Onitsha, 7 July 1911.

[205] See CSE: 192/B/VI, "Shanahan to Father Neville," Calabar, 20 September 1912:
"Although they have by no means renounced the idea of eating human flesh, yet they
think it would be well if they had a few good schools.... The Mohammedans have a settlement in Owerri and a school attended by natives! Their presence is enough to show that
a very brisk trade in slaves must be carried on.... The old chiefs want money and are
ready to sell everything and everybody to get it. The younger generation sees this and
wants to put a stop to it at any cost."

[206] See PRO:C.O. 520/8, No. 150, "R. Moor to Colonial Office," 12 June, 1901.

respected the ancient sanctions.''[207] Similarly, the Christian Missions
'encouraged their young adherents to disobey their pagan rulers. In view
of his policy of Indirect Rule, Lord Lugard was particularly upset by this
state of affairs:

> There has been a not unnatural tendency on the part of mission ''converts''
> to repudiate the authority of their chiefs, and to ignore and flout native
> customary law. Complaints have been made that in some cases missionaries
> have sympathised with this attitude. It has now been laid down in
> unmistakable terms, both in the North and in the South, that the profession
> of any particular creed (whether Christian or Mohammedan), does not
> absolve its adherents from the authority of their chiefs, or from the native
> law and customs prevalent in their district, provided that they are not com-
> pelled to do anything which is repugnant to their religious beliefs.[208]

It is noteworthy that Lugard's views in the above passage were very
much similar to the famous Instruction of 1659 by the Propaganda Congregation. However, in this question of the true relationship between
Western education and native society, theory stood sadly at variance with
practice.

---

[207] C. K. Meek, Law and Authority in a Nigerian Tribe: A Study of Indirect Rule
(London, 1937; rpt. New York: Barnes & Noble, 1979), p. xv.
[208] F. D. Lugard, *Report on the Amalgamation*, p. 66.

CHAPTER FOUR

THE PROBLEM OF TEACHERS

I *The Village School and the Catechist*

1. *The Emergence of the Village School.*

The first phase of Catholic education in Eastern Nigeria was largely charity-oriented. By means of gifts and free education, the missionary endeavoured to lure the people to the school. Although this phase experienced a transition period under Father Lejeune, who strove, in spite of fierce opposition, to bring the school out of the confines of the Christian enclaves, it remained the most distinctive feature of Catholic education at the close of his prefectship in 1905. The missionary still built the schools, and still laboured to have pupils come to them.

A definite departure from this state of affairs was marked by the trend, from 1906 onwards, in which the people themselves came to the missionary with demands for schools, and a willingness to pay for their education. It was, in the words of the Fathers, "a happy development."[1] To give weight to their desire for education, the natives took the initiative to build the schools, erect houses for the Fathers and for the Catechists, and assemble a sufficient number of school children for a start. In the face of such adroit gestures, the Fathers found it difficult not to pay heed to their pleas. Seeing in the village school a welcome phenomenon in the growth of the Mission, they in fact actively encouraged its multiplication. Thus began a phase in Catholic missionary enterprise in which the work of the Catechist-teacher among the natives was accorded a place of paramount importance. In the same measure, the necessity of providing capable men to man the numerous village schools which sprang up at every corner of the Prefecture became a major concern for the mission leaders.

For the common man, the village school was a factor of great significance. Emerging at a time when Catholic education was showing a tendency towards elitism, it offered the village folk the best opportunity of getting some involvement with the school trend. We recall that the first Catholic educational effort in Calabar was made primarily for the sons of chiefs and wealthy traders of the coastal city-states. Although the schools at Onitsha were started with liberated slaves and out-casts, they

---

[1] CSE: *Bulletin*, 24 (1907-1908), 148.

had, by 1905, been predominantly filled with members of the upper class, especially at Onitsha-Ogboli. A report from this station in 1912 will serve as an illustration:

> At Onitsha-Ogboli, our school shelters more than 600 pupils and young men. They come from more than 30 different villages...and are the elite of the Black society—princes by birth, sons of chiefs, small and big. They have been sent to learn the ways of the White Fathers, after which they will return to their localities to teach the people in their turn.[2]

In a similar report, we learn that the first students of the Teacher Training College at Igbariam, which was established in 1913, were the elites of the Christian community.[3] The village school was therefore the only means open to the masses to exploit the appeals of education.

For their part, the missionaries saw in the village school the most effective means to ensure the presence of the Church among the people. With the school, they could penetrate any locality, as this report by Father X. Lichtenberger discloses:

> From every corner we are being requested to establish not missions, but schools. In many cases, if the local chiefs were to know that our arrival in their district was only for the purpose of preaching the truths of our sacred religion, they would not accept us; but once the pretext is a school, access to a town or village is made easy for us.[4]

Having realized the inestimable value of the school in the work of evangelization, the Fathers went all out to ensure its presence in every nook and corner of the prefecture. Accordingly, the running of schools became the principal activity in the mission outstations, which, as has been seen, were set up by community effort. There were eleven such outstations in the Onitsha district at the beginning of 1908 which were reported to be largely paying the salaries of their Catechist-teachers.[5] By 1909 two of these—Ozubulu and Igbariam—had become independent mission centres with resident priests.

In the Calabar district, Father Biéchy was reported as having opened a record number of three to four schools a day among the Anangs of Ibibioland. To ensure that his quick transactions took firm roots during his unavoidable long absence, he grouped the new schools around existing outstations, whose Catechist-teachers got the orders to cater for them and to recommend able young men from the villages concerned for

---

[2] CSE: *Bulletin*, 26 (1911-1912), 872.
[3] CSE: *Bulletin*, 29 (1918-1920), 197.
[4] CSE: 192/B/V, Report by X. Lichtenberger, 1 April, 1910.
[5] See CSE: 192/B/V, "Shanahan to LeRoy," Onitsha, 20 February, 1908.

employment as Catechist-teachers.[6] This brilliant organization eventually became, with slight modifications, a model for the organization of
missionary and educational efforts in the whole Prefecture.

The use of the village school in the advancement of missionary cause
was most successful in the Owerri district. Following the general practice
in other districts, the people of the Owerri region approached the Fathers
for missionaries and Catechists only after having built schools, chapels,
and dwelling houses. As has been seen in the preceding chapter, Father
Krafft of the Calabar Mission made the first contact with the Owerri
natives in July 1911. But the first great apostle to the Owerris was Father
John Féral. He was saddled with the difficult task of studying the hitherto
unexplored Igbo heartland. Within four months he had visited fifty
villages in and around Owerri, and on the strength of the report on his
findings, it was decided at a mission Council meeting at Onitsha on 28
October 1911 to found, without a loss of time and without awaiting the
approval of the Mother House in Paris, a mission centre at Ulakwo. Taking with him Brother Joseph and fifteen Catechists who were chosen from
among the best pupils of the Onitsha school, Father Féral set out from
Onitsha on 15 November 1911 for eight villages in the Owerri district.[7]
The team that undertook this missionary enterprise in 1911 had little idea
that on them rested the greatest missionary break-through in Eastern
Nigeria. In the 1920s hundreds of teachers were sent From Emekuku to
open schools in various districts of the Igbo heartland, including Aba and
Umuahia. By 1930, Owerri had become the most important Catholic
stronghold in the whole of Nigeria.

Paradoxically, Emekuku, which by 1912 had superseded Ulakwo as
the centre of this great mission, was not one of the eight pioneer villages
ministered to in 1911. The reason for this conspicuous omission was not
so much the lack of Catechist-teachers as the fact of indecision on the part
of the Fathers. In the face of a situation in which almost every village had
already constructed, or was in the process of constructing, a school, a
chapel, and dwelling houses, it was not easy for the missionaries to make
up their minds about where to go first. "So far, we think Ulakwo will
be the most suitable for a missionary residence," wrote Father Shanahan
in 1912. "We don't know enough about the country to make a definite
choice."[8] In January 1914, the Prefect wrote to the Superior General

---

[6] CSE: 556/VIII, J. Kirchner, "Heidentum und Christentum im Lande der Ibibios,"
(MS. n.d.), p. 82.
[7] See CSE: 192/B/VI, "Shanahan to LeRoy," Onitsha, 27 November, 1912. The
eight villages included: Osu, Eziobaku, Emii, Naze, Awaka, Okigwe, Nebuku, and
Ulakwo.
[8] CSE: 192/B/VI, "Shanahan to Father Neville," Calabar, 20 September, 1912.

THE PROBLEM OF TEACHERS

asking for permission to transfer the mission residence from Ulakwo to Emekuku, which meanwhile was functioning as an outstation. Among other things, he noted that it was hard to say if Emekuku should be the definite centre because the people themselves had not yet come to an agreement on the issue.[9]

When Father Féral and his successor at Ulakwo, Father Delisle, left the mission on health grounds, the task of building up the most important mission in Igbo heartland fell on Father Daniel Walsh. Between 1912 and 1915, he had constructed at Emekuku a magnificent Fathers' house, a school, and a church capable of taking in 1500 persons. Emekuku thus marked a definitive departure from the normal Catholic practice of using an *école-chapelle* or *école-église* (school-church) in the evangelization of a town or village. In this combination, a single simple building served as prayer house on Sundays, and as school room on week-days. Emekuku was the first mission in the Prefecture to achieve the separation of school and church right from the start.[10]

The phenomenon of the école-église has remained till this day a symbolic reminder of the dual motivation which the people and the missionaries brought to bear on the work of evangelization in Eastern Nigeria. Mention has often been made of the pragmatic strand in the acceptance of Christianity by the people. If a shrewd Igbo or Ibibio chief were given the option to choose between a cathedral and a mud school, he would certainly have opted for the latter. The missionary, who knew well this disposition, achieved his aim all the same by making the mud school building a functioning church house. This compromise was frowned at by some superiors, and firmly acclaimed by others. When, for instance, Father Joseph Soul, the Visitor of the Spiritans, made an inspection tour of Nigeria from August to November 1929, he was surprised to notice that there were "no churches in Nigeria except at Calabar,...Adazi and Emekuku."[11] By contrast, another Church dignitary, Archbishop Hinsley, the Apostolic Delegate to British Africa, found the heavy leaning on the school to be a normal approach to the special situation of the missionary in Africa. Speaking at a gathering of Bishops in Dar-es-Salam in August 1928, he had the courage to say: "Where it is impossible for you to carry on both the immediate task of

---

[9] See CSE: 192/B/VI, "Shanahan to LeRoy," 3 January 1914. The strongest case against Ulakwo was that it was unhealthy to dwell in.

[10] Calabar attained this goal in 1912, nine years after its foundation. Onitsha, the seat of the Prefect and future Apostolic Vicar, had to wait until 1935 to have its cathedral.

[11] CSE: 554/V, J. Soul, "General Report to the Superior General on the Visit to the District of Southern Nigeria," Onitsha, 12 November, 1929.

evangelization and your educational work, neglect your churches and perfect your schools."[12]

Bishop Shanahan needed little urging in this matter. Ever since he became head of the Mission in 1905, the Vicar had namely turned to the school in such a measure that left little room for the sparing of resources for the building of churches. Put simply, he firmly believed that his educational programme was of such overriding importance as to render other considerations trivial. This belief was expressed without reservations in a letter to the Superior General:

> They [the Calabar Mission] wanted a High School and got money for it.... Now that everything is set, Father Léna appears not to be enthusiastic anymore. He has already started making bricks for a new Church.... To attempt carrying abreast a new High School, a new station, and a new church is a thing which surpasses me.[13]

The village school was, by modern standards, a very modest undertaking. In fact a typical bush school in a locality differed from the surrounding huts only by having an oblong shape, and by bearing the name "school." Its construction was achieved everywhere with relative ease, and given the poor equipment and management in such a school, it was not surprising that the standard of efficiency was, to a large extent, deplorable. Nevertheless, the village school continued to multiply at a rate that was beyond the control of the missionaries.

This was for the Missions a frustrating dilemma, and for the Government an outrageous phenomenon. During the Governorship of Sir Hugh Clifford (1919-1926), a serious attempt was made to halt the spread of what had been dubbed "hedge schools." Among other things, it was decided to close down schools that were found to be "inadequately equipped, housed or managed or in which the teachers are themselves too ignorant to be able to impart education of a really sound character."[14] This and similar government measures reflected a skimpy appreciation of the complexities of what Phillipson rightly called "a healthy and vigorous social phenomenon...which...was the inevitable resultant of the forces playing on the community at that time."[15] With the people's appetite for education seeming almost insatiable, the Missions made desperate efforts to keep the village schools supplied with teachers, a commitment which, despite its shortcomings, ought to have deserved nothing but praise.

---

[12] Quoted in A. Hastings, "Patterns of African Mission Work," in *African Ecclesiastical Review*, 8 (1966), 293.
[13] CSE: 192/B/VI, "Shanahan to LeRoy," Onitsha 29 April, 1911.
[14] Quoted in S. Phillipson, *Grants in Aid*, p. 18.
[15] *Ibid.*

2. *The Catechist-Teacher.*

The Catechists occupy a place of prominence in the history of Christian Missions in Nigeria. It was they, simple and extremely pious Africans, who laid the foundation of the Christian faith in Nigeria. Although these men have remained obscure, it is generally recognized that the success of the missionary enterprise rested, to a large extent, on their shoulders. There were, for instance, thirty-five Catechists-teachers in Onitsha-Ogboli and its dependent outstations in 1912, and of these men was written: "Their services are for us indispensable. For without them we would be incapable of carrying out our undertakings."[16] These undertakings included: the daily ministration to the people, the teaching work in the schools, and, above all, the preparation of catechumens for the sacraments. None of these obligations could be thought of without the Catechist, who was interpreter, evangelist, teacher, and village counsellor, all in one person.

The dependence of the Fathers on native Catechist-teachers was particularly necessary in the early years of missionary work in Africa. The fact that the fundamentals of education—reading, writing, and arithmetic—could not be taught exclusively in English to the pupils made the use of teachers who were native speakers inevitable. Furthermore, since the small number of European missionaries did not increase in accordance with the growth of the Missions, recourse to local helpers became a compelling necessity. In 1887, for instance, the Fathers at Onitsha reported that because of their dwindling number and increasing responsibilities, they were obliged to leave all the teaching in the Wharf school "exclusively" to a native Catechist, a former printer in the service of the Anglican Mission at Lokoja.[17] It was not until 1893 that an European missionary—Brother David Doran—could be found to relieve him of that responsibility.

The use of converted Protestants as Catechists in Catholic schools was about the only solution to the problem of teachers, especially between 1890 and 1900. During this period, many Protestant teachers sought employment in Catholic schools after having become converts to the Catholic faith. It is hard to say how many of those veterans changed camp out of conviction, and how many by coercion. That many of them were men of integrity who sincerely followed their religious persuasions is hardly controvertible. Mention may be made here of such men as Samuel Okosi Okolo, who became the Obi of Onitsha in 1901, and Ephrem Agha, who was a deacon of the Anglican Church before he

---

[16] *CSE: Bulletin*, 26 (1911-1912), 872.
[17] CSE: *Bulletin*, 14 (1887-1888), 469.

joined the Catholics in 1896. However, there is ample evidence that many of the renegade Protestants were guided by considerations of material gains. In the days when the success of the Catholic educational programme depended almost exclusively on native Catechist-teachers, the Fathers were rather generous to any person who offered his services to them. In Appendix "A" of this work, a clear picture of the concessions made to qualified Protestant teachers in the service of the Catholic Mission is got from a contract made by Father Kuntzman with Mr. Ephrem Agha in 1896. Apart from a lucrative salary, which was to increase in accordance with the number of his children, Mr. Agha got from the Mission a guarantee for continuous employment at Onitsha Wharf, the promise of European provisions, and a financial contribution to the building of his personal house.

Father Lejeune showed strong antipathy towards Catechists who had Protestant backgrounds. Right from the beginning of his prefectship in 1900, he criticised his predecessors for their absolute dependence upon people he had come to regard as fortune seekers. According to his own report, as many as ten Protestant teachers came forward every month in 1900 to be admitted into the Catholic Church on the condition that they were granted favours that were similar to those given to Mr. Ephrem Agha in 1896. But the new Prefect endeavoured, at the detriment of his popularity, to put an end to this kind of conversion, which, in his opinion, had approached the threshold of simony.[18]

The growth of the Mission and its schools brought a new problem with it, namely, the difficulty of coping with a correspondingly growing number of Catechists and teachers. As the educational fever began to take hold of even the most remote villages, the station Catechists became more and more isolated from the mission residence and the Father in charge. Since most of these auxiliaries resented being posted to the interior, they often developed lackadaisical attitudes to their jobs. The success of any missionary or educational enterprise in remote areas, therefore, depended to a large extent on the discipline and administrative abilities of the Catechists. To ensure these, emphasis was laid on their formation and their being closely supervised.

The most effective measure taken to ensure an effective coordination of the work of Catechist-teachers was to group them into sub-stations and head-stations. To this we shall return later; for the moment let us consider some special aspects of the formation given to Catechists.

As has been noted above, the Catholic Fathers depended heavily on Catechists who were converts from Protestantism. Since these men were

---

[18] See CSE: 192/B/III. "Lejeune to LeRoy," Onitsha, 1 May, 1903.

qualified school masters, their formation as Catholic Catechists was usually a matter of formality, consisting mainly of re-baptism, and instructions on specific Catholic doctrines.[19] After 1900, Father Lejeune gradually replaced these Catechists of the old order with what he called "a new generation of Catechists."[20] These consisted mainly of people chosen from among the best pupils of the Onitsha school. They differed from the old generation of Catechists by having done their primary education under the supervision of Catholic Fathers and Brothers. However, their choice as Catechists depended more on their piety than on any formal training in the principles of catechetics. In 1907, for instance, Father Shanahan noted that "hitherto no attempt has been made to train the Catechists." He went on to say that anyone—slave or freeman—who was interested could be chosen as Catechist at the monthly salary of 30 to 40 Shillings.[21]

The necessity of a thorough and adequate training for the lay helpers of the Mission began to be more generally felt after 1906 following the prominence which the school had attained in the work of evangelization. However, opinion remained divided on the issue of the kind of training they were to receive in view of their dual function as Catechists and Teachers. Among the Fathers of the Prefecture, there was a general consensus on the need to lay emphasis on the training of Catechists as teachers and school masters. In the opinion of Father Vogler, it was "an established reality...in Southern Nigeria that a Catechist who has not been to school is only a poor assistant."[22] Father Lichtenberger wrote in a similar vein when he said that an uncertificated Catechist "would be looked upon unfavourably, and would do very little at the moment."[23]

The Mother House in Paris was of a different opinion. In accordance with the practice of the Holy Ghost Congregation in other parts of the world, Paris insisted that the Nigerian Mission should establish an institution where men would be trained as Catechists only. On the contrary, Father Shanahan opted for a "High School" for Catechist-teachers with the argument that the special vocation of the Nigerian Catechist was a thing that did not admit of general rules:

> It is no use proposing to have the youth trained exclusively as Catechists. We have tried it before without success. It is inexpedient to take away from

---

[19] In 1892, the Catechist-teacher of the Wharf school and his wife were said to be among the Catechumens. See CSE: *Bulletin*, 16 (1891-1893), 335.
[20] See CSE: *Bulletin*, 22 (1903-1904), 788.
[21] CSE: 192/B/V, "Shanahan to LeRoy," Onitsha, 28 May 1907.
[22] CSE: 192/B/V, Father Vogler, "Question des Frères et des Ecole," n.d.
[23] CSE: 191/B/V, "Report by X. Lichtenberger," 1 April 1910.

a Mission its special characteristic, and to demand that it does what is done in other Missions where all the conditions are absolutely different.

Here [in Nigeria] the people are clamouring for schools, and nothing but schools, at the moment. They do not want the missionary as such.[24]

The extraordinary quest for education in Nigeria was, therefore, a phenomenon which called for a radical departure from several accepted practices, principles, and norms of the Holy Ghost Congregation. After relentless struggles, Father Shanahan succeeded in joining the formation of Catechists inextricably with the training of teachers, first in the primary schools, and later in the Teacher Training Colleges. Even the establishment in 1930 of a special school for Catechists at Eke was not a turning away from the old practice of training Catechist-teachers. The specifically new thing in the school was that all the in-mates were boarders who lived with the common awareness of their special vocation as Catechist-teachers. Otherwise, the training they received at Eke did not differ substantially from the one given in Normal Schools to designated Catechists. The candidates, a selected group of brilliant pupils, were given normal school lessons in the mornings, and catechetical courses in the afternoons.[25]

This special emphasis on the teaching mission of the Catechists found ultimate expression in the official policy of the Nigerian Catholic Ordinaries. During their annual meeting in 1937, the question of whether Catechists should be Catechists only, or whether they should also be school teachers constituted a major subject for careful debate, and in the end the Conference agreed that "Instead of having merely Catechist training schools, these training schools should be always teacher training centres as well, and the students should get full training as teachers."[26] The main argument which was advanced in favour of this position was that there was hardly any part of the country where the people were not anxious for schools. Accordingly, the suggestion of some members of the Conference that Catechists without teachers' qualifications be trained for the ministry in undeveloped areas was dismissed with very little sympathy.

It is noteworthy that the Conference of Nigerian Ordinaries made the educational interest of the people a determining factor in the training and function of the Catechists, just as Father Shanahan had advocated in 1910. No matter how strange this may seem today, it reflects the extent

---

[24] CSE: 191/B/VI, Shanahan, "Training School for Southern Nigeria," Onitsha, 6 May, 1910.

[25] See CSE: *Bulletin*, 34 (1929-1930), 846.

[26] CSE: 554/II, "Extracts from the Minutes of the Meeting of the Ordinaries of Nigeria" (1937), p. 9.

to which the work of evangelization in Nigeria depended on Catholic involvement in education. Nobody at that time possessed the competence to comprehend the complexity of the problem better than the various Mission leaders in Nigeria, who were all Europeans by 1937. Father Joseph Soul, the Spiritan Visitor to Nigeria in 1929, endeavoured, in his report, to bring this truth home to his Superior General in an attempt to temper the general prejudice over the educational upheaval in Nigeria:

> The school is presently the big question in Nigeria. Although the whole world will never understand such a radical change in the methods of evangelization, there is nothing one can do than to accept the directives which come from local ecclesiastical authorities.[27]

It may not be totally wrong to say that the liberality with which the Mother House sanctioned the educational programmes of her Congregation in Eastern Nigeria in the 1930s and the 1940s owed a great deal to the above report. But in earlier years, her attitude was rather conservative, especially with regard to the foundation of a Normal School for the training of teachers.

II. *The Formation of Teachers*

The lack of well-trained teachers was the thorniest problem that faced government and missionary endeavours in Nigeria. In 1882, an attempt was made, for the first time, to provide a solution in the British West African possessions. In that year, the Secretary of State for the Colonies proposed to W. W. Streeten, the Governor of Sierra Leone, the sending of some Africans by each of the Colonial Administrations to England for teacher training courses.[28] However, no use was made of this proposal on the grounds that British colleges were not equipped to meet the exigencies of such a project. Similar attempts to train African teachers in India and the West Indies also collapsed on technical grounds. In the end, the West African Colonies were left to deal with the problem the best they could.

Of all the British possessions in West Africa, Nigeria was, in the nineteenth and early twentieth centuries, the most backward with regard to the number of qualified teachers, as indeed with regard to the number of capable clerks and artisans. As a result, some educated Africans were drawn from the Gold Coast and Sierra Leone to fill government and mis-

---

[27] CSE: 554/V, J. Soul, "General Report to the Superior General...," Onitsha, 12 November, 1929.

[28] See F.C.O.L./8234, M. Sunter, *General Report on Elementary Schools in the Gambia* (1885).

sion posts in Nigeria, a practice which was as expensive as it was unpopular.[29] The effect of the use of this small group of foreigners as teachers in Nigeria could not be more than that of a drop of water on a burning house.

Nor was the contribution of the poorly trained Nigerian teachers encouraging. Reporting on the government schools in the Central Province in 1908, Mr. Cummins, the Inspector of schools, said that lessons were given "haphazardly without any definite aim," and that "system and correct method" of teaching were lacking. He went on to say that all these resulted in "the production of pupils who are little better than parrots."[30] As a remedy, he urged for better training for teachers.

The Christian Missions, who were the first to provide education for the people of West Africa, also grappled with the problem of teachers, with the Catholics lagging behind the Protestants for a long time. Like the Colonial Government, the Catholic Missions in West Africa sought for a collective solution, which envisaged the training of African teachers in Europe. For this purpose, a college was established in Andalusia, Spain, in 1861, but the experiment did not produce the desired result.[31] Thereafter, the various Missions resorted to the method of using Pupil Teachers until they were in the position to establish Teacher Training Colleges.

1. The Pupil Teacher

The Education Code of 1908 as amended and approved in 1909 defined a Pupil Teacher as "a boy or girl who has passed Standard V and has been selected and engaged by the Managers of a school under a binding contract...to assist the teacher of a school in maintaining discipline and imparting instruction."[32] Furthermore, it required that a Pupil Teacher be given teaching lessons outside the school hours for at least one and a half hours a day by a qualified teacher.

This use of pupils as teachers was not a new idea, but rather an official recognition of an old practice which was born out of necessity in the Mission schools. The method was employed in Catholic schools initially as a solution to the problem posed by irregularity both in the registration of school children and in their attendance at school. There was no com-

---

[29] For further details, see A. C. Burns, *A History of Nigeria* (London: George Allen & Unwin, 1936), p. 263; also PRO: C.O.520/8, No.180, 6 May, 1903.

[30] PRO: C.O.590/5, *Annual Report on the Education Department of the Colony and Protectorate of Southern Nigeria* (1908).

[31] See M. J. Walsh. "The Catholic Contribution to Education," p. 86.

[32] Colony of Southern Nigeria, Education Department, *Code of Regulation for Primary & Secondary Schools* (Lagos, 1909), p. 8.

pulsory education, no general knowledge about opening dates, and school children were hard to find. More often than not, pupils who came later during the year had to be placed in the same class with those who had been there right from the start. Added to this special problem of "late-comers" was the more troubling one of irregularity in attendance. The parents and guardians, who expected their children to help them on the farms, did not always give them the permission to attend classes. Given the heterogeneous composition of the first year classes in particular, the often-lone teacher found it exceedingly impossible to coordinate his lessons. To solve this thorny problem, brighter pupils were selected to help those who lagged behind.

With the expansion of schools at the beginning of this century, the Catholics relied extensively on the help of Pupil Teachers in an effort to meet the great demand for teachers. In contrast to the Pupil Teachers of the late nineteenth century, who were chosen mainly to assist the teachers, those of the early twentieth century were mostly employed as independent teachers in the lower classes.[33] The amended Education Code of 1908 gave them an official recognition by enlisting them among the three types of teachers who were eligible to teach in schools, the other two being Assistant Teachers, and Schoolmasters or Principal Teachers. Father Shanahan had strongly opposed the original draft of the Code on the grounds that it had "a killing effect" on Catholic schools. Had it become law, it would have meant that the few Fathers and Brothers who had teaching certificates would have been the only teachers qualified to teach in Catholic schools. The inclusion in the amended Code of Pupil Teachers, a group which was already employed in Catholic schools, was therefore a major concession.

Since the Code had no provision for Catechists, the major group of teachers in Catholic employment, the Fathers were obliged to style them "Pupil Teachers."[34] This was relatively easy to do, since the Code stipulated the minimum age of a Pupil Teacher to be 14 years, and said nothing about a possible maximum age. It was therefore possible for the Catechists, most of whom were men with families, to be suddenly called "pupils". In this way, the Fathers were able to retain them and to obtain grants-in-aid from the Government.[35]

---

[33] When a vacuum was created in the Onitsha Girls' school as a result of the departure of the Sisters to Calabar in 1908, the school, which had a total of 60 school children, was taught by three grown-up girls who were themselves pupils. See CSE: 192/B/V, "Shanahan to LeRoy," Onitsha, September, 1908.

[34] CSE: *Bulletin*, 26(1911-1912), 872.

[35] Apart from grants paid as augmentation to the salaries of Pupil Teachers, the Government paid the Mission £3 and £4 respectively for first and second year Pupil Teachers who passed the special examination arranged for them each year.

The training of Pupil Teachers was a kind of private tuition, involving the assignment of a few pupils to a Father or Brother for extra instructions out of school hours. The duration of the training was two years, and each year, the candidates were required to sit for a special examination. According to J. Jordan, the average number of Pupil Teachers trained annually from 1909 to 1911 was over 20. In this way, the 43 new schools which were opened between 1906 and 1912 were able to be supplied with sufficient teachers.[36]

To the Catholics in particular, the practice of employing Pupil Teachers was of paramount importance in the production of qualified teachers. Whereas the Protestants and the Government could boast of many certificated teachers from Hope Waddell Training Institute and the Government school at Bonny, the Catholics relied on the Pupil Teachers trained in the central schools. Recognized as Assistant Teachers after a successful completion of two years of training, the Pupil Teachers were thus the first qualified African teachers in the Catholic schools of Eastern Nigeria. The self-sufficiency that was thus reached in Catholic schools served as a strong argument in Father Shanahan's efforts to convince his superiors in Paris that the establishment of a proper Training College for teachers would not require elaborate provisions of European staffs. Requesting for one qualified Father or Brother to act as Director in the proposed Catholic "High School" for teachers, he said:

> The schools are producing their personnel.... Who are those running the school at the moment? Of course they are our school children who have become Pupil Teachers; we are doing no more than to direct. Hitherto the Brothers have sufficed at Onitsha, but they don't possess the necessary qualification to educate the children much further.[37]

Until the Catholics were able to establish Teacher Training Institutions, the method of forming and employing Pupil Teachers in Catholic primary schools remained the only way of providing these schools with recognized teachers.

2. Catholic Teacher Training Institutions

a) The Lejeune Plan

It was to Father Lejeune's credit that a new impulse was given to the formal training of teachers for Catholic schools at the beginning of this cen-

---

[36] Cf. J. Jordan, *Bishop Shanahan*, p. 82.
[37] CSE: 191/B/VI, J. Shanahan, "Training School for Southern Nigeria," 6 May, 1910.

tury. Shocked by the idea of Catholics employing Protestant teachers in their schools, he strongly recommended the provision of a Catholic "High School" for the training of teachers. In a moving letter to the Propaganda Fide in 1904, he gave a serious thought to the problem:

> The Missions in Lagos and Sierra Leone are sometimes obliged to employ Protestants in their schools. This is an error and a pity!
>
> Not one of the [Catholic] Missions in the English territories of West Africa educates its pupils beyond the primary school.
>
> When I look at Sierra Leone, Ivory Coast, Benin, and Nigeria..., I see at least five Black Anglican Bishops—Johnson, Oluwole, Phillips, Smith, Crowther, the latter being a former Yoruba slave; I see a number of Black medical doctors, barristers, magistrates with degrees from Oxford and Cambridge, but I do not see a single Black Catholic priest, and not even a Seminarian. At least some efforts are being made in the French colonies, but in the English territories—nothing![38]

Lejeune's observations in this report are centered on two main issues: the absence of Catholic post-primary education in Nigeria and its consequences, and the lack of Catholic initiative in the English colonies to provide for a native clergy. Discussions on the second issue shall be carried out in a later chapter. With regard to the first point, it was clear to the Prefect that the absence of a Catholic Secondary Institution was hampering the progress not only of Catholic adherents in their struggle with their Protestant counterparts over social positions in the Colony, but also of the Mission itself. "It is the reason why everything is vegetating," he said in another letter, and regretted that "the Wesleyans, the Presbyterians, the Anglican Church are all in all."[39]

This Protestant superiority was particularly pronounced in the Western region of Nigeria. As the Reverend Metcalfe Sunter, Inspector of Schools for the Lagos Colony, discovered during his inspection of the Catholic Boys' High School in Lagos, the success of Catholic educational enterprise in the late nineteenth century depended, as it were, on the availability of competent Protestant schoolmasters. "I trust this school may become more of a useful reality than it seems to be at present," he wrote, and sincerely asked: "Could not one of the 'Christian Brethren' or some trained man, be found to supervise the Catholic schools in Lagos?"[40]

---

[38] CSE: 192/A/V, "Lejeune to Propaganda Fide," Calabar, 20 October, 1904. It is noteworthy that Lejeune did not include Eastern Nigeria among the Missions which were obliged to employ Protestant teachers in their schools. By the time he wrote his report, he had succeeded in halting the practice in his Prefecture.

[39] CSE: 192/A/IV, "Lejeune to the Directors of Propaganda Fide," Calabar, 20 October, 1904.

[40] SMA: 14/80205, 1887, M. Sunter, "First Inspection of Schools Under the Ordinance of 1887," Lagos, 1887.

However, such well-meaning "ecumenical gestures" did not appeal to Father Lejeune who, with good reasons, saw the use of Protestant teachers in Catholic schools as a flawed policy. It was "an error" first and foremost with regard to the explanation of Catholic doctrines in the schools. The great value placed on the school in the propagation of the faith demanded that a man who professed Catholicism be made the custodian of Catholic doctrinal interests in the school, and not one who was fundamentally opposed to it.

Furthermore, it was "a pity" to engage teachers of alien denominations in Catholic schools because the Fathers had no other option open to them. By 1904, the Protestants had an uncontested monopoly of secondary education in West Africa. The wellspring of their post-primary schools and Teacher Training Institutions was Fourah Bay College, which was founded in 1827 in Freetown, Sierra Leone by the Church Missionary Society. From the time of its foundation till 1950, about 50 per cent of its student population either came from Nigeria or had Nigerian backgrounds.[41] These Sierra Leonians, as the ex-students of Fourah Bay College were styled, formed the majority of the Nigerian educated elite, and contributed immensely to the development of secondary education in the country.[42] Their impact on education in Nigeria had an important bearing on the comfortable lead of the Protestants in the possession of qualified teachers, especially in Western Nigeria.

Since Father Lejeune resented the idea of sending Catholic pupils to Protestant post-primary schools, he proposed, shortly after his arrival on the Niger in 1900, to Bishop Gorman of Sierra Leone the foundation of a joint Catholic High School for the pupils of the two Missions, the Vicariate of Sierra Leone, and the Prefecture of the Lower Niger.[43] Emphasis was to be laid on the training of teachers, and the preparation of priest candidates. For some undeclared reasons, Bishop Gorman did not so much as give a reply to Lejeune's letter. However, the records show that the bishop may not have found favour with the idea of a joint High School, for by June 1905 he was getting ready to open his own High School, the Father Brown Memorial School.[44] When no positive response was made to his proposal, Father Lejeune concentrated his efforts on the

---

[41] Cf. A. B. Fafunwa, *History of Education*, p. 139.

[42] For the importance of the Sierra Leonians for Christian evangelism in West Africa, see: A. F. Walls, "A Christian Experiment: The Early Sierra Leone Colony," *The Mission of the Church and the Propagation of the Faith*. Studies in Church History, Vol. 6, ed. G. T. Cuming (Cambridge: The University Press, 1970), pp. 107-129; A. F. Walls, "Black Europeans, White Africans," pp. 339-348.

[43] See CSE: 191/B/VI, Shanahan, "Training School for Southern Nigeria," Onitsha, 6 May 1910, p. 1.

[44] See CSE: 200/A/II, "Gorman to LeRoy," Sierra Leone, 16 June, 1905.

prospects of founding a Training Institution at Calabar. But his premature death in 1905 left Shanahan, his successor, with the difficult task of executing this plan.

b) Controversy over the Calabar "High School"

The question of establishing a Catholic "High School" or "Training Institute" at Calabar for a post-primary education was, perhaps, the most prolonged controversy in the history of the Lower Niger Mission, lasting from 1903 to 1911. In many letters and reports to Paris and Rome, Shanahan endeavoured, like Lejeune did before him, to convince his superiors of the necessity of having a Catholic High School in which teachers would be trained. This had become absolutely necessary in order not to be thrown out of the all-important educational contention in Nigeria. In the main, three problems had to be solved before the project could be a reality, namely, the assurance of an adequate financial backing, the provision of a Father or Brother with a B.A. or B.Sc. to head the school, and the approval and support of the Mother House in Paris. The third problem, on which the solution of the first two depended, was paradoxically the hardest to solve. Mention has often been made in the preceding chapters of the marked disinclination of the authorities in Paris to follow the pace of the educational movement in Nigeria. It was an attitude which featured most prominently in connection with the proposed Calabar High School. In a particularly striking manner, it demonstrated the general contention that the true judgment of the actual state of affairs in any Mission land belonged to the Mission head—the Apostolic Prefect or Vicar—and not the Superior General.

In 1910, Shanahan risked a plunge in the dark by declaring at a general meeting of the Provincial Board of Education, of which he was a member, that the Catholics would have a Training Institute by the end of the year. Afterwards, he explained to his enraged Superior General that his action was merely a bluff. According to his own report, the Presbyterians at the Board meeting had namely "boasted" that they were going to build a Training Institute, and that half of the money required for the project was already at their disposal. "Accustomed though I am to the bluff of the Protestants," he said, "it appears to me that there are moments when it is necessary not to hesitate paying them back bluff for bluff."[45]

To the extent that Shanahan's declaration of intention was ostentatious, it nevertheless reflected the mind of someone acting in despera-

---

[45] CSE: 191/B/VI, Shanahan, "Training School for Southern Nigeria," 6 May, 1910.

tion. For five years, he had endeavoured to emphasize the fact that the Catholic Mission in Eastern Nigeria would survive only by possessing a post-elementary institution. That the Catholic schools did not get "killed" by the 1908 Education Code was, as has been seen, due largely to his own personal influence in the Provincial Board of Education. But he was aware, like every other school proprietor in Nigeria, that the slackening of government insistence on the use of certificated teachers was only temporary. By 1910 he had become so frustrated by the hesitation of the Mother House to come to terms with the predicaments of the Mission that he threatened, at the beginning of the year, to resign his office as Prefect and return to Europe.[46]

The personal reports of Fathers Léna and Lichtenberger to the Superior General in support of a "High School" seemed to have had a great impact on Paris. As has been seen, the Superior General had demanded the opinions of Fathers Léna and Lichtenberger on the idea of having a post-primary school in the Mission. His choice of these two Fathers was significant: they belonged to the Mission Council, and Shanahan was often blamed for putting through his educational policies without consulting its members. Furthermore, the Superior seemed to have put the international composition of the Mission into consideration. It was clear that Shanahan would, and did, speak the mind of the Irish; Léna was expected to give the opinion of the French missionaries, and Lichtenberger, that of the Germans. In a rare consensus where the interest of the Mission was placed above national whims, all the Fathers agreed that a High School was absolutely necessary, and that an Irish Father with a B.A. or B.Sc. was the best possible Director for it.[47] This common and democratic decision, and the public declaration by the Prefect about the imminent availability of a Catholic Training Institution had no small influence on the authorities in Paris. For after years of hesitation and detailed scrutiny, the Mother House finally granted permission and money for a "High School" in September 1910. In Shanahan's words, it was "the most superb of the things done by the Superior, since it corresponded with the twenty-fifth anniversary of the foundation of the Mission."[48]

The next question was what to make out of the proposed "High School"—a Secondary school or a Training School? Ever since the days of Lejeune, the names "High School" and "Training Institution" had

---

[46] See CSE: 192/B/VI, "Shanahan to Superior General," Calabar, 18 January, 1910: "Je prie que la chose s'arrange sans que je dois obligé de quitter Nigeria."
[47] See CSE: 192/B/VI, "Léna to LeRoy," 18 March, 1910; see also CSE: 191/B/V, "Report by X. Lichtenberger," 1 April, 1910.
[48] CSE: 192/B/VI, "Shanahan to LeRoy," Onitsha, 27 September, 1910.

been used synonymously when talking about a Normal School for teachers. This is hardly surprising since almost all post-primary institutions at that time were concerned, in one way or the other, with the training of teachers. However, by 1910 the name "Training Institution" had been restricted to any College, School, or Institute in which candidates for the teaching profession were instructed in specifically prescribed subjects. After long considerations, Father Shanahan decided to establish a Training College for teachers, instead of a Secondary School.

For his part, Father Léna, the Head of the Calabar Mission, was strongly in favour of a Secondary School. Despite his support for a Training Institute, he nevertheless had the following remark to make to the Superior General:

> I hope that I have answered the different points of Your Majesty's [enquiry]; however I must assert that I was surprised to be obliged to give my opinion on a *Training School*. At the time Father Shanahan wrote to you, he was here at Calabar, and we talked about a Secondary School. This school would, in my opinion, be more advantageous....
>
> After having proposed a Secondary School, Father Shanahan later proposed a Training College. The ideal thing would be to have both.[49]

Father Léna's option would certainly have been the best thing for Nigeria: it would have, at a very early stage, brought native attention on the local Church and her problems. As has been seen, Lejeune's primary objective in having a post-primary institution was, besides the training of teachers, the formation of Seminarians. In pursuit of that same goal, Father Léna rightly argued that a Secondary School offered the best prospects for a Junior Seminary. His main contention was that since the subjects taught in a Secondary School included Latin, French, Mathematics, and Elementary Science, it would be practicable to send priest candidates to a school of that nature. Furthermore, he argued that the Fathers, who had been trained according to the curriculum of French Junior Seminaries, would be able to teach easily in Secondary Schools after having learnt English.

By contrast, Shanahan's Training College-cum-Seminary plan for a native clergy contained a very vague feasibility. Not only was the programme of a Training College too specialized, it was also subjected to frequent changes from the Colonial Education Department. By 1933, it had become clear that a Teacher Training College with a Seminary was an awkward combination. With the establishment in that year of the first Secondary School in the Vicariate—Christ the King College—the real

---

[49] CSE: 192/B/VI, "Léna to LeRoy," Calabar, 18 March, 1910.

union which had been advocated by Father Léna in 1910 was finally made.

However, it must be conceded that many irresistible forces played on Shanahan's decision to found a Training School in the place of a Secondary School. In fact, he was equally well disposed towards the latter school, seeing in it an essential factor in the important question of a native clergy. Although no explanation was given for his sudden change of mind, two major considerations must have influenced his option for a Training School. The first would be financial. Whereas the highest government grant to a Teacher Training Institution was £15 for each student, it was only £3. 8s for a Secondary School. By opting for a Training School, the Prefect must have wished to get the best out of government aid for education, and by so doing be financially independent of Rome and Paris, who had been very reluctant, in the past, to sanction his educational designs.

Secondly, Shanahan's preference for a Training school for teachers was a logical corollary to his educational ambition. The Education Code of 1908 had touched this ambition where it hurt most—the question of certificated teachers. For a man whose objective was to be right in the vanguard, the insistence of the Government on recognizing and aiding only schools with certificated teachers was nothing short of a catastrophe. He had no facilities for training certificated teachers, and the fear that the new measure was a government prescription for impotence in Catholic schools loomed large in his mind:

> I have already said it many times, all the other denominations have already got their Teacher Training Institutions. We alone have nothing. But I want to go much further [than the others]. By this Code, we are directly being aimed at.[50]

Given this special predicament of the Catholic schools, it was plausible that the Prefect should give priority to a Teacher Training School in order to avert the danger once and for all. He was able afterwards to meet the great demand for teachers.

The much publicized Calabar High School finally took off in 1911 in a much humbler form than was originally envisaged.[51] Instead of establishing a Training Institution with an independent existence, a *High School* was made out of the existing Calabar primary school by the addition of a special course for teacher candidates. This arrangement was possible by virtue of a major concession in the Education Code. Becoming law in 1911, the Code had removed a sting in its former prescription

---

[50] CSE: 192/B/VI, "Shanahan to LeRoy," Calabar, 18 January, 1910.
[51] See CSE: 191/B/VI, "Léna to LeRoy," Calabar, 8 July, 1911.

by granting the Voluntary Agents the freedom to train their own teachers in the Central Schools, provided that certain conditions were fulfilled. The most important of these conditions was the engagement of a certificated Principal Teacher. Having been awarded honorary certificates in 1907, Fathers Léna and Krafft were already teaching in the Calabar school as Principal teachers. Since Catholic authorities considered the government Teacher Training School at Bonny to be too expensive, and since they would not want to have anything to do with the Presbyterian Hope Waddell Training Institute, they decided to start a special course for teachers at the Calabar Central School in 1911.

Meanwhile money from Paris and from the Colonial Government was put into the construction of a building worthy of the new status of the school. This objective having been achieved, the school was officially opened on 7 June, 1913, with a festivity that was very rare at Calabar. There was now enough room for a total of 600 pupils, fifteen of whom were said to be following a post-primary course for teachers which included French and Latin.[52]

The special class for teachers comprised chiefly school children who had spent the last two years of their primary education as Pupil Teachers. Recognized as Assistant Teachers, they were required to teach while in training. The course lasted for five years, at the end of which the successful candidates became certificated teachers.[53]

In justifying the establishment of a "High School" at Calabar, Father Shanahan emphasized a most familiar driving force in Catholic educational policy—the urge to achieve parity with the Protestants. In order to give Catholic pupils a chance of doing their post-primary education, it was necessary, he argued, to have a school comparable to those of the Protestants.[54] However, the Calabar "High School" would easily have become a match to the famous Protestant Institutions like Hope Waddell and Fourah Bay College if the Prefect had followed his original plans. But there are indications that he had, by 1911, had a second thought about Calabar remaining the principal centre of Catholic education in the Prefecture. In that year, he had written to the Superior General complaining about Father Léna's dampened enthusiasm over a High School at Calabar. "Some time ago," he said, "it was the High School that was the talk of the day. Now that the desired object is at hand, he wants nothing more other than to be preoccupied with the building of a

---

[52] See CSE: 191/B/VI, J. Shanahan, "Report on the New School at Calabar," Onitsha, 21 June, 1913; see also CSE: *Bulletin*, 27 (1913-1914), 203.

[53] Cf. "Höhere Schule in Kalabar," *Echo aus den Missionen der Väter vom Heiligen Geist*, 15 (1914), 150-152.

[54] CSE: 192/B/VI, "Shanahan to LeRoy," Onitsha, 27 November, 1912.

church.''[55] For a second time since 1910, Shanahan called for a separation of the Calabar Mission from the rest of the Prefecture. Given this disposition, it was no wonder that he reserved for the Onitsha district his long-standing conception of a respectable Catholic post-primary Institutionone run by a Principal Teacher who possessed a B.A. or B.Sc. honours.

c) Teacher Training Colleges

The first Catholic Teacher Training College was established at Igbariam in 1913. The Annual Report on the Education Department, Southern Provinces, for 1916 gave only two Training Colleges on the Assisted List—Igbariam and the Hope Waddell Training Institute. Among other things, it said that the Igbariam Training College was established in 1915.[56] This was, no doubt, the date the College was taken into the Assisted List, and not the foundation date. The College was under construction in 1912, and in August 1915 Shanahan wrote that "fourteen excellent young men" were passing their "second year" in the College.[57] The end of 1913, therefore, was the actual starting date of the Training College.[58] It was run by capable Irish Fathers, first by Father T. O'Connor, and later by Father G. O'Sullivan.

It was at Igbariam that some privileged pupils of the Prefecture were called "Students" for the first time.[59] It was also there, more than in any other Mission, that the saying that the Missions produced teachers who were more of theologians than schoolmasters was given a sound justification. According to Shanahan, the first priorities in the new College were discipline, character formation, religious and moral education.

To a large extent, Igbariam represented the first honest attempt to form capable Africans to relieve the European missionaries of their most important activity in the Mission—the supervision of schools. This intention was given expression in the following report:

> [From] this elite class of young men, we hope to select and specially form some true Inspectors. These Inspectors, possessing a knowledge of the sacred and profane sciences that is above the average, shall be placed at the service of the principal stations. Some experiments have already been made, this encouraging us to put the project under way. It shall be a considerable relief for the Father to have these devoted and educated scouts.

---

[55] CSE: 192/B/VI, "Shanahan to LeRoy," Calabar, 29 April, 1911.
[56] See PRO: C.O.657/5, "Sessional Papers, No. 8 of 1916," *Education Annual Reports for 1916.*
[57] CSE: 192/B/VII, "Shanahan to LeRoy," Onitsha, 24 August, 1915.
[58] Compare, J. Jordan, *Bishop Shanahan,* p. 110.
[59] See CSE: *Bulletin,* 29 (1918-1920), 199.

In a word, they shall fulfil the role of our young apostles of Europe. This is not a mere vision, nor a fugitive idealism....

Yesterday we longed to have Catechist-teachers capable of replacing the Father in the school: Igbariam has produced them. Today we require Catechist-missionaries; tomorrow Igbariam shall, by the continued support of Divine Providence, provide them to double the efficacy of the work of missionaries.[60]

Although the Igbariam Training College had such good promises for the future, it was short-lived, lasting from 1913 to 1918. The scarcity of qualified personnel kept enrolment down to a bare minimum, the number rising from fourteen students in 1915 to seventeen in 1916. By 1917, Father T. O'Connor was alone in the College, following the departure of Father O'Sullivan on health grounds. The Government offered to prop up the staggering establishment on two conditions: firstly, that the number of students be raised to thirty-six, and secondly, that two Fathers with the required academic qualifications be resident in the College. Since none of these conditions could be fulfilled, the College was closed down in 1918. For a decade thereafter, the training of certificated teachers was carried out only in the central schools, especially at Onitsha-Ogboli, Emekuku, and Calabar.

A major turning-point in the history of Catholic Training Colleges was necessitated by the Education Ordinance of 1926. Desirous of a greater control of schools in Southern Nigeria, the Government introduced on 26 May 1926 some changes which, like in previous Education Codes, laid emphasis on the qualification of teachers. The most remarkable of these changes was the requirement that teachers be registered in order to be allowed to teach in any school. This register was to be kept in three parts, part "A" for certificated Teachers, part "B" for Technical Teachers, and part "C" for Uncertificated and Probationary Teachers. Furthermore, the teaching of English in all standards, including the lowest, was made the prerogative of only the pupils who have passed a special examination for teachers. According to Catholic estimates, there was little likelihood that more than 50 per cent of the pupils trained in Catholic Central Schools would have been able to pass this examination.[61] The danger for Catholic schools of this possibility was particulary grave because of their known record of heavy involvement with the English language. Consequently, it was considered expedient to resuscitate the ill-fated experiment on a Teacher Training College.

By 1928, a Teacher Training College—St. Charles College—was already in operation at Onitsha-Ogboli. It had thirty-two students, and

---

[60] CSE: *Bulletin*, 29 (1918-1920), 199-200.
[61] Cf. J. Jordan, *Bishop Shanahan*, p. 247.

among the teaching staff were Fathers Richard Daly, who was the Principal, MacCloskey, James Hagan, and two senior Seminarians. Later, the management of the College was handed over to a group of Franciscan Brothers.

To qualify for admission into St. Charles' Training College, the pupils, most of whom had had some previous teaching experience, were required to pass a special entrance examination. After a four-year course in the College, the students sat for a Government Teachers' Higher Certificate Examination. The successful candidates became Higher Elementary Teachers, and were entitled to teach in the upper classes of primary schools.[62]

No sooner did the realization of a Training College for Higher Elementary Teachers become a reality than a new education crisis threatened to ruin the whole effort: Mr. E. R. J. Hussey became the Director of Education in 1929, and in Catholic opinion, his avowed objective was "to overthrow everything his predecessor had done."[63] The most controversial of the new changes introduced by Hussey was the reorganization of the school system in Nigeria.[64] Prior to 1929, the duration of primary education was eight years, Classes I and II for Infants, and Standards I to VI. On assuming office, the new Director proposed a limitation of Primary education to six years, a measure that foresaw standard IV, and not VI, as the ultimate goal of primary education. The former standards V and VI were to be converted into secondary school grades called Lower Middle Schools. To Mr. Hussey's reorganization of the school system we shall return; for the moment let us consider the new elements he introduced into the training of teachers, and Catholic reaction to them.

d) Elementary Training Centres

In order to focus the interest of the school children on their local environments, Mr. Hussey proposed the establishment of Elementary Training Centres in which precedence would be given to practical train-

---

[62] Cf. ODA, S. Milburn, Chief Inspector of Education, Eastern Provinces, "Inspection Report on St. Charles' Training College, R. C. M., Onitsha," Enugu, 27 August, 1945. According to this report, there were 153 Students in the College in 1945, distributed in two groups of each stream, except the second year, which had only one group. The average size of each class was 20.

[63] CSE: 554/VII, "Etat Statistique Annuel pour la Propaganda Fide," 1 December, 1929.

[64] The new changes applied to the whole of Nigeria because in July 1929, the new Director had united the hitherto separate Education Departments of Northern and Southern Provinces under one Department.

ing in such subjects as Agriculture, Handicraft, and Hygiene. Furthermore, he insisted that teachers for Middle Schools be trained only in
quasi-universities known as Higher Colleges, which were to be provided
by the Government. However, the Voluntary Agencies were reluctant to
follow his scheme, and in 1935, the Director conceded that for many
reasons, it would take a long time before the measure could be "universally applied."[65]

For the Catholics in Eastern Nigeria in particular, Hussey's scheme
was extremely unpopular for two main reasons. In the first place, their
only Teacher Training Institution, St. Charles' College, Onitsha, had
been conceived chiefly for Higher Elementary Teachers in the former
eight-year primary school system. It therefore had no facilities that were
comparable to those of the proposed new Elementary Training Centres.
Secondly, since there were, by 1930, no Catholic Secondary Schools in
Eastern Nigeria, the Catholics found it much harder than the Protestants
to carry out Hussey's reorganization plans. To be on the safe side, however, they were wise to prepare for the eventuality of a binding order
from the Government. Accordingly, a decision was made at a general
meeting of all the Fathers of the Vicariate at Ihiala in 1929 to start special
courses at St. Charles' Training College in January 1930 for elementary
school teachers.[66] But, as we shall see later, this statement of intent did
not become a reality until 1947.

Catholic prejudice over Elementary Training Centres was tempered in
the 1930s, following the adverse effect of the World Depression on
Nigerian economy. The optimistic government education plan of 1926,
which had promised massive grants-in-aid on a scale that was commensurate with the economic prosperity of the country, had become abortive
in the 1930s. Consequently, the educational efforts of the Voluntary
Agencies were placed in jeopardy. Table 4 shows a conspicuous decline
in Catholic schools in 1932. The most painful aspect of this educational
set-back was the steady decrease in the number of certificated teachers
throughout the 1930s. By 1938, this decline had attained alarming proportions, with more than half the certificated teachers in the Owerri Province, and about one-third in the Enugu and Onitsha districts, resigning
from the mission service.[67] A good majority of those who drifted away
from the teaching profession were Higher Elementary Teachers, who not

[65] E. R. T. Hussey, "Some Aspects of Education...," p. 16.
[66] CSE: 554/I, "Minutes of the Fathers' Meeting Held at Ihiala after the Annual
Retreat," 11 November, 1929.
[67] See CSE: 556/VII, J. Jordan, Catholic Education Adviser, "Organization of
School Effort: Circular to Managers, Supervisors, and Principals," Onitsha, 15 July,
1948.

only were not paid on their appropriate scales, but also saw their salaries drastically reduced.

With little or no aid coming from the Government, the Catholic authorities found it unprofitable to insist on training only Higher Elementary Teachers, whom they were no longer able to pay. They discovered, on the contrary, that it was not only cheaper, but also easier to get involved with Elementary Training Centres, where students got only two years of training and yet were recognized as certificated teachers. Furthermore, in view of renewed Catholic efforts to organize more village schools, it was conceded that the training given in government Elementary Training Centres was best suited to the needs of rural communities. At a Conference of the Nigerian Ordinaries in 1937, it was therefore recommended that the Missions ought to "keep closely to Government policy in giving this kind of training, and should even take the initiative in the matter."[68]

Table 4

Catholic Education under Bishop Shanahan 1921-1932

Year	Pupils	Teachers	School-Churches
1921	41,455	927	721
1924	41,050	1,178	1,026
1929	37,275	1,947	1,403
1932	30,390	1,773	1,386

Source: J. Jordan, *Bishop Shanahan of Southern Nigeria*, p. 140.

Accordingly, a Catholic Elementary Training Centre was established at Okpala at the end of 1937 in order, as it was put, "to meet the new requirements of Government for rural education."[69] The decision to embark upon the project rested, however, on a faint hope that the Government would eventually provide a building grant. But when no such aid was forthcoming, the Centre was quickly closed down in 1939. In his letter of explanation to the Assistant Director of Education, Bishop Heerey revealed that financial considerations were, beyond any doubt, responsible for the premature termination of the Catholic educational venture at Okpala:

---

[68] CSE: 554/II, "Extracts from the Minutes of the Meeting of the Ordinaries of Nigeria, 1937," p. 9.
[69] CSE: 556/I, "Bishop Heerey to Cardinal Fumasini-Biondi, Prefect of Propaganda Fide," Onitsha, 3 September, 1937.

If there were any hope of a building grant even in the distant future I would not have taken this decision, but the present world crisis completely dispels this hope.

Sometime in the future when the world returns to normal we shall give it another trial.[70]

However, even as the Bishop was writing his report, the world was set for yet another round of abnormality—the Second World War. On account of the decimation of the European teaching staff in Nigeria during the war, nothing tangible could be done for the training of teachers.

The post-war years were a period of unprecedented boom in teacher training facilities. Conceived at the end of 1929, the plan to introduce in St. Charles' College a professional course of two years which corresponded to the type given in Elementary Training Centres was finally executed in January 1947. In that same year, a separate Catholic Elementary Training Centre was also put under construction in Orlu to take in students who had finished their Middle VI in Catholic secondary schools. The Training College was opened in January 1948.[71] The beginning of 1949 saw the opening of two Elementary Training Colleges at Nsukka (St. Theresa's), and at Agulu (St. Anthony's). Assisted by Father J. Halpin, Father W. Butler, hitherto a staff member of Christ the King College, directed the College at Nsukka, while Fathers A. Chamberlain and Horkin were assigned to Agulu. Both Colleges were officially approved by Paris on 3 January 1950. In the Owerri district, a College was also established at Azaraegbelu in 1949, the Mount St. Mary's Teachers' College. Fathers P. Gallagher and W. Mackenna were the first European staff of the new College.[72]

The enormous achievements made in training facilities for women shall be treated in a later chapter. For the moment, it suffices to say that the emphasis placed on practical skills in education was strongest in Catholic Training Centres for women. This was due principally to the extraordinary efforts of European Sisters, especially at Calabar and Onitsha.

---

[70] ODA: "Heerey to Assistant Director of Education," Onitsha, 15 September, 1939.

[71] See ODA: J. Jordan, Education Adviser, "Circular to all the Secondary Schools," Onitsha, 7 October, 1947.

[72] The new residence at Azaraegbelu was officially approved by Paris on 16 September 1950 together with Sacred Heart Nguru, where Father A. Stiegler was assisted by an African priest, Father D. Panaki. Surprisingly, the residence at Nguru was authorized a second time on 11 December 1951 together with some other new residences in the new Diocese of Owerri. This time, the Nguru Parish got the name St. Charles'. It is noteworthy that the parish church at Nguru still bears a large painting of the Sacred Heart in front of the sanctuary—a lasting vestige of the former parish Patron.

In spite of the colossal strides which teacher training had taken in the late 1940s, the acute shortage of certificated teachers persisted for the next decade. In 1958, for instance, it was estimated that of the eighteen thousand teachers in Archbishop Heerey's metropolitan See only one-fourth were professionally trained. But thanks to the many established Training Colleges, as many as two thousand trained teachers were being reckoned with annually.[73]

Table 5

Higher Elementary Teachers in the Onitsha-Owerri Vicariate, 1938-1948

DISTRICT	1938	1942	1948
Enugu	25	31	40
Onitsha	45	50	60
Owerri	53	68	120

Source: CSE:556/VII, J. Jordan, "Organization of School Effort," Onitsha, 15 July, 1948.

Meanwhile, however, the authorities had to put up with a disastrous shortage in the number of Higher Elementary Teachers (H.E). Table 5 shows the growth of their number in the Onitsha-Owerri Vicariate from 1938 to 1948. During these years, the number of school children had risen by 100 per cent in almost all the centres. By contrast, except in the Owerri Province, the number of certificated teachers experienced a near stagnation throughout the Vicariate. Owerri could boast of a marked increase in the number of qualified teachers in 1948, thanks to the concentration there of Higher Elementary Teachers who had been trained at St. Charles' Onitsha. In the words of the Catholic Education Secretary, Owerri was a Province in which "pressure from the people was perforce a potent factor in determining the timing and location of Standard V and VI schools, and where the Church stood to gain or lose more through education than in any other Province."[74] For this reason, teachers that were actually trained for the Onitsha areas of the Vicariate were used to reinforce the vital educational struggle in the Owerri Province.

The repercussion of the shortage of Higher Elementary Teachers was the lowering of Catholic control over schools in the big cities. In Onitsha town, for instance, the Catholic share of education in 1948 was only 25 per cent, as opposed to 60 per cent in 1942. At the root of this dramatic

---

[73] ODA: "J. Jordan to Father Heinzman," Onitsha, 5 July, 1958.
[74] CSE: 556/VII, J. Jordan, "Organization of School Effort," 15 July, 1948.

weakening of Catholic educational hold on the cities was the inability of the authorities to admit hundreds of pupils to the meanwhile restored standards V and VI of the pre-1930 primary school system. The decision in the late 1940s to establish Elementary Training Centres instead of normal colleges for Higher Elementary Teachers rested on the belief that it was better in the long run to reduce the widening ratio of trained to untrained teachers in Catholic schools, a ratio which stood at 1 to 15 in 1948 in the Onitsha-Owerri Vicariate, the stronghold of Catholic education in all Nigeria. More Higher Elementary Teachers would, it was conceded, lead to expansion in the top classes, but Catholic schools as a whole would be predominantly staffed with untrained teachers. With many new certificated teachers passing out of the Elementary Training Centres, it was hoped that quality, not quantity, would be the hallmark of Catholic education in the 1950s and 1960s. The procedure and merit of this educational strategy were outlined in 1948 by the Catholic Education Secretary as follows:

> It is a pressing necessity...to supply our schools in all areas with sufficient certificated teachers for the top primary classes. This is essential. Yet it is not the final aim of present Mission policy. That aim must be the dilution of our teaching establishment by 50% certificated personnel within some twelve years. It may or may not be possible to stave off State control of education for that period. If it is, and if we succeed in reaching the 50% target, we shall be in a strong position to face State control, because the larger the number of qualified Catholic teachers in the schools, the greater our influence. Indeed, if our schools are in high regard for efficiency and tone we shall probably never lose full control of them.[75]

This judgment had all the elements of a prophetic insight: the State control of education dominated the political climate in Eastern Nigeria in the 1950s, and if the Regional Government was unable to put through its designs, it was largely as a result of the opposition from the strongest educational force in the region—the Roman Catholic Mission.

III. *Setbacks and Conflicts in the Teaching Field.*

1. *The Effects of the Two World Wars.*

Generally speaking, the First World War did not seriously impair the progress of the Mission. Nevertheless, it led to a considerable reduction of Catholic missionaries in Nigeria. In the Annual Report on the Education Department of Southern Nigeria for 1915, it was reported that "a

---

[75] CSE: 556/VII, J. Jordan, "Organization of School Effort," 15 July, 1948.

large proportion of the European staff of the Roman Catholic Assisted Schools had to leave the country for military duty."[76] This concerned chiefly the French Fathers, who were required by their Government to take up military services in France.[77] Furthermore, the Catholic Fathers and Brothers from Alsace who were of German origin were temporarily interned at the out-break of hostilities in 1914. But they were later released and allowed to carry out their duties without molestation, thanks to the intervention of Father Shanahan.[78]

The situation was not as sanguine during the Second World War. In 1940, some 36 German missionaries from the Prefecture of the Benue and the Cameroons were deported to Jamaica, Bishop Heerey of the Onitsha-Owerri Vicariate having being assigned the administration of the territories vacated by them a year before. This led to a considerable reduction of staff in the schools, so much so that the Bishop could not meet the demand of the Assistant Director of Education that Catholic teachers should help in the correction of the General Certificate of Education examination papers.[79]

As has been seen, the establishment of Teacher Training Colleges during the war years was seriously hampered by the scarcity of European missionaries. However, after the war, the Catholics, more than their Protestant counterparts, enjoyed a steady flow of European missionaries into Eastern Nigeria.

2. Manager-Teacher Tensions.

For many Nigerians, the State take-over of schools in 1970 is a crime whose atonement can only be assured by a return of the schools to the Voluntary Agencies. However, the only group of persons who are of a different opinion are the teachers. Eighteen years after mission management of education in Eastern Nigeria, their strong determination to oppose any idea of a return to mission education, or what, in their opinion, was a humiliating bondage, has not shown, and may not show, any signs of slackness. In fact, it has become customary for the federal and regional Governments to use this antipathetic attitude of the teachers

---

[76] PRO: C.O.657/3, Sessional Papers No. 13 of 1916, *Annual Report on the Education Department of Southern Nigeria for 1915.*

[77] The Fathers who left in this manner were: Léna, Delisle, Douvry, Grandin, Bindel, and Féral. See *Echo aus Afrika*, 28 (1916), 136-137.

[78] See CSE: 191/A/V, J. Shanahan, "The Missionaries from Alsace and Their Difficulties with the British Government During the First World War, 1914-1919," 20 March 1920; also CSE: 192/B/VII, "Shanahan to LeRoy," 9 January, 1915.

[79] ODA: "Heerey to Assistant Director of Education, Enugu," Onitsha, 18 September, 1939.

towards mission education as a justification of their continued refusal to return the schools to their former proprietors. Chief Jim Nwobodo, the Governor of the defunct civilian Government of Anambra State, claimed in 1981, for instance, that the teachers in his State "threatened a showdown if the schools were returned to their former owners." He therefore decided to retain them in order not to "disrupt the education system of the State."[80] Why, one may ask, do the teachers choose not to be one with the majority of their countrymen? How is it that the old wounds of the past are still very tender today? No one may be able to explicate adequately the complexities of the manager-teacher tensions of the mission era. But this should not preclude a humble attempt which purposes to do justice to the positions of both parties.

Dissension between teachers and School Managers may be traced to a number of causes, and among them, financial squabbles and the insistence of the Missions on a close supervision of teachers were, beyond doubt, the most prominent.

a) The Economic Factor.

Manager-teacher tensions assumed the dimension of open confrontation for the first time during the Prefectship of Father Lejeune, 1900-1905. A determining factor in Lejeune's revolutionary policy was his unwavering resolve to break the dependence of the people on the charity of the Mission by making them pay for their education. This policy brought him into conflict with the older generation of Catechist-teachers, who saw their age-long privileges directly threatened. A clear picture of Father Lejeune's financial squabbles with the Catechist-teachers, and of his revolutionary policy, can be seen in this report by him in 1904:

> The resources of the Prefecture do not permit us to maintain three Catechists at Ossomari, as was the practice in the past. They were paid between 35 and 100 francs a month.... At the moment we are keeping only one Catechist there who is paid £24 per annum on the condition that the inhabitants provide half of this salary. In this way, the natives shall appreciate more the blessings of education, and the Catechists themselves shall be obliged to keep a better watch over their conduct and their work.[81]

By 1904, the value of one British pound was approximately 25 French francs. That means that the lone Catechist at Ossamari in 1904 was, at £24 per annum, receiving half of the salary of the best paid Catechists who, with their 100 francs a month, were the first to be dismissed from

---

[80] Quoted in *The Nigerian Daily Times*, Monday, 5 January, 1981, p. 1.
[81] CSE: *Bulletin*, 22 (1903-1904), 788.

their jobs. Is it any wonder, therefore, that the Catechist-teachers had a most strained relationship with Father Lejeune? At a time when they were agitating for more pay, they were given the option to choose between drastic reductions of their salaries and dismissal from their cherished positions. Furthermore, they bitterly resented the idea of their salaries being made dependent on the benevolence of local communities.

Although Lejeune's policies were extremely unpopular, their results demonstrated in a most striking manner that the most hated Prefect of the Niger Mission was also a man of extraordinary foresight and originality. For within a short period of time, his revolutionary measures began to have important consequences for the set- up of Catholic education in Eastern Nigeria. Called upon to bear the cost of educating their children, the natives quickly met the challenge with enthusiasm. When, for instance, a Catechist was installed at Ndoni in 1904, the people gave him a present of 500 francs over and above their readiness to contribute to his monthly salary. The significance of that new gesture did not escape the careful judgment of the exhilarated prefect. "If they are donating," he wrote afterwards, "then it is a sign that they want to educate themselves, and that they value religion and the missionaries."[82]

Although the pay-rolls of the Catechist-teachers were, by modern standards, very modest, they constituted a perennial obsession for Mission leaders. Father Shanahan, Lejeune's successor, also grappled with that thorny problem. In 1905, for instance, he strongly criticized the Catechists for demanding a salary of £30 per annum. By 1907, he was spending £40 a month on the salaries of his Catechist-teachers, a burden which certainly had an important bearing on his decision in that year to dismiss many of the teachers suspected of doubtful character.[83]

The establishment of training colleges in later years added a new dimension to the strain in the alliance between School Managers and their teachers. To make sure that teachers trained in Catholic Colleges fully refunded the money spent on them, the Managers got them to make bonds with the Mission, in which they promised to be in the service of the Mission for a period of time which ranged from five to ten years. During this period, monthly fees were deducted from their salaries. Such arrangements, however justified, engendered deep-seated resentments. A realistic observation of a Church dignitary in 1929 conceded that to treat a native in this manner was to make an enemy out of him.[84]

---

[82] Ibid.
[83] CSE: 192/B/V, "Shanahan to LeRoy," Onitsha, 28 May, 1907.
[84] CSE: 554/V, J. Soul, "Report to the Superior General," Onitsha, 12 November, 1929. In 1937, the Catholic Ordinaries of Nigeria decided that the Bond with teachers trained by the Mission should be for eight years. Conscious of the unpopularity of this

The bond system was a measure which left the teachers little room for manoeuvres. To terminate this binding agreement with the Mission prematurely was to ask for an unfavourable "character" or discharge certificate from the School Manager, a thing which inevitably hindered re-employment in Government service or in another Mission. The case of one Mr. Agu may serve as a paradigm here for the nature of the predicaments of mission teachers. For some undisclosed reasons, the quick-spirited teacher showed his back on the Mission without counting the consequences. However, from a letter of a government official to Bishop Heerey, it becomes evident that Mr. Agu, and all those found guilty of similar behaviours, did not rank as wise men:

> Mr. Agwu [sic], lately teacher in St. Patrick's School, Enugu, has shown me your letter to him of March 25th, 1942, and inquires whether this sets up a bar to his employment in a Government Department. You know, of course, that Heads of Departments are not allowed to engage Mission teachers unless these have a discharge certificate from their previous employer.[85]

Bishop Heerey's reply to this letter did not contain any facts that the Director of Education was not already aware of. "No doubt," it said, "that you will understand how difficult it would be for us to keep our schools in any state of efficiency if our teachers are free to walk out as Mr. Agu has done without a moments notice."[86] The fear of losing their jobs and remaining unemployed afterwards usually made the teachers more or less resigned to their fate.

The main issue in the bond arrangement, however, was not so much an effort to enforce loyalty on the teachers as an imperative that came from financial exigencies. For a private agency that grappled with a financial burden that was obsessively present, to train teachers for several years only to set them free shortly afterwards to seek their fortunes elsewhere, was an insuperable challenge. No proprietor, however open-handed, could have done that without upsetting the ordered development of mission education.

b) The Close Supervision of Teachers.

Catholic education in Eastern Nigeria is best remembered in connection with the perfect machinery of supervision with which School Managers

---

measure, the Church leaders solicited the Government for its "sanction." Cf. CSE: 554/II, "Extracts from the Minutes of the Meeting of the Ordinaries of Nigeria, 1937," p. 21.

[85] ODA: "Mr. Baldwin, Assistant Director of Education, Southern Provinces, to Heerey," Enugu, 8 April, 1942.

[86] ODA: "Heerey to Assistant Director of Education," Onitsha, 12 April, 1942.

computed the efficiency of their teachers. This included, besides a training that emphasized discipline and hard work, a thorough control of class-work, organization of general meetings, conferences, and refresher courses. It was these measures, more than any other thing, that accounted for much of the success and quality of mission education.

Still, the lauded machinery of supervision did contain some excesses which greatly antagonized the teachers. Teachers were, for instance, not allowed to be absent from their stations, even on their free days, without the permission of the Father in charge. When schools closed for holidays, teachers were held back and given some duties to keep them busy, the idea being to ward-off idleness, or what was described as "a great moral danger to the station."[87]

If the restrictions on the personal freedom of the teachers were, in themselves, distasteful, some of the disciplinary measures employed to enforce them were simply outrageous. One such measure was the principle which said "no fees no salary." Put in other words, teachers were to receive no salaries if the pupils did not pay their school fees. Introduced in 1929 by Father Biéchy in the Uyo District, this measure had no other justification except an inordinate desire to exercise a perfect control over the teachers. "At present," wrote the Manager, "we have not got enough control or supervision to see what each Teacher has been doing during the month."[88] While conceding that the no-fees-no-salary principle was "very hard," Father Biéchy still carried it through, in spite of strong opposition from the enraged teachers. His argument was that the people would willingly pay their school fees if they were satisfied with the work of a teacher, and withhold them if they objected to his inefficiency. What this argument did not take into consideration, however, was the general knowledge that there were some other factors which did prevent the people from paying their school fees, such as poverty. In that case, even teachers who had done their duties well and had kept all the rules still got no guarantee for their livelihood.

The controversial principle which said "no fees no salary" seemed to have fallen out of use too soon, for in 1930, a year after its introduction, it did not appear in the "General Notice to Teachers" issued by Father Biéchy. However, the teachers had no reason for jubilation: they still had to face drastic reductions of salaries in cases of indiscipline. According to the general notice, Head-Teachers disobeying any orders had their

---

[87] CSE: 554/V, "Decisions Made at the General Meeting of the Fathers Held at Onitsha Town after the Annual Retreat," 8 August, 1937.

[88] CSE: 191/B/VIII, "Biéchy to Shanahan," Anua, 31 July, 1929.

salaries reduced by seven and a half shillings, Sub-Teachers by five shillings.[89]

It was generally acknowledged that the life of a teacher was one of sacrifice and service. This credit was even given an official acclamation by the Nigerian Ordinaries in 1937. "Many of the...teachers," they conceded, "have given their lives to the service of the Mission, sometimes when they could have obtained good pensionable positions under Government."[90] Of all the Catholic leaders in Nigeria, if not in all Africa, Bishop Shanahan was, perhaps, the one who had the most elaborate dealings with native teachers, and for him they were simply "the real apostles of the people."[91] But, unfortunately, the teachers were not always given a treatment that was in tandem with this benign image they had in the Mission.

A factor of determinate significance in the manager-teacher tensions of the Mission days was the fact that the teachers were not accepted as equal partners in an alliance in which they played a vital role. Even some educational decisions that concerned them directly were often made without their knowledge. When, for instance, Mr. J. E. Odunjo founded a Catholic Federation of Teachers in 1937 to ensure a close liaison between Catholic teachers and the Nigerian Union of Teachers, which was predominantly Protestant in character, the Nigerian Ordinaries dissuaded Catholic teachers from joining it on the mere assumption that it might be used against the Mission.[92] This decision showed how unfortunate the exclusion of the teachers from the policy-making apparatus of the Mission was. Had some representatives of the teachers been consulted, they might have succeeded in convincing the Ordinaries that the Catholic Federation of Teachers in fact purposed, as one of its aims, to structure teacher-mission relations on friendly terms, and was therefore far from being reactionary. But for the Ordinaries, the traditional government-from-above relationship had a constraining priority over a Union whose constitution smacked of democracy. Accordingly, they strongly recommended, in the place of a Federation of Teachers, the organization of Teacher Congresses in which "instructions would be given by the Fathers on matters of importance and interest to the Teachers."[93]

---

[89] See CSE: 191/B/VIII, Father Biéchy, "General Notice to Teachers," Anua, 31 March, 1930.

[90] CSE: 554/II, "Extracts from the Minutes of the Meeting of the Ordinaries of Nigeria," 1937, p. 20.

[91] Quoted in J. Jordan, Bishop Shanahan," p. 155.

[92] CSE: 554/II, "Extracts from the Minutes of the Meeting of the Ordinaries of Nigeria," 1937, p. 20.

[93] Ibid.

Such patronizing arrangements developed, with the passage of time, an attitude in the Fathers which tended to degrade the personality and dignity of the teachers, an otherwise mature and critically minded group of persons. When a high-ranking Church dignitary made a tour of the Owerri and Rivers' provinces in 1948, for instance, he was shocked to notice in almost all the seventeen Missions he visited the same contemptible attitude of the Fathers towards their teachers. His message to the Fathers afterwards was: "Watch and watch over your teachers. Try to make of them helpers [in the ministry].... To correct a teacher in the presence of his pupils is unsound pedagogy."[94]

Such was generally the fate of the teachers in Eastern Nigeria: they found life much harder than ordinary Christians. But, a teacher in the Mission era was no ordinary Christian: he was more of a missionary than a school master. The school of the Mission era was the nucleus of the visible Church among a pagan community. It was there that the seed of the faith was sown, and, above all, it was to its teachers and catechists that the natives, most of whom were either neophytes or pagans, looked for guidance and inspiration. Was it any wonder, therefore, that the teachers were given a Seminary type of training, and expected to follow a standard of morality that was above the ordinary? The need to teach the people by good examples was of such overriding importance as to make the Fathers willing to employ any means in order to bring this about. Furthermore, whatever excesses the Fathers indulged in in their dealings with the teachers were always geared towards the achievement of efficiency in the schools. The general consensus today is that Mission education was of a first-class quality. That quality, it must be emphasized, had also its price—a very high price.

---

[94] CSE: 556/IV, "F. Griffin, Visitor, to the Fathers of the Owerri-Rivers Vicariate," 20 November, 1948.

CHAPTER FIVE

MISSION AND EDUCATIONAL ACTION

I. *The Burden of Proprietorship*

For the work of evangelization in Nigeria, the school was, in the words of Father J. Krafft, "the most appropriate and, unfortunately, the most expensive method."[1] There were teachers' salaries to be paid, buildings to be constructed, equipped, and maintained, and boarders to be fed. All these responsibilities, together with other huge expenditures connected with the management and coordination of schools, made the spiritual development of the people—the main objective of Christian evangelism—a very costly enterprise. Yet, the Catholic missionaries were not debarred from shouldering the burden of school proprietorship. We shall consider three great issues in that educational challenge—the financing of schools, the choice of subjects of instruction, and the organization of schools.

1. *The Financing of Catholic Schools*

The funding of Catholic educational effort in Eastern Nigeria was achieved through three main sources—Mission funds, local contributions, and government grants. Mission education, especially the advanced form it assumed after 1906, could not be thought of without any of these main sources, and for convenience, we shall discuss them separately.

a) Central Mission Funds

These came chiefly from overseas, namely, from Propaganda organizations in Europe with headquarters in Rome, from various other charitable organizations, such as the Anti-Slavery Society, the Sainte Enfance in France and the St. Peter Claver Sodality in Austria, and from direct appeals to private benefactors and parishes in Europe and America. These mission funds were particularly beneficial in the early years of the Christian Missions in Africa. Since the central funds from Rome came initially as 'anti-slave' funds, they enabled the Fathers to

---

[1] J. Krafft, "Aus der Mission von Calabar," in *Echo aus Afrika*, 19 (April, 1907), 130.

'buy' their pupils. These were then housed, fed, clothed, and educated gratuitously. The other funds were also employed in charitable works, often with the purpose of enticing the natives into the Christian flock. The poor went to the Missions not to give, but to be presented with clothing, medicine, and food. It was, in the words of Father Biéchy, "the golden age of the poor."[2] As we have seen in the preceding chapters, Father Lejeune forcefully put an end to that 'poor age' when he took charge of the Mission in 1900.

When the school finally triumphed as the best method of evangelization, the Mission's financial burdens became larger and heavier. Table 6 shows an interesting interchange of progression in the expenditure figures for 1889 and 1916.[3] Whereas the expenses on orphanages had declined in 1916, those on schools, an insignificant figure in 1889, had risen by an extraordinary proportion. In the same measure, appeals for aid from overseas were intensified, as this report from Father Krafft shows:

> The school has proved to be the best method of evangelization, so much so that nothing is going to stop us from establishing as many of them as possible, even at the risk of appearing too demanding in the eyes of our European benefactors.[4]

Table 6

Expenditures on Orphanages and Schools, 1889-1916

Year	Orphanage	School
1889	5,040 Francs	25 Francs
1890	5,540 Francs	250 Francs
1916	2,130 Francs	21,000 Francs

Source, CSE:192/A/II, and 192/A/IV, Statistics for the Sainte Enfance.

The contributions from overseas greatly lost their importance for primary schools after 1910, the natives and the Government having become the financial backbones for education in the colony. Thereafter, the Mission Central Funds were employed primarily for the maintenance of the increasing number of European missionaries, as is evident in Table 7. In an effort to get Paris send more missionaries to the Mission, Father

---

[2] CSE: 556/VII, P. Biéchy, "L'Organization du Denier du Culte et des Ecoles en Nigeria," *Extrait du Compte rendu de la ixe Semaine de Missiologie du Louvain*, (1931), p. 3.
[3] The statistics were compiled specifically for the Sainte Enfance, and it is not clear whether the expenditure included funds from other charitable organizations.
[4] J. Krafft, "Aus der Mission von Calabar," p. 132.

Shanahan claimed in 1905 that one European Father would cost the Mission "only a little bit more than a Catechist."[5] A comparison of the expenses on the maintenance of the thirty-four European missionaries in 1909—fifteen Fathers, twelve Brothers, and seven Sisters—with those on the upkeep of forty-two Catechists shows that the Prefect missed the mark by a very wide margin.

Table 7

Capital Expenditures of the Prefecture in 1909

Purpose	Amount in French Francs
Upkeep of European Missionaries (Including travel expenses)	36,569 F.
Maintenance of 42 Catechists	9,200 F.
Schools, Freed slave homes and Orphanages	7,340 F.

Source: CSE:192/A/V, Shanahan, "Report For Propaganda Fide, Rome," 1909.

There were two areas of huge expenditures which perennially worried the Prefects of the Mission, namely, the salaries of Catechists, and voyages of the missionaries to Europe, the former a particular misery for Father Lejeune, and the latter for Shanahan. In 1909, for instance, Shanahan complained to the Superior General about frequent trips to Europe of sick missionaries:

> I think that there are rather too many trips to Europe. The spirit of the governmental and commercial people has invaded us. Here, we have hospitals and medical doctors that are also as good as the ones in Europe. Furthermore, one no longer suffers from the privations of former days. I wish the missionaries would have the courage not to run away at the first stroke of discomfort or even illness of any kind.[6]

With the establishment of Teacher Training Colleges and Secondary Schools in later years, the Central Mission Funds were used in paying part of the salaries of white mission teachers. Table 8 shows the allowances of the expatriates in Catholic colleges in the 1940s. The various allowances were met on a 50/50 basis from Mission Funds and School Funds. The School Funds came from government grants, school fees, and local contributions. Since the missionaries lived in communities and did not keep private property, the school fund share of their salaries was paid into their community funds for their upkeep. The mission fund

---

[5] CSE: 191/B/IV, "Shanahan to LeRoy," Onitsha, 13 November, 1905.
[6] CSE: 192/B/V, "Shanahan to LeRoy," Onitsha, 9 December, 1909.

share was paid into a central fund called Mission Reserves. It was from this source that capital expenditures were made, such as travel expenses, extra spending on important constructions, and compensation for deficits in the funding of Unassisted Schools.

Worthy of note is the underlying significance of the Mission Reserves. Through a symbolic transformation, the Central Mission Funds, which were officially given as overseas contributions to the Mission, took the form of teachers' allowances, and finally emerged as Mission Reserves, a mutation which made apparent the central position of the school in the work of evangelization. Since the school was the chief activity of the missionary, it also served as a justification for his claim over mission funds.

Table 8

European Mission Teachers' Allowances

Grades of Teachers	Salaries per annum	Sources		
		Mission Funds	School Funds	
			Grants	Fees
	£	£	£	£
Graduate Principals	360	180	135	45
Graduate Assistants	300	150	90	60
Non-grad. Principals	300	150	135	15
Non-grad. Assistants	250	120	90	30

Source: ODA: R. Daly, "European Teachers' Allowances," Onitsha, 1941.

b) Local Contributions

A factor of great significance in the rapid expansion of schools was the willingness of the local communities to bear the cost of the education of their children. Ultimately, community effort emerged as the biggest and most important source of revenue for both government and mission schools. The means by which schools were financed by the natives varied from village to village, and from district to district. Nsukka and Nnewi were two typical regions of Eastern Nigeria where education was pursued with varying degrees of enthusiasm, the former being the most backward, and the latter the most progressive. Accordingly, the readiness of the natives to assume educational responsibilities was stronger at Nnewi than at Nsukka.[7]

---

[7] Cf. J. Jordan, "A Memorandum on the Financing of Catholic Primary Schools," in S. Phillipson, *Grants in Aid*, Appendix L. pp. 113-118.

Since the success of an educational venture depended, to a large extent, on the financial support of the local people, a village school was either run in an unsatisfactory manner, or left to collapse altogether wherever this support was lacking. In 1907, for instance, eight village schools in the sub-stations of Aguleri were abandoned when no money could be found to pay the salaries of the Catechist-teachers. In an effort to isolate the cause of that educational fiasco, Father Alphonse Bisch, the then resident Father at Aguleri, pointed out the practice by parents and guardians of sending their boys to the farms instead of sending them to school. To be more precise on the matter, Father Shanahan named other causes, two of which were significant, namely, the inability of the Mission to provide 300 francs monthly for the salaries of the Catechists, and the "refusal" of the eight villages in question to defray part of the cost of the salaries of their Catechists.[8]

The Mission and the people were in agreement to share equally the cost of engaging Catechists, and in this regard, both parties were indeed guilty of a breach of contract: the Mission could no longer pay its quota, and the people allegedly placed their farms above the school which they had asked for. However, there was much more to the people's alleged "refusal" to contribute for the upkeep of Catechists than a precedence placed on their farms. Beginning from 1906, the chiefs and elders of the people, who were in most cases still pagans, enthusiastically mounted the school stage wagon with the primary objective of exploiting the promises of education. Convinced that the school would bring progress and honour to their villages, they willingly financed it out of community funds. But suddenly they discovered that the school also brought something else to their villages—civil disobedience by the youth. Influenced by the Christian doctrines taught them at school, the children no longer took part in pagan rites and practices, and were prone to debase pagan sacred places. This factor was principally responsible for the decision of the pagan chiefs and elders to repudiate their educational commitments, a phenomenon which was discernible between 1907 and 1910 not only around Aguleri, but also in many other parts of the Prefecture.[9]

The 'unholy' alliance between the idol and the cross having been severed, there began an interim period in the financing of schools which was characterized by the determination of the youth to keep the schools in their villages functioning by bearing the financial burden which was once the responsibility of the whole community. By doing a variety of

---

[8] CSE: *Bulletin*, 25 (1909-1910), 366f.
[9] See P. Biéchy, "L'Organisation du Denier...," p. 6f.

petty jobs, they were able to procure the money necessary to keep the one-teacher schools alive.

The interim period was superseded by the "Christian era," the time when the Christians in a given village had sufficiently grown in number to finance their schools collectively. This they did through school fees, monthly and annual collections, proceeds from annual harvest, and various other means. The education funds which emerged from all these local contributions were particularly indispensable for the running of the Unassisted Schools, whose organization and financial management were entirely in the hands of the Missions. By contrast, they played a secondary role in the Assisted Schools, which were massively supported by the Government.

c) Government Grants-in-Aid of Education

The decisive criterion for government aid to Voluntary Agency schools was the efficiency of schools, which was determined first and foremost by the academic qualifications of the teachers, examination performances of the pupils, and the worthiness of school buildings and equipment. An Assisted School could get a grant-in-aid which ranged from 50 to 100 per cent, depending on the degree with which the conditions listed above were fulfilled. After official annual inspections, a school was declared to belong to any of the following classifications:

> "A + " (Excellent)   = 100 per cent aid.
> "A"   (Very Good)   = 80 ,,   ,,   ,,
> "B"   (Good)   = 70 ,,   ,,   ,,
> "C"   (Satisfactory)   = 50 ,,   ,,   ,,
> "D"   (Unsatisfactory) = 00 ,,   ,,   ,,

The "A + " classification was a coveted honour which was very rarely got by any school. The Calabar Convent School was about the only Catholic school in Eastern Nigeria to attain that goal. Under the able leadership of Sister Magdalene Walker, the school was classified as "A + " in 1926 primarily because of the innovatory Montessori method of education employed in it. As a general rule, Catholic central schools were usually classified as "A" and "B". In 1928, for instance, the Anua primary school was classified as "good," a grading which merited it a 70 per cent aid from the Government. Accordingly, it received £284 in grant-in-aid as part of the total expenditure of £365 it made that year.

However, it was not unusual for Catholic schools to be graded much lower than "A" and "B". In 1939, for instance, six Catholic Central Schools in the Onitsha-Owerri Vicariate got the classification "D". The

Central Schools in question were those in Ekeagu, Nsukka, Amawbia and Umuoji in the Onitsha Province, and Nsu and Port Harcourt in the Owerri Province.[10] Following the report of the government Inspector of Education, the then Catholic Supervisor of Schools, Fr. J. Jordan, took adequate measures to ensure improvements in the unfortunate schools.

As is evident in Table 9, government total expenditure on education before 1951 was, in comparison with the revenue allocated to other government departments and services, a mere triviality. This underlines the unduly long hesitation of the Colonial Administrations in Nigeria to assume educational responsibilities. In 1938, the Board of Education for the Colony and Southern Provinces conceded that Nigeria was "in the invidious position of providing fewer opportunities in regard to elementary education than any other British possession in Africa."[11] It was not until the late 1940s that the Government began to allocate a fair proportion of the national revenue to education. However, even in the days when education did not feature very prominently on the list of government classified duties, the meagre grants to the few Assisted Schools nevertheless boosted the educational efforts of the Voluntary Agencies. Later, Father J. Jordan, the long-time Education Adviser to the Catholic Missions of Nigeria, conceded that "without the state aid it would [have been] impossible for the Church to carry on."[12]

Table 9

Government Expenditure on Education in Nigeria, 1918-1952

Year	Expenditure on Education	Total Expenditure	% of Total Expenditure
	£	£	%
1918	45,747	3,459,774	1.0
1923	100,063	6,509,244	1.5
1925	116,301	6,136,621	1.8
1929	263,457	6,045,621	4.3
1933	237,732	6,898,816	3.3
1936	231,983	6,585,458	3.5
1939	282,820	6,576,835	4.3
1951/52	8,324,000	49,131,000	16.9

Source: J. S. Coleman, *Nigeria: Background to Nationalism* (Berkeley: Univ. of California Press, 1965), p. 126.

---

[10] ODA: Letter No. A. D. S.6914/38, "Acting Chief Inspector of Education, Southern Provinces, to Bishop Heerey," 11 August, 1939.

[11] Quoted in J. S. Coleman, *Nigeria*, p. 125.

[12] ODA: "J. Jordan to Father Heinzmann," Onitsha, 5 July, 1958.

For many decades, teachers in Voluntary Agency schools were paid on scales that were very much lower than in government schools and establishments. In an effort to redress this anomaly, the Education Ordinance of 1916 stipulated that about one-third of the grants to Assisted Schools be used to augment any salaries of teachers considered insufficient by the Director of Education. The Code of 1926 went a step further by laying down, to the chagrin of school Proprietors, the minimum wages which teachers in Assisted school may be paid. The rates were as follows:

Probationary Teachers	= £9	per annum.
Uncertificated Teachers	= £18 ,,	,,
Elementary Teachers	= £30 ,,	,,
Higher Elementary Teachers	= £40 ,,	,,

These scales were constantly revised and augmented in later years.[13] It must be recalled that many Higher Elementary Teachers resigned from mission service in the 1930s because the Proprietors could not pay them on their right scales.

Whereas the teachers in Assisted Schools benefited from government grants, those in Unassisted Schools—the bulk of the staff in Voluntary Agency schools—remained abandoned to their fate. Given the great importance of the Unassisted or "Mission" Schools for Catholic school offensive in the East, the authorities made relentless efforts to get government aid extended to them. It was in this regard that the Conference of Nigerian Ordinaries gladly endorsed in 1929 a resolution of the Le Zoute International Mission Conference of 1926 which had called on the Government to adjust its grant to aided schools in such a way as to help them attain the same measure of efficiency as obtained in government schools.[14] The primary objective of the Le Zoute resolution was to get the Government correct the practice by which teachers with the same academic qualifications were paid on different scales, depending on whether they were employed in government schools or in Voluntary Agency schools. But for the Catholic Ordinaries, the objective was much wider: whereas the International Conference spoke specifically of "aided schools," the Nigerian Ordinaries aimed at getting financial aid also for qualified teachers in the numerous Unassisted Mission Schools. Accordingly, their final resolution on the issue was presented as an addendum to the Le Zoute position:

---

[13] For the scales of 1947, see S. Phillipson, *Grants In Aid*, pp. 150-152.
[14] For the Le Zoute resolution, see E. W. Smith, *The Christian Mission in Africa: A Study Based on the Work of the International Conference at Le Zoute, Belgium* (London, 1926), p. 111.

In pursuance of [the] principles [of the Le Zoute recommendations] we claim that all qualified teachers, who have satisfied the Government test, should receive equal salaries from the Government according to the same scale, either native or non-native, irrespective of the school in which they are employed.[15]

However, since a major objective in its grant-in-aid policy was to reward efficiency in schools, the Government considered it inexpedient to give aid to Unassisted Schools, which were *unassisted* by virtue of their inefficiency. It was not until 1940 that some relief was provided for qualified teachers in this category of schools. In that year, the Government provided the sum of £26,000 to help the Voluntary Agencies pay their certificated teachers on the approved scales, thanks to the recommendation of the then Director of Education, Mr. E. G. Morris. However, this revolutionary measure was made *ad interim*, and concerned only certificated teachers, who formed an insignificant minority of all the teachers in Voluntary Agency schools.

In an effort to build the system of grant-in-aid on a more solid basis, and to induce the Missions to train their teachers, a Ten-Year Plan was also worked out in 1940 which proposed to pay 100 per cent of the salaries of teachers, a measure which would have changed the criterion for government grant from the efficiency of schools to the qualification of teachers. However, the plan was not ratified by London on the grounds that it would, among other things, weaken local initiatives in the funding of schools, and make the teachers less dependent on the Missions.[16] In 1942, the Colonial Administration under Sir B. Bourdillon made a compromise by allocating a special grant to meet the cost of living allowances of all grades of teachers employed in Voluntary Agency schools. For the first time, government aid was extended, however minimally, to thousands of probationary and uncertificated teachers in Unassisted Schools. However, that cost of living allowances, popularly known as *COLA*—meaning "favour" in a Nigerian context—was granted only after bitter struggles for wage increases by nationalist trade unions in 1941 and 1942.[17] Government grants to all schools on behalf of teachers increased considerably after 1950, and by 1960, the Government was meeting about 70 per cent of the total salary bills of the 30,000 teachers in Catholic schools.[18]

---

[15] CSE: 554/I, "Conference of the Ordinaries of Nigeria...1929," p. 12.

[16] See S. Phillipson, *Grants in Aid*, p. 36.

[17] See T. Hodgkin, "Background to Nigerian Nationalism," in *West Africa*, 18 August, 1951, p. 751.

[18] See J. Jordan, "Catholic Education and Catholicism in Nigeria," in *African Ecclesiastical Review*, 2 (1960), 61.

Of great importance to Catholic educational effort were also the special building and equipment grants from the Government. By the provision of the 1908 Code, up to one-half of the cost of school equipment, and one-third of the cost of new school buildings were paid by the Government. This was particularly helpful between 1911 and 1913, when the Catholic Mission grappled with unprecedented huge expenses on school buildings. It was at this period, for instance, that the Calabar "High School," the Igbariam Training College, and a large school building at Onitsha-Ogboli were simultaneously constructed.[19] Under the 1926 Code, the building and equipment grants were increased to cover half of the total expenditure on new Voluntary Agency schools. However, the World Depression of the 1930s made it impossible for the Government to meet its obligation in this regard. As we saw earlier, the Catholic Elementary Training Centre at Okpala was closed down in 1939 because no building grants could be expected from the Government. In 1942, the building and equipment grants were limited to only Secondary Schools and Teacher Training Colleges, and in that way, the huge expenses on the Catholic post-primary institutions constructed in the 1940s and 1950s were met.[20]

2. *The Subjects of Instruction*

a) Secular Subjects

In the main, the drawing up of educational programmes was the responsibility of the Colonial Government, whose primary concern was, for many decades, not so much to provide education as to guarantee the adequacy of what was provided by the Voluntary Agencies. More often than not, the tone of government despatches to the Colonial Office was one of criticism of mission education. There were endless reports of educational objectives which were excessively missionary in character, of teachers who lacked the skill to make meaningful interpretations of the issues treated in their subjects, and of pupils who tended to learn by rote. Such critical tones were very seldom heard in reports on other Departments and Ministries where responsibility rested solely on the Government. In other words, the Colonial Government in Nigeria recognized the Christian Missions as the principal educators of the people, provided that they proceeded on the lines carefully marked out for them. They

---

[19] See CSE: 192/B/VI, "Shanahan to LeRoy," Onitsha, 4 June 1912; also CSE: 192/B/VII, "Shanahan to LeRoy," 13 September, 1913.

[20] See ODA: "J. Jordan to Father Carroll," Onitsha, 23 December, 1947.

Fig. 3

The Funding of Catholic Schools in Graphic*

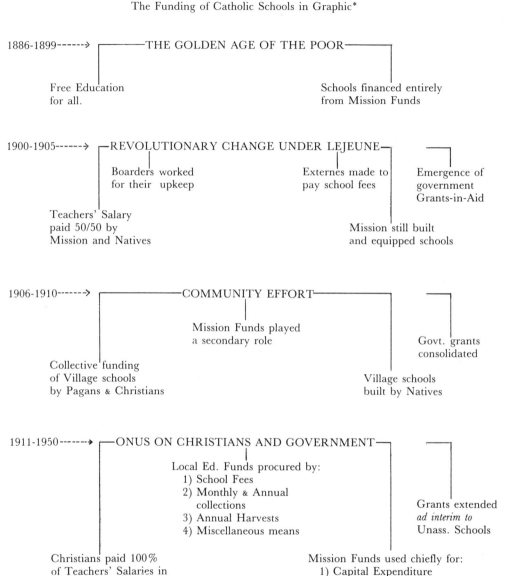

1886-1899------→ ┌────────THE GOLDEN AGE OF THE POOR────────┐

Free Education   Schools financed entirely
for all.   from Mission Funds

1900-1905------→ ┌─REVOLUTIONARY CHANGE UNDER LEJEUNE─┐   ┐

          Boarders worked   Externes made to   Emergence of
          for their upkeep   pay school fees   government
                                                           Grants-in-Aid
Teachers' Salary
paid 50/50 by   Mission still built
Mission and Natives   and equipped schools

1906-1910------→ ┌────────────COMMUNITY EFFORT────────┐   ┐

                    Mission Funds played
                    a secondary role
                                                           Govt. grants
                                                           consolidated
Collective funding
of Village schools   Village schools
by Pagans & Christians   built by Natives

1911-1950------→ ┌─ONUS ON CHRISTIANS AND GOVERNMENT─┐   ┐

                 Local Ed. Funds procured by:
                 1) School Fees
                 2) Monthly & Annual
                    collections
                                                           Grants extended
                 3) Annual Harvests   *ad interim to*
                 4) Miscellaneous means   Unass. Schools

Christians paid 100%   Mission Funds used chiefly for:
of Teachers' Salaries in   1) Capital Expenditure
Unassisted schools   2) Salaries of Expatriate
                                          Teachers in Colleges
                                       3) Deficits in Unass. schools.

* This graphic is only an approximation and should be read accordingly.

were obliged, within the grant-in-aid partnership, to follow programmes of education which were devised and supervised by the Government.

However, in its formulation of syllabuses for Nigerian schools, the Administration often portrayed heavy leanings on the curriculum of English schools, an attitude engendered by untoward patriotism and sustained by colonial ties. In the original draft of the first purely Nigerian Education Ordinance in 1887, for instance, the Lagos Colonial Administrators made no bones of their chauvinism by suggesting "History of England up to 1066" for Standard VII, "History of England from 1066-1660" for Standard VIII, and "History of England from 1666" for Standard IX. The Colonial Office rightly referred to these prescriptions as "absurd," and suggested in their place the history and geography of West Africa.[21] However, it was not until the 1930s that attempts were made to provide some treatment of Nigeria in school textbooks. In 1931, the history syllabus for primary schools prescribed for Class III the study of the indigenous life and government of Nigeria. The pupils of Class IV were required to have an elementary knowledge of the History of Nigeria under British rule. In 1932, the syllabus for the Middle Schools laid some emphasis on the history and geography of Nigeria.[22]

A factor of determinate significance in the choice of subjects of instruction was the availability in Nigeria of overseas examinations, especially the Cambridge and London local Examinations. In a measure designed to safeguard the reputation and quality of these English School-Leaving Certificates, the curriculum of Nigerian schools was carefully sculpted to fit the patterns followed in English Grammar schools. As a result, little or no room was left for manoeuvres with regard to the introduction of local elements in the syllabus for Nigerian schools. The effects on pupils of this educational aberration were considerable: it was not unusual to find school leavers who were at home with the names of major European cites, and who could quote freely from Shakespeare and the Bible, but who had no knowledge of the geography, history, and cultural backgrounds of their own country.[23]

It must be conceded, however, that the natives themselves were partly responsible for the defects in their system of education. Some critics have pointed out that the Africans did not avail themselves of the willingness of the overseas examination syndicates to make allowances for special

---

[21] See PRO: C.O.147/60, "A. Meloney to Colonial Office," Despatch attached to Education Ordinance, 1887.

[22] See P. Peshkin, "Education and National Integration," in *The Journal of Modern African Studies*, 5 (1967), 325.

[23] J. S. Coleman, *Nigeria*, p. 115.

syllabuses with distinct local characteristics.[24] The fact that some African languages were ultimately included in the syllabuses of the Cambridge and London Examinations seemed to vindicate that position. In a letter to Bishop Heerey in 1941, Mr. Baldwin, the Chief Inspector of Education for the Southern Provinces, disclosed the preparedness of the Cambridge Syndicate to include the Igbo language in the syllabus of examination on the condition that an Advisory Committee was formed in Nigeria.[25]

It may be argued that before the late 1950s, the educational committees were overwhelmingly dominated by European officials who would, perhaps, not have been willing to go too far with the "Africanization" of the foreign examinations. However, the truth remained that no sufficient pressure came from the natives to fashion a syllabus that was relevant to Nigeria. On the contrary, it was the educated Nigerians themselves who vehemently opposed every attempt to educate the Africans along their own lines. Regarding the English School Certificate as an essential factor in their aspiration towards equality with their colonial overlords, the Nigerian elite took the proposals to base the curriculum on African standards as a measure designed to perpetuate their inferiority.[26] Much of that fear stemmed from lived experiences of the Nationalists at a time when the opinion of the colonialists was largely opposed to educating the African to a point where he could be a threat to their colonial rule. However, even in an independent Nigeria, the West African Examinations Council has continued to model its syllabus largely on the tradition of the Cambridge and London Examinations.

b) Religious Instruction

The area where the initiative in determining the content and scope of instruction lay exclusively with the Missions was religious education. In both Protestant and Catholic schools, religion was the primary subject of instruction, even though the Government never recognized it as such. In his Education Ordinance of 1916, Lord Lugard at least made it obligatory in all grades of schools. Shanahan described that measure as "a noble example for Governments all over the world."[27] Recognizing

---

[24] See L. J. Lewis, "Prospects of Educational Policy in Nigeria," in *Education and Politics in Nigeria*, ed. H. N. Weiler (Freiburg: Rombach Verlag, 1964). p. 248.

[25] ODA: Letter No. A.D.S. 87/882, "Baldwin to Bishop Heerey," Enugu, 18 September, 1941.

[26] Cf. J. S. Coleman, *Nigeria*, p. 120f; see also M. Perham, *Native Administration in Nigeria* (London: Oxford Univ. Press, 1937), p. 282f.

[27] CSE: 191/B/VI, Shanahan, "Apostolic Prefecture of Southern Nigeria," 1916.

the supremacy of the Missions in matters religious, Lugard had invited Church leaders in 1915 to draw up schemes of religious and moral instructions for both Assisted and Unassisted Schools. The official Catholic programme has been reproduced fully in Appendix B:1 of this work. Of remarkable interest is item 9 of the scheme for Standards V and VI which reads: "Special insistence on a) Character and its application, b) Respect for lawful authority, c) Good example, its effects, d) Sobriety etc etc." This cosy arrangement was designed, no doubt, to appeal to the Governor General, who had stumbled upon moral instructions in his search for law-abiding citizens.

For some undeclared reasons, the Catholic authorities declined, in later years, from cooperating with the Education Department on the question of religious instructions in their schools. In answer to government demand that these classes in both Assisted and Unassisted Schools be registered, the Conference of Nigerian Ordinaries insisted in 1937 that the only persons who deserved to be informed were those local authorities who were directly involved with the maintenance of law and order, namely, the District Officers and their agents. The Catholic authorities probably felt that a close tie with the Education Department would not only give the Government the occasion to affix restrictions on religious freedom, but also the opportunity of exerting control over the Unassisted Schools, where classes such as reading, writing, arithmetic, and hygiene were often taught during religious classes.[28] In fact, in 1937, the Catholic Ordinaries described the amount of control which the Government already had over the Unassisted Schools as "unfortunate."[29]

c) Industrial and Technical Education

For any educational system to succeed, there must be a definite purpose attached to it. In Nigeria, that all-important prerequisite was usually lacking with regard to industrial education in the schools. By 1934 the Government had given up most of the technical and industrial activities in its schools, and in the Educational report of that year, one of the explanations given for this turn of events was that Nigeria did not possess the large scale industry that was necessary to absorb skilled artisans. Furthermore, it was stated that the few existing industries trained their own personnel better than any school would have done.[30]

In former days, the situation was not so grim for trained artisans: the

---

[28] See CSE: 554/II, "Extracts from the Minutes of the Meeting of the Ordinaries of Nigeria, 1937, p. 18.
[29] Ibid.
[30] Cf. M. J. Walsh, "Catholic Contribution to Education," p. 137.

Missions had need for them, and so had the trading firms, and for a long time the responsibility of providing them fell on the former. The Catholic Mission in Eastern Nigeria had its share of that vital obligation, thanks to the services of the Brothers. These were religious men who were chosen from the rank and file of professional laymen. They carried out their different trades among their religious communities, and their duties later became indispensable in the Missions. To these duties belonged, above all, the planning and construction of mission houses and churches. Furthermore, the Brothers filled an educational gap by bringing up the Africans in various trades. At the Onitsha Wharf school, Brother Hermas taught boys carpentry, while Brother Bernabé unfolded to them the secrets of shoe-making.[31] To provide manpower for their various agricultural economies, the Brothers taught Africans methods of farming and gardening. At Aguleri, a brick-making factory was established, and by 1907, it was producing as many as 22,000 bricks a week.[32] Through industrial and technical activities in their schools, the Brothers and Fathers served the needs of their Missions, of those of the trading firms and of the Government. By doing so, they advanced the cause of nation-building in the colonies.

The first Administrator in Eastern Nigeria to give official recognition to this great service of the Missions was the High Commissioner, Sir Ralph Moor. With his moral and financial support, Father Lejeune formed the Onitsha vocational undertakings into a proper industrial school in 1901. As the Annual Reports on the Education Department for the Southern Provinces bear witness, this school was, besides the C.M.S. Onitsha Industrial School, the most important industrial school in the whole of Southern Nigeria between 1906 and 1914.[33]

The tradition of providing industrial instructions in Catholic schools persisted in the Colleges till well into the 1950s. The following report on Christ the King College in 1939 gives a clear picture of the emphasis laid on industrial education in Catholic Secondary schools:

> The College workshop is a centre of lively interest and practical results. Useful articles are planned, sketched and made in metal and brass. Iron window frames and gates are to be made by the senior classes. Physical training, games and the vegetable garden receive adequate attention.[34]

---

[31] See CSE: *Bulletin*, 17 (1893-1896), 418; see also CSE: *Bulletin*, 18 (1896-1897), 413.

[32] CSE: 192/B/IV,"Shanahan to LeRoy," 7 February, 1907.

[33] The government Hussey Charity Institution in Lagos was closed down in 1905, and by 1910, the famous Catholic Industrial Centre at Topo had lost most of its former glories. (See PRO: C. O.592/9, *Annual Report on the Education Department, Southern Provinces, for 1910*).

[34] ODA: "Catholic Education Secretary (for Proprietor) to Director of Education," Onitsha, 18 February, 1939.

With the disappearance in later years of a compelling necessity in technical studies, industrial instructions ceased to be part of the curriculum in normal schools and colleges. For studies in this field, pupils had to go to separate trade schools and handicraft centres belonging either to the Government or to private institutions. The Catholics ran a few of these schools, and to train manual instructors for them, they sent candidates with Middle IV Certificates or similar qualifications to the Yaba Technical Institute. The instruction provided in this establishment included: English, Technical Drawing, Mathematics, Technology of Tools and Materials, Engineering Science, Principles of Teaching, and Workshop Practice—metal and wood work.[35]

Industrial education managed to survive in the Primary Schools in the form of rural Science. By 1909, agricultural training was carried out only in a few government schools and in three mission schools—the Onitsha Industrial Mission, the Catholic School at Onitsha, and the Hope Waddell Institute at Calabar. The Annual Report of that year described this poor provision in a country that depended heavily on agricultural exports for its revenue as "preposterous."[36] After Hussey's reorganization of schools in 1930, emphasis was more effectively placed on rural science in the primary schools. For this purpose, Rural Education Centres were established at Umuahia and Ibadan for the training of Rural Science Teachers. These teachers were usually exempted from teaching ordinary subjects. However, from a letter of a teacher in the Catholic school at Oghe, it is evident that they were extremely disinterested with their work. Obliged to perform manual labours in the school farms and gardens, the Rural Science Teachers got no extra pay for their sweat.[37] In the primary schools, pupils were taught principles of agriculture, prevention of soil erosion, and soil fertility. To ensure that these subjects were given some practical handling, schools were obliged to keep and maintain school farms and gardens. The regulations on how to run them have been reproduced in appendix C of this work.

d) Physical Education

Another subject which was used advantageously in Catholic schools as a means of propaganda was physical education. At first this was limited to

---

[35] ODA: Letter No. D.D.E.9586 L/47, "W. E. Holt, Acting Deputy Director of Education, Eastern Provinces, to J. Jordan," Enugu, 6 September, 1949.

[36] PRO.C.O.592/7, *Annual Report on the Education Department, Southern Provinces, for 1909*, p. 355.

[37] See ODA: "A. M. Ebunoha to Supervisor of Catholic Schools, Enugu Division," Oghe, 6 June, 1949.

daily drills of twenty minutes. The drills acquired a measure of grace and attraction with the introduction of school bands in most of the central schools. Although these bands specialized exclusively in Irish and Scottish airs, they nevertheless thrilled Christians and non-Christians on important feasts, such as the Empire Day, and Corpus Christi processions.

In later years—especially after 1930—school sports greatly enhanced the prestige of the Roman Catholic Mission in Eastern Nigeria. Founded in 1933, Christ the King College, Onitsha, was renowned and greatly coveted not only for its academic excellence, but also on account of its popularity in sports, especially in the field of soccer.

With regard to the introduction of games in the schools, the Catholic missionaries were confronted with two main problems. Firstly, there was the difficulty of providing capable teachers for the games. Since the European missionaries hardly got any formal training in sports back home, they naturally introduced only the games most commonly played in Irish and English schools. These included, football, tennis, net-ball, and cricket. The success of any of these games in the mission schools in Nigeria depended, to a large extent, on the degree of interest with which the Father or Brother in charge participated in them in his school days.

Secondly, there was the problem of providing adequate equipment for the major school games, which were all European. It was in the solution of this problem that the teachers and the taught most notably displayed their sense of improvisation. In order to play tennis, for instance, wooden bats, artistically fashioned in the carpenter's shop, were used in the place of racquets, and bamboo fences stood in the place of nets.

3. *The Organization and Management of Schools*

a) The Group System

To achieve a greater coordination of the numerous clandestine bush schools, a need was felt to group them around principal stations. After years of experiments, there finally emerged in the Anua Mission a workable system which quickly became a model for the whole Prefecture. In 1917, Father P. Biéchy, the author of the Anua model, grouped the outstations of his Mission into Head-stations and Sub-stations. Of the seventy stations of the Anua Mission, nine were made Head-stations. The Catechists of Sub-stations were placed under the direct supervision of the Head Teachers or Chief Catechists of the Head-stations.

The grouping of outstations was first experimented in the Prefecture between 1907 and 1909, at a time when Anua itself was an outstation of the Calabar Mission. However, this earlier grouping was designed chiefly to reduce the number of outstations and their Catechist-teachers, who were all under the direct supervision of the resident priest.[38] By contrast, the Anua model came to terms with the factor of expansion, the Head Catechist-teachers being advised and encouraged to establish and supervise new schools and outstations.

It was the duty of the teachers of the Sub-stations to collect the school fees and mission dues of their stations. They made accounts to the Head-teachers, from whom they also received their salaries. On fixed Account Days, the Head-teachers, for their part, presented their carefully kept financial records and reports on their managerial areas to the Father in charge. To do this, they often had to travel up to sixty miles or more on foot or on bicycle to the Father's residence. This inconvenience, and the expansion of the Missions in later years, necessitated the division of the principal stations into mission districts, which were placed under the supervision of Catechist-Inspectors. In 1927, for instance, the Anua Mission was divided into four districts—Ifuho, Essene, Oron, and Anua. Until the first three were supplied with resident priests, the Catechist Inspectors supervised the work of the Head-teachers, organized building projects, and settled conflicts and financial squabbles in their respective districts, activities which were hitherto carried out by the Manager from Anua.

The group policy had its bad and good sides. Since the Father had direct dealings with only the Head Catechist-teachers, he lost contact with the local Catechists of the numerous bush schools. His monthly visits and ministrations were limited to the principal stations, to which the neophytes and school children from surrounding villages must come on such occasions. However, the group system was the only reasonable answer to the otherwise insuperable problem of one Father being in charge of a vast Mission.

Furthermore, the educational reforms of 1926, and Hussey's reorganization of schools in 1930 did not find the Catholics totally unprepared, thanks to their existing group administrative system. In response to government call for quality rather than quantity, the Missions began to group their schools under the different Head-stations. The new central schools of the Head-stations, or "clan schools," as they were called in the Anua Mission, were equipped in such a way as to cater for the educational needs of their dependent sub-stations. As a result, many village schools were closed down, and where a sub-station was too far away from a central school, an Infant School or "Vernacular School"

---

[38] See CSE: *Bulletin*, 25 (1909-1910), 357.

was allowed to exist. Bishop Shanahan was apparently alarmed at the rate with which village schools in the Anua Mission were closed by Father Biéchy who, in an effort to keep the number of schools to the barest minimum, went as far as establishing only one central school for each clan, even where a clan had two or more Head-stations.[39] The very man who held excellent records in the opening of new schools, exhibited similar qualities in closing them down. Doggedly optimistic about good results, he endeavoured to calm the fears of his worried bishop. "I am convinced," he wrote in 1928, "that once these preliminary difficulties are over, the scheme shall work well."[40] The following year, he was able to report that "the new system of Central Schools or 'Clan Schools'... [was] working well, except for usual little troubles and palaver."[41]

Established indiscriminately between 1906 and 1926, the one-teacher village schools had served a useful purpose—the foundation of the Christian Church among pagan communities. The suppression of a great number of these schools after 1926 was a consolidation, rather than a weakening, of that foundation. By means of the group system, a meaningful administration of the scattered mission possessions was ensured. Ultimately, the reduction of bush schools led to the expansion of central schools. For with the growth of the number of Catholics, and changes in the political boundaries of the regions, the establishment of more central schools became inevitable, a necessity which was further boosted by petty village jealousies and squabbles.

b) The Supervision of Schools

To ensure adequate supervision of Assisted Schools, the post of Mission Supervisor of Schools was created in the Education Code of 1926. The Catholic Ordinaries welcomed this provision and recommended the appointment of one or more Catholic Supervisors in each Vicariate or Prefecture.[42] In later years, Mission Supervisors of Education became paid civil servants. With effect from 1 April, 1942, Father J. Jordan was

---

[39] Cf. CSE: 191/B/VIII, P. Biéchy, "Regulations re New Schools- or Group Schools," n.d.

[40] CSE: 191/B/VIII, "Biéchy to Bishop Shanahan," Anua, 31 July, 1928.

[41] CSE: 191/B/VIII, "Biéchy to Bishop Shanahan," Anua, 31 July, 1929. An official government report in 1928 is strikingly similar to the views of Father Biéchy: "Efforts of Missions have generally been concentrated upon re-organizing the large number of 'bush' schools. The policy of 'group' schools has reduced the number considerably. There is intense village jealousy and thus a tendency to secede from the group. But the chief hope of improving the quality of such schools lies in the group policy. *Annual Report on the Education Department, Southern Provinces, For the Year 1928*, p. 8.

[42] Cf. CSE: 554/I, "Conference of the Ordinaries ...1929," p. 18.

appointed paid Supervisor of Roman Catholic schools in the Onitsha and
Owerri provinces at the annual salary of £350.[43]

Following the administrative structuring of Southern Nigeria into
Judicial Divisions in April 1936, the Anua group model was modified in
the Onitsha-Owerri Vicariate in 1937. Based closely on the government
judicial divisions, the new Onitsha group model was designed to bring
the work of the Supervisors to the centre stage of the educational coordination of the Missions. In it, Areas and Districts replaced the Head-
stations and Sub-stations of the Anua model. As can be seen in Table 10,
each Area was supplied with one Supervisor. Working in collaboration
with two Visiting Teachers each, the Supervisors of "A1", "A2", and
"B1" were saddled with the task of coordinating and supervising the
educational work in their respective Districts. In effect, they replaced the
former native Catechist-Inspectors whose office terminated with the
arrival of resident Fathers in their districts. Kirchner reported, for
instance, that the Catechist-Inspectors for Ifuho, Essene, and Oron in the
Anua Mission were relieved of their duties when their districts were
assigned to European priests in 1928.[44] The inclusion in the Onitsha
group model of Visiting Teachers or "Supervising Catechists" was an

Table 10

Supervisory Divisions of Mission Schools in the Onitsha-Owerri Vicariate, 1937

Areas	Districts and Missions
"A1"—Onitsha (About 3085 sq. miles) One Supervisor	No.1 (1420 sq.m.): Missions of Onitsha, Aguleri, Nnewi, Ihiala No.2 (1665 sq.m.):Amaibo, Nsu, Uruala, Uturu, Umuahia.
"A2"—Enugu (About 3675 sq. miles) One Supervisor	No.3a (1900 sq.m.):Eke, Nsukka. No.3b (1775 sq.m.):Adazi, Awgu, Enugu.
"B1"—Okpala (3880 sq. miles) One Supervisor	No.4 (1475 sq.m.): Ahiara, Emekuku, Okpala. No.5 (2405 sq. m.):Aba, Elele, Port Harcourt, and part of Ahoada.
"B2"—Degema Division (4265 sq. miles)	Yet to be developed.

Source: CSE: 554/V, Bishop C. Heerey, "Circular to Fathers," Onitsha, December
1937.

---

[43] See ODA: "Director of Education to Bishop Heerey," 5 June, 1942.
[44] See CSE: 556/VIII, J. Kirchner, "Heidentum und Christentum im Lande der
Ibibios," (TS, n.d.), p. 112.

attempt to resuscitate the invaluable services of the experienced native teachers. Among other things, they were "to advise and assist the [school] Managers" in their areas.[45]

On the School Managers rested the responsibilities that were involved in the actual running of the individual schools. Their work included, among other things, the foundation and location of schools, the selection and supervision of teachers, the drafting and control of school programmes, and all other aspects of school organization and management. They were obliged to refer all educational problems to their area Supervisors.[46]

Managers of schools were also the ministers of their parishes. However, they did not see their educational and religious activities as separate entities, but rather as integral parts of their unique evangelical mission. Worthy of note is, in this regard, the fact that the educational divisions in both the Anua and Onitsha group models were at the same time the administrative units of the various Missions, a fact which demonstrates that the school was the pivot on which the whole evangelization process in Eastern Nigeria revolved.

The educational innovations described above evolved primarily out of pressure from the Government in its grant-in-aid policy which emphasized efficiency as a necessary reciprocity for the aid given to Assisted Schools. However, thanks to the selfless efforts of the Voluntary Agencies, the drive towards change and improvement also found ultimate expression in the Unassisted Schools, which were not, in spite of sporadic interim settlements to the benefits of their teachers, under the direct control and supervision of the Government. On their own initiatives, Mission Supervisors of Education saw to the pruning and reorganization of their Unassisted Schools.[47] In 1929, an Education Council was appointed in the Vicariate of Southern Nigeria which consisted of Fathers D. Walsh, T. J. O'Connor, T. Ronayne, and R. Daly. Their duty was to give instructions and educational advice to Managers of both Assisted and Unassisted Schools.[48] This Education Council was superseded in 1947 in the Onitsha-Owerri Vicariate by a Board of Education Governors.[49]

---

[45] CSE: 554/V, Bishop C. Heerey, "Circular to Fathers," Onitsha, December, 1937.

[46] There were three Supervisors in the Onitsha-Owerri Vicariate in 1948: "A1": Father Woulfe, Catholic Education House, Onitsha; "A2": Father Smyth, C.I.C., Enugu; "B1": Father J. B. Whelan, St. Paul's Seminary, Okpala. (See ODA: J. Jordan, "Teacher Training for Middle Six Students: Circular to Principals," Onitsha, 14 July, 1948).

[47] Cf. Annual Report on the Education Department, *Southern Provinces,* for 1928, p. 3.

[48] See CSE: 554/I, "Minutes of the Fathers' Meeting at Ihiala, 1929."

[49] See ODA: "J. Jordan to M. Flanagan, Principal of C. K. C.," Onitsha, 20 June, 1947.

As part of the measures taken in 1937 to ensure uniformity in all schools of the Onitsha-Owerri Vicariate, Managers of Schools were enjoined to meet three or four times a year. The aims of such meetings were:

> to discuss methods of expansion, school problems, and to arrange for the supply and exchange of teachers, the salaries of teachers in their non-assisted schools, and for time-tables, syllabuses, schemes of work, and making out of returns, etc. etc.[50]

These and similar measures helped greatly to lessen the efficiency gap between the Assisted and Unassisted Schools in Eastern Nigeria.

On the national level, measures were also taken to form a common front in the educational endeavours of the Catholic Missions in Nigeria. The Government had always insisted on the establishment of a close liaison between the Education Department and the Voluntary Agencies. For this purpose, the different proprietors of Schools were, in one way or the other, represented in the national and provincial Boards of Education. However, with the steady increase in the number of mission jurisdictions—the Catholics alone had eight in 1937—the Government saw it as appropriate to have mission representatives reduced to denominations. A proposal to the Right Rev. Bishop Taylor in this regard was unanimously welcomed by the Board of Catholic Ordinaries in December 1941.[51] The following year, the Ordinaries nominated Father J. Jordan as representative of all the Catholic Missions in Nigeria, and saddled him with the task of presenting Catholic educational policy to the Government.

It was no accident that the Nigerian Ordinaries chose as their representative a man from the Onitsha ecclesiastical province. It was there that Catholic educational reputation had attained its greatest heights, and in his capacity as Education Adviser to the Catholic Missions in Nigeria, Father Jordan endeavoured most successfully to give that reputation a nation-wide boosting. Calling on all Catholic Supervisors of Education, Managers of Schools, and Principals of Training Colleges and Secondary Schools to "get together" by holding annual conventions of an exclusively educational character, he prophesied in 1948 that the Catholics could make themselves "the strongest single educational influence in the country."[52] By the late 1950s, that prognosis was no more a statement of intention but an accomplished reality.

---

[50] CSE: 554/V, Bishop Heerey, "Circular to Fathers," December, 1937.

[51] See ODA: "Secretary to the Board of Catholic Ordinaries to the Director of Education," Onitsha, 22 December, 1841.

[52] CSE: 556/VII, J. Jordan, "Catholic Educational Policy: Annual Conventions," Onitsha, 4 August, 1948.

II. *Catholic Role in the Development of the Vernacular**

1. *The Igbo Language and Its Predicaments*

In what has now become a prophetic utterance, Ida C. Ward wrote in 1939 that the development of an Igbo literature would be held up if some specific problems connected with the language were not solved.[53] She was referring particularly to the existence of a baffling great number of Igbo dialects, and a lack of uniformity in the orthography used in reducing them to a written form. Fifty years after her observation, none of these problems has been conclusively solved, and the development of an Igbo literature has not yet come out of the foundation stage.

Apart from the Hausa and Yoruba, the Igbo constitute the largest ethnic group in Nigeria. Their progressive bent and intellectual achievements have already received worldwide acknowledgment. Yet, unfortunately, their language has yet to achieve that special honour. In an attempt to discover what had gone wrong, a consensus of opinions seems to point to the irony in the psychology of the Igbos themselves—a people who, in the past, loved every knowledge, except the knowledge of their language. Parents sent their children to school to learn English, and would not have anything to do with the vernacular. In their case, the remark of some participants at the International Mission Conference at Le Zoute in 1926 was pathetically correct, namely, that certain classes of literate Africans knew the importance of the White man's language, and would strongly oppose any attempt to make the vernacular the medium of instruction in the schools.[54]

Nevertheless, all the evidence that history affords shows that the Government and the Christian Missions were largely responsible for the retarded development of the vernacular in Eastern Nigeria. The Government, for instance, paid attention to the vernacular only after repeated pressure from humanitarian organizations and mission supporters in England, most of whom were private anthropologists, sociologists, and philologists. Otherwise, its attitude towards the vernacular, especially

[*— This chapter is an improved version of the article, N. Omenka, "The Role of the Catholic Mission in the Development of Vernacular Literature in Eastern Nigeria," *Journal of Religion in Africa* XVI, 2 (1986), 121-137.

[53] I. C. Ward, *Ibo Dialects and the Development of a Common Language* (Cambridge: Heffer and Sons, 1941), p. 1.

[54] E. W. Smith, *The Christian Mission in Africa: A Study Based on the Work of the International Conference at Le Zoute, Belgium* (London, 1926), p. 68. According to Mr. Ukong Ibekwe, many educated Nigerians regarded the prominence given to the vernacular in the 1930 Education Code as a deliberate action by the Government to lower the standard of education for the natives. See U. Ibekwe, "On the Teaching of Vernacular Languages," in *The Nigerian Teacher*, 1, Nos. 2 and 3 (1934), p. 42.

before the 1920s, was negative and, to a large extent, scornful. It was no accident that the Education Ordinance of 1882, the first of its kind in the British possessions of West Africa, made no provisions for the promotion of the vernacular. Mr. Metcalfe Sunter, the then Inspector of Schools, even went as far as opposing the efforts of the Anglican Niger Mission to reduce the *Nago* or Yoruba language to writing. During the controversy which erupted, the Catholics raised no single voice against government policy, an attitude which merited them a pat on the back from the Inspector. "With regard to the Roman Catholic schools," he said, "I do not think one question has been raised on the vernacular agitation; they—alone—have been prepared from the first to accept the Ordinance and make the most of it."[55] Recognizing English as "the only medium for the teaching of secular subjects", he advised that the vernacular be confined to the region of "theological or sectarian dogma".[56] For the Igbo language and a host of other Nigerian languages, Lugard's concessions in later years did not represent any significant change in government policy over the vernacular. Recognizing only Hausa, Yoruba, and Arabic as media of instruction, the Governor eagerly agreed with Lord Kimberley who had said that instruction in the native languages should be left to "the stimulus of self interest", and that government grants were "not required for its encouragement".[57]

In general, the colonial Governments regarded the vernacular as a necessary evil, deserving attention only as long as it served official interest. Accordingly, European officials in the various Departments were required to pass a "Lower Standard Examination" in a number of native languages, the procedure of which included "simple conversations with natives ignorant of English on subjects relating to roads, distances, water, carriers, markets, method of government, land disputes etc. etc."[58] This careful selection of subjects accentuated the naked pragmatism in government involvement with the vernacular. There was lacking in it a necessary stimulus for the development of a viable literature in the native language.

The first steps towards the attainment of that goal were taken by the Christian Missions. However, their often acrimonious divisions seriously undermined their efforts. In the all-important question of Igbo dialects

---

[55] Quoted in M. J. Walsh, "The Catholic Contribution to Education in Western Nigeria, p. 51.

[56] F.C.O.L./ 8234: M. Sunter, *General Report on Elementary Schools in the Gambia Colony, 1885.*

[57] Quoted in F. D. Lugard, *Report on the Amalgamation*, p. 61.

[58] "Rules Relating to the Examination in a Native Language of European Officers of the Southern Nigeria Civil Service, 1908," in *West African Pamphlet*, No. 47.

and the use of a common orthography, for instance, they could not come to an agreement on a solution. The Protestants accepted—at least in principle—the use of a "Union Igbo", but strongly opposed the new or "African" orthography of 1929. The Catholics, for their part, rejected the Union Igbo, but adopted the new orthography. In this contrariety, the progress of the Igbo language was greatly impaired.

Concealed in the different positions of the Christian Missions were efforts designed to safeguard denominational interests. When the new orthography was introduced in 1929, the Church Missionary Society was understandably unwilling to abandon its enormous achievements in the old orthography.[59] Having experimented with the old script for almost a century, the Society considered it inexpedient to embark upon a costly reprinting of its many works in the vernacular, or to carry out a massive re-education of its adherents on the use of the new invention.

Besides the difficulties mentioned above, there were other undesirable elements in the new orthography itself which somehow vindicated the Protestant position. Worked out by the International Institute of African Languages and Cultures, the new orthography was designed primarily to simplify the work of European linguists involved with African languages.[60] Divorced of the old "abominable" signs, as the diacritic marks used by earlier writers were called by printers in England, the new orthography was universally applied on a large variety of African languages without due considerations given to their distinctive local characteristics.[61]

It was no wonder that much prejudice was heaped around the new orthography in Nigeria, where the existence of many completely different languages posed great problems for the Church and the State. During its meeting in February 1939, the Board of Education came to the conclusion that the use of either the old or the new orthography in the vernacular texts should be left optional. Meeting later in the year, the Onitsha Provincial School Committee also reached a deadlock over the

---

[59] For the pioneer accomplishments of the Anglican Niger Mission in the reduction of Nigerian Languages to writing, see J. F. A. Ajayi, *Christian Missions in Nigeria* (London, 1965), pp. 126-131; P. E. Hair, *The Early Study of Nigerian Languages* (Cambridge, 1967).

[60] Cf. I. C. Ward, *Ibo Dialects*, pp. 2-4.

[61] It must be conceded, however, that the new orthography contained some good elements, such as the use of the digraphs "kp", "kw", "gb", "gh" for exclusively African consonant sounds. Unfortunately, however, these digraphs were for an ordinary European more abominable than the use of diacritic marks. Since it was naturally impossible for him to reproduce the single sound—the phonetic value of a digraph—of the African digraphs, he simple pronounced one letter and completely ignored the other. Thus he wrote and pronounced "Ibo" instead of "Igbo". The havoc done by the new orthography still survives today in the names of many Nigerian towns and villages.

question of orthography. On a vote being taken, nine members opted for the new, and six for the old, orthography. This was by no means a victory for the innovators since nine members of the committee withheld their votes.[62]

The Protestants eventually dropped their opposition, and the new orthography triumphed in the production of Igbo literature until 1961, when it was superseded by the present official or "Onwu" Igbo orthography.

Of a more serious nature was the controversy over the use of a "Union Igbo". Created by the Anglican Niger Mission, the Union Igbo was a concoction of five different Igbo dialects—Bonny, Owerri, Arochukwu, Ngwana, and Onitsha.[63] In the main, it resembled the *Isuama*, an Owerri related dialect that was favoured by the Anglican Niger Mission throughout the nineteenth century.[64] For practical purposes, the Union Igbo was a failure: it was a dialect spoken and written easily by no Igbo district. Furthermore, the prospects for its success were dimmed even among the Protestants by fierce opposition from the Onitsha elite, the intellectual backbones of Anglican Protestantism in Eastern Nigeria.

Yet, the idea of a "Union Igbo" was the first genuine effort to overcome the frustration created by a multiplicity of Igbo dialects. When the Catholic authorities officially rejected it in 1929, they did so not so much for its inherent weaknesses as for the fear that its growing popularity might adversely dilute the extraordinary concentration of native interest in Catholic schools, where English was given a place of prominence. In the words of the Nigerian Catholic Ordinaries, the use of "a new scientific language", as they called the Union Igbo, would be "a hindrance to the propagation of Catholic Faith and Teaching."[65] In what appeared as a demonstration of Catholic opposition to the idea of a unified Igbo language, two Igbo Readers for Catholic schools were issued in two different dialects—Owerri and Onitsha.[66]

To understand this rather puzzling Catholic position, one must bear in mind the overriding importance of English and the school for Catholic evangelism in Eastern Nigeria. Father J. Kirchner, one of the missionaries in the Ibibio District, painted a clear picture of the pre-eminence of these closely related issues in the following observation:

---

[62] See, ODA: "Minutes of the 15th Meeting of the Onitsha Provincial School Committee held at the Resident's Office", Onitsha, 5 May, 1939.

[63] Cf. I. C. Ward, *Ibo Dialects*, p. 10.

[64] Cf. P. E. Hair, *Early Study of Nigerian Languages*, p. 93f.

[65] CSE: 554/I, "Conference of the Ordinaries of Nigeria and the British Cameroons, Held at Lagos, 31 August-3 September, 1929," p. 22.

[66] Cf. I. C. Ward, *Ibo Dialects*, p. 18, n. 4.

To open an outstation or Catechist-post, and to establish a school, were one and the same thing.

If a missionary entered a village which possessed no school, his first action was not to preach about the Kingdom of God, rather he endeavoured, first and foremost, to win the people over for the school. He had to speak only about the school, for the people either did not understand much about religion and the foundation of a Mission, or they did not want to know anything about these things. But if he spoke to them about intelligent and educated people (like the Whites), about well instructed and neatly clothed school children who even understood and spoke the language of the Whites, the whole crowd would send out an outburst of enthusiasm and would say: "That is excellent ! we too would want our children transformed in this way".[67]

The language of the Whites referred to in this report was neither German—the mother tongue of the author—nor French—the official language of his congregation; it was English, the language of progress in colonial Nigeria, the greatest single influence in Catholic schools, and the pivot on which the people's interest revolved. Any attempt, therefore, to develop and popularize a vernacular language to the point of its becoming a match for English was looked upon as detrimental to the Catholic cause. It was against this background that Shanahan regarded the clause in the draft of the 1908 Education Code which had made the vernacular compulsory for all schools as a deliberate act designed to "kill" Catholic schools. The aim of his proposal to the Government not to make that subject obligatory was, according to him, to put a check on the vast Protestant vernacular publications which were circulating all over the country.[68]

From a missionary point of view, Shanahan's antipathy towards the vernacular was an attitude with a sardonic twist. He was the Prefect who fought hardest to win approval for the apostolate of the school in Eastern Nigeria. But by moving squarely against the vernacular, he unfortunately missed the most important issue in any balanced education. While the school method of evangelization he propagated made some use of the vernacular, it was not prepared to go all out to discover and promote its inherent cultural values. It was against this background that

---

[67] CSE: 556/VIII, J. Kirchner, "Heidentum und Christentum im Lande der Ibibios" (TS, n. d.), p. 81.

[68] CSE: 192/B/IV, "Shanahan to Superior General," Calabar, 21 January, 1908. Between 1857 and 1893, agents of the Anglican Niger Mission, most of whom were Black Africans from Sierra Leone, had published over fifty books and booklets in the languages of the Lower Niger and Benue regions alone. See P. E. Hair, *Early Study of Nigerian Languages*, p. 87f. By 1908, when Shanahan wrote his letter, the number of Protestant vernacular publications must have increased enormously, especially in the Yoruba speaking Western Nigeria.

Professor D. Westermann wrote that "any educational work which does not take into consideration the inseparable unity between African language and African thinking is based on false principles ...."[69]

2. Catholic Vernacular Publications

Despite the shortcomings in Catholic policy towards the native language, one can, with propriety, speak of a Catholic role in the development of the vernacular in Eastern Nigeria. It was to the credit of the Christian Missions that the African languages were reduced to writing in the first place, and the Catholics in Nigeria made a number of important contributions to that great undertaking.[70]

With regard to the Igbo language, the first, and perhaps the greatest, of these Contributions was an Igbo Grammar which was published in 1899. The author, Father Aimé Ganot of the Holy Ghost Congregation, was a French linguist whose ambitious enterprise and achievements in the development of Igbo literature were never matched by those of any other Catholic missionary. When he came to Nigeria in 1894, there was only one worthwhile Igbo Grammar in print, *Oku Ibo* by Friedrich Schön of the Anglican Church. However, Schön's work had, in his opinion, two serious flaws—untoward generalization, and the use of grammatical rules that were "more or less hazardous", such as inexact conjugation of verbs, and the presentation of the suffix *ga* as a general sign of the plural form of a substantive.[71] Indeed, these evaluations were, to a large extent, perfectly in line with those made by Schön himself, namely, that many things in his "Grammatical Elements" were "left doubtful, and must wait for further explanations."[72]

To all appearances, however, Ganot's *Igbo Grammar* was not a continuation of Schön's work, but rather a pioneer undertaking containing grammatical elements which were based mainly on his own findings in a dialect different from the one studied by Schön.[73] With its 209 pages, it has remained till this day a monumental work in Igbo studies.

---

[69] D. Westermann, "The Place and Function of the Vernacular in African Education," in *IRM*, 14 (1925), 28.

[70] By 1926, the Bible, or parts of its, had been translated into 243 African languages by the Christian Missions. Of these languages, 190 had publications on subjects other than the Scriptures. See E. W. Smith, *The Christian Mission*, p. 116.

[71] A. Ganot, *Grammaire Ibo* (Paris, 1899), p. 1.

[72] J. F. Schön, *Oku Ibo: Grammatical Elements of the Ibo Language* (London, 1861), p. 3.

[73] Father Ganot was careful to distance himself from the Protestant author in words that smacked very much of denominational rivalry: "Le livre de J. F. Schön n'a donc pu me servir; je ne l'avais pas d'ailleurs entre les mains quand j'ai commencé travail. Mais je me suis dirigé d'après les études de mes confrères du R. P. Lutz, du R. P. Lécuyer, et surtout du R. P. Pawlas, actuellement Préfet apostolique de la Mission du Bas-Niger." *Grammaire Ibo*, p. 1.

Equally of great importance was Ganot's English-Igbo-French dictionary which was published in Salzburg, Austria, in 1904. It contained over 17,000 words collected by him and by several other Catholic missionaries before him. Ganot's dictionary was the first work by the Holy Ghost Fathers in Nigeria to be printed outside France. To promote vernacular literature in the Catholic Missions of Africa, the Sodality of St. Peter Claver, Salzburg, Austria, set up a special printing press in 1899, and by 1950, it had gratuitously published over 325 works for the Missions, and these included: catechisms, scripture translations, prayerbooks and hymnals, school textbooks and dictionaries.[74]

Father Ganot's Igbo Grammar and Igbo Dictionary were primarily designed for the use of European missionaries, and there is no indication that they were ever utilized in the schools. Generally, vernacular education in Catholic schools was limited to the Infant Classes, where the intellectual capacity of the pupils allowed only drills on the alphabets, and elementary reading exercises. However, Ganot's linguistic publications rendered invaluable service to the production of religious books for the Mission.

The first of these books was *Katekismi Ibo* which was published by Father Ganot himself in 1901. Like every other thing written by him, this was a pioneer work. It was divided into two parts—twenty-eight pages of prayers, and thirty-six pages of Igbo catechism. This arrangement points to a possible influence from another veteran linguist, Father Nöel Baudin of the Apostolic Vicariate of the Bight of Benin.[75] Baudin's *Katekismu L'Edo Yoruba*, which was published in 1884, also comprised two parts: ten pages of prayers, and ninety-eight pages of Yoruba Catechism. Besides, Father Baudin also published a Yoruba grammar book, and a large French-Yoruba dictionary.[76] Ganot must have drawn much inspiration from his countryman: to do for the Igbos what Baudin had done for the Yorubas.

In 1903, barely two years after the publication of Ganot's Catechism, a much more voluminous Igbo Catechism was published by Father Charles Vogler with the English title, *Catechism of the Catholic Faith in the Igbo Language*. The Igbo title, *Katechisma Nk'Okwukwe Nzuko Katolik*

---

[74] See R. Streit & J. Dindinger, *Bibliotheca Missionum*, Vol. XX (Freiburg: Herder, 1954), pp. 704-716.

[75] Until 1883 the Apostolic Vicariate of the Bight of Benin included the Missions of Dahomey, Togo, and Lagos. Yoruba was the main language spoken in this ecclesiastical province which was under the direction of the Society of African Missions, Lyon. Most probably, the French Holy Ghost Fathers, who came to Eastern Nigeria in 1885, must have made use of the vernacular literature produced by their countrymen west of the Niger.

[76] See Streit & Dindinger, *Bibliotheca Missionum*, XVIII, p. 90.

N'Asusu Igbo, was given only after the introduction by Father Lejeune. A second edition was published in 1913 with the Igbo title on the front cover, and the English title after the introduction. 1924 saw the publication of a sixth, and perhaps the last, edition of Father Vogler's Igbo Catechism. Apart from the renunciation of the guide to the orthography, and the discarding of the grave accent employed in the first edition to show the Igbo open vowels è, ŏ, and ù, the later editions did not differ in any other way from the first.

Apparently, Ganot's *Katekismi Ibo* must have fallen short of expectations, a fact which is implicit in the following remark by Father Lejeune on Vogler's catechism:

> This work, written with the help of our Catechists, is excellent from a linguistic standpoint: the natives themselves do not find any [grammatical] error in it. Furthermore, the religious truths in it have been exposed in a way that meets the principal objections which are spread in this country against our holy religion.... [77].

The emphasis on the language of the Igbo Catechism underscores Lejeune's flair for essentials. Himself an author of a Catechism in an African language, the Prefect ordered and directed, shortly after his arrival on the Niger in 1900, the production of an Igbo Catechism that would stand the test of time.[78] Convinced that Vogler's Igbo Catechism had that quality, he made its use obligatory in the whole Prefecture, which comprised almost exclusively the Igbo-speaking districts of Onitsha by the beginning of 1903. As we shall see later, the propagandist bias of the new Igbo Catechism made it a favorite Catechism throughout Shanahan's tenure of office, when the Prefecture (later Vicariate) of Southern Nigeria embraced many non Igbo-speaking territories.

Worthy of note is the part played by native Catechists in the production of the Igbo Catechism. Without in any way depreciating the merits of the European writers, one may say that the success of their vernacular publications depended primarily on the efforts of native speakers. Since most of the White missionaries did not possess a commanding knowledge of the native languages, their credit lay chiefly in the use of their linguistic expertise to get the right information from the native speakers. However, the latter were very seldom cited as co-authors. According to Professor D. Westermann, there were in fact cases where vernacular works written exclusively by natives were published under the names of

---

[77] Quoted in CSE: *Bulletin*, 22 (1903-1904), 788.

[78] Lejeune's vernacular publications in Gabon included: a catechism in the Fang language in 1891, a French-Fang dictionary in 1892, and hymnals and prayer-books in several Gabonese languages between 1892 and 1896. See Streit & Dindinger, *Bibliotheca Missionum*, XVIII, p. 293.

White authors.[79] It was to dispel the suspicion of a possible cheat that Father Ganot went all out to emphasize his exclusive authorship of his Igbo Grammar. "The grammatical notions," he wrote in the Preface, "have demanded long and tedious research, and are not the fruit of the labours of the natives."[80] By acknowledging the cooperation of native Catechists, especially those of Ephrem Agha, Samuel Ekpundu, and Jacob Chukwuamaka,[81] in the production of the Igbo Catechism, Father Lejeune made a significant departure from a well-known practice.

West of the Niger, a French-Ika-Ibo dictionary was published in 1907 by Father Carlo Zappa of the Society of African Missions, who was Apostolic Prefect of the Upper Niger Mission (Later Prefecture of Western Nigeria) from 1894 to 1917. A highly intelligent man who wrote his reports to Rome freely in classical Latin, Father Zappa personally addressed himself to the excruciating problem of heading a Mission where Igbo was just one of the many languages spoken by his faithful.

Father Léna produced a catechism in the Efik language in 1908, five years after the foundation of the Calabar Mission. Like most of the catechism publications in the vernacular, Léna's Efik Catechism was a translation from an original in an European language. It is not clear whose work he used, but there are indications that he must have used LeRoy's *Catéchisme de la Foi Catholique* which was published in the late 1880s. Alexander LeRoy was the Superior General of the Holy Ghost Congregation, and his catechism served as a standard work for his Society, being translated into several African languages. It was, for instance, translated into Swahili in 1900 by Father Charles Sacleux. Talking about the orthography of his Efik Catechism, Father Léna remarked that he based it on Sacleux's system. There is a close probability that he must have also used LeRoy's French Catechism, just as Sacleux had done for his Swahili translation.

Father Léna was, like most of his colleagues, not a trained linguist. He had therefore to face great difficulties in the production of his Efik Catechism, which he himself described as "very imperfect".[82] Nevertheless, matching unprofessionalism with ingenuity and hard work, he succeeded in producing a catechism whose use in the Calabar Mission

---

[79] D. Westermann, "The... Vernacular in African Education," p. 29.

[80] A. Ganot, *Grammaire Ibo*, p. 2.

[81] L. Lejeune, Introd., *Catechism of the Catholic Faith in the Igbo Language*, by C. Vogler (Strassburg, 1903), p. iii.

[82] CSE: 192/B/IV, "Léna to LeRoy," Calabar, 19 October, 1907. The Efik Catechism was greatly improved in the second and third editions which were published in Abbeville, France, in 1912 and 1915 respectively. A fourth edition was published in 1919 in Angers, France.

lasted from 1908 to 1929, a record span of life for a catechism of that period.

After the production of the Igbo and Efik Catechisms, there set in a long period of linguistic inactivity. This was interrupted in 1921 with the production of an Efik hymnal by Father Joseph Krafft, and in 1922 with the production of an Igbo Prayer-book and hymnal (in one volume) by Father Joseph Treich. In 1924, Bishop Shanahan introduced a number of measures which were designed to invigorate religious activities in his new Vicariate. These were presented to the Fathers in the form of a twenty-two-point promulgation of directives. In one of these, the Igbo Catechism was made the standard catechism of the Vicariate, to be translated into English and given to Fathers working in districts where other native languages were spoken.[83] Although the Fathers were not explicitly asked to make vernacular translations from their English copies, they were required to submit for approval "literal or word-for-word translations in English" of any proposed vernacular versions.[84]

This rather paradoxical duplication of translations in English was designed to guard against any possible deviations from the Igbo original. As has been seen, the recommending factor in the Igbo Catechism was its presentation of Catholic teachings in a manner that came to terms with the doctrinal squabbles between Catholics and Protestants in Nigeria.[85] To ensure homogeneity in Catholic teaching, the Apostolic Vicar saddled his ministers with the task of popularizing the Igbo Catechism in the whole Vicariate, each in his own way. To all appearances, however, that objective was accomplished through the medium of English rather than by a recourse to translations into the numerous languages of South-Eastern Nigeria. For apart from Father Biéchy's Efik translation of 1929, the Igbo Catechism did not exist in any other vernacular version.

In his 1924 promulgation of directions, Bishop Shanahan also endeavoured to promote the production of the Scriptures in the vernacular. For this purpose, Father Treich was put in charge of translating the epistles and gospels into the Igbo language, Father Biéchy in charge of translating them into Efik, and Father Groetz in charge of Ogoja language. Since vernacular education in the Ogoja Province was particu-

---

[83] CSE: 191/B/III, J. Shanahan, "Circular no. 10: Promulgation of Directions Relative to the Administration of the Sacraments in the Vicariate of Southern Nigeria and Some Other Matters of General Importance," August, 1924, item viii.

[84] Ibid., item ix.

[85] For instance, after enumerating in question 168 the four hallmarks of a true Church, namely, that it must be one, holy, Catholic, and Apostolic, the Igbo Catechism went all out to explain, in footnotes, why the Protestant Church cannot be such a Church. See *Katekisma Nk'Okwukwe Nzuko Katolik N'Asusu Igbo* (1924), pp. 29-31.

larly weak, consisting mainly of very trivial use of Igbo and Efik in its periphery,[86] the inclusion in 1924 of Ogoja in the list of privileged languages to receive linguistic attention was therefore very promising. However, that favour was short-lived. In 1929, two standing committees were appointed to deal with language questions in the Vicariate, one for Igbo and the other for Efik. There was no longer any mention of Ogoja, or any other language group in South-Eastern Nigeria.

The chief task of the language committees was the translation of the New Testament and school text books into Igbo and Efik. Father Treich, who was in charge of Igbo publications, was assisted by three natives, John Anyogu, John Dureke, and Joseph Modebe. Father Biéchy, in charge of Efik, was assisted by Mauria Archibong, Thomas Asuguo and Leo Tom Okon.[87]

In spite of the singular efforts made in 1924 and 1929 to have the Sacred Scriptures written in the vernacular, both projects yielded no concrete results. This was by all account an unfortunate shortfall. Whereas Christian Missions all over the world, including the rest of Nigeria,[88] could look up to the versions of the Holy Bible in the vernacular as a crowning reward for their missionary enterprise, the Mission of the Holy Ghost Fathers in Eastern Nigeria, which is regarded as the most successful in Africa, could not boast of an Igbo version of the Bible. The reasons behind this most paradoxical omission are not hard to find.

One of the thorniest problems which faced the Scripture Committees was, undoubtedly, the disarming Igbo dialect question. The Protestants were able to score a partial victory here by the use of the Union Igbo in their Igbo Bible. Having rejected the Union Igbo, the Catholics could not afford to undertake the arduous task of producing the whole Bible in two or more Igbo dialects. However, their efforts to find a solution were disastrously undermined by the force of habit which accrued from their rather excessive dependence on native Catechists. On coming to Nigeria after more than five years in Gabon, Father Lejeune saw the use made by the Lower Niger missionaries of their catechists as too extraordinary to be good. In his very first report on the Mission, he highlighted the defeatist attitude of the Fathers towards the study of the vernacular:

---

[86] See *Annual Report on the Education Department, Southern Provinces, for 1928*, p. 9.

[87] Cf. CSE: 554/I, "Minutes of the Father's Meeting Held at the Annual Retreat at Ihiala, 11 November, 1929."

[88] A version of the Holy Bible in Yoruba was published in 1929—*Itan Inu Iwé Mino* (Salzburg: St Peter Claver Sodality)—and in the same year, the gospels were translated into Hausa. These publications in 1929 certainly must have had some bearing on the decision in Shanahan's Vicariate to set up standing committees for translating the New Testament into Igbo and Efik.

One hears here through the Catechists, the interpreter of the Mission, and the three teachers. These are the ones who teach catechism to the children, and not the Fathers. None of the latter goes to the village. Not one of them is capable of teaching catechism in Igbo. None has yet preached in this language, and when I said that I expected them to preach in Igbo after six months, they replied that it would be impossible, and that it would also be impossible to teach catechism in Igbo. [89]

Having had the opportunity of witnessing the missionary methods employed in other African Missions, where the necessity of ministering directly to the natives was instrumental in the study of their languages, Father Lejeune sensed that the wholesale use of Catechists did not augur well for a healthy presentation of the good news to the people. Two decades after his report, another Church dignitary, Father Joseph Soul, the Spiritan Visitor to Nigeria in 1929, made some independent observations whose tone and content are strikingly similar to those of Father Lejeune:

No Father teaches catechism: this is the responsibility of the Catechists, just as in Cameroon. I would also say that no Father gives his Sunday sermon in the native language: one preaches in English and an interpreter translates each sentence. Even the gospel itself is also read and translated [in this manner]; but I really wonder what a poor translation a Catechist would make of issues that are very difficult, and which generally demand the greatest of care.... There is still neither a prayer-book, nor a translation of the Sunday gospels in Igbo. [90]

The machinery of evangelization in Eastern Nigeria, which had as its driving force the services of Catechists and Teachers, functioned perfectly everywhere except in the promotion of vernacular literature. The Fathers, who were able to say the Mass and administer the sacraments among any language group through the help of native interpreters, did not see any immediate compelling need to translate the scripture readings for their own use, or to learn the native languages for their sermons.

Sometimes they went so far as to use Igbo Interpreters in areas where no Igbo was spoken or understood, a practice which adversely fanned the

---

[89] CSE: 192/B/II, "Lejeune to LeRoy", 18 September, 1900. In 1908, one of the Fathers succeeded in preaching in Igbo after eight months in Nigeria. Commenting on this singular achievement, Father Shanahan noted that "one can [after all] master the Igbo language" (CSE: 192/B/V, "Shanahan to Superior General," Onitsha, 2 September, 1908).

[90] CSE: 554/I, J. Soul, Visitor, "General Report to the Superior General on the Visit to the District of Southern Nigeria, August to November, 1929," Onitsha, 12 November, 1929. Father Soul's belief that a prayer-book did not exist in the Mission in 1929 was an indication that the use of Father Treich's Igbo Prayer-book of 1922 was, by 1929, not so common as to be noticed by a visitor.

embers of ethnic feelings. On Christmas Day 1925, for instance, Father O'Sullivan of the Calabar Mission preached his sermon in English as usual, but got an Igbo Catechist to interpret it for his Efik audience. The "Catholic Old Boys", a radical group which featured in the 1920s as the mouthpiece of the Calabar people, regarded that "affront" as a deliberate action designed to punish the natives of Calabar.[91]

It is possible that Father O'Sullivan grasped at a most effective punitive measure against the attendants of the Mass on Christmas Day 1925, who, according to the report of the "Old Boys", were refused participation at the mid-night Mass on the grounds that they possessed no sacrament permits—cards that showed that Christians had paid their Church dues. But it is also possible that after staying many years in the Igbo country before being posted to Calabar, Father O'Sullivan chose an Interpreter who spoke a language he already understood but could not speak. In that way he would be able to assure himself of the correctness of the turbulent translations of his thoughts.

Our chronological survey of the vernacular publications by the Catholics took us to 1929, the year Father Biéchy produced an Efik version of the Igbo Catechism. The 1930s ushered in a number of changes in the Vicariate with far-reaching consequences. Firstly, there was a change in the leadership of the Mission. Bishop Heerey, Coadjutor since 1927, succeeded Bishop Shanahan in 1931. To a large extent, the new leader was a personification of the new generation of missionaries whose dispositions towards the vernacular were not as sympathetic as those of the older generation. Is it any wonder that the 1929 resolution of the Catholic Ordinaries which rejected the Union Igbo was proposed by Bishop Heerey?[92]

Secondly, the vast territory of the Vicariate of Southern Nigeria was divided into three different Missions in 1934. This measure, rather than giving a greater scope to the attention hitherto paid to the individual languages, seemed to have achieved the opposite: it led the standing language committees to disperse for good.

However, a few useful publications were added to the vernacular list in the Igbo speaking district. Chief among these was what may have been the most popular Christian literature of the mission era in Eastern Nigeria, namely, *Ndu Dinwenu Anyi*, a narrative Igbo prose which touched on some major issues of the Christian story from Creation to

---

[91] See CSE: 554/IV, Catholic Old Boys, "Petition to the Superior General of the Holy Ghost Congregation", Duke Town, 24 April, 1926.

[92] See CSE: 554/I, "Conference of the Ordinaries of Nigeria and the British Cameroons...," p. 22.

Doomsday. Published in 1940, the biblical narrative instilled in those who could read it some measure of that popular delight which was associated with English Mystery Cycles and Morality plays. It was intended to serve as a supplement to the doctrinal Catechisms.

Another major contribution to the vernacular Christian literature was the Igbo Catechism published in 1944. The authorship of the book was not stated, but to all appearances, the production must have been largely directed by Father John Jordan, who wrote the Foreword. The new Igbo Catechism contained a number of changes, one of which was the order of presentation which, according to Father Jordan, "differs from that found in most modern Catechisms in that it is based mainly on the Catechism of the Summa Theologica [sic] of St. Thomas Aquinas".[93] This curious renunciation of the modern elements in Catechisms underscores the Irish conservatism which has left an indelible mark on the Catholic Church in Eastern Nigeria.

As a further innovation of the new Catechism, the famous questions and answers of the old Igbo Catechism were drastically reduced from 550 to only 251. Gone were also the prayers at the end of the old Catechism. To compensate for these losses, recourse was had to frequent doctrinal instructions and biblical narratives, which were to be referred to in *Ndu Dinwenu Anyi*. This innovation no doubt had its advantage: it diminished the chances of learning by rote, and allowed the people a measure of personal reflection. However, that utility was greatly undermined by the fact that many of the Catechumens could not read Igbo, a handicap whose adverse effect Bishop Heerey himself recognized in 1944. In an appeal which revealed the sordid nature of Igbo studies, the Bishop urged teachers to "encourage those non-scholars who attend Religious Instruction Classes to learn to read Igbo".[94]

Worthy of mention are two vernacular books which were published shortly after the creation of the Owerri Diocese in 1950, namely, an illustrated *Catechism Nke Mbu*, 1951, and an educational Reader for infants entitled *Central Igbo Primer*. By using an Igbo dialect that had great affinity to the dialects of the Owerri districts, the authors of these two books seemed to have disapproved of the age-long practice of imposing on all Igbo Catholics publications that were heavily influenced by Onitsha elements. Their triumphant return to Owerri Igbo also underscored the insuperable nature of the Igbo language problem.

---

[93] J. Jordan, Foreword, *Igbo Catechism*, by the Holy Ghost Fathers (Onitsha-Owerri: Catholic Mission, 1944), p. 2.

[94] Quoted in ibid., p. 4.

3. Contrasts in Irish and French Approaches to the Vernacular Problem

A close look at nearly all the linguistic works whose authors were specified reveals an astonishing sameness in the nationality of the writers. With the exception of Father Carlo Zappa, who was an Italian, the rest of the authors were French missionaries, the majority of whom came from the German-speaking province of Alsace. One meets the same picture in the linguistic publications in Western and Northern Nigeria by the Society of African Missions. This occurrence was no mere accident; it was a glaring evidence of the fundamental differences between the French and Irish missionaries in their missionary conceptions, and in their approach to the English language.

The apostolate of the school which Father Lejeune initiated between 1900 and 1905 brought conflict upon the French, and convenience for the Irish: the course which the school method of evangelization took after his prefectship meant for the French Fathers the renunciation of their favoured direct evangelical method, and their replacement with Irish missionaries, the dedicated advocates of the school. Although the French were also supporters of the school method, they had clearly different conceptions as to its application. Whereas the Irish tended to achieve their missionary ideals through an absolute dependence on the school apostolate,[95] the French Fathers took the school to be merely ancillary to the traditional evangelical method. The French position became evident in a communiqué issued in 1914 by four renowned French Fathers:

> We are of the opinion that one should adopt, develop, and perfect the school, because we believe that its disadvantages can be remedied. We take the liberty of suggesting a few [of these] remedies:
> a) That the Fathers become teachers only in very rare cases.
> b) That Catechism classes be run by the Fathers in the schools of their stations.
> c) That these Catechism classes be prepared and organized, and that they should never, under any pretext, be changed to a history class or to any other profane subject.
> d) That the teaching profession be confined to the Brothers or to certificated natives ....
> e) That Catechism examinations be carried out in all the grades, and that prizes and certificates be awarded to successful pupils.
> f) That special religious instructions be given to our native teachers.
> Signed: Fathers L. Léna, F. Sinner, J. Krafft, P. Biéchy.[96]

---

[95] An official report on the Prefecture in 1909, written most probably by Father Shanahan himself, had the following to say: "...if we had no schools, we would have a fairly easy life, with little work, little worry, and plenty of free time. The number of baptisms would not reach a fifth of what it is at the moment." CSE: *Bulletin*, 25 (1909-1910), 357.

[96] CSE: 191/B/V, "Notes made by the Fathers of Calabar and Anua Missions on Niger Schools," Calabar, 26 April, 1914.

This programme of evangelization which gave such a detailed scope to the teaching of catechism by the European Fathers implicitly took the mastery of the vernacular by the Fathers for granted. Through their linguistic publications, the signatories of the above communiqué managed, despite the fact that most of their "remedies" were never endorsed, to remain faithful to their missionary conceptions.

Anybody who wishes to isolate the reason why the Irish missionaries should have difficulties in sanctioning the above remedies, especially items a) and d), must necessarily grasp at the factor of English in the acclaimed school method of evangelization. The Irish missionaries came to the Niger in the first place because they were native speakers of English. When Father Lejeune, a Frenchman, started the call for English-speaking missionaries, he demonstrated that he was a man whose judgment was not swayed by national predilections: he genuinely addressed himself to the political and social realities in Nigeria where no future was seen for a Catholic Mission without schools, and without English-speaking missionaries.

The Irish came to Nigeria primarily as school masters, a reality which was sensitively at variance with the missionary ideals of the French. Asked why it was necessary to found a new Irish missionary congregation—the Saint Patrick's Society—for work in Nigeria, Shanahan once said that the use of French Fathers was not appropriate in a Mission "where the school holds such a permanent position as a means of evangelization."[97] The French, for their part, regarded this excessive emphasis on the school as incompatible with a true and effective Christian ministry. When at the beginning of this century the wish was expressed for a Catholic High School run by Irish Fathers, Father Léna supported the idea primarily because of his strong conviction that the Irish were good only for the school. His recommendation to the Mother House was:

> It appears to me more preferable that the Irish Fathers be put in charge of the [proposed High School] because they are generally ineffective in the [pastoral] ministry. By contrast, we [the French] have a bent for the ministry.[98]

These conflicting approaches of the Irish and French missionaries to the ministry inevitably found expression in their attitudes towards the all-important language issue. While the former emphasized English—the language of the school—the latter busied themselves with the study of the

---

[97] Quoted in J. Jordan, *Bishop Shanahan*, p. 254.
[98] CSE: 192/B/VI, "Léna to Superior General," Calabar, 18 March, 1910.

vernacular—the language of catechism. It was no accident, therefore, that the few works in the vernacular by the Catholics were produced by the French missionaries.

The fact that most of the Alsatian Fathers were bilingual held huge significance for their study of languages. Their study of English in preparation for missionary work in English-speaking territories further equipped them with linguistic experiences which made the study of native languages more natural to them than it was to the Irish. Furthermore, as pioneers in the Mission, the French Fathers lived with the people in an intimacy that had all the primitive ramifications in food and housing. That closeness brought a compelling need to learn the language of the people. By contrast, the Irish were a new generation of missionaries who came to the Mission when the Fathers' houses were built in total isolation from the villagers. Whatever chances they had of mingling with the people got lost in exclusive preoccupation with the school, where the vernacular was often a taboo. As Father J. Soul noted in 1929, the Fathers who had completely renounced the study of the vernacular were those engaged with teaching work in the Seminary and in the Training College.[99] Had he written his report a few years later, he would certainly have included the Fathers engaged in the Secondary Schools. With the establishment of Secondary schools in the 1930s and 1940s, the emphasis on the school apostolate was rapidly diverted from the primary to the secondary level. Since no catechism was taught, and no vernacular education offered, in the Secondary Schools, the Fathers were at last relieved of the only exigencies that had hitherto compelled them to study the native languages beyond the elementary knowledge required for the hearing of confessions.

For Catholicism in Eastern Nigeria, the school was both a strength and a weakness. Extolling the existence of a perfect organization of the work of Catechists and Teachers in the Niger Mission, Father Soul recommended it as a model for the Missions of the Holy Ghost Congregation in Africa. But in a rather pathetic tone, he remarked that with regard to the availability of vernacular literature, the Niger Mission was one of the most backward.[100] In other words, the Catholic Niger Mission in Eastern Nigeria disregarded what has now become the most important criterion for measuring the success of Christian education among the nations of the world. A mission which saw men like Fathers Ganot, Vogler, Léna, Treich, and Biéchy had the opportunity of carrying the development of vernacular literature to a very high level. But that tantalizing possibility

---

[99] CSE: 554/V, J. Soul, "General Report...1929."
[100] Ibid.

was permanently eclipsed by the overriding priority given to the English language.

III. *Educational Opportunities For Women*

1. *Drawbacks In Girls' Education*

A look at Table 3 of this work reveals a most curious, but predictable, disproportion in. the number of boys and girls in all the schools of the Christian denominations in 1928. This imbalance approached the threshold of absurdity chiefly in Catholic Unassisted Schools, the mainstay of Catholic educational establishments before the 1930s. If the Annual Report on the Education Department for 1928 did not make a grave mistake in its statistics, there were, for instance, 6,782 boys on the attendance list in Catholic Unassisted Schools in the Owerri Province, as opposed to only 42 girls. The Anglicans had, in the same year and in the same Province, 6,587 boys, and 1,006 girls. The figures for Onitsha and Calabar Provinces show similar discrepancies.[101] At the root of the abysmally low rating of girls in Catholic schools lay two main factors, namely, Catholic official policy towards mixed schools, and the discrimination of women in traditional society.

a) Catholic Policy on Mixed Schools

The underprivileged position of women in native society posed an educational problem for both Catholics and Protestants alike. Nevertheless, girls had a comparatively easy passage in Protestant schools, a discrepancy whose cause may be sought in the different attitudes of the two confessions towards mixed schools. Table 11 makes the divergence of policy in this regard very apparent. Of the twenty-five Assisted Protestant Infant Schools in 1913, only two were not mixed, one for boys and one for girls. By contrast, all the thirty-six Assisted Catholic Infant Schools, save three, were strictly segregated according to sex, twenty-seven for boys and only six for girls. This had nothing to do with anti-feminism; it was the logical corollary to a religious outlook which looked upon the daily gathering of boys and girls under one roof with abject indignation. In 1919, the Sacred Congregation for the Propagation of Faith in Rome was so obsessed with the hazards of mixed schools as to issue a questionnaire to Catholic Missions all over the world in an effort

---

[101] Cf. *Annual Report on the Education Department, Southern Provinces, for the Year 1928* (Lagos: Government Printing Office, n.d.), p. 24.

to give an official ruling on "the religious and moral education of children."[102] The consensus in the opinions of the Church leaders was that mixed schools were detrimental to the morality of children. It was against this background that the Mother House of the Holy Ghost Congregation frowned at the practice of Father Lutz and his Confrères of keeping both boys and girls in their only school at the Onitsha Wharf. They were advised to stick to the Church's tradition of separating boys and girls at school.[103]

However, the problem involved in running separate schools for girls at a time when most pupils had to be boarders was for a few male missionaries insurmountable. Until Catholic religious Sisters were found to take over that duty, the education of girls was carried out at a very low scale.

Table 11

Assisted Infant Schools in Southern Nigeria in 1913

Agency	Mixed Schools	Boys' Schools	Girls' Schools	Total
Government	21	—	—	21
Anglican	23	1	1	25
Catholic	3	27	6	36

Source: PRO:C.O.657/3, "Sessional Paper No.1 of 1915," *Annual Report on the Education Department for 1913.*

b) Discrimination of Women in Traditional Society

In the main, the drawbacks in the education of women was largely due to the attitude of native society towards the weaker sex. All the opportunities which the school brought—the teaching profession, work in government offices, and employment in the factories—were looked upon by parents and guardians as privileges worth the aspiration only of their male children. Thus, only the education of boys was eagerly pursued as a most profitable asset. Devoid of this vocational trend, girls' education was, by contrast, either rejected or confined to the infant classes of primary schools.

Furthermore, the hope for economic and social gains which dominated native marriage laws and customs was a stumbling block on the way of

---

[102] CSE: *Bulletin,* 29 (1918-1920), 329f. Since "mixed school" also means "non-denominational school" in French terminology, it is possible that Rome spoke in this sense.

[103] See CSE: 192/B/I, "Superior General to Father Lutz," Paris, 2 November, 1888.

girls' education. Girls were usually betrothed while still very young, and as soon as the bride prices were paid off, they were withdrawn from school and married to their waiting husbands.[104] Those lucky enough to complete their education sometimes ran the risk of not being married by prejudiced non-Christians. It was this last experience which filled Father Lejeune with misgivings about the propriety of severing the young women from their all-important native ties. He wrote:

> [The] greatest shame for a [Nigerian] woman is to have no children, a case that always calls for divorce in this country. Let us leave these girls with their parents, instead of inuring them to luxury; let us be contented with giving them only religious instructions. Besides, a married woman here adopts the religion of her husband, and the latter generally does not seek a wife among the emancipated young girls of Catholic and Protestant making, rather he goes to the pagans, who are at home with the loyalty prescribed for women by native laws. They are, perhaps, right.[105]

2. Girls' Education Under the Sisters of St. Joseph of Cluny

Despite all the apprehensions of the Mission and the people, education of women had many triumphs to point to. Chief among these was certainly the mere fact that the care of girls featured in mission educational programme right from the start. At the instigation of Father Lutz, the founder of the Lower Niger Mission, four Sisters of St. Joseph of Cluny arrived at Onitsha on 15 November 1889. To have volunteered for the Niger Mission at a time when that spot on the globe was widely known as *the White-man's grave*, was in itself a triumph of will on the part of the Cluny Sisters. The choice of a congregation of Teaching and Nursing Sisters, such as they were, was significant: it underscored the concern of the founding Fathers for the educational and medical care of the natives.

Under the Cluny Sisters, girls' education in the Prefecture received an innovatory impetus. A clear picture of that pioneer enterprise can be got from a letter of Father Lejeune to Lord Lugard in 1905. Asking for permission for girls from Dekina in Northern Nigeria—a separate political jurisdiction by 1905—to be sent to the Sisters at Onitsha, the Prefect hoped to get them trained in "washing, hand and machine sewing, ironing, cooking, the speaking, reading, and writing of English, etc, etc."[106]

---

[104] By 1893, the bride price ranged between 150 and 200 French francs, a fabulous sum at that time. See CSE: *Bulletin*, 17 (1893-1896), 418.

[105] CSE: *Bulletin*, 21 (1901-1902), 518f. This prejudice over girls' education was also expressed at Aguleri in 1912. "As for the girls," it was reported, "we have long hesitated to call them to school. "See CSE: *Bulletin*, 26 (1911-1912), 867.

[106] CSE: 192/B/IV, "Lejeune to Lugard," Bassa, Dekina, 15 January, 1905.

These were new avenues in girls' education in Eastern Nigeria, thanks to the vocational training and experiences of the Sisters.

Following a Mission Council decision in which Sister Anne-Marie, a Visitor of the Cluny Sisters, was present, the Onitsha Convent was closed down in 1908, and the Sisters sent to Calabar to aid the members of their congregation in that region. In the light of the singular services of the Sisters to the girls of Onitsha, their withdrawal appears to many as incomprehensible. Although the actual reason for the decision to send the Sisters to Calabar has remained shrouded in mystery, one explanation may have been Shanahan's obsessive quest for school buildings, a passion which was intensified by the controversy triggered off by the Education Code of 1908. Especially the strong emphasis on certificated teachers had made the lack of a Catholic *High School* an existential problem for the Catholic education-orientated missionary enterprise. In a letter to the Superior General in January 1908, the Prefect made no bones of his willingness to allow the convent and the invaluable services of the Sisters swept away in the turbulent educational waves of Nigeria. He wrote:

> If the Sisters were to quit Onitsha, we would immediately have a magnificent building for our school, Training Institution, etc etc. It is certain that if they gave me the occasion to make them leave, I would not hesitate to do so.[107]

It is not clear what occasion the Sisters eventually gave, but the Prefect probably did not have to wait too long for it. For in May 1908, he informed his Superior General of the decision of his Mission Council to close down the Onitsha Convent, and to abandon the native hospital at Calabar.[108] Only three nuns were left behind in Onitsha to care for the sick. Also left behind were sixty female pupils whose education was entrusted to three pupil-teachers who worked under the direction of Father Vogler.

Although the Cluny Sisters were sent to Calabar in 1904 primarily for medical services, it was their educational work that ultimately triumphed there. On the advice of two colonial medical doctors, Dr. Allman and Dr. O'Dey, who were "scandalized" to see that no Father or Sister had set foot in a hospital for natives at Calabar, Father Lejeune had proposed to the Colonial Administrator in 1903 to send the Sisters to the hospital.[109] Posted to Calabar in 1904, two sisters worked in the hospital, and two others in a girls' school which was quickly established for their

---

[107] CSE: 192/B/V, "Shanahan to LeRoy." Calabar, 21 January, 1908.
[108] CSE: 192/B/V, "Shanahan to LeRoy", Onitsha, 22 May, 1908.
[109] CSE: *Bulletin*, 22 (1903-1904), 799.

management. As has been seen, the hospital work was "abandoned" in 1908 under the same Mission Council decision that closed down the Onitsha Convent. The services of the reinforcement from Onitsha and those of all the Sisters already at Calabar were thereafter concentrated exclusively on educational work among the girls.

For a while, the Sisters scored glaring successes at the St. Joseph's Convent School Calabar, the number of pupils rising from 82 in 1904 to 112 in 1905. According to the Annual Report on the Education Department, Southern Provinces, there were 98 girls receiving instruction in domestic economy under the Cluny Sisters in 1908.[110] However, by 1919, illness and fatigue had greatly undermined the labours of the Sisters, and in 1920, the last three left the Mission and returned to France. Although the boarders were sent home to their families after the departure of the Sisters, the Convent school continued to function.[111]

The work of the Sisters of St. Joseph in Eastern Nigeria was essentially a pioneer undertaking, and as such it was encompassed with bitter trials and failures. Measured in terms of quantity, the success of the Cluny nuns was nothing compared with the colossal achievements of the Holy Rosary Sisters in later years. Yet, it was a success which scaled the heights of excellence chiefly by the force of its novelty. Through the vocational touch they gave to girls' education, the Sisters endeavoured, for the first time in the Prefecture, to extricate the African women from their underprivileged position in society. As their primary objective in girls' education, they emphasized the production of useful Christian mothers. The dogged enthusiasm with which they tried to reach this goal can be seen in an address of welcome which the girls of St. Joseph's Convent School presented to Lady Egerton, the wife of the Governor, when she visited their school in 1906. Part of that address, which was of course written by the Sisters, reads as follows:

'You count for little now,' it's thus they say,
The boys who rival us across the way!
'Tis true, like them we cannot aim so high,
We cannot for the bigger places try.
But we intend some day, to sell and buy,
Eén now the busy needle we have learned to ply.

Nor do we think too lowly we must bend,
When taught to wash, to iron and to mend,
Not less than boys useful ambitions spur,
We also wish to make our little stir;

[110] PRO: C.O: 592/5, *Annual Report on the Education Department, Southern Provinces, for the Year 1908.*
[111] Cf. CSE: *Bulletin*, 30 (1921-1922), 516.

We also wish to act our humble part,
To practice, as a woman should, each useful art.

This doing we may hope one day to be
Of help to make our people really free
And make them fit to share the boon with thee,
O Gentle Lady, and thy race across the sea;
The boon, which in thy person seems so good,
Of true, but rare, and fair and noble womanhood![112]

It was the coupling of education with the fulfilment of this far-reaching purpose that inspired the first moves of the natives towards the education of their daughters. The use of education in the production of enterprising and useful wives was so appealing that it could not remain unnoticed. In fact it served as a norm with which parents and guardians were to measure girls' education in the future. In 1932, for instance, the *Catholic Old Boys*, the self-proclaimed spokesmen for the Calabar people, sent a protest letter to the Superior of the Calabar Mission in which they demanded, among other things, that the education of their future wives include domestic science, and that it should not be confined to mere book-learning and religious instruction. They claimed that "a woman may obtain such degrees...as B.A., M.A., etc., and yet if she is [lacking] of a good domestic training, that is if she has no knowledge of domestic economy and needlework, her education is not worth anything."[113]

3. *Sister Magdalene C. Walker and Girls' Education Among the Efiks and the Ibibios*

The management of the St. Joseph's Convent School after the departure of the Cluny Sisters was undertaken by two Irish lay women who volunteered for the Mission in 1921. Although highly qualified, the two ladies could not address themselves adequately to the diversified vocational activities which were carried out by the Cluny Sisters. Consequently, emphasis in the girls' school gradually shifted from practical skills to literary studies, a change which was received with indignation by the natives. This is evident from the protest of the *Catholic Old Boys* referred to above. The arrival in 1924 of Sister Magdalene C. Walker, an Irish Holy Child Sister, promptly set the doubts of the natives to rest.

In an outline of her plan for girls' education, she rejected any attempt to disguise an English system of education in the curriculum for African

---

[112] Quoted in *Illustrated Catholic Mission*, 22 (1907-1908), 71.
[113] CSE: 554/IV, "Catholic OLd Boys to Father O'Sullivan, Superior of Calabar Mission," Calabar, 13 October, 1923.

schools. In the place of such a camouflage, she pleaded for an "objective" education which would come to terms with the specific situation of the African women.[114] For the realization of her designs on education, she adopted the Montessori method in the infant classes. The astonishing results which she achieved brought her praise from government officials in Nigeria, and admiration from educationists in Europe and America.[115]

Essentially, Sister Magdalene's educational plan was built on a long-term basis which looked forward to a time when the Africans themselves would take charge of their education. That involved the careful selection and education of few girls who would in turn extend their knowledge to other girls. By 1929, that strategy was already bearing fruits among the Efiks and the Ibibios: the teachers trained by her at Calabar were opening schools for girls in the villages. In a letter to Bishop Shanahan on July 31, 1929, Father Biéchy, Superior of the Anua Mission, gave a vivid description of the responsibilities entrusted to the African lady teachers, and the conditions under which they carried them out:

> When Sister M. Magdalene was here [Anua] last December, we spoke of a girls' school. I found her very enthusiastic about it and ready to spare her best girls to start the work. With your approval we have started the work on trial. Five girls have come up this month to get the place ready, two of them are elder girls, with many years of training and experience; I am sure they shall do very good work for our women. We have built at present a native house large enough to accommodate from ten to twelve girls.
> The school is a native building quite temporary. A small rest house is under construction. This is very [solid]: concrete pillars, iron roof, mud walls, and will serve as an emergency building in case anything goes wrong with the native building. Three of the girls have bicycles and they will see the women of the nearest outstations for catechism and needle work. Nsukara, Abak, Aka, Anua Obio, Isiene have been visited already. The Convent and the school will be opened officially in August 5th. Sister M. Magdalene shall be present herself for a fortnight to get the work well started. Once the work is going on she will come up monthly for a few days. Already, we have had... many applications to take in girls as boarders, mostly children of Christian parents or fiancees to Teachers.[116]

Worthy of special note in this letter is the role played by the school in the evangelization of the people. Called to Anua to found a girls' school, the

---

[114] M. C. Magdalene, "Education of Girls in Southern Nigeria," in *IRM*, 17 (1928), 505-514.
[115] For details on Sister Magdalene's educational achievements, see Handmaids of the Holy Child Jesus, *A Tribute to a Valiant Pioneer Missionary: Sister Mary Charles Walker* (Calabar, 1974), pp. 10-13; also L. Okure, *Centenary Reflection: A Tribute to Sister Mary Charles Walker* (Calabar, 1981), pp. 23-39.
[116] CSE: 191/B/VIII, "P. Biéchy to Bishop Shanahan," Anua, 31 July, 1929.

five highly trained girls—true apostles by any standard—did not confine their educational activities within the makeshift mud school which existed for only a privileged few. Rather, they used the school as a springboard for a larger and more profound missionary campaign in the surrounding villages, a practice which was not peculiar to the Anua Mission, but a *modus operandi* in the whole of the Vicariate.

The greatest achievement of Sister Magdalene Walker was, perhaps, the foundation of the first African religious Sisterhood in Nigeria. By virtue of her relentless option for a truly local Church, Calabar became the first place after Onitsha to experience a historic moment in the indigenization process. When the foundation members of the Handmaids of the Holy Child Jesus were consecrated in 1931, Father John Anyogwu, the first African priest of the Vicariate,[117] ordained priest a year earlier, was present at the ceremony, and the message which the whole spectacle conveyed to the local inhabitants was more than words could have said.

With the creation in 1934 of the Prefecture of Calabar, the task of educating the women of the new mission territory fell exclusively to the Holy Child Sisters of Ireland and their offspring, the Handmaids of the Holy Child Jesus founded by Sister Magdalene Walker.

4. *The Achievements of the Holy Rosary Sisters in Igboland*

Evolving an educational system which was at the same time solid and universally attainable was not the responsibility of one person, even if she were to have the extraordinary strength and ability of a Sister Magdalene. Bishop Shanahan came to terms with this reality by founding the Congregation of the Missionary Sisters of Our Lady of the Holy Rosary in Ireland in 1924. To the duties of the new religious Sisterhood belonged, first and foremost, the intellectual and moral formation of women in the Vicariate.

The arrival at Onitsha in 1928 of the first five members of the new congregation marked a turning-point in the history of girls' education in Igboland. Without a loss of time, the Sisters established a comprehensive school at Onitsha whose orbit included formal education for School Leaving Certificates, vocational classes for Housecraft Certificates, and teacher training courses for Teacher Certificates. Commenting on the success of the Sisters at Onitsha, Bishop Shanahan said that the educa-

---

[117] The first Catholic priest ever to be ordained in Nigeria was Father Delany, an Irishman who was ordained in July 1919. Contrary to popular belief, Father J. Anyogwu was not the first Igbo priest. That honour belonged to Father Paul Emecheta, an Ika-Igbo of the Vicariate of Western Nigeria who was ordained January 6, 1920.

tion of young women was "an indispensable groundwork in the establishment of a Christian family."[118] This great service was enthusiastically extended to other parts of the Vicariate, and by 1940 there were flourishing Holy Rosary Schools at Ihiala, Adazi, and Enugu, in the Onitsha Province, and at Emekukwu, Nguru, Ahiara, and Port Harcourt, in the Owerri Province. Later, Holy Rosary Schools sprang up at Umudioka, Aguleri, Nsukka, Eke, Mbieri, and Uzoagba.

An achievement of the Holy Rosary Sisters with far-reaching consequences was the establishment at Onitsha of a Training College for girls. It was this College that served as a wellspring for the staffing of Catholic girls' schools in Igboland. By 1929, the training department of the Onitsha Holy Rosary school had been recognized by the colonial Government as a Training Institute.[119] However, it was not until July 2, 1935, that the school was officially inaugurated as a full-fledged Training College for Higher Elementary teachers. In 1937, the first group of students sat for a public examination with "very satisfactory" results.[120]

So far, girls' education in Eastern Nigeria had been restricted to primary education. In the 1940s, efforts were made to extend secondary education to girls, a privilege which the boys had been enjoying since 1933. "We are anxious," wrote Bishop Heerey in 1941, "to do something for girls' secondary education if we could hope for any assistance."[121] Much of that anxiety was consequent on repeated pressure from Miss G. Plummer, the Lady Education Officer for the Southern Provinces, who understandably was the greatest advocate for women education in Nigeria. Anxious to bring the East at parity with the West with regard to the educational opportunities for women, she had made suggestions in 1940 to the Bishop on three issues concerning the education of girls in his Vicariate. These included: a) the Extension of facilities for teacher training, b) the provision of secondary schools for girls, c) the provision of domestic science centres. Since these questions dominated girls' education in the 1940s and 1950s, it may be appropriate to deal with them in some detail. By 1940, there were two Catholic training colleges for women in Eastern Nigeria—the Holy Rosary Training College for Higher Elementary Certificate with campuses at Onitsha and Ihiala, and a Teacher Training Centre at Ikot Ekpene for Elementary Teacher Certificate. With a view to making the two grades of certificates

---

[118] Quoted in CSE: *Bulletin*, 35 (1931-1932), 84.

[119] See CSE: 554/VII, "Etat Statistique Annuel Pour la Propagande," 1 December, 1929.

[120] ODA: "The Proprietor, Catholic Mission School, Onitsha-Owerri Vicariate, to Director of Education," Onitsha, 18 February, 1939.

[121] ODA: "Heerey to Director of Education," Onitsha, 7 March, 1941.

available in both the Onitsha and Calabar Provinces, the Lady Education Officer strongly suggested the introduction of exchange programmes which would enable students from the Onitsha-Owerri Vicariate to study at the Calabar College, and students from the Prefecture of Calabar to study at Onitsha. The funds for the inevitable building extensions in both colleges was to come from the Colonial Development fund as decided by the Board of Education at its meeting in April 1940.[122]

It is not clear what Bishop Heerey's reaction to Miss Plummer's proposal was, but Father Richard Daly, his Education Secretary, did not receive the idea of exchange schemes with much enthusiasm. He argued that since parents in rural areas were still not very keen on educating their daughters, turning out large numbers of teachers would be "to force" a demand for girls' schools. In his opinion, the demand for teachers should always remain "greater than the number trained."[123] Given the speed with which Holy Rosary Schools were established in the 1940s, Father Daly's rejection of extensions in teacher training facilities may appear as a paradox. However, as a dedicated Education Secretary, he was in the position to judge the situation better than anybody else. In his memorandum on Catholic educational work in 1938, he in fact revealed that considerable expansion had already been carried out in the Onitsha Training College to meet the demand for more schools.[124] It would seem therefore that the scope of expansion suggested by the Lady Education Officer in 1940 was in fact out of proportion with the actual need of the Catholic girls' schools in the East.

However, behind the immediate reason given for the rejection of the expansion proposal lay the fear that the Government, represented by Miss Plummer, was meddling with the affairs of the Church. In fact, the Education Secretary did remark that the establishment of inter-mission institutions could be arranged by "ecclesiastical authorities" at the suggestion of designated staff, and not of "people other than the staff."[125]

The second issue treated by Miss Plummer was about the necessity of establishing a secondary school for girls in the East. In this regard, a suggestion was made in Catholic circles—probably by the Bishop himself— to start a school of that nature at Onitsha in January 1941, a proposal which was also received with dampened enthusiasm by his Education Secretary. Fearing that the secondary education of girls did not have "a

[122] ODA: Letter No. L.E.O.186/18, "Lady Education Officer to Bishop Heerey," Ibadan, 13 May, 1940.
[123] ODA: R. Daly, "A Commentary," n. d.
[124] ODA: "R. Daly [for Proprietor] to Director of Education," Onitsha, 18 February, 1939.
[125] ODA: R. Daly, "A Commentary," n. d.

definite purpose", namely, job opportunities, Father Daly urged for caution in dealing with the issue. "The demand for a girls' Secondary
School," he said, "must be treated very carefully and slowly."[126]

On the question of domestic science centres for girls, the Lady Education Officer had given a venture at Oyo in Western Nigeria by the Native
Administration as a possible model. In that centre, girls from various
schools met about two times a week for instructions in African Cookery,
Laundry, Housewifery, Needlework, Infant Welfare, and Weaving.
Given the qualifications and activities of the European Catholic Sisters
in these fields of study, the project easily won the approbation of Catholic
authorities. Accordingly, a scheme of domestic science training was
worked out for a centre at Umudioka, and eventually spread through the
training colleges to other towns and villages in the East.

Apparently dissatisfied with Catholic stand on the question of secondary schools for girls in the East, the Lady Education Officer came up
again in August 1941 with a more controversial proposal than the one she
had made a year before. In a memorandum to the Catholic Ordinaries
of Nigeria, she offered to move Queens College from Lagos to the East
if the existing Mission girls' colleges in Lagos gave the guarantee that
they would sufficiently cater for the secondary education of girls in Lagos
and the Western Region for the next five years. From her memorandum,
it was also very clear that the acceptance of the proposal would render
the establishment of Voluntary Agency girls' secondary schools in the
Eastern Province superfluous.[127]

The readiness to transfer the best government educational institution
for girls to the Eastern Region was an indication that the Government
took the encouragement of girls' education in that Region very seriously.
It also revealed the difficulty with which the Government met its educational obligations during the war years. Under normal circumstances,
the Government would not have hesitated to establish a new government
college for girls in the East. But during the War, the necessary funds for
such projects were hard to come by. If the Lady Education Officer
resorted to elaborate consultations with, and proposals to, the Voluntary
Agencies, it was a sign that the success of her educational designs rested
solely on their cooperation.

However, for Bishop Heerey the idea of leaving the secondary education of Catholic girls entirely in government hands was an unacceptable
proposition. The specifically Catholic policy of resisting both Protestant

---

[126] Ibid.
[127] See ODA: G. Plummer, Lady Education Officer, Southern Provinces,
"Memorandum No. L. E. O.186/75," Lagos, 15 August, 1941.

and government educational superiority was in no way undermined by the special honour to have Queen's College—the *crème de la crème* of girls' colleges in the whole of Nigeria—transferred to his Vicariate. Accordingly, in his letter to the Lady Education Officer, the Bishop made it sufficiently clear that the Catholic Missions, which possessed in the Sisters the best qualified women educators, were not prepared to lose a grip on the education of girls in the Eastern Region. He wrote:

> We have been making preparations in our Mission to start, in January next, a post primary course for girls; but the future of educated girls is so uncertain that we feel, and indeed hope, that the numbers will remain low. There does not seem to be any opening in the country for educated girls....
>
> For the above reason, if for no other, it does not seem necessary to transfer Queen's College to the Eastern Provinces. The Missions are in a position, if they get the funds, to train the girls of the Eastern Provinces to be suitable wives and mothers. Even if Queen's College were transferred, we feel it would be a mistake to take this work out of the hands of the Missionaries....[128]

If there was a tendency in Catholic policy to proceed with the secondary education of girls slowly and cautiously, it was quickly discarded as soon as it became clear to the Catholic authorities that the designs of the Lady Education Officer could not be held off indefinitely. Consequently, a Catholic Secondary School for girls, the Queen of the Rosary College, was established at Onitsha in 1942. The school started with only thirteen students as was anticipated, but by 1949, the number had risen to a hundred and twenty.

That the College was founded at Onitsha was a personal defeat for Father R. Daly, the Catholic Education Secretary. Moved by a rather conservative outlook on the moral education of the Africans, he had vehemently opposed the idea of establishing another educational institution for girls at Onitsha with the argument that that would provide "further distractions for Students in the Boys' Secondary institutions."[129] For the same reason, he had criticized the idea of keeping some of the students of the Holy Rosary Training College at Onitsha instead of moving all of them to the new site at Ihiala. "The system of keeping the first year students at Onitsha," he said, "seems to be an utter mistake, if these young bush girls are to be allowed to attend football-matches etc. 'under escort' with students of C.K.C. and others."[130] However, the

---

[128] ODA: "Bishop Heerey to the Lady Education Officer," Onitsha, 4 September, 1941.
[129] ODA: R. Daly, "A Commentary," n. d.
[130] Ibid.

Holy Rosary College was eventually moved to Enugu not necessarily because of pressure from the Education Secretary, but possibly because of political changes in the administration of the colony.

In a series of constitutional changes that were made between 1947 and 1954, education in Nigeria became a regional service under Regional Education Authorities, most of whom were Black Nationalists.[131] Because of the deteriorating relationship between the Church and the Nationalists over education in the 1950s, the establishment of new Voluntary Agency schools was no longer looked upon with favour by the reformed Ministry of Education. Gone were the days when the Education Department in Lagos was urging the Catholic Missions in the East to establish schools. In fact, the request of Bishop Whelan in 1954 to found a Holy Rosary College for girls at Owerri was turned down by the Regional Education Authorities at Enugu. The College was established in 1955 only after repeated pressure from the Owerri local communities. The name of the school—Community Girls Secondary School—was a reminder of the part played by the natives in winning approval for its foundation,. and a conspicuous departure from the practice of naming girls' schools after the Holy Rosary.[132] Appearing at a time when secondary education was being shifted to the centre stage of Catholic educational enterprise, the negative attitude of the Regional Education Ministry forced the authorities to lift the concentration of schools at Onitsha in order to serve other commercial centres in Eastern Nigeria, such as Enugu and Port Harcourt.

In the main, girls' education in Eastern Nigeria, as in other parts of the country, was started on a very low scale chiefly as a result of the absence of a positive response from the natives. A revision of Catholic policy towards the education of women was undertaken in the 1940s as a result of pressure from the Government, and a change of attitude in the natives. It was against this background that Father J. Jordan emphasized in 1948 that securing a wider Catholic control over girls' education was "an all important matter." That objective was favourably within the reach of the Catholics because, as he rightly pointed out, they alone possessed "the personnel for supervising girls' schooling."[133] He was referring primarily to the existence of qualified European Sisters, who were

---

[131] See Eastern Nigeria, Ministry of Education, *Report on the Review of the Educational System in Eastern Nigeria*, (Enugu, 1962), pp. 7-8.

[132] Cf. R. A. Njoku, *The Advent of the Catholic Church in Nigeria: Its Growth in Owerri Diocese* (Owerri, 1980), pp. 127-132.

[133] CSE: 556/VII, J. Jordan, "Catholic Education Policy: Annual Conventions," 4 August, 1948.

instrumental in making Catholic educational institutions for girls coveted goals in the educational quests of the natives. Especially in the Eastern Provinces, it was not unusual to see children of pagan and Protestant families in schools run by Roman Catholic Sisters. That most of these girls eventually became Catholics was a predictable outcome.

CHAPTER SIX

CATHOLIC SCHOOLS IN THE STRUGGLE BETWEEN MIS-
SION AND COLONIAL POLITICS, 1920-1950

I. *Colonial Education Policy*

Before the 1920s, the educational involvement of the Colonial Administrations in Nigeria, as well as in all British dependencies in Africa,
was of a most superficial and secondary character. Given the fact that
there was lacking, on the part of the Imperial Government, a formulation
of a general policy for the guidance of education in Africa, it was not surprising that education rated very lowly among the responsibilities of the
individual Colonial Governments. A revision of that attitude became
apparent in the 1920s, when new educational conceptions and opportunities in Europe and America were also having important consequences in the colonies.

1. *The Phelps-Stokes Commission*

Of all the forces which acted on the British Government's awareness of
its educational responsibilities towards its African dependencies, the
work of the Phelps-Stokes Commissions was, perhaps, the most important and, to all appearances, the most immediate. A singular example of
the magnitude of private initiative and benevolence, the Commissions set
up by the Phelps-Stokes Fund and Foreign Mission Societies of North
America and Europe made educational tours of Africa from 1920 to
1923. The aim of the enterprise was to use experiences gained from working among American Negroes to determine current educational conditions in Africa and to make suggestions for improvements. The final
reports of the Commissions—*Education in Africa* (1922), and *Education in
East Africa* (1924)—exercised enormous influence on the direction of
educational principles and developments in the African continent.
Among other things, the Commissions urged the Colonial Governments
and the Voluntary Agencies engaged with educational work in Africa to
aspire towards "a correct appreciation of Africa and the Africans."[1]
They emphasized that the nature of the education to be given to the

---

[1] T. J. Jones, *Education in Africa: A Study of West, South, and Equatorial Africa* (New York:
Phelps-Stokes Fund, 1924), p. 1.

Africans should be determined not by the needs of the traders, settlers, administrators, and missionaries, but by the welfare of the natives.[2]

Following the reports and recommendations of the Phelps-Stokes Commissions, an Advisory Committee on Native Education in Tropical Africa was established in 1923 by the British Government, and in 1929 the name of this Committee was changed to the Advisory Committee on Education in the Colonies. Its members included renowned politicians, former Colonial Administrators, Church dignitaries, and representatives of the Christian Missions. As its name implied, the task of the Committee was chiefly to advise the Secretary of State for the Colonies on matters of Native Education in the British dependencies.[3] It quickly became instrumental in the formulation of British educational policy in the colonies.

2. *The Parliamentary White Paper of 1925*

The most significant result derived from the work of the Advisory Committee on Native Education was the issue in March 1925 of a Parliamentary White Paper on Educational Policy in British Tropical Africa. The principles laid down therein were designed to act as guidelines for the Colonial Directors of Education and the various Voluntary Agencies with a view to using education effectively "to raise the standard alike of character and efficiency of the bulk of the people."[4] In the main, these principles formed the basis of all educational policy in the colonies from 1925 till the late 1940s. For our purpose, we shall highlight that section of the White Paper which treated on the issue of partnership and collaboration between the Government and the Voluntary Agencies, and which were to be a source of great concern in Catholic quarters. It concerned the following statement on grant-in-aid policy:

> Government welcomes and will encourage all voluntary educational effort which conforms to general policy. But it reserves to itself the general direction of educational policy and the supervision of all educational institutions....
>
> The policy of encouragement of voluntary effort in education has as its corollary the establishment of a system of grants-in-aid to schools which conform to the prescribed regulation and attain the necessary standard.

---

[2] See P. Bovet, "Education As Viewed By The Phelps-Stokes Commissions," IRM, 15 (1926), 482-492.

[3] For more details on the constitution and function of the Advisory Committee, see J. H. Oldham, "Educational Policy of the British Government in Africa," IRM, 14 (1925), 421-427; R. J. Mason, *British Education in Africa* (London: Oxford University Press, 1959), pp. 40-43.

[4] Quoted in J. S. Coleman, *Nigeria: Background to Nationalism*, p. 117.

> Provided that the required standard of educational efficiency is reached, aided schools should be regarded as filling a place in the scheme of education as important as the schools conducted by the Government itself.[5]

The stress laid on the rights of the Government to direct educational policy and to supervise all educational enterprise was received with great concern by the Voluntary Agencies, especially the Catholic Missions. That attitude was sustained, and to a large extent vindicated, by the activities of some local Directors of Education whose interpretation and use of the 1925 White Paper left no doubts that government educational policy was largely built on criticism of mission methods of, and aims in, education. Something of that official bent was given expression in Nigeria in 1928 by C. B. Smith, the Acting Director of Education, Southern Provinces, when he noted that the missionary and the official educationists found it hard "to see eye to eye in the matter of schools and education" because of the former's religious interpretation of education, and the latter's "purely secular outlook" of it.[6] It was this disharmony in educational objectives—whether real or fancied—that lay at the root of the controversies which erupted between the Catholic Missions and Colonial Governments during the educational reforms that were carried out between 1926 and 1929 throughout the British African Dependencies.

II. *Colonial Educational Reforms*

1. *The Education Code of 1926*

In Nigeria, a new Education Code which was based closely on the White Paper of 1925 became operative on May 26, 1926, and its Regulations on 1 September 1927. In a nutshell, the main provisions of this educational reform included:

1) The registration of all teachers, without which no person was allowed to teach in the schools of the Colony and Southern Provinces.

2) The order to obtain government permission for the opening of new schools, and the right of the Governor to close those considered ineffective or unnecessary.

3) The fixing of minimum wages for teachers.

---

[5] *Education Policy in British Tropical Africa*, (Cmd.2347, HMSO, 1925), quoted in J. Mazé, *La Collaboration Scolaire des Gouvernements Coloniaux et des Missions Afrique Britannique, Afrique Belge, Afrique Française* (Alger, 1933), pp. 168f.

[6] *Annual Report on the Education Department, Southern Provinces, for the Year 1928*, (Lagos: Government Printing Office, n.d.) p. 5.

4) The creation of Mission Supervisors of Schools who received grants-in-aid for their services to Assisted Schools.

5) The assurance of mission representation on the Board of Education.

Although these educational measures and similar ones carried out in other African colonies in the late 1920s were essential for greater efficiency in schools, they nevertheless represented an unwelcome encroachment upon a province that had hitherto belonged almost exclusively to the Voluntary Agencies. If their advent had the effect of a bomb, the reactions of the Catholic Missions were no less explosive. That became evident in some of the terminology employed by mission leaders in referring to them. Some, like Bishop Herman, the Apostolic Vicar of the Lower-Volta, spoke of a devastating blow on Christianity and Civilization.[7] In a measure that further underscored the magnitude of the controversies that erupted over these educational reforms, the Pope appointed an Apostolic Visitor to the British African Colonies—Bishop Hinsley—and saddled him with the task of touring these territories for deliberations with mission leaders and Colonial Governments. What was in the Educational Ordinances and Regulations of the 1920s that brought such tensions as were made manifest in Catholic African Missions?

The answer, in the case of the Nigerian Education Code of 1926, lay primarily in the restrictions placed on the opening of new schools, and the regulation requiring all teachers to be registered. As has been seen in the preceding chapters, the multiplication of Catholic village schools in Eastern Nigeria was carried out between 1906 and 1914 with unprecedented intensity. That rapid expansion continued unabated in the post-war years. For the Administration headed by Sir Hugh Clifford from 1919 to 1926, the restrictive measures of the 1926 Code were necessary in order to stop the spread of the "bush" schools.

But, given the enormous missionary significance of these makeshift village schools, the restrictions placed on their expansion were understandably a matter of grave concern for the Missions. Following the educational reforms of the 1926 Code, hundreds of village schools were shut down, and the people's cravings for new schools left unattended.[8] It was against this background that some mission leaders spoke of the British Government as encouraging illiteracy and paganism in Africa. The future of the Catholic Missions in the British colonies was seen as holding no prospects for effective expansion, and it was to avert that danger that the Ordinaries of Nigeria and the British Cameroons gathered at Lagos

---

[7] See, G. A. Lutterbeck, S.J., "Das Schulwesen in den Britischen Kolonien Afrikas," in KM, 60 (1932), 309.

[8] See CSE: *Bulletin*, 34 (1929-1930), 839.

from 31 August to 3 September 1929 for a Conference presided over by
Bishop Arthur Hinsley, the Visitor Apostolic.

From an interview given to the *Nigerian Daily Times* by Bishop Hinsley
at the end of the Conference, it appeared that the primary objective of
the Catholic leaders was the formulation of a common Catholic education
policy in answer to British moves in this direction. "As far as Catholic
Missions were concerned," he said "they were prepared to co-operate
with the governments of the various British territories in Africa in the
education and general improvement of the native African..." He went
on to emphasize that the Catholic Missions would resist any attempt to
educate the African "as part merely of a machine for production of
wealth for the benefit of others."[9] For their part, the Catholic Ordinaries
held the view that co-operation with the Government should not infringe
their rights as missionaries, and insisted that Catholic children should be
educated in Catholic schools by Catholic teachers and in a Catholic
milieu. Furthermore, the mission leaders demanded complete freedom in
the opening and conducting of Unassisted Schools.[10]

In spite of their unpopularity, the British colonial education reforms
of the late 1920s were productive of very useful results, especially with
regard to the formulation and direction of Catholic educational policy.
With official sanction from Rome, the Catholic African Missions
definitely placed the school at the centre stage of their missionary enterprise. Although such a revolutionary change had long taken place in
Nigeria, the Ordinaries were induced to give it an official declaration in
a resolution that was similar in tone and content with another formulated
by the Catholic Ordinaries of East Africa:

> While paying due tribute of admiration and praise to the work of the mis-
> sionaries in the past, we resolve that in view of the rapidly changing condi-
> tion of Africa, of the needs and demands of the Natives themselves, of the
> attitude of the Government towards African education, and in ready obe-
> dience to the direction of the Holy See, as set forth in the Encyclical
> "Rerum Ecclesiae," increased stress should be laid on the importance of
> the school in every Mission. While the essential ministerial work of the mis-
> sionary can never be neglected, the school should be regarded as the heart
> of missionary organization in each Vicariate and Prefecture.[11]

To equip the missionary for this important educational task, the
Ordinaries recommended a training for him which was above the

---

[9] CSE: 554/VI, "Bishop Hinsley in Conference with Nigerian Bishops: A Statement
of Policy," 1929.
[10] See CSE: 554/I, "Conference of the Ordinaries of Nigeria and the British
Cameroons," Lagos, 1929, resolution III and IV.
[11] Ibid., p. 10.

average. Instead of the simple training he got in Philosophy and Theology, he was to be trained also "in the best and most approved modern methods."[12] It was this stress on modern educational qualifications which constituted the greatest hallmark of the majority of the Irish Fathers who came to Eastern Nigeria after the Second World War. In 1946, Bishop Heerey and his council of missionaries endeavoured to explain to their Superior the necessity of such a phenomenal change:

> At the recent meeting of the Council of [the Onitsha-Owerri] Vicariate, it was unanimously decided to put before you and your Council some points regarding the supply of Fathers to the Vicariate and more particularly regarding the academic qualifications which it would be well for many of the Fathers to possess... There was a time in the history of this Mission when the great cry was for priests...and still more priests. So dire was the need for men that scant attention was paid to their academic qualifications. It was not felt that such qualifications were necessary because the work of the Fathers was to live in close contact with the people and catechist-teachers. Today the position is very different... A growing percentage of future missionaries *MUST* have University degrees if the Vicariate is to progress.[13]

Of great significance to Catholic education in Africa was the uniformity which was thenceforth sought in the presentation of Catholic opinion to the Colonial Governments. That procedure was initiated and greatly enhanced by Bishop Hinsley who, by presiding over the Conferences of Catholic Ordinaries in all the British African Colonies, except South Africa, was able to transfer official Catholic policies from one country to another. The choice of an English man as Apostolic Visitor, and later as Apostolic Delegate, to the British African Colonies was in itself a feat of high papal diplomacy. Through his regional visits and deliberations with leaders of local Colonial Governments—his fellow countrymen—Hinsley was able to secure for the Missions concrete concessions from the pledge of the Colonial Office to base its educational policy on the principle of collaboration and partnership. As a South African journal—*The Argus*—put it, it was afterwards no longer possible for the Governments to ignore Catholic mission schools in matters concerning the education of the masses, thanks to the intervention of the Pope through his Apostolic Visitor.[14] In Nigeria, where different missionary societies were more or

---

[12] Ibid., Resolution XIV.

[13] "Bishop Heerey to Provincial Superior," Onitsha, 1 May 1946, quoted in K. B. C. Onwubiko, "The Catholic Church and the Development of Education in Eastern Nigeria, 1885-1984," in C. A. Obi, ed., *A Hundred Years of the Catholic Church in Eastern Nigeria, 1885-85* (Onitsha: Africana-Fep Publishers, 1985), p. 245f.

[14] See G. A. Lutterbeck, "Das Schulwesen in den Britischen Kolonien Afrikas," p. 311.

less working in complete independence of one another, efforts were made to speak with one voice in all dealings with the Government.[15] This drive towards a concerted action was perfected in later years with the appointment of Father J. Jordan as Education Adviser to the Catholic Missions of Nigeria.

Besides these new perspectives in the direction of Catholic educational enterprise which were derived primarily from confrontations with colonial educational policy, considerable gains were also ultimately registered with regard to the efficiency of schools. That was made possible chiefly because of a consolidated grant-in-aid partnership which placed substantial resources at the disposal of the Assisted Schools. Before the 1926 Education Code, the Missions had established schools in a measure they themselves found very hard to cope with. In order to keep pace with a rapidly expanding enterprise, they had had to rely on badly trained teachers to run very ill-equipped schools. These were among the anomalies which the Government sought to eliminate with the promise of vital financial aids.

Furthermore, government intervention in education proved to be an indispensable factor for the working spirit of teachers in mission schools. Although they were not given the much coveted civil-servant status, the teachers were grateful to have minimum wages stipulated for them, and their names written in official registers.

If the educational reforms of the 1920s caused popular uproar, it was because at that period there was no way the Catholic Missions could have discerned their outcome, if only for their scope and novelty. When Bishop Hinsley declared in 1929 that the aim of education should be ''the uplifting of the whole of mankind and the development of the individual man for the sake of his temporal well-being as well as of his eternal happiness,''[16] he in fact touched on the same principles which gave being and direction to the colonial education policy. The 1926 Education Code ultimately proved to be a move in the right direction. Among other things, it improved the quality of education given to the natives, and did not stand in the way of evangelization as was initially feared. On the contrary, the increase in the number of school children, and perforce of Catholic adherents, continued its upward surge even after the closure of many inferior schools. As has already been seen, the re-grouping of village schools around central schools led to a consolidation of missionary gains after many decades of uncontrolled expansion.

---

[15] See CSE: 554/I, ''Minutes of the Fathers' Meeting Held at the Annual Retreat,'' Ihiala, 11 November, 1929.

[16] CSE: 554/VI, ''Bishop Hinsley in Conference with Nigerian Bishops-A Statement of Policy,'' 1929.

However, one major criticism of the 1926 educational reform in Nigeria was its failure to prevent the production of a discontented generation who were too many to be all given employment, and too far removed from their coherent backgrounds to be profitably integrated into indigenous society. The efforts of the Government to come to grips with this social and political malaise were to plunge the Voluntary Agencies too soon into yet another educational crisis.

2. *The Reorganization of Nigerian School System*

The most notable feature of the 1930s was a tendency in government policy to restrict educational opportunities in Nigeria. The architect and most articulate defender of that policy was E. R. J. Hussey, the Director of Education from 1929 to 1936. In his opinion, the eight-year primary school system which existed in Nigeria till 1929 had the serious defect of concentrating attention on the Standard VI Examination which fetched pupils a certificate that had become worthless for employment purposes. To reduce the number of pupils who would emerge from the primary schools with this certificate, to eliminate the spirit of competition among parents and pupils, and to prevent poor village schools from stretching beyond their means, he proposed in 1929 a re-organization of the Nigerian educational system. In the new system, three distinct phases of education were envisaged. The first phase was to offer a six-year primary education made up of a two-year Infant section, and a four-year Primary section. The aim of this phase was to provide a simple and general education for the majority of the masses, an education for life which was to make the improvement and conservation of local environment and tradition its *raison d'être*.

The second phase of education contemplated an intermediate stage of six years duration to be given in Lower and Higher Middle Schools. The Lower Middle Schools were in effect the former Standards V and VI of the old eight-year primary system.

A third and final stage of education was to be given in vocational schools or Higher Colleges whose objectives were the provision of qualified medical and engineering assistants, as well as teachers of Higher Middle Schools, and staffs of other vocations. Hussey published these reorganization proposals in 1930 in a memorandum on Educational Policy in Nigeria.[17]

As has been seen, these educational innovations met with fierce opposition from the Voluntary Agencies. Catholic sources spoke of "a

---

[17] See PRO: C. O. 657/28, Sessional Paper No. 31 of 1930, *Memorandum on Educational Policy in Nigeria.*

new educational crisis" that was capable of bringing "death" to Catholic schools.[18] In 1929, Father Joseph Soul had rightly noted that the aspect of the new educational programme that was likely to provoke strong Catholic objections concerned the clause on Higher Middle Schools.[19] According to the Hussey plan, teachers of this grade were to be trained exclusively in a government Higher College established at Yaba, Lagos, for the purpose of vocational education. Furthermore, on account of a reformed basis for financial assistance, the mission leaders feared that the Government was aspiring towards absolute control over secondary education in Nigeria. Once more the Catholic Ordinaries formed a common front to oppose those designs.

During their Conference in Lagos in 1929, the Ordinaries had agreed to meet annually, with the first meeting scheduled to take place at Onitsha. Under the presidency of Bishop Heerey, the Nigerian Mission leaders accordingly convened at Onitsha in February 1930. Hussey's reorganization of the Nigerian school system, and how this affected Catholic education were themes which dominated their deliberations. Among other things, the Ordinaries reiterated their rights to take the education of their adherents in their own hands, and their wish to have the teachers in all grades of Catholic schools trained in Catholic Institutions. To prevent Catholic pupils from entering into government Middle Schools, the Ordinaries decided to establish Catholic Lower Middle Schools for pupils who wanted to go beyond Standard IV. This measure was also considered necessary in order to provide the primary schools with the needed qualified teachers.

Eventually, the Voluntary Agencies succeeded in getting the Nigerian Board of Education to organize a "First Leaving Examination" for pupils who had completed a two-year course in the Lower Middle Schools as an alternative for the abolished Standard VI Examination.[20]

Some critics have suggested that Hussey's re-organization of the Nigerian educational system was a product of a most questionable intention. In the words of David Abernethy, for instance, the primary motive of his curriculum changes was "to limit the employment opportunities of educated Southern Nigerians."[21] Before Hussey's Directorship, Sir Hugh Clifford, the Governor of Nigeria from 1919 to 1926 had accused British expatriates of being fearful of educating the Africans to the point

---

[18] See CSE: *Bulletin*, 34 (1929-1930), 536; CSE: 554/VII, "Etat Statistique Annuel Pour La Propagande," 1 December 1929.

[19] See CSE: 554/V, J. Soul, Visitor, "General Report for the Superior General...," Onitsha, 12 November 1929, p. 21f.

[20] See E. R. J. Hussey, "Some Aspects of Education in Nigeria," p. 18f.

[21] D. B. Abernethy, *The Political Dilemma* , p. 94.

THE STRUGGLE BETWEEN MISSION AND COLONIAL POLITICS 227

of "lowering the prestige of the European officials."[22] Indeed there were
some elements in Hussey's educational innovation which did make the
Governor's charges applicable to it. In the first place, his programme for
elementary schools was designed, as he often emphasized, to give large
numbers of pupils a simple education that was fit only for work "on their
father's farms."[23] Secondly, a new West African School Certificate
which was considered inferior to the coveted Oxford and Cambridge
School Certificates was to be awarded to the finalists of the new Middle
Schools. Thirdly, the diplomas from the Higher College at Yaba was
officially declared to be inferior to similar degrees and diplomas from
British Institutions. These measures were designed, according to D.
Abernethy, "to consolidate the British position within Nigeria," and to
place "definite limits on further upward mobility within the colonial
framework."[24]

The timing of the controversial Hussey reforms also seemed to vindicate these charges. The late 1920s and early 1930s were a period described by Lord Lugard, the first Governor General of Nigeria, as a "psychological moment."[25] He was referring to the first signs of organized
opposition to British rule in Nigeria which culminated in the embarrassing *Women Riot* of late 1929 in Eastern Nigeria. Although the women,
massively supported by their husbands, took to violent protests against
colonial tax practices, there were no doubts in the minds of the
Administrators that their action signalled a deep-rooted rebellion against
British rule in general. Nothing would have influenced the educational
and political decisions of a new Director of Education and a new Governor General—such as Hussey and Donald Cameron were in 1930—more
than efforts to keep their subjects servile and amenable. To achieve that
objective, they readily grasped at the adoptionist theories of the 1920s
which advocated the education of the Africans "along their own lines."
That involved, in the case of Hussey's educational programmes, giving
the masses a simple education that would leave them contented with
aspiring towards rural activities.

This restrictive tendency in government educational policy was to
meet with unexpectedly strong opposition not only from educated
Nigerians, but also from the Christian Missions. Some Catholic mission
leaders accused the British law-makers of wanting to push the Africans
back to illiteracy and paganism under the guise of preventing detribaliza-

---

[22] Quoted in F. K. Ekechi, *Missionary Enterprise*, p. 181.
[23] Quoted in D. B. Abernethy, *The Political Dilemma*, p. 94.
[24] D. B. Abernethy, *The Political Dilemma*, p. 94.
[25] F. D. Lugard, "British Policy in Nigeria," p. 386.

tion.[26] At the root of Catholic objection lay the fact that by imposing a limit to educational expansion, government policy perforce retarded the growth and development of the Missions. That reality was particularly present in Eastern Nigeria. Encouraged by the people's quest for knowledge, the Catholic Missions in that region had built their missionary endeavours exclusively around the primary schools. By drastically limiting the scope of education offered in these schools and by rendering them, as a result, unattractive, the future of the Missions was being put in jeopardy.

Hussey's educational reforms may have been born of very dubious intentions. Nevertheless, they were productive of some welcome results. By emphasising the study of agriculture, handicraft, and hygiene, the pupils and their teachers were induced to show a greater interest in their local environments and habits than was hitherto the case. As has already been seen, the Catholic Ordinaries conceded in 1937 in connection with the formation of teachers in Elementary Training Centres that training in subjects that were relevant to local environments was the best educational approach to the needs of rural communities. Furthermore, by making the vernacular the medium of instruction in the Infant Classes, and the training of vernacular teachers for these classes, Hussey's innovations reawakened some interest in the local dialects. Finally, the establishment of a Higher College at Yaba as a matter of fact raised the level of education obtainable in Nigeria. However, the ownership and management of the College were the exclusive prerogatives of the Government, and the number of persons who were privileged to attend it was very limited. These restrictive factors fitted awkwardly into the educational conceptions of the Catholic Missions.

In the main, many of Hussey's reforms were not brought to fruition chiefly because of the World Economic Depressions of the 1930s, and because of substantial shifts in government educational policy in the 1940s.

3. Reorientations In Colonial Educational Policy

The most notable change in colonial policy which had important consequences for Nigerian educational development was a departure from the view firmly held by the Imperial Government before the Second World War that the Colonial Governments should be economically and financially self-supporting. That change of policy gave birth in 1940 to the establishment of a Colonial Development and Welfare Fund, and soon

---

[26] See G. A. Lutterbeck, "Das Schulwesen in den Britischen Kolonien Afrikas," p. 309.

afterwards large sums of money were made available to the Colonial Administrations in Nigeria for educational purposes. Encouraged by this turn of events, Governor B. H. Bourdillon's Administration drew up an ambitious Ten Year Educational Plan in 1942 whose chief aims were to provide:

a) A Type of Education more suitable for the needs of the country.
b) Better conditions of service for teachers employed by the Missions and other Voluntary Bodies, in order to provide a better trained and more contented staff.
c) More adequate financial assistance to Missions and other Voluntary Educational Bodies.
d) Financial assistance to Native Administrations in order to assist them to maintain an efficient staff of teachers and expand education in their areas.
e) Controlled expansion within financial limits.[27]

The Colonial Office did not sanction this plan not so much because of its financial ambitions as for the fact that in the opinion of the Advisory Committee on Education in the Colonies, it merely touched the fringes of Nigerian educational needs.[28] Before and during the deliberations on the Ten Year Educational Plan, criticism had grown loud in London about the failure of the Nigerian Colonial Governments to stop the uncontrolled expansion of Mission schools. Because of the large scope given in the plan to teachers in Voluntary Agency schools, it was felt that ordered educational development could be guaranteed only by a complete overhaul of the whole system on which grant-in-aid policy had operated for so many years. Until such a reorganization was implemented, grant-in-aid arrangements on behalf of Voluntary Agency teachers were made, as has been seen, *ad interim*.

The beneficiaries of such interim agreements were usually all grades of teachers employed in Voluntary Agency schools, a development which accentuated the fact that the grants-in-aid system which had drawn a distinction between Assisted and Unassisted schools had outlived its usefulness. In 1948 Sir Sidney Phillipson was saddled with the task of working out a new scheme of grants-in-aid which would extend official responsibility to the numerous mission and Native Administration schools which had hitherto not fallen within the grant-aided orbit. The recommendations of his erudite report—*Grants In Aid of Education in Nigeria*—were incorporated in a new Education Ordinance which became operative in 1948. Some of the most important provisions of the new Ordinance were:

[27] PRO: C.O. 657/53, Sessional Paper No. 6 of 1944, *Ten Year Educational Plan*, 19 November, 1942; quoted also in S. Phillipson, *Grants in Aid*, p. 34.
[28] See L. J. Lewis: *Society, Schools, and Progress in Nigeria* (Oxford: Pergamon Press, 1965), p. 43f; see also S. Phillipson, *Grants in Aid*, p. 36.

a) The establishment of Central and Regional Boards of Education, with advisory and executive powers.
b) Provision for the establishment of local education authorities or local education committees in suitable circumstances.
c) That the amount of the grant-in-aid payable in respect of a recognized school should consist of the recognized expenses, less an assumed local contribution.
d) That there should be uniformity in the salary paid to each category of teachers.[29]

To a large extent, the Education Ordinance of 1948 was based on the principle formulated both in Phillipson's report and in a new memorandum on Education Policy in Nigeria which was presented to the Legislative Council as Sessional Paper No.20 of 1947, namely, that the local communities should be drawn more effectively into the financing and management of schools. The emphasis laid in the Code of 1948 on the educational involvement of a hitherto neglected third party—the local authorities—precipitated substantial shifts in the traditional relationship between the Government and the Christian Missions.

III. *Native Administration Schools*

Local councils and units of native administration were usually useful instruments in the hands of British Colonial Administrations in the pursuit of their acclaimed policy of Indirect Rule. However, before the First World War, the direct management of schools by these local authorities was almost non-existent in the Southern Provinces, the stronghold of the Christian Missions. During the war, the British occupied the Cameroons, and deported the German missionaries. To make up for the resultant set-back in missionary education, Native Administration schools were established there. This educational experiment was soon afterwards carried out in the Oyo Province, and by 1934 there were a total of twenty-one Native Administration schools in the Southern Provinces of Nigeria.[30]

The impression which Miss Margery Perham got after her tour of these schools was that they were everywhere "highly popular."[31] The popularity of the Native Administration schools may have been real in the Northern Provinces, where they greatly bridged the wide educational gap between that region and the South, a disparity caused by a near

[29] See Eastern Nigeria, Ministry of Education, *Report on the Review of the Educational System in Eastern Nigeria* (Enugu: The Government Printer, 1962), p. 7.
[30] See M. Perham, *Native Administration*, p. 283f.
[31] Ibid., p. 284.

absence of Christian evangelism in the North. But in the Southern Provinces, curiosity rather than any genuine liking must have had a definite
bearing on the people's hankering after schools managed and financed
by local authorities.

This was particularly the case in the 1920s and 1930s, when the Native
Authorities were still dominated by often illiterate native rulers and
subservient Warrant Chiefs. To a large extent, these local authorities saw
in the management of schools a consolidation of their shaky powers and
some promises of financial gains. Their requests for Native Administration schools did not always have a popular mandate, especially in districts
with large Christian populations, such as in the Eastern Provinces. Nor
did their educational schemes receive support and approval from a rising
educated class, which not only regarded the Native Authorities as stooges
of the colonial overlords, but also received the moves to educate the
Africans on their own lines with skepticism and suspicion. The only road
to self-government, they believed, was through advancements in education which were best guaranteed in mission schools, and not through the
retrogressive measures which they saw purported in the Native
Administration schools. An editorial in the *Nigerian Daily Times*—a
popular organ of the nationalist movement—delineated this viewpoint,
and revealed that the educated class, infinitely anxious to see executive
powers in their own hands, did not show much sympathy to the Native
Administrations and their educational flirtations:

> The real future of education in this country, as we have been often told,
> is in the hands of the people themselves, for they only can, when they have
> reached the right standard, know exactly what they require and how best
> they can have it supplied. In the meantime, the highest credit must be given
> to those who have come to us in the spirit of true Christian brotherhood
> from across the seas in order to put us in the right path towards the
> *LIGHT*—the light of true knowledge. Referring to [Bishop O'Rourke's
> address condemning overlapping in the administration of education funds],
> we quite agree that the policy of breaking up educational authority into
> several distinct compartments between the Central Government and the
> Native Administration is one that should be very definitely discouraged.[32]

Catholic opposition to Native Administration schools was given its first
official declaration in 1929, when the Western Cameroons was being
administered by Shanahan's Vicariate. Being in possession of no "full"
Catholic study of their own on the new educational development, the
Catholic Ordinaries of Nigeria and the British Cameroons readily

---

[32] "Missionaries and Education," *The Nigerian Daily Times*, Tuesday, 6 February,
1934.

adopted the resolution of a Nairobi Mission Education Conference which
had outlined the following points:

> 1) That the present effort to promote Local Native Council Schools is a
> violation of the understanding between Government and Missions and co-
> operation, because of the introduction of a third party, namely, the Local
> Native Council Schools, without the consent of one of the original contrac-
> ting parties.
> 2) That because of proximity to our existing schools, these Local Native
> Council Schools introduce unfair competition.
> 3) That they are an encouragement to pagan elders to perpetuate through
> these schools their pagan customs. (They are contrary to the Recommenda-
> tions of the Colonial Office Memorandum on "Educational Policy in
> British Tropical African Dependencies," March 1925, p.4: Religion and
> Character Training).
> 4) The taxation of all Natives by Local Native Councils for Native Council
> Schools is often unfair, because such schools satisfy only the non-Christian
> section of the people.[33]

Commenting on mission opposition to Native Administration schools,
Miss Perham suggested that the only challenge these schools should offer
to the Missions would be to force them "to adapt their methods and
organization so as to assist in the building up of healthy local native
government."[34] But the truth was that the Missions did not hold local
governments in great esteem. The Catholic Missions in particular found
it preferable to have direct dealings with the Central Government rather
than having to deal with a local administration whose members were
either pagans or persons imbued with anti-Catholic sentiments. When
Bishop O'Rourke of the Vicariate of Western Nigeria opposed Native
Administration schools in 1934, he emphasized the fact that he was
"interpreting the minds of the Catholic Mission Authorities in the whole
of Nigeria and Cameroons under British Mandate."[35] According to him,
Catholic opinion was that Native Administration schools were
superfluous and a "waste of money."[36]

However, a major issue in Catholic opposition was the ever increasing
control which the Native Authorities were beginning to have over educational funds. In former days, government grants came exclusively from
the Educational Department. But with the establishment of Native
Treasuries, the Native Administrations were often required to provide
financial resources for education in their respective districts. But given

---

[33] CSE: 554/I "Conference of the Ordinaries of Nigeria...1929," Resolution XII, p.
14f.
[34] M. Perham, *Native Administration*, p. 284.
[35] Quoted in *The Nigerian Daily Times*, Tuesday, 6 February, 1934.
[36] Ibid.

the great importance which the Missions attached to the school apostolate, this duplication of authority and bureaucracy in the administration of educational funds inevitably brought dissension between them and the Native Administration.

But, the greatest cause of Catholic opposition to Native Administration Schools was neither the unpleasant competition which these schools brought, nor the diminution of educational grants which they threatened to be. Rather it was the emphasis placed in these schools on non-denominationalism. That emphasis was actively encouraged by the Government, which saw these schools as providing a useful option to the often criticised mission education. The great distinction which every Colonial Administration desired to see made was between "evangelization" and "education." But since the Christian Missions were generally unwilling, and to a large extent unable, to make that distinction, the Government grasped at the non-denominational school as its first priority in every effort to base educational development on community need.

For their part, the Missions were not as confident as the Government that morality and true Christian principles would be guaranteed in a non-denominational school run in a pagan milieu, if not by the pagans themselves. When the first Native Administration Schools were established in the Cameroons after the First World War, the Government did envisage getting some Mission influence to bear upon them in order to "develop those moral sanctions without which all knowledge becomes harmful to the individual and a danger to the State."[37] But according to Miss Perham, that plan was never executed, a failure which vindicated any charges of the practice of paganism in those schools. Degeneration of morals, religious indifference, the dearth of vocations to the priesthood and to the office of catechist were among the chief evils which the Catholic authorities considered inherent in fostering non-denominationalism in a predominantly pagan community.

Furthermore, non-denominationalism mitigated against the *raison d'être* of Catholic missionary enterprise in Nigeria—the making of proselytes, and the maintenance of sectarian integrity. These were missionary objectives whose ordered achievement could not be thought of without Catholic schools. In fact, throughout the nineteenth century, and for the greater part of the twentieth, Catholic authorities had a genuine belief that a school closely supervised by a Father, a Brother, or a Sister was the only ideal place to nurture true Christian principles in the child. Accordingly, a Catholic school was passionately viewed as having a

---

[37] Quoted in M. Perham, *Native Administration*, p. 283.

pastoral value which was considered lacking not only in a non-denominational school, but even also in a Nigerian Christian community. This belief was given expression during a Catholic Education Conference held in Leopoldville in August 1965:

> Can we rely on the family and the Christian community to complete the children's education and avoid a lack of balance between their secular and religious education? It seems not.
>
> The educational level of the mother and that of the Christian community are on the whole decidedly lower than that of the children: therefore, the mother and the community are not able to help the children to cope with the problems facing them.
>
> Being a member of a religion which is at once social and personal, the Christian needs to meet the priest. And it is noticeable that when a child had had personal contact with a priest he retains a certain relationship with him even though he may have given up all religious practice.[38]

This mistrust of the ability of the family and the Christian community to impart intellectual and moral stability to the child was a real problem which was obsessively present in the mind of every average missionary. In 1941, when the issue of a secondary school for girls was being discussed, the greatest problem which preoccupied Father Richard Daly, the Catholic Education Secretary in the Onitsha-Owerri Vicariate, was first and foremost, the responsibility for the overall morality of the ladies in a rapidly growing metropolitan, such as Onitsha was. His arguments revealed some of the sad European misconceptions of the native society which had, among other things, made the practice of paternism a missionary necessity:

> There must be a definite purpose in girls secondary education, otherwise they will be "on the street" immediately. The position is very different in this country from that in Europe, where educated girls have somebody to control and look after them, but here, all the responsibility will fall on the institutions.[39]

The strong antipathy which the Catholics showed towards the non-denominational school or its correlative, the inter-denominational school, was generally recognized, and to a large extent respected, by the British Imperial Government. In its study of educational policy and practice in British West Africa, a Commission headed by G. B. Jeffery described as a flawed policy any attempt "to make arrangements which the Roman Catholics, who are doing excellent work in many areas, are

---

[38] P. Peillon, E. Navigué, "The Pastoral Aspects of Catholic Education in Africa," *Catholic Education in the Service of Africa: Report of the Pan-African Catholic Education Conference, Leopoldville, 16-23 August* (1966), p. 194.

[39] ODA: R. Daly, "A Commentary," n.d.

unable to accept.''[40] Although the preference of the Colonial Administrations was generally with government and Native Administration schools, there was no likelihood that the Christian Missions would have been totally excluded from the management of any grades of schools by official legislation. In the 1950s, the reformed Local Authorities were partially able to achieve what their colonial masters were reluctant to enforce, namely, the restriction of missionary educational expansion on the primary level, thanks to inevitable political changes after the Second World War which had brought internal self-government to the regions.

The rise after the war of two super-powers who did not hold the concept of empire in great esteem had forced the British Government to develop a new policy towards its colonies. Among other things, it was felt that the dependencies should be gradually trained for self-government. This view was given an official expression by the Advisory Committee on Education in the Colonies in a report published in 1948 under the title, *Education for Citizenship in Africa*. For the furtherance of this type of education great emphasis was laid on the use of native administrations and local government bodies. The aim was to give the natives a share in political responsibility. "People who have learnt new ideas," it was emphasized, "must be given the chance of putting them into practice."[41]

The publication in 1947 of a Memorandum on Educational Policy in Nigeria had already set the stage for a greater control of education by Local Education Authorities. In chapter five of the Memorandum, it was stated that

> Increased educational facilities cannot be provided with advantage except with the active co-operation of the communities concerned. The stage has been reached at which popular education will cease to be popular unless the communities concerned have a measure of control: and popular share in the control depends on the creation of some machinery of local government. It is recommended, therefore, that Education Committees be established in each Province with the avowed object that they should become Committees of "Local Education Authorities" in the technical sense of the term.[42]

As has been seen, this recommendation was incorporated in the Educational Ordinance of 1948. Soon afterwards Local Education Authorities were set up in the Northern and Western regions, and so were Local Authority schools, which catered mainly for the education of the large Moslem populations of these two regions. As late as 1950, there were yet

[40] F.C.O.L. / LA 1611, "A Study of Educational Policy and Practice in British West Africa" (TS, 1951), p. 92.

[41] Colonial Office, Advisory Committee on Education in the Colonies, *Education for Citizenship in Africa* (London: His Majesty's Stationary Office, 1948), pp. 30-33.

[42] Sessional Paper No. 20 of 1947, *Memorandum on Educational Policy in Nigeria* (Lagos: The Government Printer, 1947), p. 7.

no Local Education Authorities in the Eastern region, except for *de facto* local education committees which were educationally active in Abakiliki Division, Orlu and Ikot Ekpene.[43] Generally, Local Education Authorities and schools managed by them remained very unpopular in the Eastern region, a phenomenon which may be explained by the absence of a Moslem population and the extraordinary educational activities of the Christian Missions in that region.[44]

The difference between Native Administrations and Local Authorities was that whereas the former were made up of native rulers with very limited powers, the latter were predominantly members of the educated class with executive powers. The emergence of the latter marked the beginning of the decentralization process which was the characteristic feature of the political development of the 1950s. For many decades, educational decisions were made by a Central Board in Lagos. But by virtue of several constitutional changes which began in 1947, the regions had by 1954 attained substantial legislative powers over the direction of education within their respective borders. The consequences for the Christian Missions of this regionalization of education were grave and far-reaching: it permanently weakened missionary influence over primary education in the country. According to Father J. Jordan, 60 per cent of all new schools opened after 1955 in the Western region were allocated by law to Local Authorities, and in the Eastern region only Local Authorities could open new elementary schools with government grants.[45] The strongest argument advanced by the Local Authorities to vindicate the restrictive measures of the 1950s was that denominational segregation and rivalry had made possible the existence of three or more schools in a locality where only one would have been sufficient. With the administration of educational funds exclusively in their own hands, the Local Authorities felt that public money should not be used to promote what they saw as unnecessary expansion.

For the Catholics, the fact that the Voluntary Agencies were permitted to retain the proprietorship of their existing primary schools removed a sting from the aura of secularization that hung over educational policy in Eastern Nigeria. To make up for the weakening of their educational influence on the primary level, they intensified their efforts in the area where aided expansion was still possible—the secondary level.

---

[43] Eastern Nigeria, Ministry of Education, *Report on the Review of the Educational System*, p. 8.

[44] Of the 5,076 primary schools in Eastern Nigeria in 1956, only 42 were Local Authority schools. See D. B. Abernethy, *Church and State in Nigerian Education*, p. 28.

[45] J. Jordan, "Catholic Education and Catholicism in Nigeria," in *AFER*, 2 (1960), 60.

CHAPTER SEVEN

SECONDARY EDUCATION AND NATIONAL CONSCIOUSNESS

I. *The Development of Catholic Secondary Schools*

1. *The Belated Approach*

One sombre aspect of Catholicism in colonial Nigeria was the political inferiority of its adherents which resulted from Protestant dominance in post-primary education. Writing in 1957, Bishop J.B. Whelan, an Irish missionary who considerably influenced Catholic educational policy in Nigeria, touched on this issue with the following remark:

> One must recall that the conquering power in Nigeria was Protestant. The Church which followed the flag was Anglican or creation of a Protestant government. Consequently the first educated elite was Protestant in religion or in sympathy. This naturally bred a sense of inferiority in Catholics. Within the past twenty years Catholic high schools have been established in increasing numbers, and Catholics in government high schools receive regular attention.[1]

A point which is not expressly stated in this observation, but which is implicitly understood, is the belatedness with which the Catholics pursued secondary education in Nigeria. It was this fact, rather than the alleged Protestant advantage, or a possible government discrimination against Catholics, which accounted for much of the sustained hegemony of the Protestants. It was true that the Protestants drew considerable gains from their affinity to the colonial Government. That close relationship enabled them, first and foremost, to secure a comfortable lead of over 40 years in Nigeria, and placed considerable educational resources at their disposal. But, the speed and thoroughness with which the Catholics took a firm hold on primary education in the East adequately demonstrated that the Protestant advantages did not possess an indelible permanence.

Furthermore, it would be incorrect to suggest, however tacitly, that the discrimination of Catholics constituted an official issue in government policy. Of all the colonial powers in Africa, the British were, as is generally known, the most liberal. The singular religious tolerance which

---

[1] J. B. Whelan, "Our School: Victory in Nigeria," *World Mission*, 8 (Fall, 1957), 25.

existed in British colonies was a thing which even Catholic authorities remembered occasionally with gratitude. In 1955, for instance, Father J. Jordan, the Education Adviser to all the Catholic Missions in Nigeria, wrote expressly that "There is no State interference with religious teaching or practice. All our schools are Catholic schools in the strict sense of the word. We own them, control them, and appoint every teacher in them."[2] It would seem, therefore, that the tardy growth of Catholic secondary education was largely a self-imposed inhibition.

There was in Catholic educational policy an unduly long emphasis on elementary and vocational schools. One possible explanation for that would be found in the constitutional tradition of the Holy Ghost Congregation. As has been seen, Father Libermann, the Founder of the Society, placed emphasis on the elementary character of the education envisaged in his mission plan. His "central school" for the very best pupils—future priests, catechists and teachers—was no secondary school in the modern sense. Its idea was to bring primary education to a more solid basis than was possible in the public rudimentary schools. Latin was added to its curriculum for priest candidates, and church songs and liturgy for the Catechists. Ultimately, this plan of education took firm roots in the missionary strategy of the Spiritans, and although later changes in their constitution made provisions for secondary schools and colleges, the original plan was doggedly adhered to until political and social realities in the individual mission lands made a change of policy inevitable. Table 12 shows that as late as 1926, only very few Missions of the Holy Ghost Fathers around the world were offering secondary education to their pupils. By contrast, primary and vocational education were fairly well developed. With about 1,200 primary schools and more than 45,000 pupils, Nigeria was at the apex of the educational pyramid of the Congregation in that year, but like the greater majority of the society's Missions, it did not possess a single secondary school.

Since the school was essentially seen as serving the work of evangelization, the primary school, through which the masses found allegiance to the Church, was considered as deserving an overriding priority over the secondary school which, in view of financial handicaps, could only be offered to a privileged few. The conspicuous absence of Catholic postprimary education in Nigeria, a lack which Father Lejeune bemoaned as early as 1904,[3] was therefore more a matter of policy than of chance or compulsion.

---

[2] ODA: J. Jordan, "Background Note to Nigeria, With Special Reference to Catholic Education," Onitsha, 31 May, 1955.

[3] Cf. CSE: 192/A/V, "Lejeune to Propaganda Fide," Calabar, 20 October, 1904.

Table 12

Educational Establishments of the Holy Ghost Fathers in 1926

| Mission Territories | Primary Schools | | | | Secondary Schools | | | | Vocational Schools | | | |
| | Boys | | Girls | | Boys | | Girls | | Boys | | Girls | |
	Sch.	Pup.	Sch.	Pup.	Sch.	Pup.	Sch.	Pup.	Sch.	Pup.	Sch.	Pup.
Latin America												
St. Pierre/Miquelon	3	117	3	284	—	—	—	—	—	—	—	—
Guadeloupe	a	a	5	651	—	—	—	—	—	—	—	—
French Guiana	a	a	4	800	—	—	—	—	a	a	1	45
Teffé	1	84	1	28	1	16	—	—	2	52	—	—
West Africa												
Senegambia	6	612	10	866	1	54	1	50	2	53	10	289
French Guinea	14	942	3	207	1	4	—	—	7	326	2	138
Nigeria	1,190	44,846	a	225	—	—	—	—	16	124	a	32
Gabon	14	1,625	6	715	a	—	—	—	8	238	a	265
Loango	77	5,486	a	a	6	495	1	60	10	366	a	52
Portuguise Congo	24	799	2	209	a	a	a	a	3	30	a	54
East Africa												
Zanzibar	a	a	a	a	1	20	1	90	14	139	10	244
Kilima-Ndjaro	106	3,201	a	2,750	—	—	—	—	—	—	a	a
Katanga	84	6,764	3	a	—	—	—	—	22	674	a	a
Majunga	5	320	6	350	—	—	—	—	1	10	a	55

Source: CSE: *Bulletin*, 32 (1925-1926).

a = Figures not given; Sch = Schools; Pup. = Pupils.

Note: This Table does not contain all the educational establishments of the Holy Ghost Fathers in 1926.

To the extent that this policy was untoward, it nevertheless conformed closely to the judgment of most educationists and economists in the nineteenth and early twentieth centuries. That judgment was highly critical of any attempt to place literary education above agricultural and industrial education in colonies which depended almost exclusively on the land for their economic development. However, although the colonial Governments and Christian Missions in Nigeria were convinced of the propriety of this viewpoint, they were ultimately forced to lean rather heavily on an education that was more literary than practical because of insufficiency of funds to establish and maintain the laboratories and workshops that were necessary for an education based on practical utility. A famous Nigerian historian has painted a clear picture of this ironical twist with the following pun:

> The cartoonist might well picture His excellency the Governor, reading out a speech condemning literary education as he was laying the foundation of yet another grammar school on the abandoned site of an old industrial institution.[4]

This disparity between theory and practice also found expression in the educational conception of the Nigerian Nationalists. Although a good number of them recognized the merits of agricultural and industrial education, a consensus in their opinion pointed decisively to literary education, such as is offered in the secondary grammar schools. If the Africans were to be prevented from being for ever "hewers of wood and drawers of water,"[5] they argued, then something higher than the primary and vocational schools must be offered them in increasing numbers. It was thus for this purpose that Black members of the Protestant communities in Nigeria defied the criticism of their White Church leaders and founded the first secondary schools in Nigeria—C.M.S. Grammar School, 1859, the Methodist Boys' High School, 1876, and the Methodist Girls' High School, 1879.

Catholic reaction to these phenomenal developments in the Protestant camp was rather cautious. In Lagos, a Catholic Boys' High School—St. Gregory's R.C.M. College—was established in 1881 probably as an answer to the Protestant challenge. However, as the Reverend M. Sunter noted in 1887, the Catholic institution was in reality nothing other than a higher form of a primary school with facilities for Book-keeping and French.[6] Also in its report of 1903, a committee of the Lagos Education

---

[4] Cf. J. F. Ajayi, "The Development of Secondary Grammar School Education in Nigeria," *Journal of the Historical Society of Nigeria*, 2 (1963), 517.

[5] Quoted in J. S. Coleman, *Nigeria*, p. 119f.

[6] S. M. A. : 14/80205, 1887: M. Sunter, "First Inspection of Schools Under the Ordinance of 1887."

Board stated that apart from occasional flirtations with Euclid and Geometry, the Catholic Mission in Lagos had "no school or other arrangements for carrying on secondary education."[7] Father Lejeune confirmed this in 1904 when he complained that "Not one of the Catholic Missions in the English territories of West Africa [educated] its pupils beyond the primary school."[8] These observations were an indication that at the beginning of this century, St. Gregory's R.C.M. College had little or no impact on secondary education in the country.

From an economic standpoint, it was generally considered inexpedient to establish full-fledged secondary schools, if only for the fact that only few pupils actually attended them at the beginning of this century. Even the Protestant grammar schools were, in actual fact, also advanced forms of primary schools. It was with the establishment of the first government secondary school at Lagos in 1909, the King's College, that the real beginning of secondary education in Nigeria was made. The college was designed to act as a model for the Voluntary Agencies. Whereas Catholic authorities in the West addressed themselves fairly early to the changing realities in secondary education in the country, those in the East were rather slow to come to terms with them.

A considerable shift in Catholic policy on post-primary education in Eastern Nigeria became evident in the 1920s as a result of some major educational developments in the country. By 1925, the Church Missionary Society had established a secondary school at Onitsha, the Dennis Memorial Grammar School. The following year, the Government, in an effort to ensure a more effective control over the Voluntary Agency schools than was hitherto the case, issued an Education Ordinance in which considerable emphasis was laid on secondary education. In the face of these developments, the Catholic authorities began to give a serious thought to the possibility of having Catholic secondary schools. The following report which was written on February 20, 1926, signalled a turning-point in Catholic stand on post-primary education in the East:

> Education has taken such proportions in Nigeria that it is now necessary to think of entrusting it to better hands [to a congregation of Teaching Brothers]. Well organized by the Apostolic Vicar, the apostolate of the school has made a considerable advancement in the Vicariate since 1904, and the ministry has been on equal footing with the school. Nevertheless, the ministry ought to be the province of the missionary, and the school that of a teaching congregation. High schools are absolutely necessary; the Protestants have a dozen of them, and we do not possess any. As the staff

---

[7] F. C. O. L./10940, *Report of Committee of the Education Board*, (Lagos, 1903).
[8] CSE: 192/A/V, "Lejeune to Propaganda Fide," Calabar, 20 October, 1904.

[required for a secondary school] cannot be found among us, why don't we look for them where they are available? To neglect education in Nigeria is to lose Catholic influence completely, and that in a matter of a few years.[9]

This grave concern for *High Schools* notwithstanding, Catholic reaction to the 1926 Education Code was the establishment not of a secondary school, but of a Training College for teachers of higher elementary schools, a measure which accentuated the depth of Catholic involvement with primary education, and demonstrated that nothing short of a catastrophe was strong enough to sever that commitment.

An event that approached the thresholds of such a catastrophe was Hussey's reorganization in 1930 of the educational system in Nigeria. The central issue in that educational innovation was, as we have seen, the forcible elimination of Standard VI as the crowning point in the educational quest of the masses, a measure which made nonsense of the entire Catholic educational set-up. To qualify for government and commercial posts, pupils were required thenceforth to possess the Cambridge Certificate—the ultimate goal of the Middle or Secondary schools. With the weakening of their educational edifice, the Catholics were forced to give a new purpose to their greatest missionary enterprise. That need, more than any other consideration, was responsible for the foundation of the first Catholic secondary school in Eastern Nigeria.

2. *The Advent of Catholic Secondary Schools in the East*

While discussions on Hussey's proposed educational innovations were still going on in 1929, the Educational Council of the Vicariate of Southern Nigeria decided not to send Catholic pupils to the newly established government middle schools, but rather to start Catholic "Lower Middle Schools" in January 1930 in all the major stations.[10] In what was undoubtedly the moment of conception for Christ the King College, Onitsha, it was further decided that at least one "Higher Middle School" should be started "later" for the Vicariate.[11]

That memorable event took place on February 2, 1933. With a staff of three Europeans—including the Principal, Father W. L. Brolley—and two African teachers, a college section comprising thirty students was started in one of the dormitories of St. Charles Teacher Training College, Onitsha. The number of students rose rapidly, and later in the year the college took permanent quarters with about sixty students. Referring to

---

[9] CSE: *Bulletin*, 32 (1925-1926), 580.

[10] See CSE: 554/I, "Minutes of the Fathers' Meeting held at the Annual Retreat," Ihiala, 11 November, 1929.

[11] Ibid.

that humble beginning, the Inspector of Schools spoke of "the promise shown for good in educational and social influence of the school."[12] Throughout its history, the College of Christ the King, Onitsha, lived up to those promises. After its second sitting at the Cambridge Junior Examinations in 1936, it emerged as the number one school in the whole country with regard to academic excellence. Writing to Rome the following year, Bishop Heerey told the story with legitimate pride:

> Our secondary school has become a famous educational establishment. The successes in public examinations have been the highest in all Nigeria including the various Government and Protestant Colleges. And the greatest success of all have been among our Junior Seminarists. One hundred percent of young Junior Seminarists have been successful in the Cambridge Junior and Senior Examinations.[13]

The social influence of the college was predictably commensurate with its academic excellence: the first Catholic elite, including the first native priests and bishops, were all ex-students of Christ the King College. Indeed, the establishment of the college was the first successful attempt by the Catholics to achieve political and social parity with the Protestants.

3. *The Fame of Catholic Secondary Schools as a Missionary Factor*

The post Second World War years were a period of unprecedented prosperity for Catholic secondary education. Chief among the causes was the influx of Catholic white missionaries in Eastern Nigeria. Whereas the English members of the various Protestant denominations were needed in Europe to confront the social and economic problems caused by the war, more Irish Catholic missionaries than usual began to come to Nigeria after the war.[14] This new development greatly enhanced the quality and prestige of Catholic secondary schools. As the Inspector of Education for the Eastern Provinces found out during his inspection tour of the Holy Family College, Abak, in 1945, the Fathers gave Catholic colleges a humanistic bias that was very rarely found elsewhere in the country. His report contained, among other things, this interesting remark:

---

[12] Quoted in *The Irish Independent*, Thursday, January 7, 1954, p. 6.
[13] CSE: 556/I, "Bishop Heerey to Cardinal Fumasini-Biondi, Prefect of Propaganda Fide," Onitsha, 3 September, 1937. For more information on the academic performances of C. K. C. in the first years of its existence, see also J. Gosson, "The Apostolate of the School in Southern Nigeria," *Pagan Missions*, 13 (1940), 49f.
[14] Cf. J. Taylor, *Christianity and Politics in Africa* (London : Penguin, 1957), p. 11.

> There is a very pleasant tone in the college and an air of 'humanism' which only too often is lacking in Nigerian schools. There are few schools where the History Master teaches Physics and Chemistry, and the Biology Master takes Latin and where all four subjects are effectively taught.[15]

To the extent that the presence in Catholic secondary schools of many European missionaries was a positive academic boon, it nevertheless had its bad side: it contributed immensely to the heavy leaning on literary education in Catholic colleges. According to the inspection report on the Holy Family College, Abak, the original intention of the proprietor in 1942, when the college was founded, was "to give a strong agricultural bias to the curriculum." By 1945, that intention had weaned considerably, and agriculture was "just one of the subjects of the curriculum."[16] The policy which highlighted agricultural education in theory and put a damper on it in practice was a phenomenon which was not confined to Catholic schools alone. An inspection report on Ibadan C.M.S. Grammar School in 1938 had the following to say:

> Land has been purchased and cleared for a school farm at a cost of £26 pounds. The Principal has not yet thought out what part the farm will play in the school curriculum, but it will no doubt make a good impression on visitors.[17]

Furthermore, apart from English, history, geography, mathematics, and general science, the curriculum for the Middle Schools included "workshop practice, in close relationship with the practical work in the laboratories, and agriculture, closely connected with the biological teaching."[18] But by 1945, this emphasis on practical education had been lost, as is evident in the syllabus for the Higher College Entrance and Middle VI Leaving Certificate Examinations which comprised: a) compulsory subjects—English, History, Geography, Elementary Mathematics; b) optional subjects—Biology, Chemistry, Physics, Additional Mathematics, one language (French or Latin).

Nevertheless, possibly because of the huge European presence on their staff, and the literary bias of their curriculum, Catholic secondary schools enjoyed a popularity that was equalled only by the government colleges. In the Port Harcourt district, for instance, Protestant colleges like Enitona High School and Okirika Grammar School were mere dwarfs in

---

[15] ODA: No. C. I. E. (S) 1177/62, Chief Inspector of Education, Eastern Provinces, "Inspection Report on Holy Family R. C. M. College, Abak, 10-12 September, 1945," Enugu, 24 September, 1945, p. 2.

[16] Ibid., p. 1.

[17] Quoted in J. F. A. Ajayi, "The Development of Secondary Grammar School Education," p. 531.

[18] E. R. J. Hussey, "Some Aspects of Education in Nigeria," p. 17.

comparison with Catholic educational colossi like Stella Maris College and Immaculate Heart Girls' Secondary School.

The attraction and popularity of Catholic secondary schools ultimately became a factor of great significance in Catholic missionary propaganda, especially in areas where the Catholics were a minority. Such was the case among the Ibibios and the Anangs where the Holy Family College, Abak, with its 49 Catholic and 69 non-Catholic students in 1945, was regarded by many as a non-denominational college. The Inspector of Education tried to dispel that general notion with the argument that the school was "no more non-denominational than convent schools in Europe to which some English and African Protestants used to send their daughters in order that they might acquire a more cosmopolitan 'culture'".[19] He should equally well have added that some of the Protestant girls who entered such convent schools sometimes came out of them as Catholic adherents or sympathizers.

The efforts of the British Government to promote higher education in West Africa in the 1940s greatly enhanced the development of Catholic secondary schools. To ensure that Catholics had their fair share of the opportunities to be offered in the proposed University College at Ibadan, the expansion and improvement of Catholic secondary schools were considered inevitable. In a detailed outline of evidence given before the Elliot Commission on Higher Education in 1944, the Catholic Missions of Nigeria highlighted the importance which they attached not only to secondary education, but also to primary education. With regard to the former, the most prominent feature in their scheme of education was the establishment of a number of Catholic secondary schools which would run courses for the Cambridge Higher School Certificate the entrance level for Nigerian University students.[20]

By 1949, the number of the most important and full-fledged Catholic secondary schools in Nigeria had risen to sixteen.[21] Of these, nine—more than half—were located in the East, a concentration which ultimately had political consequences in the region.

---

[19] ODA: No. C.I.E. (S) 1177/62, Chief Inspector of Education, Eastern Provinces, "Inspection Report on Holy Family R.C.M. College," p. 1.

[20] See Appendix D.

[21] The Catholic secondary schools in question were: St. Gregory's College, Lagos; St. Patrick's College, Asaba; Christ the King College, Onitsha; College of the Immaculate Conception, Enugu; Holy Family College, Abak; St. Patrick's College, Ikot-Ansa, Calabar; Bishop Shanahan College, Orlu; Stella Maris College, Port Harcourt; St. Joseph's College, Sasse, Buea; Catholic College, Kaduna; Queen of the Rosary College, Onitsha; St. Theresa's College, Ibadan; Holy Child College, Ikoyi, Lagos; Our Lady's College, Kaduna; Holy Ghost College, Owerri; Cornelia Connely College, Uyo. Cf. ODA: "Father J. Jordan to Dr. K. Mellanby of the University College, Ibadan," Onitsha, 22 July, 1949.

II. *The Prospects for a Catholic University*

The Catholic origin of many Institutions of higher learning is an important legacy of Catholic educational influence in many countries and for many ages. In the African continent, something of that heritage is kept alive in a few Universities, such as Lovanium in Leopoldville, and Pius XII University College in Basutoland. However, Catholic control of the educational pyramid in mission lands was not as successful in Africa as it was in Asia and Latin America.[22] Of all the abortive plans to establish Catholic Universities in Africa, the failure at Onitsha was comparatively the saddest, if only for the fact that Eastern Nigeria was, and still is, a major Catholic stronghold in Africa. In spite of a large Catholic population, there exists in Nigeria hardly any institute of higher learning where the faithful can study Catholic theology. For someone to acquire that special knowledge, he must have to be a priest candidate, and must go to any of the few major seminaries in the country. But because of the affiliation of these seminaries to Roman, rather than Nigerian, universities, the ordinary lay Catholic may not be able to go to them in the foreseeable future to avail himself of his natural right to explore deeply the complexities of his faith.

This religious and social privation came very close to receiving a lasting solution during the missionary era. The first opportunity of establishing a Catholic university in Nigeria offered itself in 1929 during Hussey's reorganization of the Nigerian educational system. As has been seen, he proposed towards the end of that year that teachers for middle or secondary schools would be formed exclusively in higher colleges. For that purpose, the Government established the Yaba Higher College in 1930. Without expressly making the training of middle school teachers the prerogative of the Government, the Director of Education nevertheless left no doubts about that intention by denying government grants to any higher college that might be established by the Voluntary Agencies. This measure inspired the first deliberations by the Catholic missions about having a Catholic university.

At a general meeting of the Fathers at Ihiala in November 1929, Bishop Charles Heerey, Shanahan's Co adjutor, presented a resolution which called on Bishop Broderick of the Vicariate of Western Nigeria to join in "a united protest to the Government," and as a counter to government designs, he called for a Catholic higher college under mission control.[23] In December of the same year, the desirability of a

---

[22] See A. Hastings, "Pattern of African Mission Work," *AFER*, 8 (1966), 293-294.
[23] CSE: 554/I, "Minutes of the Fathers' Meeting Held at the Annual Retreat," Ihiala, 11 November, 1929.

Catholic higher college also featured prominently in a report to the Propaganda Congregation:

> The Government shall allow the missions to keep their primary schools and to train teachers for them. But with regard to the teachers of the intermediary and secondary schools, the Government reserves to itself the right to train them in a very special college, a quasi university. This quasi university shall be the only one to be maintained at the expense of the Government. But in view of the [prescribed standards] of these colleges, the missionary societies shall not be able to have theirs without government grants. There is a necessity for the Catholic missions to have, as soon as possible, their quasi Catholic university.[24]

Unfortunately, nothing of this urgency to have a Catholic university was evident in Catholic educational programme throughout the 1930s for a number of reasons. Firstly, given the near absence of Catholic secondary schools, the government measures did not pose any immediate danger for Catholic educational enterprise. As a matter of fact, there was not a single Catholic secondary school in Eastern Nigeria in 1929, and when Christ the King College was established in 1933, the staff consisted almost exclusively of expatriate teachers. Given the poor state of Catholic secondary education in the 1930s, there was no way the establishment of a Catholic university could have had a feasibility in a grand crash programme. Secondly, the Government eventually gave up its insistence on the university training of secondary school teachers, and by 1945, the staff of Holy Family College, Abak, for instance, included two seminarians with only the School Certificate, one Rural Science Teacher trained at the Umuahia Agricultural School, and one teacher with a Higher Elementary Certificate.[25]

The 1940s and 1950s saw a rapid development of Catholic secondary schools and, as a result, a resurgence of interest in the foundation of a Catholic university. By 1955, there were ten full-fledged Catholic secondary schools in the East, and four incomplete ones. The greatest single factor in that extensive buildup of Catholic secondary education was, as has been seen, the desire to catch up with Protestant dominance of the political and social life of the country. However, as Father J. Jordan frankly admitted, the mere achievement of parity in institutional strength did not bring instant equality with the Protestants. His conviction was: "It will...be many years before we can equal them in public influence.

----

[24] CSE: 554/VII, "Etat Statistique Annuel Pour la Propagande," 1 December, 1929.
[25] See ODA: No. C.I.E (S) 117762, Chief Inspector of Education, "Inspection Report on Holy Family R.C.M. College, Abak," Enugu, 24 September, 1945.

Indeed, we can *never* hope to do so if we do not find an outlet for our best boys in a Catholic university.''[26]

A search for such an outlet began in earnest in 1944 in the wake of the British Government's efforts to develop higher education in British West Africa. In the outline of evidence presented to the Eliot Commission on Higher Education, the Catholic Missions of Nigeria envisaged the elevation of a few Catholic secondary schools to the Higher Certificate level. These "Higher Schools" were to prepare Catholic students for the proposed University College at Ibadan. Furthermore, the authorities expressed the hope that one of these special schools would "ultimately develop into a constituent college of a Nigerian University, with Faculties of Science, Art, Philosophy and Divinity.''[27]

Catholic support for the establishment in Nigeria of a university college under government control was based primarily on the same belief that had prompted the British Government to come to that decision, namely, the undesirability of sending Africans to Europe and America for studies. "Spiritually poisoned,"—this was Father M. J. Bane's description of the Africans who had studied in American colleges and universities. "Is it any wonder," he asked, "that Catholic Prelates in West Africa are apprehensive and alarmed?''[28]

However, for other more serious reasons, the apprehension of the Catholic leaders did not diminish with the establishment of the University College at Ibadan in 1948. From the very beginning, the College acquired a strong Protestant bias, and by 1955, it had a divinity school for Protestant theology, and 250 Protestant students, as opposed to only 60 Catholic students.[29] As Nigeria moved closer to self-government, this strengthening of the Protestant hold on the highest echelons of society engendered renewed trepidations in Catholic leaders. Something of that obsession was given expression in Father Jordan's background note to Nigeria:

> ...Protestant leadership in higher education over the years, combined with the fact that University staff in West Africa are recruited mainly from England with its Protestant and secularist traditions has brought it to pass that Catholic influence, Catholic traditions, and Catholic life are all practically non-existent at the top of the educational ladder. This is a situation

---

[26] ODA: J. Jordan, "Background Note to Nigeria," p. 6.

[27] See Appendix D.

[28] M.J. Bane, "Educational Problems in West Africa," in *World Mission*, 1 (September, 1950), p. 90; see also ibid., p. 80: "From Nigeria in British West Africa, young Nnamdi Azikiwe came to us in the 1920's.... Unfortunately, due to the pinkish education he received in America, his facile pen is often used to try to embarrass the Catholic Church in Nigeria."

[29] See ODA: J. Jordan, "Background Note to Nigeria...," p. 7.

which obviously calls for change, particularly now that self-government for the West Coast is just around the corner, and self-government means political power in the hands of the educated few. We simply *must* produce a Catholic elite in Nigeria, or take the risk of being administered out of our whole school system by rulers with secularist traditions.... Catholic ideas and ideals must be set against these lay ones, which are rooted in Masonic and Socialist thought or absence of thought.[30]

It was against this background that efforts to establish a Catholic university were intensified in Nigeria between 1954 and 1956. Indeed, the educational developments of this period do not fall within the purview of our study. Yet, since they make for a better appreciation of the process that had gone before, it shall serve a useful purpose to give them some treatment.

By May 1955, a definite plan had been worked out by the Catholic authorities with regard to the type of University envisaged. The Faculties to be offered were given by Father Jordan as follows:

Arts and science would be sine qua non. Financial considerations would rule out medicine, except State sponsored by special arrangement. Teacher training for secondary schools would be a possibility though here Government recognition would be essential. Engineering degrees are rare in Nigeria, and this faculty would be of great value. Economics...should be an easy choice. It may be that a beginning with arts and science are at best with arts, science and economics would be a wise plan, and that other faculties including philosophy and divinity would follow at the dictation of circumstances.[31]

Worthy of note is the exclusively secular nature of the proposed Catholic University. Contrary to the wishes expressed in 1944, where Divinity was accorded a place of prominence, this official plan has little or no room for the study of Christian Theology.

Meanwhile, there were enormous financial difficulties to be contended with, and excruciating affiliation problems to be solved. At first, the Premier of Eastern Nigeria, Dr. Nnamdi Azikiwe, received the idea of a Catholic University with great enthusiasm, but he was careful not to commit his Government financially.[32] After efforts to affiliate the proposed Catholic university to the University of London had failed,[33]

---

[30] Ibid., p. 9.

[31] Ibid., p. 12.

[32] See ODA: "Mr. Glew, Private Secretary to the Premier, to J. Jordan," Enugu, 7 June, 1955.

[33] See ODA: "G. B. Jeffery, Director, University of London Institute of Education, to J. Jordan," London, 16 May, 1956. Among other things, the Director said that his colleagues would not "view with enthusiasm the establishment of other universities in Nigeria." He added that they "would probably resist any 'special relationship' of the type which applied to Ibadan."

Father Jordan concentrated his efforts on American universities.[34]

In spite of very bright prospects that had resulted from the visit of the American Jesuits to Nigeria in 1956, the possibility of a Catholic university had worn thin by the close of the decade. By that time, the Eastern Nigerian Government had put its full weight behind the search for higher education. That it appeared this time not as a distant supporter, but rather as a committed initiator, was not without serious consequences for the Catholic project. In fact, the Education Adviser to the Catholic Bishops of Nigeria had feared that the demand for an Eastern university under government control, a call which became loud shortly after the proposal of a Catholic university was made public,[35] would constitute a major obstacle. "Government is now wrestling with the problem of establishing an Eastern University," he wrote in 1955. "Does this mean that it will frown on efforts other than its own to spread universities in the East?"[36] The foundation in 1962 of the University of Nigeria, Nsukka, did in fact deliver a *coup de grace* to the ill-fated and ill-timed Catholic private enterprise.

In the failure to establish a Catholic university was best reflected that glaring flaw in Catholic educational policy in Eastern Nigeria, namely, the unduly prolonged absence of Catholic post-primary education. The best prospects for a Catholic institute of higher learning were given in the 1940s, when educational policy was still largely directed by a central Board in Lagos, and the readiness to make grants to major educational projects was notably present. But at that period, the longing for such an institution did not possess a concrete feasibility as a result of the meagre scope of Catholic post-primary education. By the late 1950s, when that scope had been considerably enlarged, the political climate of Nigeria had assumed a dramatic change: internal self-government had been achieved in the Regions, and education had become a regional affair. Catholic authorities had thenceforth to deal with the Nigerian Nationalists whom they rightly described as having secularist tendencies.

They had also to contend with the consequences of the failure to cater for sufficient Catholic representation in the political leadership of the emerging sovereign nation. While working out plans for the proposed Catholic university, Father Jordan was alert to the obvious opposition that would come from the Protestant politicians. He wrote:

---

[34] A summary of Father Jordan's contacts with American Universities was made by him in a press release which has been reproduced in Appendix E: 1 of this work.

[35] See Appendix E: 1.

[36] ODA: "J. Jordan to Private Secretary to the Premier," Enugu, 21 March, 1955.

Though I was assured verbally by the Prime Minister of the Eastern Region [Dr. Nnamdi Azikiwe] that his government would welcome a university run on the lines of Fordham or Notre Dame...I have reason to believe that his executive council with its Protestant ethos will not support him in this view.[37]

As it indeed turned out to be, the most immediate cause of the failure to establish a Catholic university in Eastern Nigeria was the opposition of the Protestants. The depth of that opposition can be measured from a letter of one Mr. S. N. Muotoe who put an application to Father Jordan for a scholarship to study Laboratory Technology at Ibadan in order afterwards to become a staff of the proposed Catholic university. "We are fully aware," he wrote, "that you will not be dismayed by some destructive criticism from some individuals appearing in the local dailies."[38] He was mistaken: judging from the evidence in Appendix E:1 of this work, the distress of the Catholic Education Adviser over the "attacks" of the Christian Council of Nigeria was manifested in no small measure. Given the enormous influence of the members of that Protestant Body on the political leadership of Nigeria, it was not surprising that by 1960 what was left of the initial support and encouragement of the former Premier of Eastern Nigeria, and then President of Nigeria, for a Catholic university was only an unconcealed indifference.

To a large extent, the Protestant opposition towards a Catholic university was an enlightened opportunism that sought to nip the rise of a Catholic intellectual class in the bud. For many decades, the Protestant Missions in Nigeria had enjoyed an unchallenged superiority in secondary education, a lead which had given them a comparable dominance over the political parties. But in the 1950s, however, Catholic efforts to redress that imbalance had taken on a dramatic turn. According to the Annual Report on the Eastern Nigeria Ministry of Education for 1956, five out of the seven secondary schools opened that year were Catholic, and seventeen of the twenty-nine new Grade Two and Three Teacher Training Colleges were also under Catholic auspices.[39] If, for the Protestants, this unprecedentedly rapid expansion of Catholic post-primary institutions was alarming, the talk of a Catholic university was simply outrageous. As it were, the Protestant leaders could not bear to see themselves and their missions outdone in educational prestige.

Furthermore, the attitude of the Christian Council of Nigeria epitomized denominational rivalry at its very worst. There was nothing in the proposal to found a university for Nigerians that was out of charac-

---

[37] ODA: J. Jordan, "Background Note to Nigeria...," p. 9.

[38] ODA: "S. N. Muotoe to J. Jordan," Ibadan, 28 September, 1955.

[39] Cf. D. B. Abernethy, *Church and State in Nigerian Education*, p. 27, n. 36.

ter with the educational objectives of these renowned "preaching-politicians," or with the aspirations of the nationalist movement, except that it was Catholic. The pledge of the Catholic Education Adviser to open the doors of the proposed Catholic institute of higher learning to Protestants and Moslems[40] did not temper the Protestant judgment that the "popish edifice" was a threat to the nation. To remove that crushing danger, the Protestant Council chose to demolish the entire building. That it thereby dug its own grave did not seem to have bothered its members. In their preference of a regional university under state control to one under Catholic auspices, they manifested the tendency of the Protestant Missions to see secularized education as a lesser evil than Catholic domination.[41] The state take-over of mission schools in 1970 certainly hurt the Protestants as much as it hurt the Catholics. But the fact remains that that measure was systematically prepared by Protestant politicians, whom Father J. Jordan rightly described as being imbued with "secularist thought or lack of thought." They readily evoked their Protestant backgrounds whenever a formidable front against Catholic expansionism was called for, but in pursuit of their secularist aspirations, they showed their anger alike to all missionary bodies and establishments—Catholic and Protestant.

A Catholic university in Eastern Nigeria may not have survived the political onslaught on mission schools in Nigeria after the civil war. But Catholic tradition and influence in such an institution would still have had some continuity under state control, just as is now the case with regard to former Catholic secondary schools.

III. Catholic Education and the National Movement

1. Backgrounds to Catholic Political Outlook

As has been seen in the foregoing chapters, the precedence which the Catholics placed on primary education was a logical corollary to a policy which laid strong emphasis on the school as a means of proselytization. There was great need, first and foremost, to catch-up with, and supercede, Protestant numerical superiority in the country, and as long as the primary school held good prospects for the achievement of that

---

[40] See Appendix E: 1.

[41] D. B. Abernethy, *Church and State*, p. 29. The same author quoted J. H. Price as saying: "It seemed...that the Church Missionary Society had slipped into the position of non-conformists in England in the nineteenth century, they would sooner have secular education for all than allow the dominant Church to run its own schools." Quoted in ibid., n. 38.

goal, some other major issues that form constituent parts of formal education, such as nation building and the advancement of an indigenous clergy, were given only a perfunctory attention. Accordingly, politics rated very lowly in Catholic institutions. The Protestants, for their part, were politically orientated right from the start. Their secondary grammar schools were established by parson politicians who saw the combination of religion and politics as belonging to a normal and healthy execution of their evangelical mission. Accordingly, Protestant pupils and students were more politically minded than their Catholic counterparts.

The lack of a sense of initiative which was discernible among Catholic pupils was, in the opinion of Dr. Alba Zizzamia, a Catholic educationist, the product of an ¡"over-protectiveness in the Catholic schools generally."[42] By "over-protectiveness," she was referring to the extraordinary paternal influence which the Catholic missionaries had on their adherents in general, an influence which made any major political decision in the country without Catholic sanction a very risky affair. To this point we shall return, but for the moment it may be a significant finding to isolate the reason behind Catholic prohibitive attitude towards politics in the schools.

Generally speaking, Nigerian political agitation in the colonial era was an expression of a popular longing for self-government. Accordingly, the cry for independence became the most distinctive characteristic of the national movement, which was largely a product of the Protestant African Missions.[43] This Protestant connection of the Nigerian Nationalists stood firmly in the way of cooperation with the Catholic authorities. Given the unrelenting Catholic antipathy towards Protestantism and Islam, Catholic schools and institutions could not easily acquire a character that had more than denominational integrity. One would not, for instance, regard as obvious the willingness of Catholic priests to organize political campaigns for Protestant and Moslem candidates. That needed some extraordinary grace, which, as we shall see later, did come in the course of time, but not necessarily from heaven.

Furthermore, the feeling of insecurity on the part of Catholic expatriates was a factor of major significance for Catholic political outlook. Since the popular demand for independence included self-government in education, the Catholic authorities understandably

---

[42] Quoted in B. Sundkler, *The Christian Ministry in Africa* (London: SCM Press, 1960), p. 78.

[43] For the background history of the Nigerian National Movement, see J. F. A. Ajayi, "Nineteenth Century Origin of Nigerian Nationalism," in *Journal of the Historical Society of Nigeria*, 2 (1961), 196-210.

looked upon the nationalist movement with disfavour. By all account, they regarded any attempt to challenge their direction of education as posing an existential problem. It was an obsession whose depth can be best determined by the following observation by Father John Grant, a member of the Society of African Missions:

> Nigeria is moving rapidly towards self-government and, almost inevitably, towards a greater measure of State control in the schools. We may be called upon for a great fight in defence of Catholic principles in our schools. In many areas we are already fighting for our existence....The position we have gained at such cost, the achievement that was bought at such sacrifice in ill-health, suffering and in so many lives lost in lonely missionary out-posts must not be surrendered without a great struggle.[44]

The first taste of this inevitable power struggle came sooner than was envisaged. In the Eastern Region, it culminated in a serious crisis in 1957 over a government plan to introduce a universal primary education. Unlike in the Western Region—a Protestant stronghold—where the Universal Primary Education programme was carried through without grave difficulties, the project was dropped in the East largely because of strong Catholic opposition. For the regional Government, it was the first bitter taste of Catholic influence.[45]

2. The Nature of the Nationalist Grievances

The grievances of the Nigerian Nationalists which ran high during the controversy over state control of education were both real and fancied. They were real in the sense that the greater majority of the Nationalists were former mission teachers who had genuine reasons to see the absolute educational hegemony of the Missions dismantled. Although they were the group that made the greatest contribution to missionary and national developments, the teachers contended with the worst pay conditions in the country. Although their salaries were, to a large extent, paid by the Government, they were denied the rights and privileges of civil servants, and often abandoned to the whims and caprices of their employers—the Voluntary Agencies. Finding themselves in high govern-ment positions, the former teachers understandably strove to achieve the emancipation of the teaching profession from its state of servitude. Accordingly, the nationalist demand for state control of education was largely made from the perspective of the plights of the teachers. The com-

---

[44] J. Grant, "Education in Nigeria and the Mission Effort," in *The African Angelus*, 7, No.4 (July-August, 1953), p. 6.

[45] See Eastern Nigeria, Ministry of Education, *Report on the Review of the Educational System in Eastern Nigeria* (Enugu, 1962), pp. 44-46.

mission that reviewed the educational system in Eastern Nigeria in 1962 left no doubts about the central position accorded to the welfare of the teachers when it stated that state control of education "must ultimately be achieved if the status of teachers and their conditions of service are to be respected and improved."[46]

Nevertheless, the legitimate disaffection of the teachers did not deduce from the fact that much of the nationalist grievances was fancied. The ultimate motives of the Nationalists were, to a large extent, based on the questionable assumption that the true measure of national "adulthood" lay in state control of education. Much of that misleading conception was acquired from examples of nationalist movements in the civilized nations of the world where state control of education was very much in vogue. The idea of non-denominational schools under government control was in fact not a creation of the Nigerian Nationalists. It was a continuation of the secularist tradition of their erstwhile British colonial masters.[47] Had the colonial Administration in Nigeria had the means and opportunity, it would also have taken the direction of education exclusively in its hands.

Seen against this background, it would seem therefore that nationalist attack on mission schools in Nigeria was motivated by the mere desire to have the direction of national destiny in the hands of Nigerians, rather than by any grave anomaly in mission schools. A major feature in the educational crusade of the nationalist movement was the eradication of illiteracy. In this regard, the selfless commitments of the Christian Missions to the education of the masses greatly surpassed anything the Government or the Native Administration Committees could offer, a thing which the Nationalists themselves remembered with gratitude. Speaking about the Catholic Priests, one of them said:

> ...it must be conceded that these clerics, most of them, are devoted and hard working. It must also be accepted that the system of education introduced by them supplies a necessary ingredient to the formation of the character of a nation—sound morality and the fear of God. Nothing should be done to minimise the immense debt we owe to them....[48]

However, despite such benign overtones, the desire for self-government in all aspects of national life was accorded an overriding priority. It was an uncompromising attitude which stemmed largely from the educational backgrounds of the twentieth century nationalists. Unlike their

---

[46] Ibid., p. 45.

[47] J. Jordan, "Background Note to Nigeria," p. 9.

[48] Quoted in Eastern Nigeria Ministry of Education, *Report on the Review of the Educational System*, p. 45.

nineteenth century predecessors, who received their higher education almost exclusively in the few Protestant colleges in West Africa, and who were, as a result, spared the worst experiences of racial discrimination, most of the twentieth century nationalists studied in Britain and America where they were confronted with the bitter realities of intense colour prejudice.[49] Consequently, their brand of Pan-Africanism held such explicit nostalgia for a free Africa that could not be tempered by anything short of self-government.

3. Catholic Approach to the National Movement

The greatest battle for self-government in Nigeria was fought between 1940 and 1950. It was a decade of seething tensions and unprecedented political activities during which nationalist newspapers, trade unions, tribal associations, progressive societies, and diverse political organizations directed public opinion throughout the country.[50] By the end of the decade, it had become sufficiently clear to the colonial Government that a revision of its position on self-government was advisable, if not inevitable. Accordingly, it began to give Nigerians a greater share in the Government than was hitherto the case, especially in the regional Education Departments.

Of a more dramatic character was the change of attitudes in the official policies of the Christian Churches. In 1950, Pope Pius XII created three ecclesiastical provinces in the British West African territories.[51] Although the provinces remained under the sovereignty of the Propaganda Congregation, and for that reason retained their mission character, they nevertheless acquired a hierarchical status for being headed by missionary bishops who had the same honours, rights, and privileges as those possessed by normal diocesan bishops, and who could be succeeded, albeit in principle, by members of the local clergy. The following year, the Pontiff, in what was undoubtedly an accommodating response to the political changes in the Missions, issued a missionary encyclical

---

[49] For the experiences of African students in Britain and America, see J. J. Considine, "African Students in American Colleges," *World Missions*, 1 (September, 1950), 90-99.

[50] For more details on the course of the National Movement in the 1940s, see T. Hodgkin, "Background to Nigerian Nationalism, 3: The Coming of Zik and the N.C.N.C.," *West Africa*, August 18, 1951, pp. 751-752.

[51] The three Ecclesiastical Provinces were: 1) Eastern Nigeria and the British Cameroons; Onitsha became a metropolitan see with three suffragan dioceses—Owerri, Calabar, and Buea. 2) Western Nigeria with Lagos as metropolis. 3) Gold Coast and British Togo; Cape Coast was made a metropolitan see with four suffragan dioceses-Accra, Kumasi, Tamala and Kala. The former Apostolic Vicariate of Sierra Leone was accorded a special union with the diocese of Liberia-Bo. See "Laeto Accepimus," in AAS, 42 (1950), 615-619.

which, among other things, called the attention of the missionaries to the educational contributions which they ought to make towards the political maturity of the mission lands.[52]

The Protestants, for their part, also marched with a pace that was in rhyme with the political tunes of the moment. In 1951, the Archbishop of Canterbury created the Ecclesiastical Province of West Africa, and with that Nigeria became, within the Anglican community, an equal partner to the white dominions and the young states of India, Burma, and Ceylon.[53]

Despite these revolutionary signals from Rome and London, the Catholic Mission in Eastern Nigeria remained largely at odds with the National Movement for the greater part of the 1950s. As D. B. Abernethy rightly put it, there was among the Irish priests a strong unwillingness "to accept the fact that the colonial era was ending."[54] The more intensive the political agitation in the country became, the more irascible the Fathers became towards any of their subjects caught meddling with politics. One of the very few missionaries who realized that such attitudes were not to the best interest of the Catholic Church in Nigeria was Father J. Jordan. Of all the Catholic priests in Eastern Nigeria in the years of political unrest, he was, perhaps, the most articulate defender of the broad objectives of the nationalist movement. Using his office as the Education Adviser to the Catholic Bishops of Nigeria, he endeavoured, in numerous written appeals, to achieve a change of heart in his fellow missionaries. In one such entreaty, he vehemently defended a native priest who was persecuted because of his alleged political leanings:

> I think X has a very poor opinion of him, possibly because he is very open in his views, and has had the reputation for sometime of being nationalistic and rather anti-white. I consider him a very reliable priest, unusually spiritual and definitely a good observer of Rule. He is rather forward in his political views, though he does not in any way take part in politics as such. Many European Fathers on the other hand are too retrograde in their political outlook and do not realise the way Nigeria is moving. Father Z's views are actually the prevalent ones among the native clergy and among educated Africans. There is nothing extreme about them. They really boil down to this: that the Africans should be prepared and prepared well with all possible speed to take over the running of their own country.[55]

---

[52] Cf. "Evangelii Praecones," in AAS, 43 (1951), 514-515.

[53] J. S. Coleman, *Nigeria: Background to Nationalism*, p. 112.

[54] *The Political Dilemma of Popular Education*, p. 166.

[55] "J. Jordan to Superior General," 18 March, 1954, quoted in E. Isichei, *Entirely for God: The Life of Michael Iwene Tansi* (London: Macmillan, 1980), p. 13. "X" and "Z" are Professor Isichei's substitutes for the names of the Fathers mentioned in Jordan's letter.

By underlining the way Africans ought to be "prepared," Father Jordan admitted what his confrères tended to deny—the propriety of a well-grounded post-primary education for Blacks.[56] By emphasizing the urgency which the provision of such an education demanded, he implied that further delay would be disastrous for the Catholic Church not only because of a possible nationalist anger over Catholic resistance, but also because the Catholic Church would have no position of influence in an independent Nigeria. In 1955 he gave an emphatic expression to his concern over Protestant hegemony in Nigeria when he noted that "the Prime Minister, the Deputy Prime Minister, together with 11 out of 12 ministers—in other words the Government of the East—are Protestant."[57]

These considerations prompted a shift in attitudes, and by the late 1950s, Catholic active opposition to the national movement had been noticeably abandoned. Gradually, Catholic adherents were encouraged to take active part in politics, especially within the National Council of Nigeria and the Cameroons (N.C.N.C.), the most influential political party in the Eastern Region.[58] As Bishop Whelan put it, "it seemed a lesser evil to campaign for non-Catholics rather than risk losing all influence in the Nationalist Party."[59] To achieve parity with the Protestants in political and social influence, Catholic post-primary education was improved and expanded in the 1950s with unprecedented rapidity. The results were reassuring, and in 1953, Father John Grant noted that "Catholic interest in education and its contribution has left it in a position where it just cannot be ignored."[60]

This brings us to Catholic influence over, and contribution to, the National Movement.

Although the Catholics lacked political prominence in government high places, they were able to counter that disadvantage by their overwhelming influence over the masses, a leverage which came about chiefly from the concentration of Catholic primary schools in the Eastern Region. According to official Catholic records, there were 388,509 children in Catholic primary schools in Nigeria in 1952. Of these,

---

[56] According to Father Jordan, some of the Catholic priests "believed that the children should be educated up as far as Standard Two or so and then sent back to the land." *Bishop Shanahan*, p. 252.

[57] ODA: J. Jordan, "Background Note to Nigeria...." In 1960, Father Jordan wrote that Protestant advantage in secondary education had given them "a dangerous degree of control at the top, both in and out of Government." See J. Jordan, "Catholic Education and Catholicism in Nigeria," *AFER*, 2 (1960), 61f.

[58] See D. B. Abernethy, *The Political Dilemma*, p. 166.

[59] J. B. Whelan, "Our Schools: Victory in Nigeria," p. 22f.

[60] J. Grant, "Education in Nigeria...," p. 6.

243,989 were in the East. Furthermore, of the 834,235 Catholics in Nigeria in the same year, as many as 603,304 were in the Eastern Region.[61] This numerical strength of the Eastern Catholics gave them a strong political influence which was never equalled in the West, the stronghold of the Protestants.

Although the failure in Eastern Nigeria to "Africanize" the Catholic Mission—the greatest single educating Body in the Region—stimulated nationalist resistance, the Eastern politicians generally refrained from religious confrontations and denominational attacks in their political campaigns. With more than 50 per cent of its electorate likely to be Catholics, the N.C.N.C. realized that it could not win any election without Catholic support.[62] A case which sufficiently demonstrated the growing political influence of the Catholics was the failure of Mazi Mbonu Ojike to be elected to the Eastern House of Assembly in 1951. Filled with the agnostic spirit that tended to be the hallmark of most of the young Nationalists, the former pupil-teacher used the *West African Pilot* as a medium for devastating attacks on the Catholic Church. Confronting that challenge in kind, the Catholic authorities used the *Catholic Herald* for their strong denunciation of what they regarded as "ungodly nationalism." When election day came in 1951, Mbonu Ojike lost not only in all major towns of the East, but also in his home town Orlu.[63]

In the main, it would be a cheap assumption to suppose that the Catholics, because of their known antipathy towards political agitations, and because of their poor standing in the political leadership of the country, were irrelevant to the nationalist cause. In an effort to dispel this notion, Father James O'Connell rightly pointed out that

> ...no matter how lukewarm was the initial reception given by the missionaries to the nationalist movements, African leaders have concluded that the logic of the Christian missionary enterprise and organization was going in the right direction.[64]

To many, this opinion would rather appear grotesque, but in actual fact it was in tandem with the truth. The political debate, it must be emphasized, could not have been called into existence in the first place without the Christian Missions: it was they who painstakingly led the

---

[61] Cf. Sr. M. Osmund, "Nigerian Schools: Politics or Education?" in *World Mission*, 5 (1954), 231-232.

[62] Cf. D. B. Abernethy, *The Political Dilemma*, p. 166f.

[63] For more details on this controversy, and on Catholic influence on the Nigerian political scene, see T. Oloko, "Religion and Politics in Nigeria," in *West Africa*, 2 and 9 February, 1951, pp. 102 and 131.

[64] J. O'Connell, "The Church in Africa—Will Its 'Success' Continue?" in *The Church in Africa*, ed. W. J. Wilson (Maryknoll: Maryknoll Publications, 1967), p. 7.

nationalists through the school to political adulthood; the mission schools equipped the nationalist movement with its most useful instrument—the English language—which formed a band of communication between the Nigerian tribes with their plurality of languages;[65] and it was the Missions who, perhaps, saved Nigeria from the worst ills of imperialism. In all these, the contributions of the Catholic Missions were considerable.

Despite their grievances, the nationalists did not lose sight of the great importance of the missionaries for their cause. One of the most prominent of them, Dennis Osadebay,[66] gave expression to that fact in what may, perhaps, be regarded as a representative opinion of most of the African Nationalists:

> The direct good from missionary service in Africa outweighs any by-product.
>   Even the Colonial Office has sounded the death-knell of the old imperialism and, when partnership between the African and the British grows to its full strength and splendour, neither the old nor the young African will have anything but praise and thanks for the missionaries who have given their lives and belongings to help to reclaim a race....
>   If the Colonial Governments now take up education they are taking it up from where the missionary stopped. If African tribes can now meet to discuss their national aspirations, they ought to thank the missionaries for preaching goodwill. When African historians come to write their own account of the adventure for Africa with imperialism, they will write of the missionaries as the greatest friends the African had.[67]

IV. *Indigenous Leadership of the Mission*

When the Christian missionary enterprise experienced a universal breakdown at the close of the eighteenth century, Church leaders and scholars realized that the unduly long racial discrimination in the choice of candidates to the priesthood and to the Orders was a precedent that must not be adopted if the Missions were to acquire a measure of permanence in a revived effort. Their emphasis on the promotion of native clergies and hierarchies was based entirely on that all-important cognizance. It was hoped that by fostering indigenous leadership in the Missions, the Church would continue to flourish in them even if the presence of foreign

---

[65] Cf. J. S. Coleman, *Nigeria*, p. 114.

[66] Dennis Osadebay was one of the foundation members of the N. C. N. C. in 1944, and in 1963 he became the Premier of the Midwest Region. He was also a renowned writer, and his most celebrated work of poetry—"Africa Sings"—was published in 1952. See J. Jahn, *The Black Experience: 400 Years of Black Literature from Africa and the Americas.* Series I (Liechtenstein: Kraus Reprint, 1969), p. 45.

[67] D. Osadebay, "Easter Reflection: The Missionary in West Africa," in *West Africa*, 5 April, 1947, p. 289f.

missionaries were to be terminated in a measure comparable to the calamities of the eighteenth century.

Such a situation did occur in Eastern Nigeria after the Nigeria-Biafra War (1967-1970). The entire force of European missionaries—some 300 priests and 200 religious men and women—were expelled from that region at the end of the war, and the Church was deprived of all its educational institutions, except for a few seminaries. Totally unprepared, the native clergy assumed the responsibilities of the expatriate missionaries, and contrary to all expectations, there followed no such thing as a total break-down of church life in Eastern Nigeria. Although the vast school system of evangelization was forcibly dismantled, the Church continued to function normally, and the 1970s even experienced an unprecedented vocation explosion.[68] That the credit of that spectacular success belonged ultimately to the Holy Ghost Fathers is beyond any possible doubt. They had left behind indigenous bishops, priests, religious Brothers and Sisters to lead the Lord's flock in their stead. Yet, the greatest single factor in that success story was the fact that the calamities of the post civil war years—the expulsion of the missionaries, and the nationalization of the mission schools—did not take place a decade or two earlier.

When Nigeria became a Church hierarchy in 1950, almost ninety years after the advent of Catholicism in the western part of the country, there were only a handful of indigenous priests and not a single native bishop. The hierarchical status conferred upon the Nigerian Church therefore brought no significant changes in its leadership. Had the expatriate missionaries been sent away that year, the missionary fiasco of the eighteenth century might, perhaps, have experienced a re-birth in Eastern Nigeria.

The reluctance and belatedness with which the native clergy was promoted in the Missions was a thing which confounded even contemporary Church leaders. As has been seen, Father Lejeune lamented in 1904 over the lack of Catholic initiative to provide for a native clergy. As late at 1929, Father Joseph Soul, a Visitor of the Spiritan Congregation, was scandalized to find only seven seminarians in Eastern Nigeria and not a single native priest. That such a thing should happen in Nigeria, a coun-

---

[68] For more details, see J. Daly, "Iboland: The Background to the Vocation Explosion," AFER, 15 (1973), 259-266; see also C. Mba, D. O'Sullivan, Progrés et situation de l'Eglise parmi les Ibos au Nigeria," in *Le Christ au Monde*," No. 6 (Rome, 1974), 491-499; C. Mba, "My Experience in Running a Seminary in the East Central State of Nigeria," in *Omnis Terra*, 64/6 (Rome, 1974), 79-83.

try with unparalleled economic and missionary successes, was for him simply incomprehensible.[69]

However, for all the bewilderment of the Visitor, the case of Nigeria was not an isolated one. Discernible in contemporary Missions in Asia, Africa, and Latin America, it was a predictable vestige of the racial discrimination which existed in the Padroada and Propaganda Missions of past centuries.[70] At the root of that colour bias was the popular belief that the stigma of heathenism in Christian converts can be washed off only after centuries of communion with Christianity. Until that gradual purification had taken place, the indigenes of the mission lands were considered unfit for the sacred orders. Some mission leaders were so sure of the propriety of this belief as to associate it with divine inspiration. In opposing the idea of ordaining American Indians as priests, Father Geronimo de Mendieta (1538-1604), for instance, had the following to say:

> ...the Church, illuminated by the Holy Spirit..., has ordained that by the determination of the high priests, the vicars of Christ, there shall not be admitted to the profession of priesthood or the Orders, the descendants of any infidel in the fourth degree.[71]

In Nigeria, as indeed in all Africa, the "recentness" of the conversion of pagans to Christianity became the greatest limiting factor in the promotion of a native clergy. In fact, it was a prejudice which, for a long time, no amount of moral excellence on the part of the aspirants to the priesthood was able to temper. Bishop Shanahan was frank enough to give an overt admission to this with the following observation:

> If our number of native priests are already not much greater, it is because we put them through a long course of preparation. This is not because they are not good students, or because they do not give sufficient promise in the Seminary. On the contrary, the general comment of those in charge of the Seminary is that they are too keen on their studies, and are over-exemplary in conduct. But these young men have only just emerged from centuries-old pagan tradition and habits.[72]

---

[69] CSE: 554/V, J. Soul, "General Report to the Superior General...," Onitsha, 12 November, 1929, p. 19: "Je n'arrive pas à comprendre pourquoi on ne pourrait pas trouver un plus grand nombre de vocations dans un pay aussi avancé que la Nigeria."

[70] See C. R. Boxer, "The Problem of the Native Clergy in the Portuguese and Spanish Empires from the Sixteenth to the Eighteenth Centuries," in *The Mission of the Church and the Propagation of the Faith.* Studies in Church History, 6, ed. G. J. Cuming (Cambridge: At the Univ. Press, 1970), pp. 85-105.

[71] Quoted in ibid., p. 92.

[72] Quoted in E. Isichei, *Entirely for God: The Life of Michael Iwene Tansi* (London: Macmillan, 1980), p. 35.

Is it any wonder then that the promotion of an indigenous clergy in Eastern Nigeria was put off for so long? It must be recalled that Father Shanahan and his confrères repeatedly supported their demands for a Catholic "High School" or Training Institution with the argument that it would serve at the same time as a seminary.[73] Paradoxically, neither the Calabar "High School," nor the Igbariam Training College had a Seminary department. Bishop LeRoy, the Superior General of the Holy Ghost Congregation, did speak of a Junior Seminary at Igbariam in 1919,[74] but what he spoke of was in fact only a standing plan. By 1919, the Igbariam Training College had been closed down, and a report on the Lower Niger Mission in 1920 spoke of only one Seminarian and one "Seminary" that was yet "to be approved."[75]

After many years of hesitation, a Seminary was finally established at Igbariam in 1924. It would be euphemistic to call the Igbariam venture a Major Seminary, for apart from John Anyogwu and perhaps one or two Irish students, the rest of the pioneer candidates had no adequate post-primary education.[76] To strike a balance between a secondary education and a Senior Seminary training, the programme of studies at Igbariam included English, Latin, Mathematics, Liturgy, Church History, and Church Music.[77]

The choice of Igbariam as a site for a Seminary was symptomatic of a universal tendency in the Missions to turn clerical institutions into semi-monasteries.[78] In the words of Bishop Shanahan, Igbariam was chosen because it was "a small station isolated from the noise of the

---

[73] See for instance, CSE: 192/B/V, "Shanahan to Superior General," Calabar, 21 January, 1908: "Les Training Institutions (puisque le Grec, le Latin, le Français etc...) seront nos Seminaires. Nos Seminaristes seront éduqués par le gouvernement." He made the same observation in September: "Nous pouvons avoir une école supérieure. Le gouvernement nous paiera £25 par enfant par an.... C'est notre petit Seminaire tout trouvé et payé par le gouvernement." CSE: 192/B/V, "Shanahan to Superior General," Onitsha, 2 September, 1908.

[74] Cf. CSE: 191/B/III, "Report by LeRoy," Paris, 29 September, 1919.

[75] CSE: 191/B/V, D. Walsh, Apostolic Pro-Prefect, "General Statistics," 1 January, 1920.

[76] It is uncertain how many students actually numbered among the pioneer members of the Igbariam Seminary in 1924. Writing in 1931, Father C. O. Donohue gave the number as ten. See "The Church in Southern Nigeria," in *The Missionary Annals of the Holy Ghost Fathers*, 13 (1931), 76. But an official report on the Seminary in 1924 put the number at seven, namely, two Irish and five Nigerian students. See CSE: *Bulletin*, 31 (1923-1924), 778. Another undated report, written most probably in 1925 or early 1926, gave the number as eight but enumerated only seven names: John Anyogwu, William Hinzepeter, Michael Iwene, William Obeleagu, Charles Nweze, Simon Okoye, and John Aghanti. CSE: 555/VI, "Le Seminaire indigène."

[77] See C. O. Donohue, "The Church in Southern Nigeria," p. 76

[78] Cf. A. Hastings, *Das Schwarze Experiment: Kirche und Mission im Modernen Afrika* (Wien: Verlag Styria, 1969), p. 260f.

governmental and commercial worlds, as well as from the distractions of
the daily routines of a parish.''[79] In reality, however, Igbariam was a
mosquito-infested vicinity, and the mud buildings set up there for
Seminarians were ''neither beautiful to look at nor comfortable to live
in.''[80] There, the students contended with a strictly guarded daily
routine—prayers, studies, and manual labour—which began at 4.50
a.m. and ended at 9.10 p.m.[81]

They had also to contend with a more serious handicap—the lack of
confidence and trust in their superiors. That attitude was largely discernible in no less a personality than the Apostolic Vicar himself. ''In spite
of undeniable qualities,'' he wrote in 1920, ''most of these young people
lack character and conviction. They are changeable, egotistical and
proud. They lack a clear idea of sacrifice and of abnegation.''[82] All these
charges were typical European conceptions of the Black man which were
very much in vogue in Shanahan's time, and which were instrumental
in his well-known antipathy towards the ''gentlemen of the coast,'' the
Sierra Leonians and Lagosians of the Protestant community, who
formed the bulk of the educated class in Onitsha in the nineteenth and
early twentieth centuries.[83]

The fact that Shanahan expressed these views about his young
Africans at a time when the Seminary had not yet been officially established proved that they were based on preconceptions rather than on
lived experience. Later in his ministry, he was to speak of the Africans
in words that revealed the depth of his conversion:

> Those teachers in the old days were wonderful fellows. They were the real
> apostles of the people. There would be no Church in the country today if
> they had not done their work so well. They never spared themselves, and
> every one of them was a catechist as well as a teacher. We cannot number
> the vast multitude of souls that has gone to heaven through their hands.
> Who transformed the dying hours of old men whose long lives had been
> passed in the darkness of paganism? The teacher. Who controlled the
> Church services on Sundays and taught the people their knowledge of God?
> The teacher. Who kept the idea of God and Church before the minds of
> the people during the long months of the Father's absence? The teacher.[84]

Any commentary on this passage would be superfluous, but it would be
useful to point out that the group of Seminarians who came to Igbariam

---

[79] CSE: 554/VI, J. Shanahan, ''Annual Report, 1923 to July 1924.''
[80] C. O. Donohue, ''The Church in Southern Nigeria,'' p. 76.
[81] See E. Isichei, *Entirely for God*, p. 28.
[82] CSE: 554/VII, ''Shanahan to Cardinal Van Rossum,'' quoted in E. Isichei, *Entirely for God*, p. 27.
[83] Cf. CSE: *Bulletin*, 24 (1907-1908), 147.
[84] Quoted in J. Jordan, *Bishop Shanahan of Southern Nigeria*, p. 155f.

in 1924 were the best of all Catholic teachers and catechist of their time. They quickly turned the Vicar's pessimism into an undisguised optimism. In 1924, the same year that the Seminary was officially inaugurated, the Bishop wrote that "The Seminarians are doing well and giving us a serious hope for success."[85] Among the great merits of the Igbariam pioneers, therefore, was their salvaging of the dignity and reputation of a whole race and of a whole generation.

On the whole, life at Igbariam was arduous and, to a large extent, inhuman. Although the Seminary was there for only five years, the name *Igbariam* still elicits in Seminarians of today notions of monasticism, asceticism, and ultra-tridentinism. An idea of the conservatism that was nursed at Igbariam may be gained from a letter of intent by Shanahan in 1924. His desire was "to use the Fathers of the Church alone as Latin authors to the exclusion of all pagan authors. But an idea of the latter's style—not of their worthless ideas—will be given to our students."[86] This position would surely have surprised even the scholastics of the most extreme right.

However, the name *Igbariam* also embodies today notions of the best qualities of a perfect priesthood—discipline, holiness, and industry. All these and many more were possessed by the few who survived the ordeals of the pioneer experiments at Igbariam, including their dedicated teachers and directors.[87]

In 1928, the Seminary was moved from Igbariam to Onitsha, rather out of necessity than of "apathy" or "hostility" on the part of the local inhabitants, as Professor Isichei seemed to suggest.[88] A Teacher Training College was established that year at Onitsha, and since the only qualified staff to run it were the Fathers of Igbariam, the Seminarians had to move with them to Onitsha. At last the long envisaged college-cum-seminary institution was called into being. However, the union brought more bruises than blessings for the Seminarians: it helped to further prolong the unusually long way to the priesthood. The Training College became a suitable place for the "probation" of Seminarians, a period of uncertainty and trial which sometimes lasted more than two years. For those

---

[85] CSE: 554/VI, J. Shanahan, "Annual Report, July 1923 to July 1924."

[86] CSE: 555/II, "Shanahan to Léna," 4 August, 1924, quoted in E. Isichei, *Entirely for God*, p. 28.

[87] Father William O'Donneli was the first Rector of the Seminary, but on account of a failing health, he was soon replaced by Father Charles Heerey, who directed the Seminary with the assistance of Father Philip O'Connor until 1927 when he was made Shanahan's Coadjutor. His place was temporarily taken by Father Richard Daly until Father Denis Kennedy replaced the latter in 1928. See CSE: *Bulletin*, 32 (1925-1926),578; 34 (1929-1930), 835.

[88] See E. Isichei, *Entirely for God*, p. 30.

so tried, the years at Onitsha were a period during which one was made to teach more than one was actually taught.[89]

The prescription of a long Seminary course for priest candidates was not peculiar to Nigeria, and not favoured only by the Holy Ghost Fathers. It was discernible almost in the whole of Africa. In Congo, where the White Fathers worked, for instance, the first stage of the major seminary course lasted five years. During this time, Seminarians were tutored in Philosophy, Dogmatic Theology, Church History, Sacred Scriptures, Liturgy, Languages, and Nature Studies.[90] At the end of the five years, successful candidates were made to go through a two-year "probation period," at the end of which those who proved worthy came back to the Seminary for another three years of study. The subjects taught at this second stage included: Moral and Pastoral Theology, Canon Law, Homiletics, and Catechetics. In all, therefore, candidates had to go through ten years of rigorous study before being ordained priests. Together with the seven or more years in the Minor Seminary, it took at least seventeen years to become a Catholic priest in the Congo. Also in Uganda, the first two priests ordained there spent between eighteen and twenty years of their lives in the Seminary.[91]

In the Vicariate of Southern Nigeria, an official ruling on the "probation of Seminarians" in 1929 stipulated that Seminarians be engaged as Catechists after their secondary education for at least one year. During this period, they were to be "given allowance for their complete support (food, clothing, etc.) at the rate of one shilling a day while so engaged."[92] The same process was to be repeated after their philosophical studies, and for a third and last time, a probational period of about six months was to be observed before ordination. Only a very insignificant fraction of the number of candidates who entered the Seminaries in the early years survived this long period of rigorous trial. Some became disillusioned and left on their own, others (the majority) were sent away for a thousand and one reasons, which ranged from a passing illness to a Superior's whim.[93]

Behind the slow pace with which Seminarians were led to the priesthood was, besides the often expressed misgivings over the pagan

---

[89] In 1930, there were 13 Seminarians at St. Charles' Training College who were studying Latin and a few other secondary subjects. Two of the Senior Seminarians—Michael Tansi and William Obelagu—were teaching members of the College staff. See CSE: 554/V, P. Biéchy, "Bulletin des Oeuvres," October, 1930.

[90] Cf. "Eine Priesterweihe am Kongo," in *Afrikastimmen*, 1 (1920), 12.

[91] See *Afrikastimmen*, 1 (1920), 13.

[92] CSE: 554/I, "Minutes of the Fathers' Meeting Held at the Annual Retreat," Ihiala, 11 November, 1929, item v.

[93] Cf. E. Isichei, *Entirely for God*, p. 29f.

backgrounds of the candidates, the popular belief that the African was intellectually inferior to the White man. Pope Pius XI endeavoured in 1926 to dispel that universal bias when he wrote:

> It is rather a flawed policy to regard the natives as inferior human beings, and as people of dull intellects. For experience has long shown that with regard to the acuteness of the mind, the peoples who live in the farthest East or South are not inferior to our people, but capable of competing with them....You, honourable Brethren and beloved Sons, can be witnesses to this yourselves. We too can also give a convincing proof here, namely, that the natives [from the Third World] who, before our very eyes, are pursuing studies in diverse disciplines in the Roman Colleges are, with regard to intellectual abilities and academic achievements, not only equal to our own students, but also outmatch them oftentimes. This is all the more reason why you should not rate the indigenous priests lowly and assign to them only mean jobs, as if they do not possess the same priestly dignity, and as if they do not share in the same apostolic vocation as you yourselves. On the contrary, you must have an eye particularly to them, because some day they will be the ones to lead both the Churches you have built up with so much sweat, and the future Catholic communities. For this reason, there should be between the European and native missionaries no distinctions made and no lines of demarcation drawn; rather the one should be united with the other in a bond of reverence and love.[94]

That the Holy Ghost Fathers discriminated between White and Black clerics in Eastern Nigeria can best be judged from the careers of the first two priests to be ordained in the Lower Niger Mission. The very first was Mr. Delaney, an Irish lay missionary who volunteered for Nigeria in 1910. After some years in the Mission, he got a vocation to the priesthood and quickly did all his studies—Latin, Philosophy, Theology—not in a Seminary, but privately with the Fathers. On 7 July, 1919, he was ordained deacon, and by virtue of a special papal Indult, he was ordained a priest *sub titulo missionis* a week afterwards by Bishop Broderick, the Apostolic Vicar of Western Nigeria.[95] He thus became the first Catholic priest ever to be ordained on both sides of the Niger. In connection with that memorable event, Father Shanahan, the Prefect of the Lower Niger Mission, made a very important observation which, had it also been designed to be taken seriously, should have spurred him on to secure for Delaney's immediate followers seminary careers that were less precarious. He wrote:

> At last one has seen here a true Catholic Bishop [Broderick] and a true Catholic priest. Bishop Tugwell [of the Anglican Niger Mission] has never

---

[94] "Rerum Ecclesiae," in AAS, 18 (1926), 77.
[95] See CSE: *Bulletin*, 30 (1921-1922), 507-508.

failed to ordain "priests" every year. One would in fact say that the Protestants alone have a truly perfect hierarchy.[96]

The second priest to be ordained in the Mission was John Anyogwu, a man whose biography, if it is written, would be a vital contribution to the study of the missionary history of Nigeria. Some time between 1910 and 1912, he and another unidentified schoolboy expressed the wish to become priests. Although the necessity of promoting an indigenous clergy had been preached for many decades, the "unusual" intention of the two young Africans landed like a bombshell amidst the expatriate Fathers. It was received by the Prefect himself with a mixture of delight and perplexity, as can be seen in his letter to his Superior. "Two of our boys of very good Christian parents," he wrote, "have expressed the wish to become priests.... Concerning so important a question, I would like to have the advice of the Mother House."[97] Meanwhile, for the next one year or two, the genuineness of the vocations of the aspirants was put to the test. But the little John could not be daunted: he came "again and again...begging 'to learn priest.'"[98]

Much of Shanahan's dilemma in this matter stemmed from the fact that he had no Seminary or secondary school to which he could send the priest candidates. The only option open to him was to send them to any secondary school in Ireland or England. This became a reality by virtue of the willingness of the Christian parents of the prospective clerics to pay for each 500 French Francs annually for their studies overseas.[99] Towards the end of 1912, the young John Anyogu was sent, probably with his comrade, to the Apostolic school of the Holy Ghost Fathers in Castlehead, England, to do his secondary education.

The course of Anyogwu's secondary career in England has not yet been studied by historians. But one thing which has become certain knowledge is that at the end of it, reality was hard to grasp in the mirror world of European colour prejudice: no religious House in Ireland or England was prepared to offer him opportunities for his priestly studies. In 1949, Bishop C. Heerey, Shanahan's successor, had the opportunity of experiencing the confounding attitude of his countrymen when he made futile efforts to place two of his native priests, Michael Tansi and Clement Ulogu, in any of the monastries in Europe. From the Abbot of

---

[96] "Shanahan to Superior General," 7 July, 1919, quoted in CSE: *Bulletin*, 29 (1918-1920), 400.

[97] CSE: 192/B/VI, "Shanahan to Superior General," Onitsha, 27 November, 1912.

[98] C. O. Donohue, "The Church in Southern Nigeria," p. 76.

[99] See CSE: 192/B/VI, "Shanahan to Superior General," Onitsha, 27 November, 1912.

·the Cistercian Abbey in Roscrea, Ireland, came a reply which may help to explain why John Anyogu could not do his theological studies in Europe after his secondary education:

> After careful consideration I have decided against giving the proposed candidates a trial in our Abbey....The *admiratio* that would be caused by coloured men in our community and the strong objection of the members to same was a big factor in deciding the issue.... Add to all this our lack of a proper appreciation of the character of the coloured race and your Lordship will readily agree that for us the suggestion is entirely out of the question.[100]

In 1919, Father Shanahan finally informed his Superior General of the decision of his mission council "that John Anyogu should leave Castlehead and return to the Niger, where he could do his studies under the direction of Father G. O'Sullivan."[101]

Given the precedents set for Father Delaney, whose ordination in Nigeria was still fresh in everybody's mind, it was but logical that Father Shanahan should think of a private tuition as the best solution to John Anyogwu's case. Paradoxically, however, when the latter returned to Nigeria in 1919, he was made to spend the next five years serving as catechist and teacher in various mission stations.[102] It was not until 1924, when the Seminary was finally opened at Igbariam, that he could start his philosophical studies. He was to spend another six and half years as a Senior Seminarian.

As he was about to receive major orders at the end of 1929, all the Fathers of the then still very large Vicariate were required to give their approvals in a private vote.[103] That not many, perhaps, were against his ordination, spoke eloquently for the candidate's moral and intellectual integrity. Many of the Fathers had had the opportunity of knowing him personally in the five long years he served as Catechist in various stations of the Mission, and during his seminary years.

However, the major issue to be determined by the Fathers was not the character of the candidate, but the religious, social, and financial status of the future first indigenous priest of the Mission. Nobody would pause for a moment today over these issues on the eve of any priestly ordination. But in 1929, they were so central a problem as to call for a private vote of all the Fathers of the Mission. In fact, the Fathers were urged to come to an agreement "before admission [of the candidate] to major

---

[100] Quoted in E. Isichei, *Entirely for God*, p. 76.
[101] CSE: 192/B/VIII, "Shanahan to Superior General," Dublin, 22 September, 1919.
[102] See C. O. Donohue, "The Church in Southern Nigeria," p. 76.
[103] CSE: 554/I, "Minutes of the Fathers' Meeting held at Ihiala," 11 November, 1929," item iv.

orders.''[104] To aid them in that all-important task, Father Joseph Soul, the Visitor of the Congregation who was present at the Ihiala Meeting, presented them with a handbook which outlined the arrangements made for native secular priests in the Belgian Congo.

Without the opportunity of reading this handbook, it is hard to figure out the details and motives of the ''arrangements'' contained therein. Such a knowledge would have offered valuable insights to the actual, as opposed to the theoretical, missionary conceptions of the Fathers on the issue of local clergy and hierarchy. Given the fact that Bishop Shanahan was not present at the Ihiala Meeting of the Fathers,[105] and the fact that it was Father Soul who put the booklet before the Meeting, it is most probable that it was the Visitor himself who raised the question of fixing the status of the future native priest before his admission to major orders. The report on his visit to Nigeria, written a day after the Ihiala Meeting, lends substance to that probability, and gives some clues as to the motives and aims of the otherwise paradoxical status question:

> A secular priest, Mr. Brown, is at present the superior of the Mission of Emekukwu. This is an abnormal situation. It is necessary to put another capable priest, a member of the Congregation, in charge of this big Mission.
>
> It is good to acknowledge the efforts of Shanahan to secure auxiliary priests. But he has the strange and impossible idea of doing every work in the Vicariate with secular priests.... These priests are only auxiliaries and should remain so![106]

If such was the conception of the official representative of the Holy Ghost Congregation of the proper place of his fellow European who happened to have the ''bad luck'' of being a secular priest, then his understanding of what a prospective African native clergy should be would be anybody's guess. The whole issue will appear less grotesque if one recalls that between the religious and the secular priest there existed a rivalry which had all the appearances of a cold war. With their elevated *vita communis* firmly propped up by the vows of poverty, chastity, and obedience, the religious tended to regard the secular clergy as their inferiors in religious life. For their part, the secular priests considered themselves to be the true vicars of the Church of Christ which the religious have unfittingly

---

[104] Ibid.

[105] In August 1929, Bishop Shanahan went to Paris to give his views on the proposal to cede the north-eastern part of his Vicariate to the German province of the Holy Ghost Fathers. See CSE: 554/I, ''Shanahan to Members of the Congregation,'' Onitsha, 23 July, 1929.

[106] CSE: 554/V, J. Soul, ''General Report to the Superior General...,'' Onitsha, 12 November, 1929.

"abandoned." This holy feud may have been contended within limited fronts in Europe, but in the Missions, it often escalated into total wars, and shaped the overall attitudes of the religious Fathers towards their secular subjects whose education and status they had the welcome opportunity of determining.

Furthermore, it must be remembered that the religious missionaries, most of whom were not even yet in their prime, had volunteered for the Missions for life. The Missions were their only homes, and it was not surprising that setting a precedent for the native secular priests with regard to their status and financial standing in the Missions was of such primary importance to them. If the secular priest was, by their definition, "merely an auxiliary," it was therefore considered necessary to give validity to that position in the future by means of a legal agreement to be secured before his admission into major orders.

At last, on the Feast of Immaculate Conception, 8 December, 1930, John Anyogu was ordained a priest. By all account, it was a triumph of will for both parties: for the candidate who had endured so many hardships, and crossed so many barriers, to reach his goal, and for the Holy Ghost Fathers, who had lived true to their better missionary ideals in spite of unrelenting prejudices and untoward attitudes that were characteristic of human frailty. The further development of the Seminary in the Mission was, however belatedly, a consolidation of that triumph.

In 1934, the Seminary, which had hitherto co-existed with St. Charles Training College, Onitsha, was transferred to Eke. Two factors were chiefly instrumental in the decision to choose a new site for the major Seminary, firstly, the establishment in 1933 of a Catholic secondary school at Onitsha, and secondly, the proposal to hand over the management of the Training College to the Franciscan Brothers. After the foundation in 1933 of the first Catholic secondary school in Eastern Nigeria, it was considered no longer expedient to keep the major and minor Seminarians together, as had been the practice since 1924. At Christ the King College, the junior Seminarians availed themselves of a proper college education, and followed their seminary formation under Father Burke, a member of the College staff.[107] For the few Senior Seminarians, the Training College was no longer a fitting place to do their studies because the administration of the Institution having been entrusted to a different congregation, the Holy Ghost Fathers must have considered it appropriate to continue to take the formation of the native priests in their own hands. They could do that only by moving the Seminary to a different location.

---

[107] Cf. *The Leader*, 24, No. 6 (March/April, 1982), p. 3.

At Eke, the major Seminarians pursued their theological studies under conditions that were reminiscent of Igbariam, as can be seen in the following report by Father Denis Kennedy, their dedicated Rector and Teacher:

> We were then housed in the big house on the top of the hill...the citing of which was such a mistake. There was no water supply, we were over two miles from the nearest river, we were many miles from the numerous mission stations of which Eke was the mother church, and a difficult half mile from the Eke church school.... At Eke we struggled through a course of theology, but with a one-man teaching staff, where the canon law requires at least five; it can well be imagined how adequate their theology formation was.[108]

Of the pioneer Seminarians whose way to the priesthood went through Igbariam, Onitsha, and Eke, only four reached the goal, namely, John Anyogwu, who was ordained in 1930, Michael Tansi, Joseph Nwanegbo, and William Obelagu, who were ordained on 19 December, 1937, by Bishop Heerey.[109]

An event of determinate significance for the promotion of the native clergy was the decision of the Nigerian Ordinaries in 1929 to found a "Regional Major Seminary" for the whole of Nigeria. In a resolution taken at their annual Conference, they elucidated this project as follows:

> We, the Ordinaries of Nigeria and the British Cameroons, recognising the desirability and the indisputable advantages of a Regional Major Seminary, established and controlled according to Pontifical Constitutions, decide to take steps at our next meeting to bring about its realization on behalf of the territories committed to our care.[110]

The advantages referred to in this resolution were essentially economical. The private rudimentary Major Seminaries of the various Catholic Missions in Nigeria, which sometimes contained no more than three to four students in the average, were a gross wastage of much needed missionary personnel. An amalgamated Seminary, it was realized, would provide better teaching for more students at the cost of only a few better qualified teachers. Furthermore, a concentration of all the library collections in one Regional Seminary would bring indisputable advantages to the teacher and the taught.

Yet, the idea of establishing one Seminary for all the missionary congregations in the country was as unrealistic as the name "regional" was

---

[108] Quoted in E. Isichei, *Entirely for God*, p. 34.

[109] See CSE: 554/V, C. Heerey, "Circular to Fathers," Onitsha, December, 1937.

[110] CSE: 554/I. "Conference of the Ordinaries of Nigeria...1929," resolution xxx, p. 23.

inappropriate. The first critic to see loopholes in the project was no less a personality than Father Joseph Soul, the Visitor of the Holy Ghost Fathers. In his report to the Superior General, he made the following prophetic observation:

> [Establishing a Regional Seminary is certainly] an excellent idea, but I believe that in practice there shall be difficulties between the different congregations. Until now there has never been much entente between the [Lyoner Society of African Missions] and our congregation in matters concerning the ministry.[111]

Meanwhile the project contended with a chequered existence. Featuring again on the agenda of the Conference of the Nigerian Ordinaries in 1937, it received no more substantial attention than the confirmation by the Ordinaries of its "desirability," and the promise of the Apostolic Delegate, Bishop A. Riberi, to canvass for its establishment before the Sacred Congregation of Propaganda in Rome.[112] It was not until 1939 that the Nigerian Ordinaries were able to make conclusive arrangements for the Regional Seminary, thanks to the success of the campaigns of the Apostolic Delegate in Rome.[113] Among other things, the Mission leaders decided that the Seminary should be located at Enugu, and that it should be called "Bigard Memorial Seminary."[114]

The choice of Enugu as a centre for a major Seminary was a significant departure from the usual practice of isolating Seminaries in remote villages. Decisive for that ruling was the central position of Enugu, which was within easy reach by rail from Lagos, Kano, and Port Harcourt. The name chosen for the Seminary was a singular act of gratitude to the French women, Jeanne and Stephanie Bigard—mother and daughter—who founded the Association of St. Peter the Apostle in 1889 for the training of native priests in the Missions. It was with money donated by this charitable organization that the buildings of the new Seminary were to be erected.

The outbreak of the Second World War in 1939 seriously undermined building projects on the site of the new Regional Seminary at Enugu. In fact it was not until January 1951 that the Seminarians began their studies there. The Major Seminary was officially inaugurated on March

---

[111] CSE: 554/V, J. Soul, "General Report to the Superior General...," Onitsha, 12 November, 1929, p. 19.

[112] CSE: 554/II, "Extracts from the Minutes of the Meeting of the Ordinaries of Nigeria, 1937," p. 6.

[113] For details of the report of the Apostolic Delegate on the necessity of a Regional Seminary in Nigeria, see A. Riberi, "Ein Stephania-Johanna Bigard Seminar in Nigeria," in *Der Einheimische Priester in den Missionsländern*, 16 (Freiburg, 1939), 48-52.

[114] See Father Spärndli, "Das Große Seminar in Onitsha Vikariate," in *Der Einheimische Priester in den Missionsländern*, 19 (1942), 48.

4, 1951, by the Apostolic Delegate to British West Africa, Archbishop David Matthew. In 1939, a Seminary capable of holding 250 students was envisaged. But when it finally took off in 1951, it had only 24 students.[115] Besides, contrary to the original plan of the Nigerian Ordinaries, the Regional Seminary was opened not for the whole of the country, but for only four dioceses—Onitsha, Owerri, Calabar, and Buea in the Cameroons. Just as Father Soul had predicted in 1929, the Missions of the Society of African Missions had gone their own separate ways, and before long, Regional Seminaries were established by them at Ibadan in the West, and at Jos in the North.

By all account, the establishment of a Regional Seminary in Eastern Nigeria was a milestone in the Mission's indigenization process. With that, permanence and efficiency replaced the elements of improvisation and haphazardness which had characterized the Seminary since 1924. Yet, the results which were eventually secured were not as sanguine as the expectations. For in spite of substantial improvements in the training of Seminarians—better equipment and accommodation provisions, and more efficient staff—ordinations to the priesthood remained conspicuously low throughout the 1950s, as is evident in Table 13. Father John Daly, an Irish Missionary who worked in Igboland, has endeavoured to explain this paradox in his article on the background to the vocation explosion in Eastern Nigeria in the 1970s. Of vital importance is the observation which reads as follows:

> Eastern Nigeria had an African government from 1952. If relatively few priests were ordained during the fifties, this may have been due to the enormous demand for secondary school graduates during the post-war period. By the middle of the sixties, most of the important posts in business and government were already held by Africans, and entries into the Major Seminary show a sharp upward rise from 1965.... In Uganda, where native priests were ordained in large numbers at a much earlier period than in Nigeria, priestly ordinations began to fall in the sixties. It may be that this fall may be partly due to the post-independence Africanization process, which began in Uganda, and in East and Central Africa in general, at a later date than in Nigeria. If this hypothesis is correct, one may expect an increase of vocations in these countries soon.[116]

A major point in this "hypothesis" is the supposition that the Africanization process inhibited the natives from embracing the priesthood, in Nigeria, as well as in Uganda. It does perforce suggest that the absence of this process was conducive to priestly ordinations. If so, one would then wonder why native priests were not ordained in large numbers in

[115] See CSE: *Bulletin*, 42 (1951-1952), 92f; see also ibid., p. 157.
[116] J. Daly, "Iboland," p. 266.

Nigeria before the Africanization process, as was the case in Uganda. This inconsistency notwithstanding, the link between the drop in ordinations and the struggle for independence is very significant.

There is a compelling evidence that the promotion of a native clergy received perfunctory attention between 1945 and 1950—the period of greatest political upheaval in colonial Nigeria. Incidentally, the influx of Catholic expatriate Fathers into Nigeria corresponded with these years of seething tensions and maintained a steep rise until 1960, the year Nigeria attained self-government. Thereafter it remained fairly constant. Table 13 shows that the number of religious priests[117] in the dioceses of Onitsha and Owerri rose from 133 in 1952 to 182 in 1955, an increase of 37 per cent. By contrast, the number rose from 238 in 1960 to 265 in 1963, an increase of only 11 per cent in spite of the creation of three additional dioceses.

There is no suggestion here that the increase in the number of expatriate missionaries in the post-war years was in any way undesirable. Indeed, Nigeria had the unenviable reputation of having the most unsanguine priest-people ratio in the whole of Africa.[118] In spite of the comparatively large influx of religious priests, that pastoral misery was never eliminated largely because of the extraordinary growth of the Catholic population. In the Owerri Vicariate, for instance, there were only 59 priests for 223,456 Catholics in 1949, a ratio of 1 priest to 3,788 souls. By 1960 there were 430,000 Catholics in the Owerri diocese, which was about half the area covered by the old Owerri Vicariate. For this large number of the faithful, there were only 98 priests, a priest-people ratio of 1 to 4,388. Since a large number of the Fathers was assigned full-time to educational duties, the actual priest-people ratio must have been much higher. The situation would have been worse had the personnel not been tripled as it was.

Nevertheless, the sustained influx of expatriate Fathers in the post-war years was not without far-reaching consequences for the advancement of a native clergy and a native leadership of the Church. For the foreign missionaries, "who never took kindly to the idea of independence,"[119] the popular demand for self-government in the late 1940s did create a conflict situation which probably had an important bearing on the sur-

---

[117] At this period there were some Nigerian Fathers who were members of the Holy Ghost Congregation, but since their number was very insignificant, the term "religious priests" has been used in this work to refer to white missionaries. In the same manner, the term "secular priests" refers to Nigerian native priests, although there were a few Irish among them.

[118] See A. Riberi, "Ein Stephania-Johanna Bigard Seminary in Nigeria," p. 49; see also A. Hastings, *Das schwarze Experiment*, pp. 276-296.

[119] J. O'Connell, "The Church in Africa," p. 10.

Table 13

Church Personnel in the Old Onitsha-Owerri Vicariate, 1949-1963

Diocese	1949 Sem.	1949 Sec.	1949 Rel.	1952 Sem.	1952 Sec.	1952 Rel.	1955 Sem.	1955 Sec.	1955 Rel.	1960 Sem.	1960 Sec.	1960 Rel.	1963 Sem.	1963 Sec.	1963 Rel.
Onitsha	4	7	47	6	5	60	21	5	92	37	16	112	41	16	56
Owerri	4	7	52	11	7	73	13	9	90	35	2	96	34	5	90
Umuahia	a	a	a	a	a	a	a	a	a	14	11	30	18	12	37
Port Harcourt	a	a	a	a	a	a	a	a	a	a	a	a	—	3	24
Enugu	b	b	b	b	b	b	b	b	b	b	b	b	20	5	58
Total	8	14	99	17	12	133	34	14	182	86	29	238	113	41	265

Source: *Annuario Pontificio* (1949-1964).

a = data contained in Owerri figures; b = data contained in Onitsha figures.

Sem. = Seminarians; Sec. = Secular Priests; Rel. = Religious Priests.

prisingly small number of natives admitted to the Major Seminary in these years. This may explain why the number of ordinations to the priesthood was abysmally low throughout the 1950s. Furthermore, a secular priest was, for the religious Fathers, essentially an auxiliary, a position which, as has been seen, was given an overt expression in 1929 by Father Joseph Soul of the Holy Ghost Congregation. That belief consequently exercised a considerable influence on the selection and training of native priests, and was doggedly adhered to in spite of frequent papal appeals.[120]

The attainment of indigenous leadership of the Mission falls outside the scope of our study. Nevertheless, it will be of interest to discuss it in a nutshell.

The forces which expedited the process of the indigenization of the Church in Nigeria came chiefly from factors that were external to the immediate bent of mission leadership. By 1960 most of the African nations had attained independence, and in keeping with its practice of adapting mission policy to international politics, a measure which received special emphasis under Pope Pius XII, Rome realized that any further delay in bringing about the indigenous leadership of the Missions would be conspicuously out of character not only with its avowed missionary motives, but also with the political realities in the mission lands. Thenceforth, the promotion of a native leadership of the Missions was to be a matter of command rather than of choice.[121] Accordingly, when new dioceses were created in Eastern Nigeria in the wake of the Nigerian Independence in 1960, they were all placed under the leadership of Black Ordinaries. These dioceses were Umuahia, Port Harcourt, Enugu, and Ikot Ekpene, and were headed respectively by Bishops Anthony Nwedo, Godfrey Okoye, John Anyogu, and Dominic Ekandem.

The reaction of the expatriate mission leaders to these phenomenal developments took various stances. In the former Owerri diocese, there took place a concentration of native secular priests in the new diocese of Umuahia which was created in 1958. By 1960, there were only two native priests left in the old Owerri diocese, as opposed to eleven in the new diocese. To all appearances, Bishop J. B. Whelan of Owerri must have had in mind two categories of Church leadership—one predominantly African, and the other European. With a Black Bishop, a Black Vicar General (Msg. Joseph Nwanegbo), and a relatively good number of Black priests, Umuahia thus became the first diocese in Eastern Nigeria to witness a sui generis indigenization experiment.

---

[120] Cf. L.J. Luzbetak, *The Church and Cultures: An Applied Anthropology for the Religious Worker* (Illinois, 1970; rpt. California: William Carey Library, 1977), pp. 104-108.

[121] Cf. ibid., p. 104.

A somewhat similar case obtained in Ikot Ekpene. Created out of Calabar diocese in 1963, the new diocese was headed by Bishop Dominic Ekandem, Auxiliary Bishop of Calabar since 1954. If the statistics of the diocese published in the *Annuario Pontificio* are to be relied upon, then Ikot Ekpene was the first diocese in Eastern Nigeria where the secular priests formed a majority of the entire clergy right from the onset. According to the data for 1963, there were 26 secular, and only 5 religious, priests in the new diocese during its foundation year. However, the possibility is that a large number of the secular priests were Irish volunteers in the service of the St. Patrick's Missionary Society.

A more realistic sharing of power was carried out in the old diocese of Onitsha under Archbishop Charles Heerey. When the diocese of Enugu was created in 1962, the native priests were not required to move from the old to the new diocese, as was generally the case in Owerri. Rather, except for a few, each Father remained at his post. Furthermore, the expatriate missionaries were divided fairly equally between the two dioceses, as can be seen in Table 13. There was in that arrangement a move in the leadership of the local Church that upheld the essential factor of co-existence between Black and White Fathers.

Worthy of special note is the fact that the first Catholic Ordinaries in Eastern Nigeria were not secular priests, but African members of the Holy Ghost Congregation, namely, Anthony Nwedo and Godfrey Okoye.[122] Although Bishop Dominic Ekandem and John Anyogu were the first African bishops of the region (both were ordained auxiliary bishops in 1954 and 1957 respectively), they did not become Ordinaries—heads of local Churches—until 1962 and 1963 respectively. The fact that Nwedo and Okoye were the first to be made Ordinaries underscored the great distinction which the Holy Ghost Fathers made between secular and religious priests.

That the relinquishing of leadership to a viable native clergy was a major objective in the missionary policy of the Catholic Missions in Eastern Nigeria cannot be doubted. However, in the minds of the foreign missionaries, the actual date for such a phenomenal change existed in an unpredictably distant future. Christian Missions—both Protestant and Catholic—now view their successes in this regard with legitimate pride, but looking back on their eventful pasts, they invariably discover that training the natives for mission leadership was a triumph which contended with an unrelenting prejudice. Although the Protestant Missions in Nigeria were far ahead of the Catholics in their indigenization process,

---

[122] These two were the first Nigerians to be professed members of the Holy Ghost Congregation. See CSE: *Bulletin*, 42 (1951-1952), 229.

their conception at the onset of the pace and depth of the transfer of authority to the indigenes did not differ much from the Catholic position. At the beginning of their ministry in Nigeria, the Reverend Henry Townsend of the Church Missionary Society vehemently opposed the creation of a "black clergy" with an argument which may be said to have found a common validity in the early missionary conceptions of the Christian Missions:

> The purely native Church is an idea, I think, not soon to be realized. The white merchant and civilization will go hand in hand with missionary work, and foreign elements must be mixed up with the native, especially in such changes as are effected by a religion introduced by foreigners. The change of religion in a country is a revolution of the most extensive kind and the commanding minds that introduce those changes must and do become leaders. It is a law of nature and not contrary to the laws of God, and efforts to subvert such laws must produce extensive evils.[123]

This argument shows how far individual predilection was at variance with official policy, and theory at variance with practice. With regard to mission objectives, the creation of a native clergy and hierarchy occupied a place of prominence in the official teachings of both the Protestant and Catholic Missions. But the deciding factor was the degree with which the missionary at the spot accepted those teachings. On his approach to them depended the success or failure of missionary ideals. Accordingly, the pace with which Africans assumed responsibility in the Church of Nigeria corresponded closely with the pace with which the missionary followed the instructions of his Church leaders. Although the forces which acted on his development were many, the greatest were undoubtedly political and social changes in the Missions. What the Reverend Townsend said in 1858 could not have been said by him in the post-independence Nigeria. In the same manner, what the Franciscan missionary, Father Geronimo de Mendieta, said in the sixteenth century of American Indians, namely, that they were "not fitted to command and rule, but to be commanded and ruled..., not fitted for masters but for pupils, not for prelates but for subjects,"[124] could not have been said by him or by any other Catholic missionary in the last two centuries.

The figures in Table 13 are indicative of the evolution that took place in the attitude of the Catholic missionaries in Eastern Nigeria towards the question of indigenous leadership of the Mission. After decades of stagnation in the number of native Seminarians and priests, a steady

---

[123] "Townsend to Venn," 18 October, 1858, quoted in J. F. A. Ajayi, *Christian Missions in Nigeria*, p. 187.
[124] Quoted in C . R. Boxer, "The Problem of the Native Clergy," p. 92.

growth became apparent in the 1960s. At last the long-awaited indigenization process had received its due élan. The attainment of self-government in the country certainly had no small bearing on that turn of events. However, because of the huge difference between the number of foreign missionaries and native priests, a disproportionate relation which comes out more clearly in Figure 4, the achievement of indigenous leadership of the Church was a long way off even in the 1960s. Besides, the decade which saw the first native Ordinaries in Eastern Nigeria was chiefly characterized by a concert of weak Black bishops and very influential White vicar generals. That union was superceded after the Nigerian Civil War by a merger of very powerful bishops with weak and ceremonial vicar generals, all Black. That means that the local leadership of the Church in Eastern Nigeria, as indeed in all Nigeria, had yet much to learn by way of power-sharing.

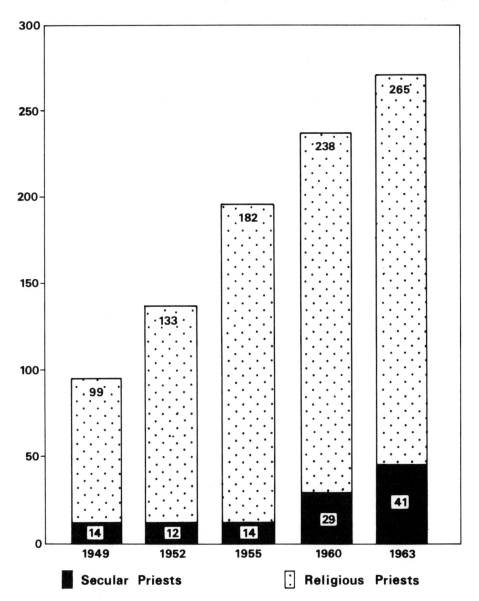

Fig. 4: Quantitative relation of religious priests to secular priests

CONCLUSION

An appreciation of Catholic educational endeavours in Eastern Nigeria from 1886 to 1950 can be made from to main perspectives: the purpose attached to the school by the missionaries, and the motives behind the people's response to mission education.

With regard to the former, two aims stand out most prominently in Catholic educational policy: conversion and the transformation of native society.

By all account, the priority given to proselyte-making in Catholic education produced phenomenal results: Eastern Nigeria is today the most important Catholic stronghold in West Africa, if not in the whole of Africa. This is, to a large extent, the outcome of a missionary enterprise which made the education of the masses its raison d'être. The decision to use the school as a medium of evangelization, as proclaimed at the beginning of Catholic missionary efforts in Eastern Nigeria, did not lose its force with the passage of time. Accordingly, Father J. Jordan, the man who held the reins of Catholic education in his hands for nearly three decades, said in 1958 that "The school is the normal road to the Church, and more than 80% of adult baptisms are provided by the primary school system."[1]

This special use made of Catholic schools perforce dictated the form and scope of education provided in them. For a long time, the tendency in Catholic educational policy was to seek large-scale conversion through the primary rather than the secondary school. A shift in this policy was made in the face of social and political changes, and as a result of pressure from the people.

Another major objective in Catholic policy was the transformation of traditional society through education. The missionaries had largely seen the wild stories told about Africa and its inhabitants by European explorers and adventurers as a confirmation of their belief in the moral depravity of the African society caused by its long contact with superstition and paganism. However, whereas the European traders and explorers tended to believe in the permanence of the harm done to the African by his environment, the missionaries, while often not seeking to correct this cliché image for financial reasons,[2] nevertheless expressed the

---

[1] ODA: "J. Jordan, Catholic Education Secretary, to Father Heinzman," Onitsha, 5 July, 1958.

[2] The numerous mission publications played a leading role in the funding of the missionary enterprise. More often than not, what captured the interest and sympathy of

conviction that the African could be improved through contact with Christianity and Western civilization. The village school, the focal point of Catholic presence within any given community, was therefore designed to provide not only spiritual strength, but also the basic cognitive skills that were necessary for the material and intellectual transformation of native society. The eradication of such evil practices as human sacrifice, cannibalism, witch-craft, and the killing of twins was the dividend of the missionary's educational optimism.

Furthermore, Catholic education in Eastern Nigeria was particularly commended for the impact it had on the temper of the natives by the emphasis it placed on discipline and character formation. These positive results were in turn instrumental in luring the colonial Administrations into the educational field after many decades of indifference and hesitation. Convinced that mission education served the interests of the colonial process, the Governments endeavoured to secure maximum control of it in return for minimum financial investment.[3]

Unfortunately, the efforts to prepare the African soil for an effective transplanting of the Christian message produced some negative results. Among other things, it led to the destruction of native culture and social institutions. This was as a result of the unrelenting conviction of the missionary that African customs and institutions were based on an evil system. Accordingly, he endeavoured to prevent every aspect of traditional life from coming within the orbit of the Christian faith. In this regard, the missionary's understanding of evangelism and education was essentially what J. Dougall has described as "a dualism which...emptied religion of its social content and society of its soul."[4]

In Eastern Nigeria, as well as in Western Nigeria, the pressure to expand education to its ultimate limits came neither from the Missions nor from the colonial Governments. It came from the natives. Among the diversified motives behind the people's quest for mission education, two are most noteworthy, namely, economic gains and emancipation from foreign domination.

For the greater majority of those who attended mission schools, the hope of better job opportunities and lucrative positions in Church and state was a principal motivation. For the various rival Christian

---

overseas donors and benefactors were not the *lettres édifiants*, but rather the abundant *lettres curieuses* of these mission journals.

[3] Cf. W. H. Taylor, "Missionary Education in Africa Reconsidered: The Presbyterian Educational Impact in Eastern Nigeria 1846-1974," in *African Affairs*, 82 (1984), 191.

[4] J. W. C. Dougall, "The Relationship of Church and School in Africa," *IRM*, 26 (1937), 206.

denominations, this was largely not an unwelcome phenomenon. A consensus in their views was that the largest number of adherents would belong to any group that best responded to the people's economic ambitions. This in turn led to an unprecedented and often untoward proliferation of schools in Eastern Nigeria.

While it would be depreciatory to suggest, as E. H. Berman has done, that the Catholics were "less interested in providing education for religious reasons than were their Protestant counterparts,"[5] one may say that on the primary level, the Catholics in Eastern Nigeria addressed themselves more positively to the economic needs of the people than did the various Protestant denominations. This strong vocational emphasis in Catholic education was greatly encouraged by the colonialists and traders in their search for qualified artisans and junior clerks. The Holy Ghost Fathers were persuaded to cooperate because they saw their response to the exigencies of the Government, and perforce of the people, as enhancing the progress of the Catholic Mission. Wherever they encouraged the people's quest for social mobility—be it by the provision of elementary education for the masses, or through the strong emphasis placed on the English language, or by the provision of vocational education in industrial schools, or simply through the establishment of special schools for the sons of chiefs—they always did so with the conviction of serving legitimate Christian objectives. This was of determinate significance for the extraordinary educational success of the Catholics in Eastern Nigeria, which by 1950 had slightly surpassed those of all the Protestant denominations taken together.

However, in spite of this benign economic strand in Catholic education, the people could not derive from it encouragement and support for their political aspirations, which were mainly geared towards emancipation from foreign domination. This appears less paradoxical when seen against the background of the difference in Protestant and Catholic educational policies. Whereas the Protestants integrated the school into the art of nation-building, the Catholics used it essentially as a medium of proselytization. This discrepancy was reflected most prominently in the attitudes of the two confessions towards: 1) the provision of post-primary education, 2) the political formation of their adherents, 3) the promotion of an independent local Church. In all these cases, the Protestants were pioneer entrepreneurs, with the Catholics following suit largely because of pressure from the people. As Father Jordan aptly put

[5] E. H. Berman, "Christian Missions in Africa," in *African Reaction to Missionary Education*, ed. E. H. Berman (New York: Teachers College Press, 1975), p. 22.

it, "A Mission had to choose between giving [the people]... further education and arousing their distrust and enmity."[6]

In the main, Catholic education in Eastern Nigeria in the period under consideration in this work was full of ambivalent features. Although it emphasized training in modern methods, it remained conservative in its content. Despite its glaring achievements in the intellectual and moral transformation of traditional society, it generally did not seek to uphold native culture and institutions. In spite of its promotion of social mobility, it was essentially not a training in leadership and self-government. These latter objectives were added after 1950.

Yet, within the context of the goal it set for itself—the evangelization mission—Catholic education in the Eastern Region was a great success. Neither its often non-religious emphasis, nor its ambitious expansion process depreciated its spiritual value. By insisting on a benign paternism, and through their dogged emphasis on discipline and character formation, the Catholic educators succeeded to cast a spiritual spell on all those who came under their sway. If the Igbos in particular disclosed a propensity for Catholicism, it was perhaps not only because of their predilection for learning, but probably also as a result of a spiritual affinity which such great leaders as Fathers Lejeune and Shanahan discovered and nursed with incomparable adroitness.

The impact on society of this religious influence is of a permanent character. The Catholic Church in present Eastern Nigeria distinguishes itself by its conservatism, dynamism and religious vocations. These are certainly the effects of its profound missionary foundation.

---

[6] J. Jordan, *Bishop Shanahan*, p. 253.

BIBLIOGRAPHY

PRIMARY SOURCES

A. *Archival Materials*

I. The Archives of Propaganda Fide, Rome

Without any doubts, this is the biggest and most systematically kept mission record office in the world. However, given the obligatory closure to public use of all documents that are less than a hundred years old, works on the mission history of this century have had to be written without recourse to the valuable records of the Propaganda archives. In 1979, a year before I made use of the archives, it was possible for researchers to consult the documents dating up to the pontificate of Leo III, namely, up to 1903. The relevant materials utilized in this work are those contained in the following series:

1. *Acta Sacrae Congregationis de Propaganda Fide*

These are the reports of the sessions of the General Congregation, where important decisions on the Missions were usually taken. The materials consulted are Vols. 211- 224 (1848-1860). They contain reports on the earliest missionary activities of the Holy Ghost Congregation along the West African Coast.

2. *Scritture Riferite nei Congresi*

These documents are the letters and reports sent to Propaganda Fide from the Missions. They began in 1893 to be arranged in a *New Series* with rubric numbers. The most relevant series are:
a) "Africa Centrale, Etiopia, Arabia," Vol. 4 (1853).
b) "Africa: Angola, Congo, Senegal, Isole dell' Oceano Atlantico," Vols. 8 and 9 (1862-1892). The records of the *New Series* used in this work include:
Vol. 49, R.141/1894.
Vol. 73, R.141/1895.
Vol. 118, R.141/1897.
Vol. 144, R.141/1898.
Vol. 168, R.141/1899.
Vol. 193, R.141/1900.
Vol. 214, R.141/1901.
Vol. 237, R.141/1902.

II. Archives of the Holy Ghost Fathers, Chevilly Larue.

The records were formally housed in the Mother House of the Congregation in Paris, and I was one of the last people to consult them there. For in 1981 they were transferred to Chevilly Larue, where there are more rooms for the documents and the researchers. This work has drawn extensively from the materials of these archives, if only because of the extraordinary involvement in education of the Holy Ghost Fathers in Eastern Nigeria, a fact which is given expression in the pages of the numerous reports, articles, and private letters of the missionaries. The most relevant series are:
Boîte 191, Dossier A, Chemises I-IX.
Boîte 191, Dossier B, Chemises IX-XIII.
Boîte 192, Dossier A, Chemises IV-VIII.

Boîte 192, Dossier B, Chemises IV-VIII.
Boîte 200, Dossier A, Chemises II & III.
The documents in Boîte 200 are those of the Mission of Sierra Leone.
Boîte 554, Chemises IV-VII.
Boîte 555, Chemises I-II.
Boîte 556, Chemises IV-VIII.

III. Archives of the Society of African Missions, Rome.

The records here are very fragmentary, but presently efforts are being made to augment them with materials from the Archives of Propaganda Fide. This involves the practice of recopying by hand the letters and reports sent to the Propaganda Congregation from the Missions of the Society. Since the archives of the S.M.A. contain the earliest records of Catholic missionary activities in Southern Nigeria in the nineteenth century, their importance can hardly be overemphasized. However, only a very meagre record was kept on educational matters. The only materials that deal specifically on education are contained in a file with the rubric number 14/80205, which comprises mainly government reports on the schools of the Society in the Lagos colony. The records for the years 1884-1929 were consulted. Also consulted were: 14/80200 (1869), 14/2w (1949). Of great importance is the archives' "Amoire" 5.9, a compartment containing books, colonial circulars and memoranda on educational policy in Nigeria.

IV. Onitsha Diocesan Archives, Onitsha.

The materials here are perhaps the most valuable of the mission records still left in Nigeria. They were kept under the Holy Ghost Fathers and were saved from complete destruction during the Nigeria-Biafra War by one of the Catholic faithful of Onitsha. This man told me the exciting story of how he risked his life carrying away the files from the Archbishop's house, with the Federal troops within sight on the Asaba bank of the Niger. The documents were preserved in several private homes throughout the war. However, it may never be known how many of the priceless records were lost during those turbulent years. When I visited the archives in 1981, the documents were still very disorderly kept in a small room marked "Education Room." It was from here that Father J. Jordan and his officials coordinated Catholic educational activities not only in the Eastern Region, but also in the whole of Nigeria and the former British Cameroons. The present state of the "Education Room" is certainly far removed from the splendour of former days. However, there is a growing awareness in the Archbishop's Secretariat of the necessity not only of saving the valuable documents from dust and pests, but also of sorting and shifting them into recognizable categories.
    The present condition of the Onitsha diocesan archives does not in any way detract from their immense value. Fortunately for this work, the documents in the "Education Room" deal almost exclusively with educational matters. Those I examined date between 1929 and 1968. Among other things, they offer valuable information on the background history of the Catholic Secondary schools, most of which were founded in the 1930s and 1940s. Since the archives have not been systematized, it is not possible to give the exact location of the documents. However, besides those taken from several unidentified dossiers, the materials utilized in this work were found in the following files:
"Secondary and Training Reports."
"Secondary, C.K.C."
"S/EN.30, Technical Institute Yaba."
"S/EN.31, Agriculture."
"Rural Science."
"University College."
"Catholic University."
"Old Onitsha (File 196)."

V. Public Record Office, Kew, London.

This office contains government records, and the most pertinent of these materials are those of the Colonial Office, especially the Original Correspondences and Sessional Papers. The former were particularly useful because of their reports of government dealings with the Voluntary Agencies involved in education in the colonies. They were usually despatched to the Colonial Office in London by the Colonial Governors and their Acting Assistants. The Sessional Papers contain the proceedings of the Legislative and Executive Councils, as well as administrative reports. The most important records of the Sessional Papers utilized in this work are the annual reports on the Education Departments of the various Provinces of Nigeria. Most of what remained obscure in the mission records became clear from these annual reports, which were usually written by the Directors of Education and their Inspectors of Schools. The main sources consulted are:
C.O. 96, Gold Coast, Original Correspondence, 1883-1886.
C.O.147, Lagos, Original Correspondence, 1860-1906.
C.O.149, Lagos, Sessional Papers, 1872-1906.
C.O.343/10, Gold Coast, Register of Correspondence, 1884-1886.
C.O.444/1, Niger Coast Protectorate, Original Correspondence, 1899.
C.O.520, Protectorate of Southern Nigeria, Original Correspondence, 1900-1913.
C.O.583, Nigeria, Original Correspondence, 1912-1943.
C.O.592, Protectorate of Southern Nigeria, Sessional Papers, 1906-1913.
C.O.657/3-64, Nigeria, Sessional Papers, 1914-1950. The records of the Foreign Office consulted are those of the F.O.2 series.

VI. Foreign and Commonwealth Office Library, London.

This is the former Commonwealth Relations Library, and the most relevant materials found here include:
10940, "Report by the Committee of the Education Board," Lagos, 1903.
LA 1611, "A Study of Educational Policy and Practice in British West Africa." A Report to the Secretary of State. TS, 1951.
8234, Sunter, M. *General Report on Elementary Schools in the Gambia Colony*, 1885.
    This Library was particularly useful because of its large collection of government published records which now lie in numerous defunct periodicals, newspapers, and magazines.

VII. Archives of the German Province of the Holy Ghost Father, Knechtsteden, Dormargen.

The German Spiritans began work in the Benue Region in 1934, but they did not stay long on account of the Second World War. Consequently, the Mission House does not contain records on Nigeria in any worthwhile quantity. However, it possesses a rich collection of mission periodicals, including the famous *Bulletin de la Congregation des Pères du Saint-Esprit*, which contains, to a very large extent, the verbatim publications of the letters and reports of the missionaries.

B. *Published Sources*

I. Mission Records

Benedict XV, "Maximum Illud." AAS. 11 (1919), 440-445.
Biéchy, P. "L'Organistion du Denier du Culte et des Ecoles en Nigeria." *Extait du Compte rendu de la ixe Semaine de Missiologie du Louvain*. 1931, pp. 1-16.
Collectanea Sacrae Congregationis de Propaganda Fide. Rome, 1892, Nos. 300 and 328.
Pius XI, "Rerum Ecclesiae." *AAS*, 18 (1926), 65-83.

Pius XII. "Evangelii Praecones." *AAS*, 43 (1951), 497-528.
Pius XII. "Laeto Accepimus." *AAS*, 42 (1950), 615-619.
Propaganda Fide. "Instructio Vicariorum Apostolicorum ad Regna Sinarum, Tonchini et Concincinae proficiscentium, 1659." *Sacrae Congregationis de Propaganda Fide Memoria Rerum, 1622-1972*. Vol.III/2. Ed. J. Metzler. Freiburg: Herder, 1976, pp. 697-704.
.Streit, R. and Dindinger, J. *Bibliotheca Missionum*. Vols. XVI & XVII. Freiburg: Herder, 1952; Vol. XVIII, 1953; Vols. XIX and XX, 1954.

II. Mission Periodicals (Primary and Semi-Primary)

The African Rosary (1936/7).
Afrikastimmen (1920).
Annales de la Propagation de la Foi (1894-1900).
Annales Spiritaines (1956)
Bulletin de la Congregation des Pères du Saint-Esprit (1883-1952).
Echo aus Afrika (1896-1916).
Echo aus den Missionen der Väter vom Heiligen Geist (1911-1914).
L'Echo des Missions Africaines (1911-1914).
Die katholische Missionen (1885-1951).
The Missionary Annals of the Holy Ghost Fathers (1927, 1931).
Les Missions Catholiques (1883-1905).
Illustrated Catholic Missions (1891, 1907/8)
Irish Independent (1930, 1954).

III. Government Records

Colonial Office, Advisory Committee on Education in the Colonies. *Education for Citizenship in Africa*. London: His Majesty's Stationary Office, 1948.
Colony of Southern Nigeria, Education Department. *Code of Regulations for Primary and Secondary Schools, Government and Assisted*. By E.G. Rowden. Lagos: The Government Printer, 1909.
Eastern Nigeria, Ministry of Education. *Report on the Review of the Educational System in Eastern Nigeria*. Enugu: The Government Printer, 1962.
Lugard, F. D. *Report on the Amalgamation of Northern and Southern Nigeria, and Administration, 1912-1919*. London: His Majesty's Stationary Office, 1920.
Memorandum on Educational Policy in Nigeria. Sessional Paper No. 20 of 1947. Lagos: The Government Printer, 1947.
Ministère des Affaires Etrangère. *Documents Diplomatiques, Afrique: Convention entre la France et la Grande Bretagne*. Paris: Imprimerie Nationale, 1898.
Phillipson, S. *Grants in Aid of Education in Nigeria: A Review with Recommendations*. Lagos: The Government Printer, 1948.
"Rules Relating to the Examination in a Native Language of European Officers of Southern Nigeria Civil Service 1908." *West African Pamphlet*, No. 47.
Smith, C. B. *Annual Report on the Education Department, Southern Provinces, for the Year 1928*. Lagos: Government Printing office, n.d. IV.

IV. Vernacular Publications

Biéchy, P. *Catechism of the Catholic Religion in the Efik Language*. Rome: St. Peter Claver Sodality, 1929.
Catholic Mission of the Holy Ghost Fathers. *Igbo Catechism*. Onitsha-Owerri, 1944.
Catholic Mission, Onitsha-Owerri Vicariate. *Ndu Dinwenu Anyi Jesu Christi*, 1940.
Ganot, A. *English-Ibo-French Dictionary*. Salzburg: St. Peter Claver Sodality, 1904.
Ganot, A. *Grammaire Ibo*. Paris, 1899.
Ganot, A. *Katekismi Ibo*. Paris, 1901.

Holy Ghost Fathers, Diocese of Owerri. *Catechism Nke Mbu*, 1951.
Holy Ghost Fathers, Diocese of Owerri. *Central Igbo Primer*, I. London: Macmillan, n.d.
Kraft, J. *Nwed Ikwö Eke Ufök Abasi Me Katolik* (Efik Hymn-Book), 1921.
Léna, L. *Nwed-Mbume Eke Me Katolik* (An Efik Catechism). Abbeville, 1908.
Nwed Akam (An Efik Prayer Book). Salzburg: St. Peter Claver Sodality, 1938.
Schön, J. F. *Oku Ibo: Grammatical Elements of the Ibo Language*. London, 1861.
S.M.A. Fathers. *Ayiyo na Ukwé Ndi Katolik*. Salzburg: St. Peter Claver Sodality, 1928.
S.M.A. Fathers. *Katechismi k'o bu Nkwuzi Ndi Katolik*. Salzburg: St. Peter Claver Sodality, 1928.
Treich, J. *Akwukwo Ekpele na Ukwe Ndi Katolik n'Onu Igbo*. Lagos Ebute-Metta: St. Paul's Press, 1922.
Vogler, C. *Katekisma Nk'Okwukwe Nzuko Katolik n'Asusu Igbo*. Strassburg, 1903.
Zappa, C. *Essai de Dictionnaire, Francecais-Ibo ou Francecais-Ika*. Lyon, 1907.

V. Newspapers and Magazines

The Nigerian Daily Times, 6 February, 1934
Le Soleil, 24 June, 1891.
The African Times, February, 1889.
Echo de Paris, 3 April, 1904.

SECONDARY SOURCES

Abernethy, D. B. *Church and State in Nigerian Education*. Ibadan: Nigerian Institute of Social and Economic Research, 1967.
Abernethy, D. B. *The Political Dilemma of Popular Education*. Stanford: Stanford University Press, 1969.
Afigbo, A. E. "The Background to the Southern Nigerian Education Code of 1903." *Journal of the Historical Society of Nigeria*, 4 (1968), 197-225.
Afigbo, A. E. "The Calabar Mission and the Aro Expedition of 1901-1902." *Journal of Religion in Africa*, 5 (Leiden, 1973), 94-106.
Afigbo, A. E. "The Missions, the State and Education in South-Eastern Nigeria, 1956-71." *Christianity in Independent Africa*. Ed. E. Fasholé-Luke, et al. London: Rex Collins, 1978, pp. 176-192.
Afigbo, A. E. "Patterns of Igbo Resistance to British Conquest." *Tahrik*, 4, No. 3 (1973), 1423.
Ajayi, J. F. *Christian Missions in Nigeria, 1841-1891*. London: Longman, 1965.
Ajayi, J. F. "The Development of Secondary Grammar School Education in Nigeria." *Journal of the Historical Society of Nigeria*, 2 (1963), 517-535.
Ajayi, J. F. "Nineteenth Century Origin of Nigerian Nationalism." *Journal of the Historical Society of Nigeria*, 2 (1961), 196-210.
Anene, J. C. *Southern Nigeria in Transition, 1885-1906*. Cambridge: The University Press, 1966.
Arnold, M. "A French Eton or Middle-Class Education and the State." *Matthew Arnold and the Education of the New Order: A Selection of Arnold's Writings on Education*. Ed. P. Smith and G. Summerfield. Cambridge: The University Press, 1969, pp. 76-156.
Aubert, R. "Die Wiedergeburt der alten Orden und das Aufblühen neuer Kongregationen." *Handbuch der Kirchengeschichte*. Ed. H. Jedin. Freiburg: Herder, 1971, VI/1, pp. 247-259.
Baëta, C. G., ed. *Christianity in Tropical Africa*. London: Oxford University Press, 1968.
Bane, M.J. *Catholic Pioneers in West Africa*. Dublin: Clonmore & Rynolds, 1956.
Bane, M. J. "Educational Problems in West Africa." *World Mission*, 1 (September, 1950), 88-90.
Berg, L. *Die katholische Heidenmission als Kulturträger*. 3 vols. Aachen, 1927.
Berger, H. *Mission und Kolonialpolitik: Die katholische Mission in Kamerun während der deutschen Kolonialzeit*. Immensee: Neue Zeitschrift für Missionswissenschaft, 1978.

Berman, E. H. ed. *African Reactions to Missionary Education*. New York: Teachers College Press, 1975.
Beyerhaus, P. *Die Selbständigkeit der jungen Kirchen als missionarisches Problem*. Wuppertal-Barmen: Verlag der Rheinischen Missionsgesellschaft, 1967.
Biermann, B., *Die Anfänge der neueren Dominikanermission in China*. Münster, 1927.
Bovet, P "Education as Viewed by the Phelps-Stokes Commissions." *International Review of Missions*, 15 (1926), 483-492.
Bowen, F. J. "La question de l'Ecole en Afrique britannique." *Revue d'Histoire des Missions*. (1931). 263-273.
Boxer, C. R. "The Problem of the Native Clergy in the Portuguese and Spanish Empires from the Sixteenth to the Eighteenth Centuries." *The Mission of the Church and the Propagation of the Faith*. Studies in Church History, 6. Ed. G. J. Cuming. Cambridge: At the University Press, 1970, pp. 85-105.
Briault, M. "La Mission du Bas-Niger après cinquante ans d'existence." *Revue d'Histoire des Missions*, 12 (Paris, 1935), 512-523.
Brucker, J. "Chinois (Rite)." *Dictionnaire de Théologie Catholique*, II (1950), 2363-2391.
Burns, A. C. *A History of Nigeria*. London: George Allen & Unwin, 1936.
Catholic Education in the Service of Africa. Report by the Pan-African Catholic Education Conference, Leopoldville 16-23 August, 1965. Tournai, 1966.
Cavazzi, J. A. *Relation Historique de l'Etiopie Occidentale*. Paris, 1732. Vol. III.
Charles, P. *Les Dossiers de l'Action Missionnaire*. Louvain, 1932.
Charles, P. "Le Probleme de l'enseingnement aux Missions." *Katholiches Missionsjahrbuch der Schweiz*, 4 & 5 (1937-1938), 5-10.
Clarke, P. B. "The Methods and Ideology of the Holy Ghost Fathers in Eastern Nigeria, 1885-1906." *Journal of Religion in Africa*, 6 (1974), 81-108.
Cockin, G. "The Land and Education in the Ibo Country of South East Nigeria." *International Review of Missions*, 33 (1944), 274-279.
Coleman, J. S. *Nigeria: Background to Nationalism*. Berkeley: University of California Press, 1958.
Considine, J. J. "African Students in American Colleges." *World Mission*, 1 (September, 1950), 90-99.
Cooke, C. M. "Church, State and Education: The Eastern Nigeria Experience, 1950-1967." *Christianity in Independent Africa*. Ed. E. Fasholé-Luke, et al. London: Rex Collins, 1978, pp. 193-206.
Cruickshank, M. *Church and State in English Education: 1870 to the Present Day*. London: Macmillan, 1963.
Daly, J. "Igboland: The Background to the Vocation Explosion." *African Ecclesiastical Review*, 15 (1973), 259-266.
Dohmen, L. "Missionsstrategische Gedanken des ehrwürdigen P. Libermann." *Zeitschrift für Missionswissenschaft*, 36 (1952), 153-155.
Donohue, C. O. "The Church in Southern Nigeria." *The Missionary Annals of the Holy Ghost Fathers*, 13 (1931), 76-78,88.
Dougall, J. W. C. "The Relationship of Church and School in Africa." *International Review of Missions*, 26 (1937), 204-214.
Dubois, H. "Les Missions et la question scolaire en Afrique." *Bulletin de la Ligne Missionnaire des Etudiants de France*, No. 8 (1932), 110.
Eggert, J. *Missionsschule und sozialer Wandel in Ostafrika*. Bielefeld, 1970.
Ekechi, F. K. "Colonianism and Christianity in West Africa: The Igbo Case, 1900-1915." *Journal of African History*, 12 (1971), 103-115.
Ekechi, F. K. *Missionary Enterprise and Rivalry in Igboland, 1857-1914*. London: Frank Case, 1972.
Engel, A. *Die Missionsmethode der Missionare vom Heiligen Geist auf dem Afrikanischen Festland*. Neuß: Knechtsteden, 1932.
Fafunwa, A. B. *History of Education in Nigeria*. London: George Allen & Unwin, 1974.
Fasholé-Luke, et al., eds. *Christianity in Independent Africa*. London: Rex Collins, 1978.
Flint, J. E. *Sir George Goldie and the Making of Nigeria*. London: Oxford University Press, 1960.

Floyd, B. *Eastern Nigeria: A Geographical Review*. London: Macmillan, 1969.

Glazik, J. *Mission — Der stets größere Auftrag: Gesammelte Vorträge und Aufsätze*. Aachen, 1979.

Glazik, J. "Die neuzeitliche Mission unter Leitung der Propaganda Kongregation." *Warum Mission: Theologische Motive in der Missionsgeschichte der Neuzeit*. Kirche und Religionen. Ed. H. Fries, et al. St. Ottilien: EOS Verlag, 1984. Vol. III/1, pp. 27-40.

Grant, J. "Education in Nigeria and the Mission Effort." *The African Angelus*, 7, No. 4 (1953), 46.

Gray, R. "The Origins and Organization of the Nineteenth-Century Missionary Movement." *Tahrik*, 3, No. 1 (1969), 1522.

Grentrup, T. "Die Definition des Missionsbegriffes." *Zeitschrift für Missionswissenschaft*, 3 (1913), 265-274.

Gosson, J. "The Apostolate of the School in Southern Nigeria." *Pagan Missions*, 13 (1940), 45-49.

Hair, P. E. *The Early Study of Nigerian Languages*. Cambridge: At the University Press, 1967.

Handmaids of the Holy Child Jesus. *A Tribute to a Valiant Pioneer Missionary: Sister Mary Charles Walker*. Calabar, 1974.

Hastings, A. *African Christianity: An essay in Interpretation*. London: Geoffrey Chapman, 1976.

Hastings, A. "Patterns of African Mission Work." *African Ecclesiastical Review*, 8 (1966), 291-298.

Hastings, A. *Das Schwarze Experiment: Kirche und Mission im modernen Afrika*. Wien: Verlag Styria, 1969.

Henkel, W. "Gestaltnahme von Bekehrungvorstellungen bei Ordens gründungen im 19. Jahrhundert." *Mission: Präsenz, Verkündigung, Bekehrung?* Ed. H. Rzepkowki. St. Augustin: Styler Verlag, 1974, pp. 102-114.

Hertlein, S. *Christentum und Mission im Urteil der neoafrikanischen Prosaliteratur*. Münsterschwarzach: Vier-Türme Verlag, 1962.

Hodgkin, T. "Background to Nigerian Nationalism, 3: The Coming of Zik and the N.C.N.C." *West Africa*, August, 18, 1951, 1951, pp. 751-752.

Hodgkin, T. *Nigerian Perspectives: An Historical Anthropology*. London: Oxford University Press, 1960.

Holmes, B., ed. *Educational Policy and the Mission Schools*. London: Routledge & Kegan Paul, 1967.

Hunne, G. H. *Generation of Giants: The Story of the Jesuits in China in the Last Decade of the Ming Dynasty*. Notre Dame, 1962.

Huonder, A. "Die chinesische Ritenstreit." *Die Katholiche Missionen*, 39 (1911), 112-115; 167-169; 219-224; 268-274.

Hussey, E. R. J. "Some Aspects of Education in Nigeria." *Some Aspects of Education in Tropical Africa: Three Joseph Payne Lectures for 1935*. London: Oxford University Press, 1936, pp. 7-22.

Ibekwe, U. "On the Teaching of Vernacular Languages." *The Nigerian Teacher*, 1, Nos 2 and 3 (1934).

Ilogu, E. *Christianity and Igbo Culture*. Leiden: E. J. Brill, 1974.

Isichei, E. *Entirely for God: The Life of Michael Iwene Tansi*. London: Macmillan, 1980.

Isichei, E. *A History of the Igbo People*. London: Macmillan, 1976.

Jahn, J. *The Black Experience: 400 Years of Black Literature from Africa and the Americas*. Liechtenstein: Kraus Reprint, Series I, 1969.

Jones, T. J. *Education in Africa: A Study of West, South, and Equatorial Africa by the African Education Commission*. New York: Phelps-Stokes Fund, 1924.

Jordan, J. *Bishop Shanahan of Southern Nigeria*. Dublin: Clonmore & Reynolds, 1949.

Jordan, J. "Catholic Education and Catholicism in Nigeria." *African Ecclesiastical Review*, 2 (1960), 60-62.

Kalu, O. U., ed. *The History of Christianity in West Africa*. London: Longman, 1980.

Kilger, L. "Die Missionsversuche in Benin." *Zeitschrift für Missionswissenschaft*, 22 (1932), 305-319.

Kinnerk, P. "La montée de l'Eglise dans l'Est Nigérien." *Vivant Afrique*, No. 205 (1959), 4344.

Koelle, S. W. *Polyglotta Africana*. London, 1854; rpt. Graz: Akademische Druck- und Verlagsanstalt, 1963.

Köster, F. "Ricci und Nobili: Der Ritenstreit." *Warum Mission*. Kirche und Religionen. St. Ottilien: EOS Verlag, 1984. Vol. III/1, pp. 41-62.

Leith-Ross, S. *African Women: A Study of the Ibo of Nigeria*. 1939; rpt. London: Routledge & Kegan Paul, 1978.

Lewis, C. S. *The Problem of Pain*. London, 1940; rpt. Glasgow: Collins, 1977.

Lewis, L. J. "Prospects of Educational Policy in Nigeria." *Education and Politics in Nigeria*. Ed. H. N. Weiler. Freiburg: Rombach Verlag, 1964, pp. 239-260.

Lewis, L. J. *Society, Schools and Progress in Nigeria*. Oxford: Pergamon Press, 1965.

Lugard, F. D. "British Policy in Nigeria." *Africa: Journal of the International Institute of African Languages and Cultures*, 10 (1937), 376-400.

Lutterbeck, G. A. "Das Schulwesen in den Britischen Kolonien Afrikas." *Die katholische Missionen*, 60 (1932), 307-311; 332-336.

Luzbetak, L. J. *The Church and Cultures: An Applied Anthropology for the Religious Worker*. Illinois, 1970; rpt. South Pasadena: William Carey Library, 1976.

Maas, O. *Die Wiedereröffnung der Franziskanermission in China in der Neuzeit*. Münster, 1926, pp. 81-134.

Magdalene, M. C. "Education of Girls in Southern Nigeria." *International Review of Missions*, 17 (1928), pp. 505- 514.

Marshall, J. *Reminiscences of West African and its Missions*. London: St. Anselm's Society, 1885.

Mason, R. J. *British Education in Africa*. London: Oxford University Press, 1959.

Mazé, J. *La Collaboration Scolaire des Gouvernements coloniaux et des Missions Afrique Britannique, Afrique Belge, Afrique Française*. Alger, 1933.

Mba, C. "My Experience in Running a Seminary in the East Central State of Nigeria." *Omnis Terra*, LXIV, No. 6 (Rome, 1974), 79-83.

Mba, C. and O'Sullivan, D. "Progrès et situation de l'Eglise parmi les Ibos au Nigeria." *Le Christ au Monde*, No. 6 (Rome, 1974), 491-499.

Meek, C. K. *Law and Authority in a Nigerian Tribe: A Study in Indirect Rule*. Oxford, 1937; rpt. New York: Barnes & Noble, 1970.

Moody, P. F. "The Growth of Catholic Missions in Western, Central and Eastern Africa." *Sacrae Congregationis de Propaganda Fide Memoria Rerum, 1622-1972*. Ed. J. Metzler. Freiburg: Herder, 1975. Vol III/1, pp. 203-255.

Moorhouse, G. *The Missionaries*. London: Eyre Methuen, 1973.

Morel, E. D. *Nigeria: Its Peoples and Its Problems*. London: Frank Case, 1968.

Mourez, M. "Le développement de l'enseignement catholique dans les colonies anglaises du Centre africain." *Bulletin des Etudiants de France*, No. 22 (1934), 101-113.

Mulders, A. *Missionsgeschichte: Die Ausbreitung des katholischen Glaubens*. Regensburg: Pustet, 1960.

Neill, S. *Colonialism and Christian Missions*. London: Lutterworth Press, 1966.

Neill, S. *A History of Christian Missions*. Middlesex: Penguin, 1964.

Neill, S. *Mission zwischen Kolonialismus und Ökumene: Die Aufgabe der Kirche in der sich wandelnden Welt*. Stuttgart: Evangelisches Verlagswerk, 1962.

Njoku, R. A. *The Advent of the Catholic Church in Nigeria: Its Growth in Owerri Diocese*. Owerri: Assumpta Press, 1980.

Nwabara, S. N. *Iboland: A Century of Contact with Britain, 1860-1960*. London: Hodder & Stoughton, 1977.

Nwaokpoh, J. *Religious Novitiate, A Fattening Room: Some Insights into this Aspect of the Nigerian Cultural Value in the Novitiate Formation of the African Sister*. Rome, 1979.

Obi, C. A., ed. *A Hundred Years of the Catholic Church in Eastern Nigeria, 1885-1985*. Onitsha: Africana-Fep, 1985.

O'Connell, J, "The Church in AfricaWill Its 'Success' Continue?" *The Church in Africa*. Ed. W. J. Wilson. Maryknoll: Maryknoll Publications, 1967, pp. 123.

Okure, L. *Centenary Reflection: A Tribute to Sister Mary Charles Walker*. Calabar, 1981.

Oldham, J. H. "Educational Policy of the British Government in Africa." *International Review of Missions*, 14 (1925), 421-427.

Oloko T. "Religion and Politics in Nigeria." *West Africa*, February 2 and 9, 1951, pp. 103 and 131.

Osadebay, D. "Easter Reflection: The Missionary in West Africa." *West Africa*, April 5, 1947, pp. 289-290.

Osmund, M. "Nigerian Schools: Politics or Education?" *World Mission*, 5 (1954), 229-235.

Perham, M. *Native Administration in Nigeria*. London: Oxford University Press, 1937.

Peshkin, P. "Education and National Integration." *The Journal of Modern African Studies*, 5 (1967), 323-334.

Porter, A. "Late Nineteenth-Century Anglican Missionary Expansion: A Consideration of Some Non-Anglican Sources of Inspiration." *Religious Motivation: Biographical and Sociological Problems for the Church Historian*. Studies in Church History. Vol. XV. Ed. D. Baker. Oxford: Blackwell, 1978, pp. 349-365.

Riberi, A. "Ein Stephania-Johanna Bigard Seminar in Nigeria." *Der Einheimische Priester in den Missionsländern*, 16 (1939), 48-52.

Ritson, J. H. "The British Government and Missions of Alien Nationality." *International Review of Missions*, 8 (1919), 331-340.

Rivinus, K. J. *Mission und Politik*. St. Augustin, 1977.

Ryder, A. F. C. "The Benin Missions." *Journal of the Historical Society of Nigeria*, 2 (1961), 231-259.

Ryder, A. F. C. "Portuguese Missions in Western Africa." *Tahrik*, 3, No. 1 (1969), 113.

Scanlon, D. G., ed. *Church, State and Education in Africa*. New York: Teachers College Press, 1966.

Scheuer, J. "Matteo Ricci and the Inculturation of Christianity, 1583-1983." *Lumen Vitae*, English ed. 40/1 (1985), pp. 79.

Schlunk, M. "Mission and Culture." *International Review of Missions*, 12 (1923), 532-544.

Schmidlin, J. "Deutsche Kolonialpolitik und katholische Heiden mission." *Zeitschrift für Missionswissenschaft*, 2 (1912), 25-49.

Schmidlin, J. *Die katholische Missionslehre im Grundriss*. Münster, 1919.

Schmidlin, J. "Katholische Missionstheoretiker des 16. und 17. Jahrhunderts." *Zeitschrift für Missionswissenschaft*, 1 (1911), 213-227.

Schwager, F. "Missionstätigkeit und nationale Propaganda." *Zeitschrift für Missionswissenschaft*, 6 (1916), 109-134.

Smith, E. W. *The Christian Mission in Africa: A Study Based on the Work of the International Conference at Le Zoute, Belgium*. London, 1926.

Smith, P. and Summerfield, G., eds. *Matthew Arnold and the New Order: A Selection of Arnold's Writings on Education*. Cambridge: The University Press, 1969).

Solaru, T. T. *Teacher Training in Nigeria*. Ibadan, 1964.

Spitz, M. "The Growth of Roman Catholic Missions in Africa." *International Review of Missions*, 12 (1923), 360-372.

Spörndli, P. "Das Große Seminar in Onitsha-Vicariate." *Der Einheimische Priester in den Missionsländern*, 19 (1942), 58.

Streit, R. "Die Missionsliteratur des 19. Jahrhunderts." *Zeitschrift für Missionswissenschaft*, 7 (1917), 108-115.

Sundkler, B. *The Christian Ministry in Africa*. London: SCM Press, 1960.

Tasie, G. O. M. *Christian Missionary Enterprise in the Niger Delta 1864-1918*. Studies on Religion in Africa. Leiden: E. J. Brill, 1978. Vol. III.

Taylor, J. *Christianity and Politics in Africa*. London: Penguin, 1957.

Taylor, W. H. "Missionary Education in Africa Reconsidered: The Presbyterian Educational Impact in Eastern Nigeria 1846-1974." *African Affairs*, 83 (1984), 189-205.

Todd, J. M. *African Mission*. London, 1962.

Van Leuven, J. H. "L'Enseignment en Nigeria." *L'Echo des Missions Africaines de Lyon*, 3 (March, 1931), 60-61.

Walls, A. F. "Black Europeans, White Africans: Some Missionary Motives in West Africa." *Religious Motivation: Biographical and Sociological Problems for the Church Historian*. Studies in Church History. Ed. D. Baker. Oxford: Blackwell, 1978. Vol. XV, pp. 339-348.

Walls, A. F. "A Christian Experiment: The Early Sierra Leone Colony." *The Mission of the Church and the Propagation of the Faith*. Studies in Church History. Ed. G. J. Cuming. Cambridge: The University Press, 1970. Vol. VI, pp. 107-129.

Walsh, M. J. "The Catholic Contribution to Education in Western Nigeria, 1861-1926." M. A. Thesis. University of London, 1951.

Ward, J. C. *Ibo Dialects and the Development of a Common Language*. Cambridge: Heffer and Sons, 1941.

Warneck, G. *Evangelische Missionslehre*, 5 vols. Göttingen, 1892-1903.

Weiler, H. N., ed. *Education and Politics in Nigeria*. Freiburg: Rombach Verlag, 1964.

Westermann, D. "The Place and Function of the Vernacular in African Education." *International Review of Missions*, 14 (1925), 25-36.

Whelan, J. B. "Our School: Victory in Nigeria." *World Mission*, 8 (Fall, 1957), 1826.

Williams, H. G. "Relations with Government in Education: British Colonies in Tropical Africa." *International Review of Missions*, 14 (1925), 324.

Wise, C. G. *A History of Education in British West Africa*. London: Longman, 1956.

APPENDIX A

COPY OF A CONTRACT MADE BY FATHER E. KUNTZMANN WITH A CATECHIST OF THE MISSION, ONITSHA 18 MAY 1896.

Mr. Ephrem J. Agha, on the one hand, and E. Kuntzmann, Superior of the Catholic Mission, on the other hand, do hereby make an agreement on the following conditions:-

The said Mr. Ephrem takes the following obligations:

1) To serve the R.C.M. as Catechist and Inspector of Schools.

2) To work only for the R.C.M. and that without interruption, unless he receives the permission for good reasons considered as such by both contracting parties.

The said Superior of the R.C.M. takes the following obligations:

1) To employ the said Mr. Ephrem as Catechist and Inspector of Schools at the monthly salary of £4. 0. 0. from the first of June 1886 and of £4. 10. 0. from the first of August, 1896. The aforesaid salary is to be increased according to the number of Mr. Ephrem's children. Other circumstances may also cause the aforesaid salary to be increased and then it will be done according to further arrangements between both contracting parties.

2) Not to dismiss the said Mr. Ephrem unless his conduct be incompatible with the work he had to do, which incompatibility takes place in the case of public scandal, of well proved machinations against the R.C.M., and the like.

3) Not to remove the said Mr. Ephrem from Onitsha-Wharf except for a short time and only in a case of necessity. And in the case of Mr. Ephrem being sent to another station, the R.C.M. shall help him in a special manner and in proportion as there his ordinary expenses are greater.

4) To supply the said Mr. Ephrem, at the cost price, with all the European provisions which the Mission uses to get [sic] and the said Mr. Ephrem requires.

5) To contribute to the building of the said Mr. Ephrem's house in the following measure: the R.C.M. shall furnish and put up the framework, and the walls will be made at the said Mr. Ephrem's expenses.

Witness our hands, the day and year aforesaid,

E. Kuntzmann, Superior, R.C.M.
E. J. Agha.

Witness:
C. Vogler.
F. Lichtenberger.

APPENDIX B:1

TEMPORARY SCHEME OF RELIGIOUS MORAL INSTRUCTION IN THE ROMAN CATHOLIC MISSION SCHOOLS BY FATHER J. SHANAHAN, APOSTOLIC PREFECT, ONITSHA, 1915.

INFANTS

Class I

1. Sign of the Cross.
2. Recitation of Our Father
3. Hail Mary.
4. The Apostles' Creed.
5. Elementary notion about God as Creator of:Angels, Men, the World.
6. Our First Parents.
7. The Garden of Eden.
8. The First Sin.
9. The Promise of a Redeemer.
10. The Birth of Jesus at Bethlehem on Christmas Night.
11. The Adoration of Jesus by Angels, the Shepherds, Kings from the East.
12. The Life of Jesus During His Childhood. His obedience to His Parents.
13. The Love of Jesus for Children.
14. The Death of Jesus. His Resurrection and Ascension into Heaven.
15. Refrains of Some Igbo Hymns.

Class II

1. Prayers learned the previous year.
2. The Commandments of God and of the Church.
3. Elementary Notions about the Attributes of God.
4. More detailed Notions about the Angels in general—Good Angels, Bad Angels, and Guardian Angels.
5. Original Sin and its Effects.
6. Short Stories taken from the Life of Christ.
7. The Passion of Christ.
8. The Institution of the Seven Sacraments.
9. Special Lesson on: Baptism, Penance, Holy Eucharist.
10. Virtues peculiar to Children, How to avoid them.
11. Vices peculiar to Children, How to avoid them.
12. Igbo Hymns.

Standards

Class I (Std. III)

1. All the Prayers learned in previous years.
2. Short explanation of the 12 Articles of the Apostles' Creed, 10 Commandments of God, Commandments of the Church, and the 7 Sacraments.

3. Special stress to be laid on the 1st, 4th, 6th, 7th, and 8th Commandments.
4. Elementary notion about the Sacraments.
5. Further details taken from the life of Christ.
6. Hymns and Serving of Mass.

Class II (Std. III & IV)

1. More advanced Lesson on nos.1), 2), 3), of Class I.
2. Explanation of the Parables contained in the New Testament.
3. Special Lesson on Pagan Customs and Practices:—a) some, good or indifferent, b) others, evil.
4. Elementary Bible History for Children. The Old Law.
5. Elementary Notion of Church History: I—IV Centuries.
6. Noble deeds performed by Christian Men and Women.
7. How character is acquired and Heaven won by those who observe the law of God.
8. Latin Hymns.

Class III (Std. V & VI)
1. All the Catechism of Christian Doctrine.
2. Special Lesson to show the authorities on which is based Christian Belief.
3. Liturgy and Ceremonies of the Church with Explanation.
4. Elementary Bible History: Old and New Law.
5. Principal events in the History of the Church up to the present day.
6. What Christianity has done for the human race.
7. What it may do for Africa.
8. Special reference to the lives of men and women who by their learning or great deeds have honoured and benefited the human race.
9. Special insistence on:- a) Character and its acquisition. b) Respect for lawful authority. c) Good example, its effects. d) Fidelity to duty. e) Sobriety etc etc.

APPENDIX B:2

APPROVED SCHEME OF RELIGIOUS INSTRUCTION FOR THE
ONITSHA-OWERRI VICARIATE, 1944.

A. *Scholars*

Infant Class I
(a) Ayiyo Ututu na Ayiyo Anyase as on pages 48 and 49 of the Igbo Catechism.
(b) Isi I and Isi II of Katikizma nke Umu-aka.
Infant Class II
Katikizma nke Umu-aka from beginning to end.
Standard I.
(a) Part One of the Igbo Catechism.
(b) From the beginning of Ndu Dinwenu Anyi to number 36 (inclusive).
Standard II
(a) Part Two of the Igbo Catechism.
(b) From number 36 in Ndu Dinwenu Anyi to the end.
Standard III
(a) Revision of the whole Igbo Catechism.
(b) Mary, Nne Jesu.

B. *Catechumens (Non-Scholars)*

First Year Catechumens
    Katikizma nke Umu-aka.
Second Year Catechumens
(a) Part One of the Igbo Catechism.
(b) From the beginning of Ndu Dinwenu Anyi to number 36.
Third Year Catechumens
(a) Part Two of the Igbo Catechism.
(b) Number 36 of Ndu Dinwenu Anyi to the end.

C. *Baptized Members*

Children's First Communion Class
    Katikizma nke Umu-aka.
Adults (receiving Sacraments).
(a) Igbo Catechism (one class per week)
(b) Ndu Dinwenu Anyi (one class per week).
(c) Mary, Nne Jesu (one class per week).

APPENDIX C:1

REGULATIONS ON THE RUNNING OF SCHOOL FARMS IN SENIOR PRIMARY SCHOOLS

1. Each class in the Senior Primary School should have a plot of land. This plot is kept by the same class from Standard III until they leave, thus the new Std. III takes over the ex- standard VI's plot.
2. The plot varies in size but should be neatly marked out and all paths should be straight, preferably lined with lemon grass or some other suitable edging plant.
3. The plot is divided into a number of sections corresponding to the number of courses in the rotation, e.g. a plot farmed on a 4 course rotation will be divided into 4 sections, each cropped with a different course.
4. The Rural Science Teacher should be able to supply a copy of the rotation and on visiting the farm an education officer could check that the required crops have been planted and growing well.
5. In some schools there may be extra plots of land cropped with oil palms, bananas, or any other permanent crop. This plot is looked after by all the classes.
6. Compost: Compost should be made in all schools and is usually made in a series of 4 to 6 pits. The refuse is put in one pit and watered and after an interval of about two weeks is turned into the next pit. This continues so that the last pit contains the Finished compost which resembles coarse soil with a little amount of dead leaves, etc.
7. The compost pits should be shallow, i.e. no more than 2 ft. deep and they should have neat, straight edges. It is preferable if the last pits are covered by a shed to prevent excess leaching by the rain.
8. Urine from the urinal should be poured over the first compost pit daily to act as a starter which enables the bacteria to commence the process of decay.
9. Cultivation is done on ridges which should be well made and straight.
10. Some fallow plot should contain icheku, fallow well covered with leguminous plants.
11. Steps should be taken to prevent erosion on the school compound.
12. Class work: Each class teacher should take his class for Rural Science with the help of the Rural Science Teacher.

APPENDIX C:2

RURAL SCIENCE IN PRIMARY SCHOOLS: CIRCULAR BY THE
DIRECTOR OF EDUCATION, EASTERN REGION, ENUGU, 26 JUNE,
1953.

1. Each class should do 5 hours of Rural Science per week.
2. The period for Rural Science should come early in the morning, the best
   arrangements being two morning sessions per class per week.
3. The periods on the time-table should not be split up into "Agriculture",
   "Nature Study", "Hygiene", but should be left as "Rural Science." The
   time devoted to the various divisions of the subject will vary according to the
   time of the year, and will be organized by the Rural Science Teacher
   accordingly.
4. On mornings on which a class is doing practical farm work, the children
   involved should not do physical training, but go straight to the farm.

OUTLINE OF EVIDENCE GIVEN BEFORE THE
ELLIOT COMMISSION ON HIGHER EDUCATION
BY THE CATHOLIC MISSIONS OF NIGERIA, 1944.

1. The Catholic Missions of Nigeria are unanimous in desiring to see a fully-fledged University in West Africa, and consider Nigeria the most suitable place for it. The need exists, the people are keen and the population is large. It is unthinkable that a population of more than twenty millions should not have its own cadre of specialists to assist in developing it and giving it leadership. According to our way of looking at things, the main point at issue for the commission is not whether there should be a University in the country or not (we assume there should), but rather whether this is the acceptable time or not. The general opinion is that the time for a Nigerian University is close at hand, and that an immediate stepping up of the educational standard in secondary schools is desirable in view of it.

2. Few of those now teaching in the top classes of our secondary schools would hold that the boy who leaves a Middle Six class is a fit subject for a normal University. The very brilliant boy may be, because he can be trusted to bridge the gap between the Nigerian secondary school and a University by sheer mental acumen. It is hardly wise, however, to legislate solely for the very brilliant. It would seem better to close the gap. This can be done in two ways:-

a) By having University preparatory classes attached to some institute like Yaba, in much the same way as preparatory classes are attached to certain secondary schools;

or

b) By raising the standard in a number of selected secondary schools from the School Certificate to the Higher Certificate level. This would seem the more logical of the two alternatives, and would provide for a wider selection of boys. Such boys would be fit for a University.

3. In the event of b) being adopted, the Catholic Missions would expect to have two such schools, one in the Eastern Provinces and one in the Western. Two would represent requirements, and should not be regarded as excessive, as about thirty per cent of the school-going population of Nigeria attends Catholic schools. We are not without hope that one of the two may ultimately develop into a Constituent College of a Nigerian University, with Faculties of Science, Arts, Philosophy and Divinity.

4. A preponderance of Government secondary schools of this Higher Certificate type cannot be recommended, because it would tend to create a narrow bureaucratic class. In addition, Government schools would not be in a position to guarantee the formation of that Christian outlook which requires special stressing in those aspiring to higher education. Individual Government teachers might be excellent, but there would inevitably be much variety in type.

5. A Nigerian University, if founded, must be run on definitely Christian lines, Otherwise it will simply turn out a godless elite, and the last state of the

country will be worse than the first. We expect a Governing Body with reasonable Mission representation and a Catholic hostel for Catholic students. There should be nothing in the nature of exclusive government control.

6. While it is recognized that a Nigerian University must have a technical and scientific bias in order to meet the needs of the country, it is hoped that some effort will be made to introduce a liberal element into University training, Over-specialization will cause Nigerians to leave the University with no general outlook and entirely devoid of the culture that goes with the Classics, Philosophy and Modern Languages. Some counter to excessive specialization must be found. It might be wise to make English Language and Literature a compulsory subject for all. This would be a partial counter. A Chair of Aristotelian Philosophy might induce general intellectual interests; one of Sociology would be extremely practicable, particularly as the very fact of a University will give rise to an *upper class* in the country.

7. If a University is to fit into a balanced system of education, then a considerable amount of reconstruction and overhaul must take place in our secondary and primary schools. As already suggested, a certain number of the best secondary schools would need to run Higher Certificate courses (but without the examination) in view of supplying alumni to the University. They would require considerable financial assistance in order to enable them to get staffs of graduates and specialists, to obtain equipment for practical work in Science, and to put students through a well-graded course in reading, under the guidance of a Reading Master. Their elevation would not mean that less privileged secondary schools could not carry on as at present. They could continue to do their valuable work of giving a far more advanced form of schooling than the primary schools. They would be useful for providing clerks for the Government service, teachers (after training) in the primary schools, technicians in the mines and the various departments which take on Middle Six boys for special training. They would not turn out a jobless class. Nigeria actually needs far more Middle Six schools than we have at present. The people are constantly crying out for an education beyond Standard VI for their children, and there is no point in constantly denying them.

8. It is in the domain of primary education that the greatest need for reorganization lies, since it is the ultimate foundation of all educational effort. It alone touches the mass of the people, and it is for them almost the sole instrument of uplift. The present state of the primary schools is somewhat pitiable. They are poorly equipped and poorly staffed. Only about one teacher in ten is trained. Medical attention scarcely exists for the rural child. (He may and does go to a Mission hospital for free treatment if he lives near one. But such hospitals have so much to do at general work and maternity that they cannot afford doctors and assistants for exclusively school work, especially as no one would raise a hand to help pay these doctors and their staffs). He generally comes from a home where living conditions are appallingly unhygienic. The school has done something to ameliorate his lot, but not enough. The blame for what has not been done is not to be laid on the Missions or on the Department of Education. Were it not for them, many rural districts would still be cannibalistic. All efforts for the betterment of the Nigerian child have been hampered by lack of funds. This has been the limiting factor for years past. It is useless to formulate plans and policies as long as funds are not available to push them through. If funds are to become available for Nigerian uplift, the Nigerian child should have first

claim on them. Incidentally, it is apposite to remark that Missions can achieve three times as much as Government with the same funds.

9. Primary education must be integrated with a wide plan of social service, especially outside the urban areas. In the sphere of social service, health should receive first consideration. There should be a school Medical and Welfare Officer attached to each Division. One would do for a beginning, but he would need a well-trained staff to run dispensaries, and these would best be placed close to Central Schools. It would then be a relatively simple matter to get school children from outlying areas in for health inspection, injections and treatment. Health courses could be given to teachers during holidays, so that they might know how to detect common ailments, inculcate the ordinary rules of hygiene and principles of dietetics, and give first aid in backward places in case of emergency. The Central School could be used for lecturing adults or giving them cinema shows to drive home simple but oft ignored facts regarding good housing conditions, pure drinking water, decent sanitary arrangements, a balanced diet and a host of other things. In this way the village school would be made organic to the rural community, instead of being a thing apart as it often is now. The grown-ups would begin to view primary education as a means of bettering living conditions and improving environment, and would gradually become education conscious. Children of school age not actually attending, but getting free medical attention at the school, would easily be induced to attend. The era of mass literacy would not then be far away, and would be ushered in with a minimum of compulsion. Finally, the Native Court, with its appendage of litigious quarrelling, would cease to be the centre of rural life, and would cede this role to the school—the main educative factor and therefore the proper centre. The cost of providing a School Medical Officer for each Division (there are about 90 Divisions in Nigeria) would willingly be defrayed in part by the Native Administrations, but would also be a most worthy absorbent of Colonial Welfare money. In areas where the Missions have large schools and a good hospital, they should be asked to supply the School Medical Officer, since this would help to unify their efforts and would double their usefulness to the people.

10. As it is futile to discuss education—higher, secondary or primary—without taking into account the teacher, who is the pivot of the whole process, it is necessary to make a few remarks about him. In the first place, he should be a professional man, trained for his job, and having his future bound up with that job. Teaching in Nigeria needs to be a permanent way of life, high in the common estimation and capable of attracting the best brains of the country. It must be a career with a future in the sense that it must hold out reasonable hopes of advancement and remuneration within the service, and offer financial security in the years that succeed retirement. There is no need whatsoever for it to be incorporated into the Government service, though there is need for more Government money to be put into it.

11. The training of teachers must be the focal point of educational policy for some years to come. It is vital to get more trained men into the schools, particularly into the primary schools, which cater for more than ninety per cent of the school-going population. Existing training facilities would need to be doubled straight away, and trebled within the next five years. The Catholic Missions are at present making frantic attempts to reduce the alarming proportion of untrained to trained personnel (about 10 to 1). All extra effort, however, means extra money drawn from Mission resources and this procedure cannot continue

indefinitely. Our secondary schools are relatively better off than our primary, because they have a leavening of European teachers. The whole question of training is one of urgency, and until it is tackled with speed and decision, the edifice of higher education in Nigeria will rest on very insecure foundations.

PRESS RELEASE ON A PROPOSED NIGERIAN CATHOLIC UNI-
VERSITY BY FATHER J. JORDAN, EDUCATION ADVISER TO THE
CATHOLIC MISSIONS OF NIGERIA, 1955.

There has been discussion recently in the press about the above, and I expect
an official and factual statement from Catholic sources will be welcomed by the
public. I therefore offer one.

In December, 1954, during the Marian Congress in Lagos, the Archbishops
and Bishops of Nigeria met under the presidency of the Apostolic Delegate to
discuss the possibility of instituting a Catholic University. This problem,
together with cognate higher educational problems, had been with them for
years but had found no solution. They decided, in understanding with Cardinal
McIntyre of Los Angeles, that a solution might be reached in the United States.
They therefore instructed me to go there and explore possibilities. This instruction was given me about two months before we first heard of a possible Eastern
University under government auspices.

I went to America in mid-May, and returned in mid-August, having visited
many universities and discussed Nigeria's educational needs with high officials
and friends in Rome and the U.S.A. My mission was successful. The greatest
educational agency in America and possibly in the world, the Jesuit Educational
Association, which controls 27 American Universities with a total of over one
hundred thousand students, has agreed *in principle* to establish a Catholic
University in Nigeria. It will be initiated most probably in the Eastern Region,
but may later shoot branches West and North.

Before going to America, I sought and obtained an interview with the Prime
Minister of the Eastern Region, Doctor the Honourable Nnamdi Azikiwe. The
purpose of the interview was to secure from the leader of the ruling party in the
East and of Government an authoritative statement that Government would be
favourable to our efforts to provide higher education. The Prime Minister was
very kind and most encouraging. He summed up his views in the following
sentence which every true-hearted Nigerian should remember with pride: "The
people of this Region desire better and better education with their whole hearts,
and we in Government must do our utmost to give it to them. Father, if you
succeed in bringing here a University on the lines of Notre Dame or Fordham,
the people will rise up to welcome it, and I shall be entirely on your side." Well,
one of the universities mentioned by the Premier—Fordham University, New
York—is controlled by the Jesuit Educational Association. It may of course take
decades to bring our Catholic University up to that level: it may even be a year
or two before we lay the first stone. Much negotiation and preparation has still
to take place. But the dawn is breaking.

It is apposite here to make a few statements about American Universities with
special reference to religion, since this aspect has received press notice. The
most outstanding universities—Yale, Notre Dame, Harvard, Princeton, Fordham, etc, etc—were established, not by the state, but by religious bodies. They
still retain their religious character and ethos, and religion has an honoured

place in them. But no narrow bigotry is tolerated, and there is full freedom of conscience for all. You find Protestants and Jews, and even Budhists and Shintoists, attending American Catholic Universities, while you find many Catholics being educated in institutions under non-Catholic control. Mutual regard and amity go hand in hand with respect for God and for religious observance. All this is as it should be. And this is the spirit which shall prevail in our Catholic University. Moslems and Protestants, as well as Catholics will be welcomed within its portals; and they will be entirely free, mentally and spiritually, to pursue knowledge and truth. We hope to find many of them among our most distinguished alumni.

It came as a great surprise to me on my return from America, to find the Christian Council of Nigeria featured in the press as "attacking" the Catholic University. I know many members of this Council, and I hold their views in esteem and their lives in respect. I know, too, their record of service. For those reasons I refuse to counter attack. But I feel that the average Catholic will not be quite so tolerant and understanding. He will feel like saying to the Council "Is thy eye evil because we are good?" The average Nigerian, also, especially the average Easterner, will certainly not support the view of the Council. He will believe that it is trying to deny educational advancement to his children just because this advancement is offered by Catholic hands. He will regard "attacks" as signs of bigotry and unchristian bitterness. I therefore invite the Christian Council to desist from attacks, and to walk hand in hand with the Catholics—as it has so often walked in the past—towards a better and more educated Nigeria.

Our reasons for starting a Catholic University are simple. Catholic policy in education is to give the people all we have at the primary, the secondary, and the higher level. "What I have, I give" said St. Peter, the head of the Apostles, in Acts III,6. We Catholics trace our spiritual lineage back to Peter. His policy is our policy. What we have, we give.

NOTE ON FINANCING THE CATHOLIC UNIVERSITY BY J. JORDAN

Capital Costs

We can assume that the University will be a separate institution, and that it will have its own independent setting in a rural or semi-urban area. It would not be possible to obtain the acreage required for it (say 150 to 200 acres) in any Nigerian city. The probable cost of building in a rural area, where practically every student must of necessity be residential, can best be arrived at by studying the costs of rural secondary schools.

The money required for erecting a non-urban secondary school of reasonable design and proportions in Nigeria today [1955] is forty thousand pounds for a single stream (120 students) and almost double that for a double stream. Staff buildings are included, also essential equipment such as desks, beds, tables, etc. The figures are for Mission schools, which are built under our own supervision, and not handed to contractors.

A University would run to about twice the above figure per student head. Better design would be needed, more lavish equipment, more costly labs, etc. Staff costs per *professional* head would far exceed the secondary average, because many secondary teachers are not fully qualified and are modestly housed. Undergraduates would naturally expect far better accommodation than secondary boys or girls, who are normally put into dormitories. So a doubling of expenditure is the minimum to be envisaged. If we accept it, it means that the 300 undergraduates we expect at the end of about five years will involve us in an expenditure of at least two hundred thousand pounds.

I do not for a moment suggest that 300 is to be the probable total number of students. Judging by the way Nigerian secondary facilities are expanding, the figure 300 will be multiplied by about four twenty five or thirty years from now. If we are to plan the University on a long term basis, we must plan for about twelve hundred students. And we must therefore look forward to an expenditure of eight hundred thousand pounds, or say 2½ million dollars.

It is possible of course to design any institution, including our University, in such a way that it contains a fair proportion of modest and inexpensive buildings. And these can easily be erected first. From experience in providing funds for Nigerian institutes, I should not hesitate to counsel starting the University with fifty thousand pounds in hand. Without that minimum sum it would be idle to begin. At least it would be idle to begin in a separate institution. One could make an alternative beginning in one of our secondary schools. But there would be no permanent future there.

Could a University begun with fifty thousand continue to function if it received no further allocations towards capital costs? The answer is that it could. But it would be completely stunted in growth, and would never provide for more than a few hundred students...and for these inadequately. I find it hard to imagine such a possibility becoming an actuality. I rather fancy that any Catholic University, however humble in origin, would succeed in pushing its way into the sun and securing financial aid from Government, from Rome, from alumni, and from various other Providential sources. Also, it would in time be able to set aside annual sums from fees for buildings and other expansionist purposes. To be a University in the accepted sense of the term, it would—even for 300 students—have to have for building purposes the £200,000 mentioned in paragraph 3.

Recurrent Costs

I think it can safely be assumed that all recurrent costs in the University will be met by fee income after the first two or three years. If the students pay 150 pounds annually—and they should—it is quite certain that not more than ninety or a hundred will be needed to feed them and to defray all other expenses incidental on their existence (games, library, water, light, travel, maintenance of buildings, etc. etc.). Thus fifty or sixty pounds per student head remains to pay or maintain staff. Allowing a ratio of ten students per teacher, there would be available five to six hundred pounds per man. This is more than sufficient for priests.

At any rate, the general principle that fees can pay for all non-building expenses is reasonably safe. In doubt, one increases fees. There would be no doubt from the moment the number on roll would reach 200. Thereafter, excess fees should help towards building and equipment, especially the latter.

It is almost certain that the Eastern Government would give staff, equipment and salary subsidies to the University if favourably impressed by it. We have not a single secondary school or normal college in Nigeria today which is not in receipt of sufficient grant-in-aid to make it a going concern. Most of them have also received building grants ranging from twenty to seventy per cent of costs. I should say that the probabilities are that the University will get from Government both capital and recurrent aid.

INDEX